Good Housekeeping™

BEST RECIPES

1999

Good Housekeeping™
BEST RECIPES
1999

Time Inc.
HOME ENTERTAINMENT

Hearst Communications, Inc.

Good Housekeeping™ BEST RECIPES 1999

GOOD HOUSEKEEPING

Editor in Chief: Ellen Levine
Food Director: Susan Westmoreland
Associate Food Director: Susan Deborah Goldsmith
Food Associates: Lisa Brainerd, Lori Perlmutter, Mary Ann Svec, Lisa Troland
Nutrition Director: Delia Hammock
Food Appliances Director: Sharon Franke
Hearst Brand Development: Carrie Bloom, Jennifer Talansky

TIME INC. HOME ENTERTAINMENT

President: David Gitow
Director, Continuities and Single Sales: David Arfine
Director, Continuities and Retention: Michael Barrett
Director, New Products: Alicia Longobardo
Group Product Manager: Robert Fox
Product Managers: Christopher Berzolla, Alison Ehrmann,
Roberta Harris, Stacy Hirschberg, Kenneth Maehlum,
Jennifer McLyman, Daniel Melore
Manager, Retail and New Markets: Thomas Mifsud
Associate Product Managers: Carlos Jimenez, Daria Raehse, Betty Su,
Cheryl Zukowski
Assistant Product Managers: Jennifer A. Dowell, Meredith Shelley, Lauren Zaslansky
Editorial Operations Manager: John Calvano
Book Production Manager: Jessica McGrath
Book Production Coordinator: Joseph Napolitano
Fulfillment Director: Michelle Gudema
Assistant Fulfillment Manager: Richard Perez
Financial Director: Tricia Griffin
Associate Financial Manager: Amy Maselli
Assistant Financial Manager: Stephen Sandonato
Marketing Assistant: Ann Gillespie

Special thanks to Anna Yelenskaya

GOOD HOUSEKEEPING BEST RECIPES 1999
Produced by Rebus, Inc.
New York, NY

First Edition
Printed in the United States of America
ISBN# 0-688-16597-4-0
ISSN# 1096-2697

We welcome your comments and suggestions about Good Housekeeping Books.
Please write us at: Good Housekeeping Books, Attention: Book Editors, P.O. Box 11016. Des Moines, IA 50336-1016

If you would like to order additional copies of any of our books, please call us at 1-800-327-6388.
(Monday through Friday, 7 a.m.–6 p.m. Central Time)

Contents

WELCOME TO GOOD HOUSEKEEPING'S 1999 edition of *Best Recipes*, our annual recipe anthology. In the 12 months since we brought you our last collection, we've turned our attention to topics of growing interest. We've devoted an entire chapter to meatless main dishes—a family-pleasing selection of hearty casseroles, stir-fries, sandwiches, and even burgers and chili. *Best Recipes 1999* also contains a whole chapter on grilling, a style of cooking that, in addition to the delicious food it produces, brings its own unique pleasures. Our creative grilling chapter offers an international array of recipes as well as all-American updates like Backyard BLT's. Baking for special occasions big and small is another passion we share, and our Breads & Pastries chapter features a special focus on coffee cakes—old-fashioned yeast-raised braids and wreaths as well as inviting fruit- and streusel-topped butter cakes. Start writing those brunch invitations!

Once again we've reviewed the latest kitchen gadgets, such as a nifty pump spray bottle to fill with your own oil (a big improvement on store-bought aerosols) and a compact electric barbecue grill that works as well as the big models. We've fully covered the equipment front with reports on stand mixers, bread machines, microwave ovens, dishwashers, gas ranges, and more. We update you on nutrition news and new food products, too.

As always, every recipe is triple-tested to ensure success. And each chapter features savvy tips and inside info—shopping helps (how to choose fresh figs, for instance), cooking tricks (like quick ways to spice up rice), and health facts (about eggs, prewashed salad greens, and more)—from the Good Housekeeping Institute and the food editors.

We think we've outdone ourselves this time around, and we hope you agree. Here's to another year of enjoyable cooking and, of course, great eating!

Good Housekeeping's food editors pictured above (left to right): Mary Ann Svec, Associate; Debby Goldsmith, Associate Director; Susan Westmoreland, Director; Lisa Troland, Associate; Marianne Marinelli, Associate; and Lisa Brainerd, Associate.

NEWS & NOTES *from the Good Housekeeping Institute*

A NEW TOOL FOR FAST FLAVOR

If you love pricey extravirgin olive oil but want to stretch your dollar—and keep calories and fat to a minimum—check out the plastic EcoPump from the California Olive Oil Corporation. It's a favorite in the *Good Housekeeping* test kitchens. Fill with regular or herb-infused oil and use to lightly mist salads, grilled meats and vegetables, or slices of crusty Tuscan bread. Or pour in safflower or canola oil, and pump to prep muffin cups and cake pans. Refillable, holds about ⅔ cup oil. For information: 800-fun-oils (800-386-6457).

SAFETY WATCH

The strawberry, America's sweetheart, has been at the center of some food-safety stories in the past few years. An outbreak of cyclospora—a microbe that causes intestinal infections—was mistakenly linked to strawberries in June 1996 when more than 100 people fell ill in Texas, Toronto, and Florida, and many of them reported eating the fruit. But the Department of Health Services in California—where 80 percent of all strawberries from the United States are grown—soon traced the outbreak to raspberries imported from Guatemala (where they were washed with standing contaminated water). And in 1997, a hepatitis A outbreak, which affected more than 250 people, was traced to frozen strawberries grown in Mexico and processed in California. As a general precaution, health officials advise consumers to wash all fresh produce to protect against contaminants; rinse with running water for 15 to 30 seconds.

DOUBLE-DUTY SPATULAS

Our vote goes to these clever, dishwasher-safe utensils for busy chefs:

Do-It-All Tool

This double-edged plastic spatula (pictured below) makes kitchen work easy. Use the transparent flexible edge to scrape the bowl when you whip cream or mix batter, to ice a cake, even to clean a wet countertop, squeegee-style. Switch to the hard edge for scooping up chopped onions from the cutting board and transporting them to the pot, dividing dough, or scraping counters after you've rolled cookies. Look for the Chef's Friend, from Frieling USA; call 800-827-2582.

Handy Spoon-Spatula

Scrape, stir, and scoop without changing utensils with this hard-working plastic spoonula from Rubbermaid. The spoonula (not shown) looks like a regular spatula, but the working end is shaped like a flat, shallow spoon; at supermarkets and mass merchandisers.

Bright & Heatproof Helpers

The best thing about Le Creuset's silicone-paddle spatulas (pictured below)—next to the fun colors and old-fashioned wooden handles—is that you can use them over heat to scramble eggs or stir sauces and they won't melt, burn, or fade. Choose blue, yellow, red, green, or white in small, medium, or large spoon-spatula. At specialty stores; call 800-827-1798.

DUCK THE DUCK

It's fair game now, even for fat watchers. For years, duck had a reputation for being high-fat, but thanks to careful breeding techniques using the leanest stock and highly nutritious feeds, this bird is now a smart diet choice. The United States Department of Agriculture recently updated its nutritional values to show that, despite its rich flavor, duckling breast or leg (thigh and drumstick) is surprisingly low in calories and fat—if cooked without skin. For example, a 3½-ounce portion of cooked breast weighs in at only 139 calories and 2.5 grams of fat (for comparison, the same amount of turkey breast is 157 calories and 3 grams of fat!). We love duck roasted, sautéed, stir-fried, or grilled. Cook's note: Duck is dark meat, so even when

Stand Mixers

Stand Mixers Baking is a breeze when you leave the tough tasks to a stand mixer. It does all the work in less time and rewards you with lighter cakes, fluffier whipped cream, and taller loaves of bread than you can get by hand or with a handheld electric mixer. We recommend mixers designated as heavyweight (they handle 8 or more cups of flour and cost the most—$300 to $425) or middleweight (most mix 3 to 4 cups of flour and range in price from $100 to $170). The lightweight models (they're the ones you can detach from their stands to use as hand mixers) are the least expensive, but they aren't durable enough for the rigors of frequent use and large quantities of ingredients.

How We Chose

We put 11 stand mixers to work, whipping cream and egg whites, mashing potatoes, mixing oatmeal-raisin cookies from scratch, making cakes from mixes, and kneading bread dough. To test each model's power, we measured the maximum amount of yeast dough it could handle and evaluated its ability to cream butter straight out of the refrigerator. We looked for little or no spattering, ease of operation, and useful owner's manuals. Our engineers also checked the construction and measured wattage, speed, and noise levels.

HEAVYWEIGHT CHAMPS

KITCHENAID CLASSIC: This basic model comes with a 4½-quart bowl and enough power to knead bread dough quickly and easily. Like the other KitchenAids, it whips up tender yellow cakes, crisp oatmeal cookies loaded with raisins and nuts, and lofty whipped cream and meringues. Most home bakers will find this more than adequate for their needs.

KITCHENAID ULTRA POWER: Identical in size and design to the Classic, but has a little more oomph so it finishes tasks quicker. Its 4½-quart bowl has a handle, making it easier to remove and pour out the contents. Also comes with a plastic shield that wraps around the bowl's rim to prevent spattering when adding ingredients while the mixer is running.

KITCHENAID HEAVY DUTY: With its 5-quart bowl and ability to knead up to 10 cups of flour (enough for 3 loaves), this is for serious bakers who want maximum power. Like professional mixers, the head doesn't lift up. Instead, the bowl hooks onto side arms and is raised and lowered by turning a crank. Also comes with a pouring shield. Note: This model is 17 inches high, while others are 12 to 14 inches.

MIDDLEWEIGHT WINNERS

WEST BEND: Offers good results (egg whites whip up high; cake batters come out thoroughly mixed) at a bargain price. But you need to occasionally scrape the sides of the bowl for even mixing. The beaters are specially marked so they're easy to insert in their proper holes. This model is also one of the quietest. Comes with 1½- and 4-quart glass bowls.

HAMILTON BEACH CHEFMIX: This solid performer is notable for a head that locks in the up position, preventing it from accidentally falling down when you stop to stir. It ties with the West Bend for quietest mixer. The cord can be pushed inside the base for easy storage. Also comes with 2- and 4-quart stainless-steel bowls and a handy mixing guide above the control dial. Weak spot: The owner's manual offers few tips and no starter recipes.

SUNBEAM MIXMASTER: This sleek, chrome model prepares bread dough faster (by up to 3 minutes) than others in its category. It comes with 1½- and 4-quart stainless-steel bowls. A guide on the control dial indicates which speed to use for each chore. The instruction book is especially helpful and filled with recipes to get you started. When tackling stiff mixtures like cookie dough, the mixer head bobs up and down and appears to be struggling, but it always does a great job.

THE NEED TO KNEAD

Many bakers prefer the convenience of making bread with a mixer but feel guilty because, deep down, they believe that hand-kneaded bread tastes better. We put this theory to the test: First, our home economists pummeled white, buttermilk, and whole wheat doughs with mixers from the heavy- and middleweight categories, then by hand. They found it hard to tell any difference in taste or texture among them. One exception: Though it didn't affect taste, loaves prepared by heavyweight mixers rose slightly higher.

Microwave Ovens

In the market for a microwave? You'll be happy to know that today's ovens boast sleek designs, quicker cooking times, and a variety of helpful features. Our top picks range in price from under $140 to over $250.

How We Chose

We zapped everything from water to chicken parts to brownies to check the evenness of cooking in 19 new models, giving high marks to ovens that were user-friendly. Our picks include 6 family-size (1 to 1.39 cubic feet) ovens with 1,000 watts (the highest available during our tests), plus a standout in the compact categories. Here are some of the features we especially liked:

Automatic-cooking pads: Control panel has pads or push buttons for preprogrammed reheating or cooking times. Some can also be adjusted to the quantity of food being cooked.

Automatic weight defrost: Defrosts at preset power levels after you've entered an item's weight and sometimes a category, like chicken or beef. An on-screen display usually tells you when it's time to turn or remove defrosted portions of food.

Quick start: Just 1 touch starts the oven for brief periods, such as 30 seconds or 1 minute. Good for adding time at the end if your food isn't hot enough.

Smart sensors: Determine cooking time by reacting to the amount of steam released by foods during cooking or reheating. They're more precise than automatic-cooking pads, but not foolproof.

SAMSUNG (compact): This petite powerhouse gives great results for key tasks like reheating and defrosting—and it bakes a mean brownie. The microwave also comes with an automatic-cooking pad for popcorn. Ideal for those who use their ovens mostly for quick heating and have limited counter space.

KENMORE: This model has "smart sensors" (see above) for precise heating every time. The display provides helpful cues, such as when to rearrange food during defrosting, and the turntable returns a cup to its starting position. Plus, unlike most, the timer can be used while the microwave is in operation—handy for those who like to use it for other tasks.

SANYO: Press the appropriate automatic-cooking pad and popcorn, potatoes, pizza, or frozen vegetables are done to perfection. Popcorn fans will appreciate that it pops the most kernels without scorching. The turntable returns to its starting position, so it's easy to remove dishes and grab piping hot coffee mugs.

GOLDSTAR: Of all our picks, this is the easiest to use thanks to a display with instructions that prompt you every step of the way. This one also has special sensor pads for various foods, like the cake button that our testers noted delivers a yummy, picture-perfect devil's food cake. This model also has a timer that works while the oven is cooking.

SHARP: This microwave boasts the most even results and quickest cooking times. It even turned out a juicy meat loaf. You'll find 8 automatic-cooking pads for popular foods. One drawback: There's no quick reference guide on the oven, so you have to refer to the manual for help.

GE: In addition to automatic-cooking pads and automatic weight defrost (good for meats), there's time defrost, which is preprogrammed for low power (handy for thawing soups and stews). The cheat sheet posted inside the oven is especially helpful because it lists what codes to push for different foods.

SAMSUNG: Has a special device that browns and crisps chops and casseroles. In addition to automatic-cooking pads for the usual suspects, this unit has one for baby food (GH moms found it warmed jars perfectly). The display prompts can be programmed for French and Spanish. And, like the compact Samsung, this model chimes instead of beeps.

CAN YOU REALLY COOK IN A MICROWAVE?

Yes. Foods that are typically steamed or poached—like fish, vegetables, and even chicken breasts—cook more quickly and actually look and taste better than when steamed on the stovetop. Brownies also come out fudgy and moist. However, most microwaves don't do a good job browning burgers or baking cakes. Intent on learning to micro-cook? The Multiple Choice from Sharp has a display with step-by-step instructions.

cooked properly (breast to 165°F., leg to 185°F.), it will look slightly pink. Overcooking will dry it out.

THE RAW TRUTH ABOUT VEGGIES

Eating food fresh and uncooked is a big trend—there's a raw-food magazine, several Web sites devoted to the craze, and juice bars aplenty. But don't stash your pots and pans yet. While it's true that heat can destroy some vitamins, cooking makes certain foods more healthful. For example, raw legumes and eggs contain substances that interfere with the absorption of some of their nutrients; heat removes these blockers.

Cooking also breaks down plant-cell walls, making important compounds more available to the body. Carrots cooked until tender-crisp deliver more beta-carotene than raw ones. And heat-processed tomatoes (like tomato paste) provide much more of the cancer-fighter lycopene than fresh tomatoes. Properly cooking eggs, seafood, and meat is also the best way to destroy any disease-causing bacteria. Just don't over-do: High temperatures and long cooking times ultimately reduce the nutritive value of all foods.

UNMASKING FAT-FREE PRODUCTS

Reality check: Most "fat-free" foods contain fat—and it's been that way since the Food and Drug Administration defined the term in 1993.

To be fat-free, a food must have "less than 0.5 grams of fat per serving." Almost all foods contain a trace, with some exceptions: salt, vinegar, pure gelatin, and sugar and sugar products such as soft drinks. Manufacturers have the right, though, to round numbers under 0.5 grams to zero—and they do. That's why you can find so many products these days proudly wearing the fat-free label. Still, the trace of fat is no great shakes. Even if you ate a whole 8-ounce bag of fat-free pretzels (with 0.4 fat grams per serving), the fat content would be under 4 grams—nothing compared to the 880 calories! The real risk with no-fat claims is that you'll ignore portion sizes and pack in calories—which does a lot more to add pounds than a tiny bit of fat does.

KNIFE POINTS: ELECTRIC VS. CARVERS

Even the most beautiful golden-brown turkey can be reduced to shreds if you don't use the right knife. To find the top one, we compared a razor-sharp carving knife and 9 electric knives, thinking the carving knife would be easier to control. Surprise: An electric model was superior for ultrathin, uniform slices. It moves quickly—so you don't have the same control as you do when maneuvering around the wings and drumsticks with a carver—but you're able to slice every last bit of meat off the bones. We found the plug-in knives also went through roast beef like butter and cut crusty rye bread as neatly as a bakery slicing machine. For perfect slices: The Black & Decker Slice Right Electric Knife was the most comfort-

able to hold and the speediest worker. The snap-on cutting guide, especially handy for bread, ensures that every slice is the same thickness. For information, call 800-231-9786.

PRESSURE COOKERS THAT MAKE SOUP FAST

A pressure cooker—a heavy, air-tight pot that cooks on the stove with superheated steam—is just the thing for making quick soups and stews that taste like they've simmered for hours. We hand-picked the following favorites, each with a 6-quart capacity and multiple safety features. [Note: For our Pressure-Cooker Chicken Broth, see page 54.]

Seeing Clearly
The Safe 2 Visio (pictured above) from T-Fal has a window in the lid so you can watch what's cooking. The price is steep, but this model is loaded with user-friendly features: a durable non-stick coating inside and a black porcelain-enamel finish (so it's a snap to clean), high- and low-pressure levels, and a quick-release setting that lowers pressure in seconds so you can serve dinner even faster.

Best Buy:
The Rapida from Fagor (not pictured), a gleaming stainless-steel

Cookware

Our pick of the pans includes 8 winners that run the gamut in price, from a complete set for just over $90 to a single saucepan that breaks the bank at $100. Two trends we applaud: nonstick finishes on interiors and exteriors, and break-resistant glass lids that let you keep an eye on what's cooking. Sure, lots of sets resemble Mom's, but heavy, professional-looking cookware is now the norm, often sold separately rather than in a set, with eclectic choices like woks and paella pans.

How We Chose

Selecting cookware can be daunting—we know because we browned flour, flipped burgers, and simmered spaghetti sauce in skillets and saucepans from 62 cookware lines. And we didn't just do cooking trials: We considered the heft of a pan, whether its handles held up to heat and felt good in our grip, and how easily it came clean after we burnt cheese in it. (To choose among metals and finishes, see "Taking the Heat," at right.)

ALL-PURPOSE BARGAINS

REGAL WARE ROYAL DIAMOND Here you get upscale touches at a down-to-earth price. An allover nonstick coating makes these aluminum pots a snap to clean and a cooking dream: Without a drop of oil, eggs glide right out of the skillet. The plastic handles come with thumb rests; lids are made of clear glass. Most lightweight of our picks, these are easy on the arm but not for cooks who like high heat because the thinner aluminum can overcook quickly.

REVERE CLEAR ADVANTAGE It's homey-looking—but there's nothing old-fashioned about how this stainless-steel set performs. Aluminum bases provide even heat distribution for perfect browning of chicken breasts and hamburgers. Pieces are user-friendly: Lids are see-through, and knobs and plastic handles fit naturally in your hand. Even after repeated use, these pans were easier to keep shiny than other stainless ware.

MID-PRICED PLEASERS

BERNDES SIGNOCAST CLASSIC COLORS These cast-aluminum pieces come with nonstick interiors and blue, green, or black nonstick exteriors. A plus if you're using the pans in the oven: Plastic handles can take higher heat (450°F.) and are angled for a comfortable grip. The skillet's low sides make it easier to flip

pancakes, but may be a bit shallow if you're cooking a one-dish dinner for 4.

FARBERWARE CLASSIC SERIES With clean lines, plastic handles, and dangling hook rings, these stainless-steel pieces look just like the ones you grew up with. But they feel more substantial; the traditional-looking pots and pans have been improved with heavier aluminum bases for even heating. We got great results every time.

T-FAL ARMARAL PERFECTION This cookware is perfect for those who love the professional look, but hate the heavy weight and high prices that come with it. Home cooks will also appreciate the convenience of nonstick surfaces inside and out. The aluminum pots have stainless-steel handles with rivets that stay cool to the touch when cooking on the stovetop. They're also safe to use in the oven.

PROFESSIONAL STYLE

CALPHALON PROFESSIONAL NONSTICK Made of hard-anodized aluminum with an allover nonstick finish, these withstand higher heat than others. Over a medium-high flame, a skillet turns out steak as brown and crusty as one from a cast-iron frypan. Skillets have sloping sides for tossing and turning foods like a pro—sans spatula. Minor drawback: Riveted stainless-steel handles become very hot.

ALL-CLAD STAINLESS We love this classic stainless-steel ware—the pots are the ideal shape for whisking; the pans are perfect for folding omelets. Because the entire inner core is made of aluminum, you get even heating throughout. Our testers found that the riveted handles stayed cool even after lengthy cooking. Some pieces come in a nonstick version.

MEYER ANOLON PROFESSIONAL This weighty hard-anodized aluminum set has an exceptional nonstick interior finish (pancakes and eggs slide right off). Serious cooks can depend on it for every task from quickly bringing water to a boil to turning out delicate crêpes. The pan maintains a constant heat to keep spaghetti sauce at a simmer (no need to adjust the burner!). Sole drawback: Riveted stainless-steel handles get quite hot.

SHOULD YOU BUY A SET?

A set will always be less expensive than buying individual pieces, but it's a good value only if it includes items you'll actually use. Unless you need a basic starter set, mix and match from different manufacturers. Select, for example, an inexpensive nonstick skillet for eggs or "reheats," and heavy, professional-style pots for sauces and stews.

Taking the Heat

The measure of cookware is the metal it's made of. Each material and finish has strengths and weaknesses that affect its price and durability as well as whether or not your potatoes brown evenly, your corn chowder needs stirring, and how big a cleanup job you're left with after the company's gone. Here are some guidelines to help you choose your cookware.

ALUMINUM Aluminum is second only to copper in evenly distributing heat. And it's far less costly. But because it reacts with food, aluminum is almost always lined with either a nonstick finish, stainless steel, or porcelain enamel. Drawback: Unless treated or coated with a harder metal, cookware is easily dented and warped.

HARD-ANODIZED ALUMINUM Hard-anodized aluminum is electrochemically treated to harden the surface so the aluminum won't react with foods or warp easily. The process gives it a dark color, making stains less likely to show. Drawback: Must always be handwashed; dishwasher detergent discolors the surface.

CAST IRON Cast iron can be used over very high heat, making it the choice for pan-seared steaks. It also interacts with food, a plus when you want to add iron to your diet. Drawbacks: You need to give it tender loving care to build up a stick-resistant patina and prevent rusting. Iron may also discolor creamy sauces. Note: When coated with enamel, cast iron is easier to maintain and won't affect foods, but can't be used over high heat. Your best bet: Buy an inexpensive, unlined pan for pan-searing—not everyday use.

COPPER Copper, lined with tin or stainless steel because it reacts with food, conducts heat quickly and evenly and is most responsive to changes in heat. Take a pot off the range and bubbling stops immediately. If you pride yourself on fancy sauces, invest in a copper saucepan. Drawbacks: The expense (a stockpot can go for more than $400). Also, not even frequent polishing will keep it spot-free.

STAINLESS STEEL Stainless steel is extremely durable and nonreactive, but it doesn't cook evenly. That's why there's always a layer of aluminum or copper on the bottom (and sometimes up the sides) to better conduct heat. Drawback: Pots made of stainless steel require a little elbow grease to keep them shiny.

ENAMEL-ON-STEEL Enamel-on-steel comes in bright glossy colors. Draw-back: We recommend it only for boiling water for tea or pasta because it doesn't distribute heat well and may chip.

NONSTICK Nonstick surfaces cut down on fat and are much easier to clean. And yes, you can brown food on them just as well as in unlined metal pans. Today's coatings are also more durable and are showing up on expensive cookware. In general, the better the quality of the pan, the better the finish. Drawbacks: Many new nonstick pans have ridges or waffle patterns for extra durability. But they make cleaning harder and leave an imprint on foods. Nonstick surfaces also need special care. Avoid using metal utensils (regardless of the manufacturer's advice) to prevent harmless but unsightly scratches. Handwash thoroughly (food residue isn't always visible on dark surfaces and can build up and cause sticking). For best cleaning results, we recommend using Bon Ami, a powdered nonabrasive cleanser, and a plastic mesh pad.

model with a potbelly shape that can hold bulky foods like chicken parts or spareribs. It has a built-in pressure valve and an extrathick aluminum base to prevent scorching—features usually found only on pricier models.

SMART SOLUTION: LITTLE ELECTRIC GRILL, BIG COOKING POWER
(pictured below)

If you have limited space or want the convenience of plug-in grilling outdoors, this one's for you. The Electric Patio Caddie from Char-Broil has a special aluminum lining that holds in heat so you can really sear a steak and uses ceramic briquettes to impart cooked-over-the-coals flavor. It's portable enough for a patio yet large enough to hold 8 burgers or even a 12-pound turkey, and has a handy thermometer built right in the hood (the grill heats up to 700°F., higher than most electric models). Available, only in cobalt blue, at home centers, mass merchandisers, and hardware stores. For information, call 800-241-7548.

A TELL-ALL PRODUCE BOOK
How many times have you been stumped in the store, unable to find an unusual fruit or vegetable that a recipe calls for? Now about 3,000 supermarkets have the *Shoppers' Guide to Fresh Produce* on hand, for quick, complete answers. It pictures, describes, and tells how to use more than

250 different fruits, vegetables, and herbs, highlights peak availability, and gives tips on selecting and storing. It's great to leaf through! You'll find it on display in produce sections at some stores in these chains: Associated Food, Giant Food, Grand Union, Kings, Kroger, Publix, Safeway, Wal-Mart Supercenter, and Wegman's. Published by Try-Foods International, the guidebook may soon come out in a less expensive softcover version for consumers. For more information, call Try-Foods at 800-421-8871.

BETTER WAYS TO MEASURE UP
Good Housekeeping Institute was instrumental in establishing the standards for measuring cups and spoons—until then, housewives relied on teacups and soupspoons. Now measuring cups are getting even more accurate. You no longer need to double up and use 2 dry measures (the ½-cup and ¼-cup size) when you could use one ¾-cup one instead. Cups come in more precise sizes so you can easily measure out every amount recipes call for.

What we've found helpful in our test kitchens: Tupperware's 6-piece plastic set (pictured above, top), including ¼-, ⅓-, ½-, ⅔-, ¾- and 1-cup sizes. (Call 800-858-7221 for a distributor near you.) If you prefer stainless steel, a handsome 7-piece set with all the above sizes plus ⅛ cup is available from The Baker's Catalogue (800-827-6836). And to eliminate

constant refilling when you need several cups of flour, get the catalogue's 2-cup stainless steel measure. Both sets have pour spouts and are clearly marked and dishwasher-safe.

Also noteworthy: At left, Tupperware's 6-piece measuring spoon set (⅛, ¼, ½, and 1 teaspoon, plus ½ tablespoon and 1 tablespoon). Each spoon easily detaches from the hook to rest level on the counter for filling—a convenience for bread, cake, and cookie bakers.

SHOULD YOU WASH POULTRY BEFORE COOKING?
Not according to experts like Margy Woodburn, Ph.D., professor emeritus in nutrition and food management at Oregon State University. "Research shows that rinsing chicken before cooking removes only a small amount of bacteria and may introduce other risks," says Woodburn. Nasty illness-causing organisms like campylobacter or salmonellae frequently contaminate raw poultry, and rinsing can transfer them, via splashing, to the sink, faucet, and countertops. Besides not rinsing, Woodburn recommends these preventive measures:
• Put packaging directly in the garbage.
• Wipe up drips promptly with paper towels (a sponge can be a bacterial breeding ground).
• Thoroughly wash all work surfaces, utensils, and your hands with hot, soapy water.

Dishwashers

These 6 quiet, energy-efficient models can handle whatever your family dishes out. They are arranged according to price, ranging from under $300 to over $600.

All models have the following cycles: normal; pots & pans or heavy wash; rinse & hold or quick rinse (rinses dishes being held until the dishwasher is full to prevent odor buildup); and energy- saver dry. But many offer more options than just the basics. Some are worth getting to know; others you may decide you can live without:

Add-a-Dish: indicates when you can open the dishwasher to add a last-minute item.

Child Lock: stops machine from starting accidentally.

China/Crystal (also Light Wash, Water Miser): offers a shorter wash cycle for china, crystal, and lightly soiled dishes.

Delay Start: lets you start wash cycle at a later time, anywhere from 1 to 14 hours.

Favorite Cycle: lets you program your machine to automatically select the options you use most often.

Water Heat (also High-Temp Wash): delays wash cycle until hottest water temperature is reached (usually 135 to 140°F.); ideal for people who keep their water heater at a low setting to conserve energy.

WHITE WESTINGHOUSE Quiet Clean I: Made by Frigidaire, this model is as quiet as more expensive ones. It cleans normally soiled dishes and glasses well. Also uses the least amount of water of our picks (5.85 gallons for a normal cycle, while others ranged from 6.38 to 7.75). Weak spot: It was the least able of our picks to handle burned-on food. You'll need to do more hand scrubbing.

ROPER: Like the deluxe Whirlpool (its parent company), this washer does a good job on dinnerware, including pots and pans. It has a delay-start feature (hard to find on low-end machines). Bottom rack fits a 13" platter upright; most others fit 12". Also has extra fold-down shelves for small cups. But it's the noisiest of our picks, and the filter for food residue must be cleaned (though it's easy to do).

KENMORE Ultra Wash: Cleans dishes and glasses exceptionally well; second only to the high-end Kenmore. It's also very quiet; you'll be pleasantly surprised by the low hum of the wash cycle. Inside, it mirrors the deluxe version, except it doesn't have fold-down tines in the upper rack. A special tray holds long utensils, such as spatulas and serving spoons.

WHIRLPOOL: Though its dimensions are the same as the others, the interior is designed for extra capacity and flexibility. (All our picks fit 10 place settings, but this one did so with plenty of leftover room.) The silverware basket is attached to the door to provide more space for dishes in the lower rack. But you have to be especially careful not to overload the silverware or it won't come out as clean. The top rack can be lowered to accommodate tall glasses. Also has extra fold-down shelves. As for performance, it does a good job on dishes, pots, and pans; some glasses came out spotty.

KENMORE: Does a superb cleaning job. This is the only one of our picks where casserole dishes with burned-on food came out spotless. An electronically controlled sensor monitors the soil level and adjusts cycles accordingly. A digital display indicates how much time is left. You can program it to select your favorite cycles. Fold-down tines in the upper rack let you make room for larger items. There are also fold-down shelves for extra cups and a compartment for long utensils. The silverware basket can be split. Plus, this has the longest warranty of our picks.

GE: You'll get excellent results on dishes, cookware, and glasses. An electronically controlled sensor "evaluates" how dirty dishes are and chooses the number of wash and rinse cycles accordingly. A digital display tells how much time is left in the cycle and registers a code if problems occur, such as a blocked drain. Six rows of fold-down tines in the bottom make room for large items. Fits a 13" platter upright. The silverware basket has covered compartments for small items like baby-bottle caps and can be separated into 2 parts.

LOWDOWN ON LOADING

- Place glasses and cups in between the prongs; never over them; make sure they don't touch each other.
- Load plates, pans, and casserole dishes with the soiled surfaces facing toward the middle (where the most forceful spray is located).
- Plastic items (only those marked dishwasher safe) should be placed on the top rack where it's coolest.
- Mix silverware—some up, some down—so the pieces don't nest against each other. This allows water to hit all surfaces.

Gas Ranges

With the right stove, you have ultimate control. You can brown food evenly, simmer gently, and bake like a pro. Our top picks below are arranged according to price, from under $650 to over $1,500.

How We Chose

To pick the top performers, our experts subjected 17 top-of-the-line models to more than a dozen cooking tasks—from heating spaghetti sauce to broiling steak to baking apple pies, biscuits, and sugar cookies. Two features we found to be essential were a self-cleaning-oven cycle and sealed gas burners, which prevent spills from dripping below the cooktop surface. Other options that might suit your cooking needs:

- Simmer burners maintain a very low flame, ideal for keeping soups warm.
- Power burners produce a superhigh flame—great for boiling water, searing steak, or stir-frying.
- Convection ovens have fans that circulate hot air, which speeds up cooking times and browns roasts to perfection.

HOTPOINT: Best value: This budget brand (made by GE) gets high marks for performance and convenience. The oven is as large as the more deluxe GE Profile's, and burner grates and drip pans are black, so they won't show stains as easily. Minor drawbacks: an old-fashioned dial knob (instead of touch-control pads) for the oven and a latch to close the unit for self-cleaning (others lock automatically).

MAYTAG: In our tests, every strip of bacon and slice of bread crisped evenly under the superb broiler. There's a bonus half-size rack to give you extra space in the oven when you have a big turkey inside. We especially like the large window. Weak spot: You can't remove the sealed burner caps for easy cleaning as you can with other ranges.

WHIRLPOOL ACCUBAKE: Our testers found this range gave even results, turning out pies with flaky crusts—top and bottom—and batch after batch of golden-brown biscuits. It also has one of the largest ovens available—about 20 percent bigger than older models—and 6 rack positions, so you can juggle items if necessary. The low-heat burner maintains a steady flame, so there's no need to adjust when simmering.

FRIGIDAIRE GALLERY: This model offers a warmer drawer in the space below the oven usually reserved for storage. Use it to heat plates, keep rolls warm, or hold a pie at the perfect temperature to melt a scoop of ice cream. Another smart feature is a preheat pad that beeps when the oven reaches the right temperature.

GE PROFILE: This model heats the most evenly of our picks. When we baked 3 sheets of cookies at once, they all came out alike. The large-capacity oven (slightly larger than the Whirlpool's) has 3 racks (most have 2). The cooktop has heavy grates and a stylish glass backsplash. Numbered pads (like those on microwaves) make setting cooking times and temperatures a cinch.

KENMORE: Closest to a professional model, this stove has a superhigh burner that boils water almost as quickly as a commercial one. Grates are durable, but at 4 pounds each, they might be too heavy for some. Its cooking performance would please any master chef: Angel food cake came out picture-perfect; broiled chicken had delectably crisp skin.

KITCHENAID: Priciest because of its many features, like a convection oven that speeds up cooking times, delivering a crusty rib roast in four-fifths the time. (You enter your usual time and temperature, and it makes the conversions for you.) Also, check out the unique bread-rising setting, and the temperature probe that indicates when food is done. The downside? Its oven is the smallest of our picks.

PROFESSIONAL-STYLE RANGES: WORTH THE BIG BUCKS?

Heavy-duty ranges like those used in restaurants look great, but what do you get for the steep price (starting at about $2,000)? We put several through our standard cooking tests, and overall, the ovens gave average results, sometimes falling short of our 7 picks. It is true that the burners are more powerful and heat faster, but you can't always adjust them to cook slowly. Still, these ranges are built to last. So, if you do tons of stovetop cooking, consider going commercial. Otherwise, know that what you're really paying for is the look. Our top choice: Viking. Its powerful burners can be turned down to a low simmer. It comes with a convection oven and an infrared broiler. But the burners aren't sealed, the oven is small, and there is no self-cleaning feature.

THE VEGGIE QUESTION: FRESH VS. FROZEN

Nine out of ten consumers think fresh vegetables are much more nutritious than canned and frozen. Surprise: Studies by the University of Illinois at Urbana-Champaign found that many processed veggies stack up favorably to fresh. "Nutrient values of fresh-from-the-field produce are not always what most consumers eventually eat," says Barbara Klein, Ph.D., principal investigator. "Produce loses vitamins from when it's harvested to the time it's eaten." Freezing and canning, on the other hand, lock in nutrients for up to a year.

DISPOSABLE GLOVES: HELP OR HINDRANCE?

When food-service employees wear vinyl gloves, do you feel confident that the food is clean and safe? It may not be. "If an employee doesn't wash his hands properly before putting on gloves, there can be a higher risk of transmitting disease-causing microorganisms than if he just left the gloves off and washed his hands," says Daryl S. Paulson, Ph.D., president and CEO of Bio-Science Laboratories, Inc., in Bozeman, MT.

A recent BioScience study showed that E. coli bacteria can be transferred from contaminated hands to the outside of gloves through an opening as small as a needle prick. Unlike sterile latex surgical gloves, "vinyl food-grade gloves commonly have pinhole punctures, and are easily ripped through normal use," says Paulson.

Another problem: Many workers get inadequate training. "They may wear the same pair all day—while handling raw and cooked food, making change, sneezing, and touching their hair, face, or the telephone," says food safety specialist Alita Rethmeyer, Ed.D., R.D., of Consulting Nutritional Services in Calabasas, CA. Vinyl gloves should be used for one task, such as slicing cold cuts, then discarded.

When you spot unsanitary practices at a lunch counter, cancel your order and talk to the manager. The more you speak up about safety hazards, the more likely it is that local businesses will take measures to train employees properly.

WHAT DOES "LOW-FAT" REALLY MEAN ON FAST-FOOD MENUS?

It's the nutritional claim you see most at fast-food restaurants. And even though federal regulations stipulate that to be low-fat, a food must have no more than 3 grams of fat per standard serving, portions are often 3, 4, even 5 times the size of the government standard, which means a dish could have 9, 12, or 15 grams of fat and still technically be called low-fat. On top of that, low-fat doesn't automatically mean low-calorie. Even if it's fat-free, a huge portion can be a calorie splurge. Other menu claims—light, lite, or heart-healthy, have legal definitions too: If nutrition information is not listed on the menu, ask for it.

FRUITS & VEGETABLES: SURPRISING WAYS TO GET 5 A DAY

Eating 5 fruit and veggie servings daily can be hard—especially during winter. Some products (like all-fruit jam or vegetable chips) sound promising, but don't deliver; others, which seem like splurges, can count toward your goal but may contain extra fat or calories. Here's the lowdown on good-for-you indulgences that help you meet your daily requirements:

What counts:
A baked apple, a banana split, a Bloody Mary, a BLT, candied sweet potatoes, chocolate-dipped strawberries, coleslaw, cranberry relish, a fruit smoothie, hot or sparkling apple cider, pumpkin pie, salsa, sauerkraut on a hot dog, tomato sauce, veggie-topped pizza.

What doesn't:
Chewy fruit snacks/roll-ups, fruit-filled toaster pastries or cereal bars, fruit-flavored cereals like Froot Loops, jam, juice-sweetened cookies, onion dip, pumpkin/banana quick bread (from a mix),

sherbet, spinach pasta, vegetable crackers or chips.

THE BURNING QUESTION

It's not enough that we worry about secondhand smoke and additives…now studies suggest a possible link between grilled foods and carcinogens.

Charring meat at very high temperatures—whether by grilling, frying, or broiling, as opposed to baking or roasting—produces chemical substances that have been shown to cause cancer in some animal studies. And when meat is browned with intense heat over a direct flame, and fat drips on the fire and coals, it creates smoke containing carcinogens called polycyclic aromatic hydrocarbons.

But there's no need to roll your barbecue off the patio and put it away. "You can still grill, and grill healthfully," says Jennifer K. Nelson, M.S., R.D., director of clinical dietetics at the Mayo Clinic in Rochester, MN. "Cook at lower heat, cook more quickly, don't char your foods, and keep the grill from flaring up." Tips for healthy grilling:

1) Trim excess fat from meat or poultry before cooking to minimize flare-ups. 2) If meat does char or burn, cut away blackened portion. 3) Raise adjustable cooking racks to their highest position above the heat. 4) Brush barbecue sauces and glazes on only during the last several minutes of grilling; if they splatter and drip down on the flames, the sugar in them can cause flare-ups and smoke. 5) Precook ribs, thick cuts of meat, and whole turkeys indoors before grilling, then sear briefly over high heat.

GRILL PANS: HOT BUY OR GIMMICK?

Stove-top grill pans are big business now, from simple ridged skillets (as low as $10) to high-end cast-iron models (over $80) and two-piece flying-saucer-type designs (under $20). The theory is that foods cooked in them contain less fat and are more flavorful than skillet-browned versions.

To find out, we cooked hamburgers in 4 different grill pans (nonstick aluminum, nonstick cast aluminum, enameled cast-iron, and a flying-saucerlike model with a drip pan you fill with water) and 2 regular skillets (nonstick aluminum and cast-iron). We used the same burner on the same range each time, preheated all pans to the same temperature, and cooked each batch of burgers for identical times. Then we sampled them in a blind tasting and asked the Chemistry Department to analyze their fat content.

The results: There was no significant difference in fat among the burgers. The ones from the first 3 grill pans had attractive sear marks, but no noticeable outdoorsy grilled flavor. The burgers in the grill with drip pan browned poorly, were least flavorful of all, and made more work, since there were 2 pieces to clean instead of 1. Ironically, the hamburgers cooked in the cast-iron skillet, which were brown and crusty on both sides, got the most votes for best backyard grill taste.

So if you put a premium on grill marks, cook your chicken, steak, or burgers on a standard grill pan. But if flavor is your priority, stick to a good old cast-iron frying pan—or the real grill, of course.

WHAT'S NEW: OSSIE BURGERS!

Made from ground ostrich, ossie burgers are showing up on menus nationwide—and with good reason. Ostrich meat is deep red with a taste and texture similar to beef, and it is as low-fat as skinless chicken breast. This new breed of burger is touted as a healthful choice. But its "good for you" claims are based on whole ostrich meat, not ground—hardly a fair comparison, since fat may be added during grinding.

To get the facts, we ordered cooked ossie burgers to go from two New Jersey restaurants and had the Good Housekeeping Institute's Chemistry Department do a nutritional analysis. The burgers averaged about 11 percent fat by weight—about 40 percent less than cooked ground beef, but substantially more than ostrich meat (2.8 percent fat) or even a lean pork loin chop (7.8 percent fat). So don't assume a birdburger is really low-fat. Even if the meat was ground without extra fat, some was probably added before or during cooking to make the superlean burger supertasty.

HIDDEN SALT IN SEASONINGS

If you're cutting back on salt—because of a health problem like high blood pressure, or to improve your diet overall—you may be shaking on a Cajun, lemon-herb, garlic-pepper, or other spicy blend instead. But salt is often a key ingredient in these products—some even contain more sodium than those with "salt" in their names. For example, 1 brand of lemon-pepper seasoning has 191 milligrams (mg) of sodium per ¼ teaspoon, while an equal amount of the same brand's garlic salt has only 120 mg. (Pure salt has about 550 mg per ¼ teaspoon.) Some better low-sodium strategies:

• Read ingredient lists carefully; check the Nutrition Facts panel for an exact sodium count. (Not all seasoning-blend labels have a nutritional rundown; because packages are small, the Food and Drug Administration doesn't require it. These products must provide an address or phone number for consumers who want information.)

• Watch portion size. The sodium content may sound moderate for a standard ¼-teaspoon serving, but some recipes—or your taste buds—may call for 2 or 3 times that.

• Compare brands. Cajun seasoning, for example, can range from 60 to 260 mg of sodium per ¼ teaspoon.

• Look for salt-free herb-spice blends, or make your own mixtures at home.

• Take another look at your whole diet. Government guidelines recommend a cap of 2,400 mg of sodium per day—even if you're in good health. And that's easy to exceed, because sodium shows up in unexpected places like cereal (up to 350 mg per cup), American cheese (400 mg per ounce), and instant pudding (420 mg per half cup).

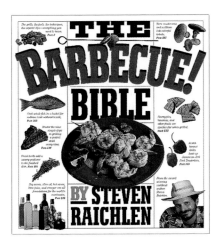

GLOBAL GRILLING

What better way to learn the ins and outs of grilling (the world's oldest cooking method), than by personally sampling barbecue in 25 countries? Award-winning cookbook author Steven Raichlen did just that for his 500-recipe book, *The Barbecue Bible*. Raichlen's 3-year, 150,000-mile odyssey resulted in a book packed with mouthwatering recipes like Pakistani "Slipper" Kabobs, Samba-style Hotdogs, Piri-piri Chicken, and a recipe for Shrimp on the Barbie from Down Under.

TASTE-TESTING CHUNK-LIGHT TUNAS

When it comes to selecting tuna, about 3 out of 4 American shoppers take the bait for chunk-light (usually a combination of yellowfin and skipjack varieties) rather than solid albacore—partly because albacore is pricier, partly because it's drier. To find the best of the chunk-light choices, we compared brands in a blind test. A panel of 8 food experts (including 2 moms who make tuna sandwiches for their families) evaluated 11 kinds. Samples ranged from inexpensive store brands to premium labels, packed in water, soybean oil, and olive oil. First, tasters examined each in its unlabeled can, undrained, then they sampled them plain to evaluate flavor and texture. Next, the tunas were drained well and combined with mayonnaise, chopped celery, and fresh lemon juice for the classic salad.

The verdict:

Flavor and texture differences were minor overall, and pronounced only in the unseasoned tuna tastings—a few brands seemed too fishy, mushy, salty, or tinny. But since most of us—except die-hard dieters—eat tuna with some garnish, we weren't really bothered; the salad ingredients masked the small flaws, but still let our winners emerge. Here, our picks for the top of each class, taking pre- and post-salad comments into account:

• Packed in water (a category that outsells oil-packed by 4 to 1): Chicken of the Sea won for its firm texture and large chunks of pale-pink fish, which could almost pass for solid white. Its fresh flavor and aroma got top marks when eaten plain and in salad. Bumble Bee, with its slightly salty notes, scored well in both rounds.

• Packed in vegetable oil: Our tasters picked Chicken of the Sea again, because it had the "most classic tuna flavor," according to one panelist. Others noted its overall clean, pleasing taste and

good texture. And Bumble Bee earned compliments once more because it made a nice salad, though some found it a bit fishy on its own.

• Packed in olive oil: Progresso and Bumble Bee both fared well—the former for its attractive pale chunks of tuna in an assertive oil, the latter for its mild, fresh taste.

MICROWAVE MYTHS

• Myth: Standing in front of the microwave oven while it's on will give you cancer.

• Fact: Federal regulations have established strict limits on the amount of energy that can be emitted by microwave ovens. These standards are much lower than the level at which any adverse health effects are believed possible. Even if an oven leaks, you may feel some warmth but you will not be at risk for cancer, says Sharon Franke, the Institute's expert on microwave cookery and food appliances. Unlike X-rays and ultraviolet light, microwave energy is nonionizing, meaning it can't damage genes or cells.

• Myth: Never put aluminum foil in the microwave.

• Fact: "Older ovens—those made twenty or more years ago— couldn't handle foil because of a problem with energy reflection and would become damaged," says Franke. "But you can use foil safely in newer models." For instance, small pieces can be folded around corners of foods like brownies and lasagna to keep them from overcooking. Note that you should keep the foil smooth and at least one inch away from oven walls; pieces that

have jagged edges may cause some sparking. Other metals, such as wire twist ties, should never be used in the microwave.

• Myth: Don't use plastic wrap in the microwave; toxic substances in the plastic can get into your food.

• Fact: Under very high temperatures (300°F. or higher), plastic wrap can melt into food. However, it's highly unlikely that food will ever get that hot unless you're cooking—not just reheating— something that contains large amount of sugar or fat, says Franke. Even if you do eat heated plastic particles, experts say there's no scientific evidence they will make you ill. But to be extra safe, advises Franke, put food in a microwave-safe bowl, then cover with plastic wrap.

A LEAN CHOICE FOR RED-MEAT LOVERS

Imagine biting into a 7-ounce filet mignon that has a mere 4 grams of fat instead of the usual 19—or a juicy 5-ounce burger with 6 fat grams instead of 20. Now you can have your meat and eat it too: Piedmontese beef is so lean that some cuts (like the New York Strip Steak) are even lower in fat and cholesterol than skinless chicken.

This trim choice originates from the Piedmont region of northwest Italy, where it's been bred for more than 100 years. The cattle are naturally leaner than their beefier, bulkier cousins and higher in protein-dense meat; they have a smaller bone structure with more muscle and less fat. The breed isn't genetically altered, or given growth hor-

mones—it's just blessed with a leaner physique. And now Piedmontese cattle are raised in the United States, too, with the meat marketed and distributed (as Better Beef) to upscale stores and through mail-order exclusively by Wooster, Ohio-based Ameri-Pied Beef. Two more big differences, in addition to the beef's nutritional profile: The price is about 25 to 30 percent higher than supermarket cuts, and the cooking time is approximately one third to one half shorter. (It's important not to overcook, or this lean beef can taste like shoe leather.)

Ameri-Pied claims its products are tender and tasty, but we wanted to find out for ourselves that this wasn't another case of sacrificing fat for flavor. So 8 experts in the Good Housekeeping test kitchens compared Piedmontese and supermarket ground chuck patties, filet mignons, cube steaks, and shell steaks in a blind sampling. All cuts were cooked separately in a nonstick skillet with just 1 teaspoon olive oil.

The burgers were the favorite lean pick, praised for being less greasy and chewy than the store-bought patties. Filet mignons and cube steaks also made the cut for good flavor. But the shell steak, generally not a tough meat to begin with, got the lowest rating because it was too tender, almost mushy.

Still, it's not a perfect world, and with so many cuts to choose from, Piedmontese beef seems a fitting solution if you make watching fat and cholesterol a top priority. For more information, call Ameri-Pied Beef at 800-611-8332.

APPETIZERS & BEVERAGES

Firecracker Mix

PREP: 10 MINUTES PLUS 30 MINUTES PER BATCH TO COOL
BAKE: 30 MINUTES PER BATCH

A spicy party snack so addictive, you can't eat just one handful! Omit the ground red pepper for kids or guests with a mild-taste preference. Make up to a week in advance—store in zip-tight plastic bags.

¼ cup Worcestershire sauce
4 tablespoons margarine or butter
2 tablespoons brown sugar
1½ teaspoons salt
½ to 1 teaspoon ground red pepper (cayenne)
12 cups popped corn (about ⅓ to ½ cup unpopped)
1 package (12 ounces) oven-toasted corn cereal squares
1 package (8 to 10 ounces) thin pretzel sticks

1 Preheat oven to 300°F. In 1-quart saucepan, stir Worcestershire, margarine or butter, brown sugar, salt, and ground red pepper over low heat until margarine or butter melts.

2 Place half each of popped corn, cereal, and pretzels in large roasting pan (17" by 11½"); toss with half of Worcestershire mixture.

3 Bake popcorn mixture 30 minutes, stirring once halfway through baking. Cool mixture in very large bowl or on counter covered with waxed paper. Repeat with remaining ingredients. Makes about 25 cups.

Each ½ cup: About 65 calories, 1 g protein, 13 g carbohydrate, 1 g total fat (0 g saturated), 0 mg cholesterol, 245 mg sodium.

Hot & Spicy Toasted Walnuts

PREP: 5 MINUTES PLUS COOLING • BAKE: 20 MINUTES

If you like, try peanuts, pecans, or almonds instead of walnuts, or your favorite combination. When cool, store in jars or tins.

1 can (8 ounces) walnuts (2 cups)
2 tablespoons sugar
1 tablespoon vegetable oil
1½ teaspoons Worcestershire sauce
½ teaspoon ground red pepper (cayenne)
¼ teaspoon salt

1 Preheat oven to 350°F. Place walnuts in 15½" by 10½" jelly-roll pan. Toast walnuts in oven 20 minutes, stirring occasionally. Meanwhile, in small bowl, mix sugar, vegetable oil, Worcestershire, ground red pepper, and salt.

2 Remove walnuts from oven. Drizzle spice mixture over nuts and toss until thoroughly coated. Spread nuts in a single layer; cool completely in pan on wire rack. Store at room temperature in tightly covered container up to 1 month. Makes about 2 cups.

Each ¼ cup: About 210 calories, 4 g protein, 9 g carbohydrate, 19 g total fat (2 g saturated), 0 mg cholesterol, 80 mg sodium.

Lacy Parmesan Crisps

PREP: 20 MINUTES • BAKE: 6 TO 7 MINUTES PER BATCH

Called *frico* in Italy, these wafers are nothing more than melted cheese! Try experimenting with any cheese you like, but don't let the crisps brown or they will taste bitter. Look for reusable nonstick bakeware liners—they yield the best end product, and make removal and cleanup a snap. You can also use a nonstick baking sheet; just remember to cool the crisps on the sheet for 2 minutes. These keep very well in an airtight container at room temperature.

1½ cups coarsely shredded Parmesan cheese (6 ounces)

1 Preheat oven to 375°F. Line large cookie sheet with reusable nonstick bakeware liner. Spoon cheese by level measuring tablespoons, about 3 inches apart, onto cookie sheet. Spread each mound into 2-inch round.

2 Bake cheese rounds 6 to 7 minutes, until edges of crisps just begin to color. Transfer bakeware liner to wire rack; cool 2 minutes. Remove crisps to paper towels. Repeat with remaining cheese. Store in airtight container up to 4 days. Makes about 24 crisps.

Each crisp: About 30 calories, 3 g protein, 0 g carbohydrate, 2 g total fat (1 g saturated), 6 mg cholesterol, 130 mg sodium.

Lacy Parmesan Crisps ➤

Parmesan Toasts

PREP: 15 MINUTES PLUS COOLING • BAKE: 35 MINUTES

We've seen these in gourmet shops for $24 a pound! A very dense loaf of bread makes cutting thin slices easier—we used a baguette-type loaf of bread, 5 inches in width. If you use a narrower loaf, cut slices on the diagonal to make them wider. And be sure to use a top-quality grating cheese such as Parmigiano-Reggiano for the best flavor.

1 loaf dense sourdough bread (about 1 pound)
1¾ cups freshly grated Parmesan cheese (about 5 ounces)
2 tablespoons olive oil
¼ teaspoon dried thyme
¼ teaspoon crushed red pepper
Pinch dried rosemary, crushed
Pinch salt

1 Preheat oven to 300°F. With serrated knife, cut off ends from bread; reserve for making crumbs. Cut loaf into slices, each slightly thinner than ¼ inch thick. Place slices on large cookie sheet. Bake slices until

Sesame Pita Toasts

dry and toasted, about 30 minutes, turning slices over halfway through cooking time. Remove cookie sheet from oven. Turn oven control to 400°F.

2 Meanwhile, in medium bowl, with fork, mix Parmesan, olive oil, thyme, crushed red pepper, rosemary, and salt until combined.

3 Top each bread slice with 2 rounded teaspoons cheese mixture; spread mixture slightly. Bake toasts 3 to 5 minutes, until cheese melts. Cool toasts on cookie sheet on wire rack at least 2 hours or overnight to allow topping to dry out. Store at room temperature in tightly covered container up to 2 weeks. Makes about 24 toasts.

Each toast: About 90 calories, 5 g protein, 9 g carbohydrate, 4 g total fat (2 g saturated), 6 mg cholesterol, 240 mg sodium.

Sesame Pita Toasts

PREP: 25 MINUTES • BAKE: 8 MINUTES

Topped with a zesty mixture called *zahtar*, these are best assembled the day of your party, not more than 6 hours before baking.

½ cup sesame seeds, toasted
2 tablespoons chopped fresh parsley leaves
2 teaspoons dried thyme
2 teaspoons grated fresh lemon peel
½ teaspoon salt
¼ teaspoon coarsely ground black pepper
1 package (7 ounces) mini pitas, 2-inch diameter
2 tablespoons extravirgin olive oil

1 Prepare *zahtar* mixture: In blender at high speed, blend sesame seeds, parsley, thyme, lemon peel, salt, and pepper until seeds are ground, stopping blender occasionally and scraping down sides with rubber spatula. Transfer *zahtar* mixture to medium bowl.

2 Brush tops of pitas with olive oil. Sprinkle olive-oil side of each pita with about 1½ teaspoons *zahtar* mixture. Gently press *zahtar* mixture onto pitas. Place pitas on large cookie sheet; cover and refrigerate up to 6 hours before serving.

3 To complete, preheat oven to 450°F. Bake 8 minutes or until pitas are crisp and golden. Makes 24 toasts.

Each toast: About 50 calories, 1 g protein, 5 g carbohydrate, 3 g total fat (0 g saturated), 0 mg cholesterol, 75 mg sodium.

Quesadillas

PREP: 10 MINUTES • BAKE: 5 MINUTES

Here is a reduced-fat version of this classic Southwestern snack.

8 low-fat flour tortillas (7- to 8-inch diameter)
1 jar (7 ounces) roasted red peppers, drained and thinly sliced
2 small green onions, thinly sliced
¼ cup shredded Monterey Jack cheese with jalapeño chiles (1 ounce)
¾ cup loosely packed fresh cilantro leaves

1 Preheat oven to 400°F. Place 4 tortillas on large cookie sheet. Top each tortilla with one-fourth of roasted peppers, green onions, cheese, and cilantro; top with remaining tortillas.

2 Bake quesadillas 5 minutes or until heated through. Cut each quesadilla into 8 wedges. Makes 32 wedges.

Each wedge: About 30 calories, 1 g protein, 5 g carbohydrate, 1 g total fat (0 g saturated), 1 mg cholesterol, 55 mg sodium.

Christmas Quesadillas

PREP: 40 MINUTES • BAKE: 8 MINUTES

Warm tortilla triangles filled with melted cheese and sautéed red and green peppers make tasty bites.

1 tablespoon vegetable oil
1 large onion, diced
1 green pepper, diced
1 red pepper, diced
1 garlic clove, minced
¼ teaspoon ground cumin
¼ teaspoon salt
2 tablespoons chopped fresh cilantro leaves
12 flour tortillas (6- to 7-inch diameter)
6 ounces Monterey Jack cheese with jalapeño chiles, shredded (1½ cups)
Cilantro leaves and 1 hot red pepper for garnish

1 In nonstick 10-inch skillet, heat vegetable oil over medium heat. Add onion and peppers and cook, stirring often, 15 minutes or until golden and tender. Add garlic, cumin, and salt, and cook 5 minutes

longer, stirring often. Remove skillet from heat; stir in cilantro.

2 Preheat oven to 450°F. Place 6 tortillas on 2 large cookie sheets. Spread pepper mixture on tortillas; sprinkle with cheese. Top with remaining tortillas to make 6 quesadillas.

3 Bake quesadillas 8 minutes or until lightly browned on both sides, turning quesadillas over once. Remove quesadillas to cutting board; cut each into 8 wedges. Top each wedge with a cilantro leaf for garnish. Garnish platter with a hot red pepper. Serve immediately. Makes 48 wedges.

Each wedge: About 50 calories, 2 g protein, 6 g carbohydrate, 2 g total fat (1 g saturated), 4 mg cholesterol, 75 mg sodium.

Black Bean Dip

PREP: 5 MINUTES • COOK 3 MINUTES

This flavorful dip is simple to whip up—even at the last minute—from ingredients already in your pantry. This dip goes well with crudités such as blanched asparagus spears and snap peas, whole cherry tomatoes, and bite-size pepper strips. You can also spread it on toasted pita triangles.

4 garlic cloves, peeled
1 can (15 to 19 ounces) black beans, rinsed and drained
2 tablespoons tomato paste
2 tablespoons olive oil
4½ teaspoons fresh lime juice
½ teaspoon ground cumin
½ teaspoon ground coriander
¼ teaspoon salt
⅛ teaspoon ground red pepper (cayenne)

1 In 1-quart saucepan, place garlic and *enough water to cover*; heat to boiling over high heat. Reduce heat to low; cover and simmer 3 minutes to blanch garlic; drain.

2 In food processor with knife blade attached, blend garlic with remaining ingredients and *1 tablespoon water* until smooth. Spoon dip into bowl; cover and refrigerate up to 2 days. Makes about 2 cups.

Each tablespoon: About 20 calories, 1 g protein, 3 g carbohydrate, 1 g total fat (0 g saturated), 0 mg cholesterol, 55 mg sodium.

Hummus

....
PREP: 20 MINUTES

Serve this thick Middle Eastern garbanzo-bean dip as an appetizer with wedges of toasted pita bread.

1 can (15 to 19 ounces) garbanzo beans, rinsed
   and drained
⅓ cup sesame tahini*
¼ cup fresh lemon juice
½ teaspoon ground cumin
½ teaspoon salt
¼ teaspoon coarsely ground black pepper
1 garlic clove, chopped

1 tablespoon extravirgin olive oil
1 tablespoon chopped fresh parsley leaves
Pinch paprika

1 In food processor with knife blade attached, blend garbanzo beans, tahini, lemon juice, cumin, salt, pepper, garlic, and ⅓ *cup water* until smooth. Cover and refrigerate Hummus if not serving right away.

2 To serve, spoon Hummus onto platter. Drizzle with olive oil and sprinkle with parsley and paprika. Makes about 2 cups.

*Sesame tahini is a creamy purée of sesame seeds, used in Middle Eastern cuisines.

Each tablespoon: About 40 calories, 2 g protein, 3 g carbohydrate, 2 g total fat (0 g saturated), 0 mg cholesterol, 75 mg sodium.

DOES "LITE" AVOCADO TASTE GOOD?

Guacamole lovers, take note: There's a new smooth-skinned avocado from Florida, the Brooks Lite, that contains 50 percent less fat and 35 percent fewer calories than the dark green pebbly-skinned Hass, the leading California variety. The Brooks has 105 calories and 7.5 grams of fat per 3-ounce serving; the Hass, 165 calories and 15 fat grams.

To find out if the slimmer pick could pass as the genuine article, we compared the two in blind tastings, first on their own and then in our favorite guacamole.

Our panelists reported that both samples of avocado chunks had the rich, mellow flavor and creamy texture they expected. But they preferred the Hass, noting that it was more buttery, denser, and more deeply colored. When it came to the guacamole, tasted on its own and with tortilla chips, they again preferred the more fattening dip, but found the Brooks version had a pleasant, delicate taste and a bright green color, even after several hours of standing at room temperature (though the guacamole got watery around the edge). The dip made with the Hass was thick, smooth, and muted green, but darkened slightly as it stood.

Our Food Department's verdict? Let them eat avocado! Tasters agreed that the Brooks Lite (avail-able July through February) was a good stand-in for waist-watchers who wanted to have their avocado and eat lower-fat too.

GH Guacamole

2 medium or 1 large ripe* avocado
2 tablespoons minced onion
2 tablespoons chopped fresh cilantro
1 tablespoon fresh lime juice
2 serrano or jalapeño chiles, seeded and minced
½ teaspoon salt
¼ teaspoon coarsely ground black pepper
1 plum tomato, finely chopped

1 Cut each avocado lengthwise in half; remove each seed. With spoon, scoop flesh from peel into medium bowl.

2 Add next 6 ingredients. With potato masher, coarsely mash mixture. Stir in tomato. Transfer to small serving bowl. Makes about 1½ cups.

*Choose perfectly ripened avocados that yield to gentle pressure when lightly squeezed in the palm of the hand.

Each tablespoon (Hass): About 35 calories, 1 g protein, 2 g carbohydrate, 3 g total fat (1g saturated), 0 mg cholesterol, 45 mg sodium.

Each tablespoon (Brooks Lite): About 25 calories, 0 g protein, 0 g carbohydrate, 2 g total fat (0 g saturated), 0 mg cholesterol, 45 mg sodium.

Mango Curry Dip

PREP: 5 MINUTES

Mango chutney gives this a subtle spiciness and a touch of sweetness. To lower the fat, substitute Neufchâtel cheese for regular cream cheese and reduced-fat sour cream for the regular kind. The flavors blend and develop nicely upon standing— up to 2 days is optimum. In addition to serving this with vegetable crudités, try apple and pear wedges.

2 packages (3 ounces each) cream cheese,
   softened
½ cup sour cream
¼ cup mango chutney, chopped
2 teaspoons curry powder
1 teaspoon ground coriander
½ teaspoon ground cumin
½ teaspoon ground ginger
½ teaspoon salt

In food processor with knife blade attached, blend all ingredients until smooth. Spoon dip into bowl; cover and refrigerate up to 2 days. Makes about 1½ cups.

Each tablespoon: About 45 calories, 1 g protein, 2 g carbohydrate, 4 g total fat (2 g saturated), 10 mg cholesterol, 70 mg sodium.

Potted Cheddar & Beer Spread

PREP: 15 MINUTES PLUS STANDING AND CHILLING

The flavors in this recipe were borrowed from the famous dish, Welsh Rabbit, where Cheddar cheese and beer are melted together and served over toast. Include some nice biscuits with this, such as water crackers or plain flatbread crisps.

1½ pounds extrasharp Cheddar cheese,
   shredded (6 cups)
1 can (12 ounces) beer
6 tablespoons margarine or butter (¾ stick),
   softened
1 tablespoon Dijon mustard
1 tablespoon Worcestershire sauce
⅛ teaspoon ground red pepper (cayenne)
⅛ teaspoon ground nutmeg

1 In large bowl, combine cheese and beer. Let stand 30 minutes or until cheese softens.

2 In food processor with knife blade attached, blend cheese mixture, margarine or butter, and remaining ingredients 3 to 5 minutes until smooth.

3 Pack cheese into crocks or airtight containers and store in refrigerator up to 1 month or in freezer up to 3 months. To serve, let cheese stand at room temperature 30 minutes or until soft enough to spread. Makes about 5 cups.

Each tablespoon: About 45 calories, 2 g protein, 0 g carbohydrate, 4 g total fat (2 g saturated), 9 mg cholesterol, 70 mg sodium.

Green Goddess Dip

PREP: 10 MINUTES • COOK: 15 MINUTES

The famous dressing for salads and fish is made with mayonnaise, tarragon vinegar, anchovies, parsley, chives, tarragon, scallions, and garlic. We came up with a slightly less complicated version that's delicious for dipping. The flavor of the tarragon will intensify slightly as it sits, so don't prepare the dip more than 2 days before serving. Serve it with a variety of crudités, or just tiny tender romaine lettuce dippers.

2 garlic cloves, peeled
1 container (8 ounces) sour cream
1 cup fresh parsley leaves, chopped
2 tablespoons light mayonnaise
2 teaspoons fresh lemon juice
1½ teaspoons anchovy paste
1 teaspoon dried tarragon leaves
2 green onions, minced

1 In 1-quart saucepan, place garlic and *enough water to cover*; heat to boiling over high heat. Reduce heat to low; cover and simmer 3 minutes to blanch garlic; drain. Mince garlic; place in medium bowl.

2 Stir in sour cream, parsley, mayonnaise, lemon juice, anchovy paste, tarragon, and green onions. Cover and refrigerate up to 2 days. Makes about 1 cup.

Each tablespoon: About 35 calories, 1 g protein, 2 g carbohydrate, 3 g total fat (2 g saturated), 7 mg cholesterol, 40 mg sodium.

Roasted Red-Pepper & Herb Dip

PREP: 20 MINUTES PLUS COOLING
BROIL: 6 TO 8 MINUTES

For a pretty presentation, line a wicker basket with foil and fill the bottom with alfalfa sprouts. Spoon the creamy dip into red- or yellow-pepper shells and serve in the basket with cut-up fresh vegetables to use as dippers. Garnish with garden flowers and bunches of herbs for a festive finish.

1 medium red pepper
1 package (8 ounces) cream cheese, softened
⅓ cup milk
½ teaspoon salt
¼ teaspoon coarsely ground black pepper
1 small garlic clove, coarsely chopped
1 cup loosely packed fresh parsley leaves, chopped
¼ cup snipped chives
1 teaspoon fresh thyme leaves

1 To roast red pepper: Preheat broiler. Line broiling pan (without rack) with foil. Cut pepper lengthwise in half; discard stem and seeds. Arrange halves, cut side down, in broiling pan. Place broiling pan in broiler 5 to 6 inches from source of heat and broil pepper until blackened and blistered, about 6 to 8 minutes. Wrap foil around pepper and allow to steam at room temperature 15 minutes or until cool enough to handle.

2 Remove pepper from foil. Peel off skin and discard. Cut each pepper half into 4 pieces.

3 To prepare dip: In food processor with knife blade attached, blend roasted pepper with cream cheese, milk, salt, black pepper, and garlic until smooth. Transfer mixture to medium bowl; stir in parsley, chives, and thyme. Cover and refrigerate if not serving right away. Makes about 1½ cups.

Each tablespoon: About 40 calories, 1 g protein, 1 g carbohydrate, 4 g total fat (2 g saturated), 11 mg cholesterol, 80 mg sodium.

Caviar Pie

PREP: 15 MINUTES • COOK: 15 MINUTES

Fast and delicious, this makes perfect party fare when prepared a day in advance. Serve with plain crackers or toasted bread rounds.

8 large eggs
⅓ cup mayonnaise
¼ cup chopped fresh dill or parsley leaves
¼ teaspoon salt
¼ teaspoon coarsely ground black pepper
1 container (8 ounces) sour cream
1 jar (2 ounces) red lumpfish caviar

1 In 3-quart saucepan, place eggs and *enough cold water to cover* eggs by at least 1 inch; heat to boiling over high heat. Immediately remove saucepan from heat and cover tightly; let stand 15 minutes. Pour off hot water and run cold water over eggs to cool. Remove shells from eggs.

2 In medium bowl, with pastry blender or large fork, mash eggs. Stir in mayonnaise, dill, salt, pepper, and 2 tablespoons sour cream. Spoon egg mixture evenly into 9-inch pie plate. Cover and refrigerate overnight or until ready to serve.

3 To complete, spread remaining sour cream over egg mixture; top with caviar. Makes about 3 cups.

Each tablespoon: About 35 calories, 2 g protein, 0 g carbohydrate, 3 g total fat (1 g saturated), 45 mg cholesterol, 50 mg sodium.

Deviled Eggs with Sun-Dried Tomatoes

PREP: 30 MINUTES • COOK: 15 MINUTES

A new twist on a traditional hors d'oeuvre, with bits of sun-dried tomatoes in the filling.

12 large eggs
½ cup mayonnaise
8 oil-packed sun-dried tomatoes, chopped
3 tablespoons capers, drained and chopped
2 tablespoons milk
¼ teaspoon coarsely ground black pepper

1 In 3-quart saucepan, place eggs and *enough cold water to cover* eggs by at least 1 inch; heat to boiling over high heat. Immediately remove saucepan from heat and cover tightly; let stand 15 minutes. Pour off hot water and run cold water over eggs to cool. Remove shells from eggs.

2 Slice each egg lengthwise in half. Gently remove yolks and place in medium bowl; with fork, finely mash yolks. Stir in mayonnaise and remaining ingredients until blended.

3 Line 15½" by 10½" jelly-roll pan with damp paper towels; place egg-white halves on top of towels. Spoon yolk mixture into decorating bag fitted with medium star tip (about ½-inch diameter). Pipe about 1 tablespoon yolk mixture into each egg-white half. (Or, use spoon to fill egg whites with yolk mixture.) Cover with plastic wrap and refrigerate up to 2 days. Makes 24 stuffed-egg halves.

Each egg half: About 75 calories, 3 g protein, 1 g carbohydrate, 7 g total fat (2 g saturated), 108 mg cholesterol, 95 mg sodium.

John's Favorite Deviled Eggs

PREP: 30 MINUTES • COOK: 15 MINUTES

John Werner, co-proprietor of the Jimtown Store in Healdsburg, California, has been making this recipe for about 25 years—it's a favorite at his family's Labor Day picnic in Connecticut.

12 large eggs
⅓ cup mayonnaise
3 tablespoons milk
1 tablespoon capers, drained and chopped
2 teaspoons Dijon mustard with seeds
¼ teaspoon coarsely ground black pepper
Snipped chives for garnish

1 In 3-quart saucepan, place eggs and *enough cold water to cover* eggs by at least 1 inch; heat to boiling over high heat. Immediately remove saucepan from heat and cover tightly; let stand 15 minutes. Pour off hot water and run cold water over eggs to cool. Remove shells from eggs.

2 Slice each egg lengthwise in half. Gently remove yolks and place in medium bowl. With fork, finely mash yolks. Stir in mayonnaise and remaining ingredients, except chives, until blended.

3 Line 15½" by 10½" jelly-roll pan with damp paper towels; place egg-white halves on top of towels. Spoon yolk mixture into decorating bag fitted with medium star tip (about ½-inch diameter). Pipe scant 1 tablespoon yolk mixture into each egg-white half. (Or, use spoon to fill egg-white halves with yolk mixture.) Cover with plastic wrap and refrigerate up to 2 days.

4 To serve, sprinkle tops of deviled eggs with chives, then transfer to platter. Makes 24 stuffed-egg halves.

Each egg half: About 60 calories, 3 g protein, 0 g carbohydrate, 5 g total fat (1 g saturated), 108 mg cholesterol, 70 mg sodium.

HOW DEVILED EGGS GOT THEIR NAME

Since the late 1700's, devil has been a culinary verb, meaning to season highly. But the term "deviled eggs" evolved over time—for a while, they were known by the French name, Oeufs à la Diable. Either way, their hot moniker comes from the flavorings, such as dry mustard, hot pepper sauce, and/or ground red pepper (cayenne). The ingredients vary, but the zesty bite is always there.

To get deviled eggs to behave like little angels (and not slip and slide around), our test-kitchen experts cut a thin slice from the rounded side of each egg-white half—after the yolk has been removed—to make a flat base. And they place the halves on a jelly-roll pan lined with damp paper towels during prep, filling, and refrigerating.

Baked Goat Cheese

PREP: 5 MINUTES • BROIL: 2 TO 3 MINUTES

Serve hot with toasted baguette slices or plain crackers.

½ teaspoon cracked black pepper
¼ teaspoon dried thyme
¼ teaspoon fennel seeds
¼ teaspoon paprika
⅛ teaspoon dried rosemary
⅛ teaspoon ground red pepper (cayenne), optional
¼ cup plain dried bread crumbs
2 tablespoons extravirgin olive oil
11 to 12 ounces plain goat cheese (chèvre), such as Montrachet
Thyme sprig for garnish

1 Prepare crumb topping: With mortar and pestle, crush black pepper with thyme, fennel, paprika, rosemary, and ground red pepper. In small bowl, toss herb mixture with bread crumbs and olive oil; store in airtight container until ready to use.

Baked Goat Cheese

2 Preheat broiler. Evenly crumble goat cheese into shallow 8-inch round gratin dish. Sprinkle crumb mixture over goat cheese.

3 With oven rack 5 to 7 inches from source of heat, broil goat-cheese mixture 2 to 3 minutes, until crumb topping is lightly browned. Garnish with thyme sprig. Makes 12 appetizer servings.

Each serving: About 105 calories, 6 g protein, 2 g carbohydrate, 8 g total fat (5 g saturated), 13 mg cholesterol, 125 mg sodium.

Country Pâté

PREP: 40 MINUTES PLUS COOLING AND CHILLING OVERNIGHT • BAKE: 1 HOUR 15 MINUTES

A French classic, pâté is wonderful for relaxed entertaining because it must be put together in advance. Our version is lower in fat than typical ones; serve with French bread or crackers.

3 slices bacon, finely chopped
12 ounces skinless, boneless chicken breast, cut up
8 ounces medium mushrooms, finely chopped
1 medium onion, minced
2 garlic cloves, minced
2 tablespoons margarine or butter
2 tablespoons brandy
1½ teaspoons salt
1 teaspoon coarsely ground black pepper
1 teaspoon dried thyme
¼ teaspoon ground allspice
8 ounces ground pork
4 ounces chicken livers, trimmed and finely chopped
⅔ cup packed fresh parsley leaves, chopped
¼ cup shelled pistachio nuts

1 In 10-inch skillet, cook bacon over medium-low heat, stirring occasionally, until browned.

2 Meanwhile, in food processor with knife blade attached, blend chicken breast until finely chopped, about 30 seconds; set aside.

3 With slotted spoon, transfer bacon to paper towels to drain. To bacon drippings in skillet, add mushrooms, onion, garlic, and margarine or butter; cook, stirring, 8 to 10 minutes, until vegetables are tender. Add brandy, salt, pepper, thyme, and allspice. Reduce heat to low; cook 5 minutes longer. Remove skillet from heat; let mushroom mixture cool to room temperature.

4 Preheat oven to 350°F. In large bowl, combine chopped chicken, bacon, mushroom mixture, ground pork, chicken livers, parsley, and pistachios. With wooden spoon, beat meat mixture until well blended.

5 Grease 8½" by 4½" metal loaf pan. Spoon meat mixture into pan, packing it carefully with back of spoon to press out any air pockets. Bake pâté 1 hour 15 minutes.

6 When pâté is done, transfer to wire rack; cover pan with foil. Place another 8½" by 4½" loaf pan on top of foil-covered pâté. Place two 16-ounce cans in top loaf pan to weigh down pâté. Let weighted pâté cool about 1 hour at room temperature, then refrigerate overnight or up to 3 days.

7 To complete, remove weighted pan from pâté. Dip loaf pan with pâté in hot water 15 seconds. With small metal spatula, loosen pâté from sides of pan. If pâté doesn't release easily, dip pan in hot water again. Invert pâté onto cutting board. Makes 16 appetizer servings.

Each serving: About 125 calories, 10 g protein, 2 g carbohydrate, 8 g total fat (3 g saturated), 68 mg cholesterol, 275 mg sodium.

Mushroom Turnovers

· ·
PREP: 1 HOUR PLUS COOLING AND FREEZING
COOK: ABOUT 20 MINUTES • BAKE 12 TO 20 MINUTES

These tender pastries are made with an easy cream-cheese dough. Freeze up to 1 month ahead—bake directly from the freezer as needed.

TURNOVER PASTRY:
1 package (8 ounces) cream cheese, softened
1½ cups all-purpose flour
½ cup margarine or butter (1 stick), softened

MUSHROOM FILLING:
3 tablespoons margarine or butter
1 medium onion, minced
8 ounces medium mushrooms, diced
1 garlic clove, crushed with garlic press
1 tablespoon all-purpose flour
½ teaspoon salt

¼ teaspoon coarsely ground black pepper
¼ teaspoon dried thyme
1 tablespoon dry sherry or dry vermouth
3 tablespoons sour cream
1 large egg, beaten with 2 tablespoons water, for glaze

1 Prepare Turnover Pastry: In medium bowl, with hand, knead cream cheese, flour, and margarine or butter until blended. Shape dough into 2 disks; wrap each with plastic wrap and refrigerate until firm enough to handle, about 30 minutes.

2 Meanwhile, prepare Mushroom Filling: In 12-inch skillet, melt margarine or butter over medium heat. Add onion and mushrooms and cook until onion is tender and liquid evaporates, about 20 minutes, stirring frequently. Stir in garlic, flour, salt, pepper, and thyme, then sherry; cook 1 minute longer. Transfer mushroom mixture to bowl to cool. Stir in sour cream.

3 On floured surface, with floured rolling pin, roll half of dough ⅛ inch thick (keep remaining dough refrigerated). With 3-inch round biscuit cutter, cut out as many rounds as possible, reserving trimmings.

4 On half of each dough round, place 1 rounded measuring teaspoon Mushroom Filling. Brush edges of rounds with some egg mixture. Fold dough over filling. With fork, press edges together to seal. Brush turnovers lightly with egg mixture; prick tops. Place turnovers on ungreased cookie sheet, about 1 inch apart.

5 Repeat with remaining dough, trimmings, and filling to make about 48 turnovers in all.

6 Cover cookie sheets tightly with plastic wrap or foil and refrigerate turnovers up to 1 day. Or, to freeze up to 1 month, place unbaked turnovers in jelly-roll pan; cover and freeze until firm. With pancake turner, remove turnovers from pan and place in freezer-safe containers with waxed paper between each layer and freeze.

7 To serve, preheat oven to 450°F. Bake refrigerated turnovers 12 to 14 minutes, until golden. Or, arrange frozen turnovers on ungreased cookie sheets, 1 inch apart, and bake 15 to 20 minutes, until golden. Serve hot. Makes about 48 turnovers.

Each turnover: About 60 calories, 1 g protein, 4 g carbohydrate, 5 g total fat (2 g saturated), 10 mg cholesterol, 75 mg sodium.

Potato Nests

PREP: 1 HOUR 10 MINUTES PLUS CHILLING
BAKE: 25 MINUTES

These beautiful appetizers are not as complicated as they look. You can bake the nests up to 4 hours ahead and then let them stand at room temperature until it's time to reheat for serving.

2 large baking potatoes (about 1½ pounds)
½ cup sour cream
1 tablespoon prepared white horseradish
1 tablespoon chopped fresh dill
½ teaspoon salt
⅛ teaspoon coarsely ground black pepper
Dill sprigs and/or smoked salmon for topping (optional)

1 Preheat oven to 425°F. Grease thirty-two 1¾" by 1" mini muffin-pan cups.

2 In 3-quart saucepan, place unpeeled potatoes and *enough water to cover*; heat to boiling over high heat. Reduce heat to low; cover and simmer 20 minutes or until potatoes are just cooked through. Drain potatoes; refrigerate about 1 hour or until chilled.

3 Meanwhile, in small bowl, mix sour cream, horseradish, and dill until blended. Cover and refrigerate until ready to serve.

4 Peel and coarsely grate potatoes. In medium bowl, gently toss grated potatoes with salt and pepper. Place about 1 heaping measuring tablespoon potato mixture in each mini muffin-pan cup; press mixture against bottom and up sides of cups, allowing some mixture to extend slightly above rim.

5 Bake potato nests 25 minutes or until edges are golden brown. Cover pans loosely with foil if nests brown too quickly. Cool nests in pans on wire racks 10 minutes. Carefully remove potato nests to jelly-roll pan or cookie sheet lined with paper towels. Let stand at room temperature up to 4 hours before serving.

6 To complete, preheat oven to 375°F. Place nests on large cookie sheet (without paper towels), and bake 6 to 8 minutes, until heated through and crisp. Transfer nests to platter. Spoon about 1 teaspoon sour-cream mixture into each nest, and top each with a dill sprig or a small piece of smoked salmon, if you like. Makes 32 nests.

Each filled nest without topping: About 20 calories, 0 g protein, 3 g carbohydrate, 1 g total fat (1 g saturated), 2 mg cholesterol, 40 mg sodium.

Stuffed Pepperoncini

PREP: 40 MINUTES • COOK: 12 MINUTES

Tuscan peppers (pepperoncini) are available in jars at your supermarket; they're slightly hot and just the right size to pop into your mouth. The heat from the peppers is complemented by the cool cream cheese and smoky bacon. These will keep perfectly overnight in the refrigerator—just bring to room temperature to serve.

3 slices bacon, finely chopped
2 shallots, minced (¼ cup)
½ medium red pepper, minced (about ⅓ cup)
1 package (3 ounces) cream cheese, softened
2 teaspoons milk
2 jars (9 to 10½ ounces each) Tuscan peppers, or pepperoncini, drained (about 28 peppers)

1 In nonstick 10-inch skillet, cook bacon over medium-low heat, stirring occasionally, until bacon is browned. With slotted spoon, transfer bacon to paper towels to drain. Discard all but 1 tablespoon bacon drippings.

2 In drippings in skillet, cook shallots and red pepper over medium heat, stirring frequently, until vegetables are tender, about 5 minutes. Remove skillet from heat.

3 In small bowl, with mixer at medium speed, beat cream cheese and milk until smooth. Add bacon and shallot mixture and beat just until combined. Spoon cream-cheese mixture into heavy-weight plastic bag with 1 corner cut to make a ¼-inch opening.

4 With small knife, cut a slit lengthwise in each pepper, being careful not to cut all the way through peppers. Squeeze cream-cheese mixture into peppers; cover and refrigerate up to 1 day. Makes about 28 stuffed peppers.

Each stuffed pepper: About 25 calories, 1 g protein, 1 g carbohydrate, 2 g total fat (1 g saturated), 4 mg cholesterol, 245 mg sodium.

Pork & Shrimp Dumplings

PREP: ABOUT 1 HOUR
COOK: ABOUT 20 MINUTES PER BATCH

Panfrying gives these Asian-style dumplings a crisp, golden crust.

DUMPLINGS:
1 package (½ ounce) dried shiitake mushrooms (about 6 mushrooms)
½ pound Napa cabbage (about ½ small head), finely chopped (1½ cups)
2 teaspoons salt
1 pound ground pork
4 ounces shrimp, shelled, deveined, and finely chopped
2 tablespoons reduced-sodium soy sauce
1 tablespoon Asian sesame oil
1 tablespoon seasoned rice vinegar
1 teaspoon minced, peeled fresh ginger
48 (3½" by 3½" each) wonton wrappers (about 12-ounce package)*
3 tablespoons vegetable oil
1½ cups chicken broth

DIPPING SAUCE:
¼ cup reduced-sodium soy sauce
¼ cup seasoned rice vinegar
1 green onion, minced

1 Prepare Dumplings: In 1-quart saucepan, heat ¾ *cup water* to boiling over high heat. Remove saucepan from heat; add dried mushrooms and soak 20 minutes or until soft.

2 Meanwhile, in colander, sprinkle cabbage with salt; set aside 5 minutes. Drain cabbage in colander, pressing down on cabbage to squeeze out all the water.

3 Drain mushrooms, reserving 2 tablespoons soaking liquid. Discard stems from mushrooms; finely chop caps. In large bowl, combine cabbage, mushrooms, pork, shrimp, soy sauce, sesame oil, vinegar, ginger, and reserved mushroom soaking liquid, stirring until well blended.

4 Arrange 4 wonton wrappers on work surface. Place 1 tablespoon pork mixture in center of each wrapper. Run finger, dipped in water, over edges of each wrapper to moisten, rewetting finger as necessary. Diagonally fold each wrapper over filling, forming a triangle.

Pinch and pleat edges of dumpling to seal in filling.

5 Place dumplings on 2 flour-dusted 15½" by 10½" jelly-roll pans. Cover dumplings with damp (not wet) paper towels to prevent drying out.

6 Repeat steps 4 and 5 to make a total of about 48 dumplings.

7 In nonstick 12-inch skillet, heat 1½ teaspoons vegetable oil over medium-high heat until hot. Add one-third of dumplings (it's okay if they're slightly overlapping), and cook until golden on both sides, turning once, about 2 minutes per side. Add ½ cup chicken broth; heat to boiling over high heat. Reduce heat to low; cover and simmer 8 to 10 minutes, until dumplings are cooked through. Remove cover; turn dumplings over and continue cooking until any remaining liquid evaporates. Add another 1½ teaspoons oil to skillet. Cook over medium heat until crisp on both sides, turning once, about 4 minutes per side. Transfer dumplings to platter; cover with foil to keep warm.

8 Repeat step 7 twice to cook remaining dumplings.

9 Prepare Dipping Sauce: In small serving bowl, mix soy sauce and vinegar until blended. Sprinkle with green onion. Serve dumplings with dipping sauce. Makes about 48 dumplings.

*Available in Asian markets or some supermarkets in the refrigerator case in the produce section.

Each dumpling with ½ teaspoon sauce: About 65 calories, 3 g protein, 6 g carbohydrate, 3 g total fat (1 g saturated), 10 mg cholesterol, 245 mg sodium.

FOOD EDITOR'S TIP

Q Though I like to cook Asian food, I don't do it often enough to use the whole piece of ginger I buy. Is there any good way to keep it from going bad?

A Yes. Peel it and place in a screw-top jar. Pour enough dry sherry (or vodka) on top to completely cover the root, then seal the jar and refrigerate for up to one year. Grate or chop the ginger as needed. (The sherry will also take on a very hot and gingery flavor; so if an Asian recipe calls for sherry, you can use some of this "ginger-ized" sherry for extra ginger flavor.)

Shrimp with Two Sauces

Though both sauces will keep nicely for up to 2 days, don't cook and chill the shrimp until the day before serving at the earliest.

SOUTHWESTERN DIPPING SAUCE:
1 cup seafood cocktail sauce
2 tablespoons minced fresh cilantro leaves
2 teaspoons fresh lime juice
1 jalapeño chile, seeded and minced

DIJON DIPPING SAUCE:
1 cup reduced-fat sour cream
¼ cup Dijon mustard with seeds
3 tablespoons chopped fresh parsley leaves
¼ teaspoon grated fresh lemon peel
¼ teaspoon salt
⅛ teaspoon coarsely ground black pepper

SHRIMP:
4 bay leaves
1 lemon, thinly sliced
20 whole black peppercorns
10 whole allspice berries
2 teaspoons salt
48 large shrimp (about 2 pounds), shelled and deveined

1 Prepare Southwestern Dipping Sauce: In small bowl, stir cocktail sauce, cilantro, lime juice, and jalapeño until well blended. Cover and refrigerate up to 2 days. Makes about 1 cup.

2 Prepare Dijon Dipping Sauce: In small bowl, stir sour cream, mustard, parsley, lemon peel, salt, and pepper until well blended. Cover and refrigerate up to 2 days. Makes about 1 cup.

3 Prepare Shrimp: In 5- or 6-quart saucepot, heat bay leaves, sliced lemon, peppercorns, allspice berries, salt, and *2 quarts water* to boiling over high heat. Cover and boil 15 minutes.

4 Add shrimp and cook just until shrimp turn opaque throughout, about 1 to 2 minutes. Drain shrimp in colander; rinse with cold running water to stop further cooking. Dry shrimp well on paper towels.

5 Serve shrimp on platter with bowls of dipping sauces. Makes 16 appetizer servings.

Each serving of shrimp without sauces: About 45 calories, 9 g protein, 0 g carbohydrate, 1 g total fat (0 g saturated), 90 mg cholesterol, 105 mg sodium.

Each tablespoon Southwestern dipping sauce: About 15 calories, 0 g protein, 3 g carbohydrate, 0 g total fat, 0 mg cholesterol, 170 mg sodium.

Each tablespoon Dijon dipping sauce: About 20 calories, 1 g protein, 1 g carbohydrate, 1 g total fat (0 g saturated), 5 mg cholesterol, 140 mg sodium.

Jamee's Little Crab Cakes with Guacamole

This appetizer was the brainstorm of Jamee Carleto, who's been the chef at the Jimtown Store in Healdsburg, California, for 5 years. Do all the prep ahead—then panfry the petite cakes just before serving. Top each with a dollop of creamy guacamole.

GUACAMOLE:
3 ripe medium avocados
2 tablespoons fresh lime juice
2 green onions, thinly sliced
2 tablespoons chopped fresh cilantro leaves
½ teaspoon salt
¼ teaspoon green jalapeño sauce

CRAB CAKES:
1 container (16 ounces) lump crabmeat
1½ teaspoons fresh lemon juice
3 tablespoons olive oil
1 medium onion, finely chopped
⅛ teaspoon ground red pepper (cayenne)
⅓ cup mayonnaise
1 tablespoon Dijon mustard with seeds
¾ teaspoon salt
¼ teaspoon dried thyme
2 tablespoons chopped fresh parsley leaves
3 large eggs
4 cups cornflakes
Lemon or lime wedges for garnish

1 Prepare Guacamole: Cut each avocado lengthwise in half; remove each seed, then peel. Cut avocados into chunks.

2 In medium bowl, with fork, mash avocados with lime juice; stir in green onions and remaining guacamole ingredients. Cover surface of guacamole directly with plastic wrap to prevent discoloration. Refrigerate if not serving right away. (Makes about 1½ cups.)

3 Prepare Crab Cakes: Pick over crabmeat to remove any pieces of shell or cartilage. Sprinkle with lemon juice; set aside.

4 In nonstick 12-inch skillet, heat 1 tablespoon olive oil over medium heat. Add onion and ground red pepper, and cook until onion is tender, about 8 minutes, stirring frequently. Remove skillet from heat.

5 In medium bowl, with wire whisk or fork, blend mayonnaise, mustard, salt, thyme, 1 tablespoon chopped parsley, and 1 egg. Stir in crabmeat and onion mixture until well blended. With hands, shape crabmeat mixture into twenty-four 2-inch round cakes.

6 In food processor with knife blade attached or in blender, pulse cornflakes until fine crumbs form; transfer to large sheet of waxed paper and toss with remaining 1 tablespoon chopped parsley.

7 In pie plate, beat remaining 2 eggs with *1 tablespoon water*. Dip each crab cake into beaten eggs, then coat with cornflake crumbs. (If not cooking right away, place crab cakes on large cookie sheet; cover with plastic wrap and refrigerate until ready to cook.)

8 In same skillet, heat 1 tablespoon olive oil over medium-high heat. Add 12 crab cakes and cook about 10 minutes, turning once, until golden brown on both sides. Transfer crab cakes to platter; cover loosely with foil to keep warm. Repeat with remaining olive oil and crab cakes. Serve crab cakes with guacamole and lemon or lime wedges. Makes 24 crab cakes.

Each crab cake without guacamole: About 85 calories, 5 g protein, 4 g carbohydrate, 5 g total fat (1 g saturated), 47 mg cholesterol, 205 mg sodium.

Each tablespoon guacamole: About 40 calories, 1 g protein, 2 g carbohydrate, 4 g total fat (1 g saturated), 0 mg cholesterol, 45 mg sodium.

ITALIAN LEMON CORDIAL

Food Director Susan Westmoreland's cousin, Paola D'Atino, makes this after-dinner cordial from the lemons that grow in her backyard near Italy's Amalfi coast. It's tastiest served from the freezer, very cold and syrupy.

PREP: 10 MINUTES PLUS 1 WEEK TO STEEP
COOK: ABOUT 5 MINUTES

6 lemons
1 bottle (750 ml) 100-proof vodka (3¼ cups)
1¾ cups sugar

1 With vegetable peeler, remove peel from lemons (refrigerate peeled lemons for juice). Pour vodka into 8-cup measuring cup or large glass bowl and add lemon peels. Cover with plastic wrap and let stand at room temperature 1 week.

2 After 1 week, line sieve with paper towels and place over a large bowl. Pour vodka mixture through sieve; discard lemon peels.

3 In 2-quart saucepan, mix sugar with 3¼ *cups water*; heat to boiling over high heat, stirring. Boil 2 minutes. Cool completely. Add cool syrup to vodka mixture.

4 Pour cordial into small decorative bottles with tight-fitting stoppers or lids. Although it is not necessary to refrigerate cordial, we recommend storing it in the freezer where it can keep indefinitely. Makes about 6½ cups or 34 servings.

Each serving: About 100 calories, 0 g protein, 10 g carbohydrate, 0 g total fat, 0 mg cholesterol, 0 mg sodium.

Sangria

PREP: 10 MINUTES

Serve this with all your summer dishes—it's great with grilled food. For a change, make our white-wine variation.

2 oranges
2 lemons
1 bottle (750 ml) dry red wine (about 3¼ cups)
⅓ cup sugar
¼ cup brandy
¼ cup orange-flavor liqueur
1 bottle (1 liter) plain seltzer
Ice cubes (optional)

1 With vegetable peeler, remove peel in 1-inch-wide strips from 1 orange and 2 lemons. Squeeze juice from both oranges.

2 In 2½-quart pitcher, stir wine, sugar, brandy, liqueur, and orange juice until sugar dissolves. Stir in orange and lemon peels. If not serving right away, cover and refrigerate. Just before serving, stir in

seltzer. Serve over ice if you like. Makes about 7 cups or 14 servings.

WHITE SANGRIA: Prepare Sangria as above, but use white wine instead of red and add 3 peaches, peeled and cut into thin wedges, and 1 orange, thinly sliced. Makes about 7 cups or 14 servings.

Each serving sangria: About 85 calories, 0 g protein, 9 g carbohydrate, 0 g total fat, 0 mg cholesterol, 50 mg sodium.

Each serving white sangria: About 90 calories, 0 g protein, 9 g carbohydrate, 0 g total fat, 0 mg cholesterol, 20 mg sodium.

Frosty Cappuccino

PREP: 5 MINUTES

Better than store-bought! A deceptively rich blender drink.

1 cup low-fat (1%) milk
1 tablespoon chocolate-flavor syrup
1 teaspoon instant espresso-coffee powder

SECRETS FOR THE BEST ICED COFFEE

Instead of paying top dollar for iced java at places like Starbucks, make your own—and make it better:

To make Iced Coffee Brew regular or decaf coffee, cool slightly, and refrigerate. Stir in milk and sugar as desired and serve over ice. Shortcut: Double the amount of grounds, then add ice to the hot coffee. If you're a die-hard caffeine fan and don't want to water down your drink with ice, make coffee cubes: Pour the cooled brew into ice-cube trays and freeze.

For Spiced Iced Coffee Put a cinnamon stick or some cardamom pods in with the ground beans before brewing.

• Buy enough beans only for the immediate future. Unless they are vacuum-packed, whole beans are at their peak for only 3 weeks, ground beans for only about 1 week.

• Despite what you've heard, don't store coffee in the fridge or freezer. The beans absorb the condensation that forms when they're exposed to temperature changes from cold to warm. Best bet: Keep coffee in an opaque, airtight container in a cool, dry place.

• Follow the manufacturer's directions for brewing in your coffeemaker. Generally, 1 to 2 tablespoons ground coffee per ¾ cup cold water is sufficient for a good cup.

• Don't leave brewed coffee on the burner for longer than 20 minutes. The heat causes the coffee to deteriorate, leaving a bitter taste. Instead, pour into an insulated pitcher.

2 ice cubes
⅛ teaspoon ground cinnamon

In blender at high speed, blend all ingredients except cinnamon 1 minute. Pour into 2 chilled glasses. If you like, add sugar to taste. Sprinkle with cinnamon for garnish. Makes 2 servings.

Each serving: About 75 calories, 4 g protein, 12 g carbohydrate, 1 g total fat (1 g saturated), 5 mg cholesterol, 65 mg sodium.

Classic Iced Tea

PREP: 5 MINUTES • BREW: 5 MINUTES

Use your favorite breakfast tea or a fruit or herbal blend.

8 tea bags, tags removed
Ice cubes
Granulated or superfine sugar (optional)
Thin lemon slices (optional)

1 In 3-quart saucepan, heat *4 cups cold water* to boiling over high heat. Remove saucepan from heat and stir in tea bags. Cover and let stand 5 minutes to brew.

2 Stir tea. Remove tea bags and pour tea into 2½-quart pitcher with *4 cups cold water*. Cover and let stand until ready to serve. (Do not refrigerate or tea will become cloudy. If this happens, add boiling water, gradually, until tea clears.)

3 To serve, pour tea over ice cubes in tall glasses. Serve with sugar and lemon slices if you like. Makes about 8 cups or 8 servings.

FRUIT TEA: Prepare Classic Iced Tea as above, except in step 2, after pouring tea into pitcher, stir in 4 cups cold fruit juice (such as peach, cranberry, raspberry, or white grape) instead of water. Garnish with fresh fruit. Makes about 8 cups or 8 servings.

Each serving classic iced tea: About 2 calories, 0 g protein, 1 g carbohydrate, 0 g total fat, 0 mg cholesterol, 5 mg sodium.

Each serving fruit tea: About 65 calories, 0 g protein, 16 g carbohydrate, 0 g total fat, 0 mg cholesterol, 15 mg sodium.

Mango-Strawberry Smoothie

PREP: 5 MINUTES

This one's brimming with fruity flavors.

1 ripe medium mango, peeled and cut into chunks
1 cup hulled, cut-up strawberries
½ cup vanilla low-fat yogurt
6 ice cubes

In blender, combine all ingredients and blend until mixture is smooth and frothy. Pour into 2 tall glasses. Makes about 2½ cups or 2 servings.

Each serving: About 145 calories, 4 g protein, 32 g carbohydrate, 2 g total fat (1 g saturated), 3 mg cholesterol, 40 mg sodium.

Peach Smoothie

PREP: 5 MINUTES

1 cup peeled, sliced peaches (about 2 medium)
1 cup peach juice or nectar
½ cup vanilla low-fat yogurt
3 ice cubes

In blender, combine all ingredients and blend until mixture is smooth and frothy. Pour into 2 tall glasses. Makes about 2¾ cups or 2 servings.

Each serving: About 160 calories, 3 g protein, 36 g carbohydrate, 1 g total fat (1 g saturated), 3 mg cholesterol, 45 mg sodium.

Lemonade

PREP: 10 MINUTES PLUS CHILLING • COOK: 5 MINUTES

Whether you're sipping this on your porch or taking a commuter mug in the car, one thing's for sure—nothing tastes as good as old-fashioned lemonade. Try the mint version for a new twist.

2 cups sugar
2 cups fresh lemon juice (from about
    10 medium lemons)
Ice cubes

1 Prepare sugar syrup: In 2-quart saucepan, heat sugar and *2 cups cold water* to boiling over high heat, stirring occasionally. Cover saucepan and boil 3 minutes. Remove saucepan from heat.

2 Stir lemon juice into sugar syrup. Pour mixture into pitcher or glass measuring cup; cover and refrigerate until cold, about 3 hours. Serve over ice, stirring in *additional water* if you like. Makes about 5 cups or 10 servings.

FRESH MINT LEMONADE: Prepare sugar syrup for Lemonade as in step 1. After removing saucepan from heat, stir in 1 cup loosely packed fresh mint leaves and let stand, covered, 10 minutes. Strain mixture and discard mint leaves. Complete recipe as in step 2. Garnish with mint sprigs.

Each serving: About 170 calories, 0 g protein, 44 g carbohydrate, 0 g total fat, 0 mg cholesterol, 1 mg sodium.

Limeade

PREP: 10 MINUTES PLUS CHILLING • COOK: 5 MINUTES

2 cups sugar
1¼ cups fresh lime juice (from about 10 medium
    limes)
Ice cubes
Lime slices (optional)

1 Prepare sugar syrup: In 2-quart saucepan, heat sugar and *3½ cups cold water* to boiling over high heat, stirring occasionally. Cover saucepan and boil 3 minutes. Remove saucepan from heat.

2 Stir lime juice into sugar syrup. Pour mixture into pitcher or glass measuring cup; cover and refrigerate until cold, about 3 hours. Serve over ice, with lime slices, stirring in *additional water* if you like. Makes about 6 cups or 12 servings.

GINGER LIMEADE: Prepare sugar syrup for Limeade as in step 1, adding 6 slices (each ⅛ inch thick) peeled, fresh ginger to sugar-and-water mixture. Cover and boil 5 minutes instead of 3. Remove saucepan from heat and let stand, covered, 5 minutes. Strain mixture and discard ginger. Complete recipe as in step 2.

Each serving: About 125 calories, 0 g protein, 33 g carbohydrate, 0 g total fat, 0 mg cholesterol, 1 mg sodium.

GH INSTITUTE REPORT

PUTTING THE SQUEEZE ON LEMONS

To find out how to get every last drop of juice from lemons—a necessity when a pitcherful calls for 10—we squeezed halves with a top-of-the-line electric juicer, a manual juicer, and an ordinary handheld reamer (a pointed, ridged kitchen tool). The results: The electric machine extracted the most juice (about 3 tablespoons per lemon), followed by the manual juicer, then the reamer. No matter which method you choose, to be on the safe side, wash the skin first—even though you're not using it. And increase your yield by zapping whole lemons in the microwave before squeezing; when they're warm, the juice flows more readily. Heat 1 medium lemon for 20 to 30 seconds; 2 for 30 to 45 seconds; 4 for 45 seconds to 1 minute.

SOUPS

Caribbean Black-Bean Soup

PREP: 45 MINUTES PLUS OVERNIGHT TO SOAK BEANS
COOK: ABOUT 2 HOURS 30 MINUTES

Our new take on black-bean soup is made with fresh cilantro for great flavor.

1 pound dry black beans
2 tablespoons vegetable oil
2 medium red onions, chopped
4 jalapeño chiles, seeded and minced
2 tablespoons minced, peeled fresh ginger
4 garlic cloves, minced
½ teaspoon ground allspice
½ teaspoon dried thyme
2 medium sweet potatoes (about 12 ounces each), peeled and cut into ¾-inch chunks
1 tablespoon dark brown sugar
2 teaspoons salt
1 bunch green onions, thinly sliced
1 cup lightly packed fresh cilantro leaves, chopped
2 limes, cut into wedges (optional)

1 Rinse beans with cold running water and discard any stones or shriveled beans. In large bowl, place beans and *enough water to cover* by 2 inches. Cover and let stand at room temperature overnight. (Or, in 6-quart saucepot, place beans and *enough water to cover* by 2 inches. Heat to boiling over high heat; cook 2 minutes. Remove from heat; cover and let stand 1 hour.) Drain and rinse beans.

2 In 6-quart saucepot, heat vegetable oil over medium heat. Add onions and cook, stirring occasionally, 10 minutes or until tender. Add jalapeño chiles, ginger, garlic, allspice, and thyme, and cook, stirring, 3 minutes.

3 Add beans and *8 cups water*; heat to boiling over high heat. Reduce heat to low; cover and simmer 1½ hours. Add sweet potatoes, brown sugar, and salt; heat to boiling over high heat. Reduce heat to low; cover and simmer 30 minutes longer or until beans and sweet potatoes are tender.

4 Transfer 1 cup bean mixture to blender and puree until smooth; return to saucepot. Stir in green onions and cilantro. Serve with lime wedges if you like. Makes about 13 cups or 6 main-dish servings.

Each serving: About 390 calories, 17 g protein, 70 g carbohydrate, 6 g total fat (1 g saturated), 0 mg cholesterol, 705 mg sodium.

Black-Bean Soup

PREP: 10 MINUTES • COOK: 20 MINUTES

This shortcut soup packs a genuine Tex-Mex wallop of flavor.

1 tablespoon vegetable oil
1 medium onion, finely chopped
2 garlic cloves, crushed with garlic press
2 teaspoons chili powder
1 teaspoon ground cumin
¼ teaspoon crushed red pepper
2 cans (16 to 19 ounces each) black beans, rinsed and drained
1 can (14½ ounces) chicken broth
½ cup loosely packed fresh cilantro leaves, chopped
Lime wedges

1 In 3-quart saucepan, heat vegetable oil over medium heat. Add onion and cook 5 minutes or until tender. Stir in garlic, chili powder, cumin, and crushed red pepper; cook 30 seconds. Stir in beans, broth, and *2 cups water*; heat to boiling over high heat. Reduce heat to low; simmer, uncovered, 15 minutes.

2 In blender at low speed, with center part of cover removed to allow steam to escape, blend black bean mixture in small batches, until almost smooth. Pour soup into medium bowl after each batch.

3 Return soup to same saucepan; heat through. Sprinkle with cilantro and serve with lime wedges. Makes about 6½ cups or 4 main-dish servings.

Each serving: About 265 calories, 22 g protein, 46 g carbohydrate, 6 g total fat (1 g saturated), 0 mg cholesterol, 965 mg sodium.

Caribbean Black-Bean Soup ➤

Creamy Italian White-Bean Soup

PREP: 15 MINUTES • COOK: 40 MINUTES

A perfect marriage of canned beans and fresh spinach, with a squeeze of fresh lemon juice for flavor.

1 tablespoon vegetable oil
1 medium onion, finely chopped
1 medium celery stalk, finely chopped
1 garlic clove, minced
2 cans (15½ to 19 ounces each) white kidney beans (cannellini), rinsed and drained
1 can (14½ ounces) chicken broth
¼ teaspoon coarsely ground black pepper
⅛ teaspoon dried thyme
1 bunch (10 to 12 ounces) spinach
1 tablespoon fresh lemon juice
Freshly grated Parmesan cheese (optional)

1 In 3-quart saucepan, heat vegetable oil over medium heat until hot. Add onion and celery and cook 5 to 8 minutes, until tender, stirring occasionally. Add garlic; cook 30 seconds, stirring. Add beans, chicken broth, pepper, thyme, and *2 cups water*; heat to boiling over high heat. Reduce heat to low; simmer, uncovered, 15 minutes.

2 Meanwhile, discard tough stems from spinach; thinly slice leaves.

3 With slotted spoon, remove 2 cups bean-and-vegetable mixture from soup; set aside. In blender at low speed, with center part of cover removed to allow steam to escape, blend remaining soup in small batches until smooth. Pour soup into large bowl after each batch.

4 Return soup to saucepan; stir in reserved beans and vegetables. Heat to boiling over high heat, stirring occasionally. Stir in spinach and cook 1 minute or until wilted. Stir in lemon juice and remove from heat. Serve with Parmesan cheese if you like. Makes about 6 cups or 4 main-dish servings.

Each serving without Parmesan: About 295 calories, 18 g protein, 46 g carbohydrate, 5 g total fat (1 g saturated), 0 mg cholesterol, 945 mg sodium.

GAZPACHO

Based on the popular uncooked soup from southern Spain, our chunky garden-fresh version is a welcome lunch or supper on hot days. The corn, cilantro, lime juice, and splash of red-pepper sauce give this a distinctly New-World twist.

PREP: 10 MINUTES

6 large ice cubes (about 1 cup)
6 ripe medium tomatoes (about 2 pounds), cored and each cut into quarters
2 medium seedless (English) cucumbers, peeled and cut into 2-inch chunks
1 cup fresh corn kernels (cut from about 2 medium ears corn)
½ cup loosely packed fresh cilantro leaves
2 tablespoons fresh lime juice
¾ teaspoon salt
¼ teaspoon ground black pepper
Hot pepper sauce to taste
Lime wedges for garnish (optional)

In food processor with knife blade attached, coarsely chop all ingredients except lime wedges. If not

serving right away, cover and refrigerate up to 1 day. Serve with lime wedges if you like. Makes about 7 cups or 8 first-course servings.

Each serving: About 50 calories, 2 g protein, 12 g carbohydrate, 1 g total fat (0 g saturated), 0 mg cholesterol, 215 mg sodium.

Cool Cucumber Soup

PREP: 10 MINUTES

All you need is a blender to whip up this refreshing, no-cook soup in no time flat.

3 cucumbers (about 8 ounces each), peeled, seeded, and coarsely chopped
1 cup plain low-fat yogurt
¾ teaspoon salt
¼ teaspoon coarsely ground black pepper
3 large ice cubes (about ½ cup)
1 cup loosely packed fresh mint leaves, coarsely chopped
Thin cucumber slices for garnish

1 In blender, combine cucumbers, yogurt, salt, and pepper; blend until smooth.

2 With motor running and center part of cover removed, add ice cubes, 1 at a time. Add mint leaves and blend 5 seconds longer. If not serving right away, cover and refrigerate up to 1 day. Garnish with cucumber slices. Makes about 3 cups or 4 first-course servings.

Each serving: About 60 calories, 4 g protein, 9 g carbohydrate, 1 g total fat (1 g saturated), 4 mg cholesterol, 495 mg sodium.

Yellow Squash & Basil Soup

PREP: 10 MINUTES • COOK: ABOUT 30 MINUTES

Float a bright edible flower, such as a pansy or nasturtium, on top of the soup—or place it on the rim of the bowl.

4 tablespoons margarine or butter
1 medium onion, finely chopped
4 small yellow squashes (about 8 ounces each), sliced
3 medium carrots, peeled and sliced
1 can (14½ ounces) chicken broth
½ cup half-and-half or light cream
1¼ teaspoons salt
¼ teaspoon coarsely ground black pepper
1 cup loosely packed fresh basil leaves, chopped

1 In 4-quart saucepan, melt margarine or butter over medium heat. Add onion and cook about 8 minutes or until onion is tender but not brown, stirring frequently.

2 Add squash and carrot slices and stir vegetables to coat with onion mixture. Add chicken broth and 1½ *cups water*; heat to boiling over high heat. Reduce heat to low; cover and simmer 20 minutes or until vegetables are tender.

3 In blender at low speed, with center part of cover removed to allow steam to escape, blend soup in small batches until pureed. Pour pureed soup into large bowl after each batch.

4 Return soup to saucepan; stir in half-and-half, salt, and pepper, and heat through. Stir in chopped basil just before serving. Makes about 8 cups or 10 first-course servings.

Each serving: About 55 calories, 3 g protein, 9 g carbohydrate, 2 g total fat (1 g saturated), 4 mg cholesterol, 845 mg sodium.

Creamy Buttermilk-Beet Soup

PREP: 10 MINUTES

Just 4 basic ingredients—perfect when the last thing you want to do is cook.

3 cups buttermilk
1 can (14½ to 15 ounces) beets, drained
½ teaspoon salt
1 tablespoon minced fresh dill
Dill sprigs for garnish

In blender, combine buttermilk, beets, and salt; blend until smooth. Pour mixture into large bowl; stir in dill. If not serving right away, cover and refrigerate up to 1 day. Garnish with dill sprigs. Makes about 4 cups or 4 first-course servings.

Each serving: About 95 calories, 7 g protein, 14 g carbohydrate, 2 g total fat (1 g saturated), 7 mg cholesterol, 655 mg sodium.

Carrot & Dill Soup

PREP: 25 MINUTES • COOK: ABOUT 45 MINUTES

Combine sweet carrots with fresh orange, dill, and a touch of milk for a refreshing creamy soup without the cream.

1 tablespoon olive oil
1 large onion, chopped
1 medium celery stalk, chopped
2 large oranges
2 bags (16 ounces each) carrots, chopped
1 can (14½ ounces) chicken broth
1 tablespoon sugar
¾ teaspoon salt
¼ teaspoon coarsely ground black pepper
1 cup milk
¼ cup chopped fresh dill
Dill sprigs for garnish

1 In 5-quart Dutch oven, heat olive oil over medium-high heat. Add onion and celery and cook, stirring occasionally, until tender and golden, about 15 minutes.

French Onion Soup

2 Meanwhile, with vegetable peeler, remove 4 strips of peel (3" by 1" each) from 1 orange, and squeeze 1 cup juice from both oranges.

3 Add orange-peel strips to Dutch oven and cook 2 minutes longer, stirring. Add orange juice, carrots, chicken broth, sugar, salt, pepper, and *4 cups water*; heat to boiling over high heat. Reduce heat to low; cover and simmer 25 minutes or until carrots are very tender.

4 Remove orange-peel strips from soup. In blender, with center part of cover removed to allow steam to escape, blend soup in small batches until pureed and smooth. Pour pureed soup into large bowl after each batch. Return soup to Dutch oven; stir in milk and chopped dill; heat just to simmering over medium heat. Garnish each serving with a dill sprig. Makes about 10½ cups or 10 first-course servings.

Each serving: About 95 calories, 3 g protein, 16 g carbohydrate, 3 g total fat (1 g saturated), 3 mg cholesterol, 335 mg sodium.

French Onion Soup

PREP: 15 MINUTES
COOK: 1 HOUR 40 MINUTES PLUS BAKING

Slowly cooked onions lend great, caramelized flavor to this classic. If you double the recipe, be sure to cook the onions in 2 skillets.

3 tablespoons margarine or butter
7 medium onions (about 2½ pounds), each cut lengthwise in half and thinly sliced
¼ teaspoon salt
1 can (13¾ to 14½ ounces) beef broth
¼ teaspoon dried thyme
4 slices (each ½ inch thick) French bread
4 ounces Gruyère or Swiss cheese, shredded (1 cup)

1 In 12-inch skillet, melt margarine or butter over medium heat. Add onions and salt and cook until onions are very tender and begin to caramelize, about 45 minutes, stirring occasionally. Reduce heat to low; cook until onions are deep, golden brown, about 15 minutes longer, stirring often.

2 Transfer onions to 3-quart saucepan. Add ½ *cup water* to skillet; heat to boiling over high heat, stirring to scrape up browned bits. Pour water from skillet into saucepan with onions. Add beef broth, thyme, and 3½ *cups water*; heat to boiling over high heat. Reduce heat to low; cover and simmer 30 minutes or until onions are very tender.

3 Meanwhile, preheat oven to 450°F. Place French-bread slices on small cookie sheet; bake 5 minutes or until lightly toasted. Place four 2½-cup oven-safe bowls in 15½" by 10½" jelly-roll pan for easier handling. Spoon onion soup into bowls; top with toasted bread, pressing toast lightly into soup. Sprinkle toast with cheese. Bake 12 to 15 minutes, until cheese melts and begins to brown. Makes 6½ cups or 4 main-dish servings.

Each serving: About 375 calories, 15 g protein, 38 g carbohydrate, 19 g total fat (7 g saturated), 31 mg cholesterol, 835 mg sodium.

Green Pea
& Lettuce Soup

PREP: 5 MINUTES • COOK: 15 MINUTES

Serve this simplified version of the delicate French classic with our Fresh Mozzarella & Tomato Sandwiches (page 153).

2 teaspoons margarine or butter
1 medium onion, finely chopped
1 can (14½ ounces) chicken broth
1 package (10 ounces) frozen peas
1 head Boston lettuce (about 10 ounces),
  coarsely chopped
¾ teaspoon salt
⅛ teaspoon coarsely ground black pepper
⅛ teaspoon dried thyme
½ cup fat-free (skim) milk
1 tablespoon fresh lemon juice
Chives for garnish

1 In 4-quart saucepan, melt margarine or butter over medium heat. Add onion and cook, stirring occasionally, 5 minutes or until tender. Stir in chicken broth, frozen peas, lettuce, salt, pepper, thyme, and *1 cup water*; heat to boiling over high heat. Reduce heat to low; simmer 5 minutes. Stir in milk.

2 In blender at low speed, with center part of cover removed to allow steam to escape, blend pea mixture in small batches until smooth. Pour soup into large bowl after each batch. Return soup to saucepan. Heat through. Stir in lemon juice and remove from heat.

Transfer soup to serving bowl; garnish with chives. Makes about 6 cups or 4 main-dish servings.

Each serving: About 120 calories, 8 g protein, 17 g carbohydrate, 3 g total fat (1 g saturated), 1 mg cholesterol, 835 mg sodium.

Curried Sweet-Potato
& Lentil Soup

PREP: 15 MINUTES • COOK: 1 HOUR 15 MINUTES

2 tablespoons margarine or butter
2 medium sweet potatoes (about 12 ounces
  each), peeled and cut into ½-inch chunks
2 large celery stalks, diced
1 large onion, diced
1 garlic clove, minced
1 tablespoon curry powder
1 tablespoon grated, peeled fresh ginger
1 teaspoon ground cumin
1 teaspoon ground coriander
1 teaspoon salt
⅛ teaspoon ground red pepper (cayenne)
2 cans (14½ ounces each) vegetable or chicken
  broth
1 package (16 ounces) dry lentils, rinsed and
  picked over
Garnishes (optional): yogurt, toasted coconut,
  and lime wedges

1 In 6-quart Dutch oven, melt margarine or butter over medium heat. Add sweet potatoes, celery, and onion, and cook until onion is tender, about 10 minutes, stirring occasionally. Add garlic, curry powder, ginger, cumin, coriander, salt, and ground red pepper; cook, stirring, 1 minute.

2 To vegetables in Dutch oven, add chicken broth, lentils, and *6 cups water*; heat to boiling over high heat. Reduce heat to low; cover and simmer 40 to 45 minutes, until lentils are tender, stirring occasionally. Serve soup with yogurt, toasted coconut, and lime wedges if you like. Makes about 14 cups or 8 main-dish servings.

Each serving without garnishes: About 295 calories, 15 g protein, 51 g carbohydrate, 4 g total fat (1 g saturated), 0 mg cholesterol, 655 mg sodium.

Sweet & Sour Cabbage Soup

PREP: 25 MINUTES • COOK: 3 HOURS

Filling and fragrant, this dish is just right for a winter day.

1 bone-in beef chuck steak, 1½ inches thick (about 3 pounds)
3 medium carrots (about ½ pound), peeled and cut into ¾-inch pieces
3 medium parsnips (about ½ pound), peeled and cut into ¾-inch pieces
1 large onion, cut into ¾-inch pieces
1 large celery stalk, cut into ¾-inch pieces
1 can (28 ounces) tomatoes
1½ pounds green cabbage (about ½ medium head), sliced, with tough ribs discarded
2 teaspoons salt
½ teaspoon coarsely ground black pepper
1 bag (16 ounces) sauerkraut, drained but not rinsed
⅓ cup packed dark brown sugar
⅓ cup fresh lemon juice
⅓ cup chopped fresh dill
Dill sprigs for garnish

1 In 8-quart Dutch oven, cook steak over medium-high heat until browned on all sides; transfer to bowl. Reduce heat to medium; add carrots, parsnips, onion, and celery, and cook, stirring frequently, until vegetables are golden, about 15 minutes.

2 Return steak to Dutch oven. Add tomatoes with their juice and *8 cups water*; heat to boiling over high heat. Reduce heat to low; cover and simmer 1 hour.

3 Add cabbage, salt, and pepper; heat to boiling over high heat. Reduce heat to low; cover and simmer 1 hour longer or until meat is very tender.

4 With tongs, transfer steak to cutting board. Skim fat from soup. Cut meat into ¾-inch chunks; discard bones and fat. Return meat to Dutch oven. Add sauerkraut, brown sugar, and lemon juice; cook 15 minutes. Stir in chopped dill just before serving. Garnish with dill sprigs. Makes 14 cups or 8 main-dish servings.

Each serving: About 395 calories, 38 g protein, 30 g carbohydrate, 14 g total fat (5 g saturated), 98 mg cholesterol, 1045 mg sodium.

Broccoli & Cheddar Soup

PREP: 35 MINUTES • COOK: 25 MINUTES

This rich soup makes a satisfying meal—serve with homemade multigrain bread (or a bakery loaf) and a crisp salad. Use a blender—not a food processor—for an extrasmooth texture.

1 tablespoon olive oil
1 medium onion, chopped
¼ cup all-purpose flour
½ teaspoon salt
¼ teaspoon dried thyme
⅛ teaspoon ground nutmeg
Coarsely ground black pepper
2 cups reduced-fat (2%) milk
1 can (14½ ounces) chicken broth
1 large bunch (1½ pounds) broccoli, cut into 1-inch pieces (including stems)
1½ cups shredded sharp Cheddar cheese (6 ounces)

1 In 4-quart saucepan, heat olive oil over medium heat. Add onion and cook until golden, about 10 minutes, stirring occasionally. Stir in flour, salt, thyme, nutmeg, and ¼ teaspoon pepper; cook 2 minutes, stirring frequently.

2 Gradually stir in milk, chicken broth, and *1½ cups water*; add broccoli and heat to boiling over high heat. Reduce heat to low; cover and simmer until broccoli is tender, about 10 minutes.

3 In blender at low speed, with center part of cover removed to allow steam to escape, blend broccoli mixture in small batches until very smooth. Pour pureed soup into large bowl after each batch.

4 Return soup to saucepan; heat to boiling over high heat, stirring occasionally. Remove saucepan from heat; stir in cheese until melted and smooth. Sprinkle each serving with coarsely ground black pepper. Makes about 8 cups, 8 first-course, or 4 main-dish servings.

Each first-course serving: About 185 calories, 12 g protein, 12 g carbohydrate, 11 g total fat (6 g saturated), 27 mg cholesterol, 485 mg sodium.

QUICKIE VEGETABLE CREAM SOUPS

Start with a package of frozen vegetable, a can of broth, and seasonings—in 25 minutes you'll have a luscious, creamy, lower-fat soup.

Master Recipe

PREP: 5 MINUTES • COOK: 20 MINUTES

1 tablespoon margarine or butter
1 medium onion, finely chopped
1 can (14½ ounces) chicken broth
1 package (10 ounces) frozen vegetables (see chart)
¼ teaspoon dried thyme
⅛ teaspoon salt
⅛ teaspoon coarsely ground black pepper
1½ cups milk*
2 teaspoons fresh lemon juice
Optional garnish (see chart)

1 In 2-quart saucepan, melt margarine or butter over medium heat. Stir in onion and cook, stirring occasionally, 5 minutes or until tender. Add chicken broth, frozen vegetables, thyme, salt, and pepper; heat to boiling over high heat. Reduce heat to low and simmer, uncovered, 10 minutes.

2 In blender at low speed, with center part of cover removed to allow steam to escape, blend vegetable mixture in small batches until pureed. Pour pureed soup into bowl after each batch.

3 Return soup to saucepan; stir in milk. Heat through over medium heat, stirring often (do not boil, or soup may curdle). Remove saucepan from

Whole-kernel corn soup with fresh cilantro garnish

heat; stir in lemon juice. Garnish, if you like. Makes about 3¾ cups or 4 first-course servings.

*Nutrition data was calculated using whole milk; you can substitute low-fat milk instead, though the soup won't taste as creamy.

Each serving corn, lima bean, or pea soup: About 170 calories, 9 g protein, 20 g carbohydrate, 7 g total fat (3 g saturated), 13 mg cholesterol, 515 mg sodium.

Each serving asparagus, cauliflower, kale, or squash soup: About 130 calories, 8 g protein, 11 g carbohydrate, 7 g total fat (3 g saturated), 13 mg cholesterol, 480 mg sodium.

Type of Vegetable	Extra Ingredient	Additional Cooking Steps	Optional Garnish
ASPARAGUS CUTS OR SPEARS	¼ tsp. dried tarragon	none	snipped fresh chives
CAULIFLOWER FLOWERETS	½ tsp. curry powder	Add curry after cooking onion; cook 30 seconds.	chopped fresh apple
CHOPPED KALE	1 garlic clove, minced	Add garlic after cooking onion; cook 30 seconds. Add milk to kale mixture before pureeing.	crumbled cooked bacon
LIMA BEANS	none	none	chopped fresh thyme
PEAS	¼ tsp. dried mint	none	swirl of sour cream
WHOLE-KERNEL CORN	¾ tsp. chili powder	Add chili powder after cooking onion; cook 30 seconds.	chopped fresh cilantro
WINTER SQUASH	¼ tsp. pumpkin-pie spices	Add spice after cooking onion; cook 30 seconds.	chopped tomato

Asian-Style Corn Chowder

PREP: 20 MINUTES • COOK: ABOUT 15 MINUTES

GH Food Appliances Director Sharon Franke's sister-in-law, Andrea Spencer, began making this spicy corn soup (adapted from Ken Hom's *East Meets West Cuisine*) about 10 years ago. Spencer likes to serve it buffet-style; each person adds chili paste to taste.

2 tablespoons margarine or butter
2 tablespoons minced, peeled fresh ginger
2 medium shallots, minced
2 medium garlic cloves, minced
1 medium onion, diced
1 stalk (12 inches long) fresh lemongrass, lightly pounded and then cut into 4-inch-long pieces or 3 strips lemon peel (3" by 1" each)
2 cans (14½ ounces each) chicken broth
1 bag (20 ounces) frozen whole-kernel corn, thawed
1½ teaspoons sugar
½ teaspoon salt
½ cup half-and-half or light cream
Chopped fresh cilantro leaves for garnish
Chili paste* (optional)

1 In 6-quart saucepot, melt margarine or butter over medium heat. Add ginger, shallots, garlic, onion, and lemongrass or lemon peel and cook until golden, about 8 minutes.

2 Add chicken broth, corn, sugar, salt, and *2 cups water*; heat to boiling over high heat. Reduce heat to low; cover and simmer 5 minutes. Discard lemongrass or lemon peel. Remove 2 cups soup; reserve.

3 In blender at low speed, with center part of cover removed to allow steam to escape, blend soup remaining in saucepot in small batches until very smooth. Pour soup into large bowl after each batch. Return blended soup and reserved soup to saucepot; stir in half-and-half. Heat soup over medium heat until hot, stirring occasionally. Serve soup with cilantro and chili paste if you like. Makes about 9½ cups or 10 first-course servings.

*Chili paste is a spicy-hot condiment that can be found in Asian markets or in the ethnic food section of some supermarkets.

Each serving: About 110 calories, 4 g protein, 16 g carbohydrate, 4 g total fat (1 g saturated), 4 mg cholesterol, 410 mg sodium.

FOOD EDITOR'S TIP

Q I have only had lemongrass in Thai restaurants yet I see it popping up in more and more recipes. Do I have to go to a Thai market to buy it?

A Most Chinese markets also carry lemongrass. This herb, which has a subtle lemon flavor, is sold by the stalk and looks something like green onions. It is very fibrous; for cooking, trim off the stalk top and use only six to eight inches from the stalk base. Some recipes (like Asian-Style Corn Chowder, above) pound the lemongrass to make the flavor more available. The fibrous lemongrass is discarded after cooking.

Puréed Winter Vegetable Soup

PREP: 20 MINUTES • COOK: 30 MINUTES

Chemistry Director Sandra Kuzmich loves to start winter meals with a batch of hearty, nutritious soup. Her family often requests this one.

1 tablespoon vegetable oil
1 medium onion, finely chopped
1 garlic clove, minced
1 bag (16 ounces) carrots, sliced
1 small fennel bulb, trimmed and diced
2 cans (14½ ounces each) chicken or vegetable broth
¼ teaspoon salt, or to taste
¼ teaspoon coarsely ground black pepper
3 medium all-purpose potatoes (about 1 pound), peeled and each cut into quarters
½ cup half-and-half or light cream (optional)
Dill sprigs for garnish

1 In 5-quart saucepot, heat oil over medium heat. Add onion and garlic and cook 10 minutes or until tender, stirring occasionally. Stir in carrots, fennel, broth, salt, pepper, and *3 cups water*. Heat to boiling over high heat. Reduce heat to low; cover and simmer 10 minutes. Add potatoes and simmer 20 minutes longer or until vegetables are very tender.

2 In blender at low speed, with center part of cover removed to allow steam to escape, blend vegetable mixture in small batches until smooth; pour into large bowl after each batch.

3 Return mixture to saucepot; add half-and-half or light cream, if desired; heat through. Garnish each serving with a dill sprig. Makes about 10 cups or 8 first-course servings.

Each serving without cream: About 100 calories, 4 g protein, 16 g carbohydrate, 3 g total fat (0 g saturated), 0 mg cholesterol, 420 mg sodium.

Shrimp Bisque

• •

PREP: 30 MINUTES • COOK: 1 HOUR 10 MINUTES

Bisque doesn't get any tastier than this—between the shrimp and the white wine, it's hard to resist.

1 pound medium shrimp
3 tablespoons margarine or butter
2 cans (14½ ounces each) reduced-sodium
   chicken broth
1 cup dry white wine
2 medium carrots, chopped
2 medium celery stalks, chopped
1 large onion, chopped
2 tablespoons regular long-grain rice
1¼ teaspoons salt
⅛ to ¼ teaspoon ground red pepper (cayenne)
1 bay leaf
1 can (14½ ounces) diced tomatoes
1 cup half-and-half or light cream
2 tablespoons brandy or dry sherry
Fresh chives for garnish

1 Shell and devein shrimp, reserving shells.

2 In 5-quart Dutch oven, melt 1 tablespoon margarine or butter over medium heat. Add shrimp shells and cook 5 minutes, stirring often.

3 Add chicken broth, wine, and *½ cup water*; heat to boiling over high heat. Reduce heat to low; cover and simmer 15 minutes. Strain broth mixture into 4-cup measuring cup or small bowl, pressing on shells with spoon to extract any remaining liquid. Discard shells.

4 In same Dutch oven, melt remaining 2 tablespoons margarine or butter over medium-high heat. Add shrimp and cook until they turn opaque throughout, about 3 minutes, stirring occasionally. With slotted spoon, transfer shrimp to another small

bowl. Add carrots, celery, and onion; cook, stirring occasionally, 10 to 12 minutes, until lightly browned.

5 Return broth mixture to Dutch oven; add rice, salt, ground red pepper, and bay leaf. Heat to boiling over high heat. Reduce heat to low; cover and simmer 20 minutes or until rice is very tender. Add tomatoes with their juice and cook 10 minutes longer. Remove Dutch oven from heat; discard bay leaf and add shrimp.

6 In blender, with center part of cover removed to allow steam to escape, blend shrimp mixture in small batches until pureed and very smooth. Pour pureed soup into large bowl after each batch. Return soup to Dutch oven and add half-and-half and brandy; heat through over medium heat (do not boil or soup may curdle). Garnish each serving with fresh chives. Makes about 10 cups or 10 first-course servings.

Each serving: About 145 calories, 10 g protein, 9 g carbohydrate, 7 g total fat (2 g saturated), 65 mg cholesterol, 750 mg sodium.

Top to bottom: Carrot & Dill Soup (page 44), Broccoli & Cheddar Soup (page 46), and Shrimp Bisque (recipe at left).

Thai Chicken & Coconut Soup

PREP: 25 MINUTES • COOK: ABOUT 45 MINUTES

Exotic and delectable—a winner when the weather is blustery.

2 cans (14½ ounces each) reduced-sodium
   chicken broth
4 garlic cloves, crushed with garlic press
1 tablespoon Thai green curry paste
1 tablespoon minced, peeled fresh ginger
1 teaspoon coriander seeds
½ teaspoon whole black peppercorns
⅛ teaspoon cumin seeds
8 ounces skinless, boneless chicken breast
1 can (14 ounces) light unsweetened coconut
   milk (not cream of coconut), well stirred
1 cup thinly sliced shallots (about 5 large)
2 tablespoons Asian fish sauce*
1 tablespoon fresh lime juice
2 tablespoons chopped fresh cilantro leaves
   and/or dill
Lime wedges (optional)

1 In 5-quart Dutch oven, heat chicken broth, garlic, curry paste, ginger, coriander, peppercorns, cumin, and *1 cup water* to boiling over high heat. Reduce heat to low; cover and simmer 20 minutes. Strain broth into large bowl; discard solids. Set broth aside.

2 While broth is simmering, cut chicken breast into thin strips.

3 In same Dutch oven, heat ½ cup coconut milk to boiling over high heat. Reduce heat to medium-high; add shallots and cook, stirring constantly, until shallots soften and liquid evaporates. Reduce heat to medium; add chicken and cook, stirring constantly, until chicken just loses its pink color throughout.

4 Stir in strained broth mixture, fish sauce, lime juice, and remaining coconut milk; heat through. Sprinkle soup with chopped cilantro. Serve with lime wedges if you like. Makes about 6 cups or 4 main-dish servings.

*Available in the Asian sections of some supermarkets. For more information, see "Food Editor's Tip," page 114.

Each serving: About 205 calories, 19 g protein, 11 g carbohydrate, 10 g total fat (6 g saturated), 33 mg cholesterol, 1325 mg sodium.

Asian Chicken-Noodle Soup

PREP: 15 MINUTES • COOK: 25 MINUTES

Ours tastes just as good as, if not better than, any noodle-shop version. Use chopsticks or a fork to pick up the long noodles. The cooked chicken called for here is the by-product of making the homemade chicken broth on page 54, but you can also make this soup with canned broth (you'll need about 5 cups) and uncooked chicken (you'll need about ¾ pound of skinless, boneless breast). Cook the chicken in the broth in step 1, then set aside to cool before cutting into thin strips. Add to the soup in step 3, as directed below.

4 ounces rice noodles or linguine
1 recipe Old-Fashioned Chicken Broth
   (page 54)
4 ounces shiitake mushrooms, stems removed,
   thinly sliced
2 tablespoons soy sauce
1 tablespoon grated, peeled fresh ginger
¾ teaspoon salt
⅛ teaspoon crushed red pepper
2 cups thin strips cooked chicken
¼ teaspoon Asian sesame oil
1 cup loosely packed fresh cilantro leaves
2 green onions, thinly sliced

1 Prepare noodles as label directs; drain.

2 Meanwhile, in 4-quart saucepan, heat chicken broth to boiling over high heat. Stir in mushrooms, soy sauce, ginger, salt, and crushed red pepper. Reduce heat to low; simmer, uncovered, 10 minutes.

3 Stir in chicken, sesame oil, and noodles; heat through. Stir in cilantro and green onions. Makes about 7 cups or 4 main-dish servings.

Each serving: About 285 calories, 25 g protein, 30 g carbohydrate, 5 g total fat (1 g saturated), 58 mg cholesterol, 1050 mg sodium.

Thai Chicken & Coconut Soup ➤

Chicken & Escarole Soup with Meatballs

PREP: 1 HOUR • COOK: 1 HOUR 15 MINUTES

Freelance Food Consultant Gina Miraglia's grandmother, Rita Pacella, of Brooklyn, makes this Italian soup every year on Thanksgiving. All the grandchildren help roll the tender meatballs— everyone's favorite part.

1 chicken (4 pounds), cut up
1 large onion, cut in half
¼ teaspoon whole black peppercorns
1 bay leaf
1 pound ground meat for meat loaf (beef, pork, and veal)
2 garlic cloves, crushed with garlic press
1 large egg, beaten
¼ cup chopped fresh parsley leaves
½ teaspoon coarsely ground black pepper
¾ cup grated Romano cheese, plus additional for serving
2¾ teaspoons salt
1 cup plain dried bread crumbs
⅓ cup milk
1 can (14½ ounces) chicken broth
3 medium carrots, sliced
2 medium celery stalks, sliced
1 small head escarole (about 8 ounces), cut into ½-inch strips, with tough stems discarded

1 In 8-quart Dutch oven or saucepot, combine chicken, onion, peppercorns, bay leaf, and *12 cups water*; heat to boiling over high heat. Reduce heat to low; cover and simmer 1 hour and 15 minutes or until chicken is tender.

2 Meanwhile, prepare meatballs: In large bowl, with hands, combine ground meat, garlic, egg, parsley, pepper, ½ cup Romano cheese, and ¾ teaspoon salt. In small bowl, mix bread crumbs and milk to form a thick paste. Mix bread-crumb mixture into meat mixture just until blended. Shape meat mixture into about seventy 1-inch meatballs and place on cookie sheet; cover and refrigerate 30 minutes.

3 Transfer chicken to bowl; cool until easy to handle. Discard skin and bones from chicken; cut chicken into bite-size pieces. Reserve 2 cups cut-up chicken; refrigerate remaining chicken for use another day. Pour chicken broth through sieve lined with paper towels into large bowl. Let stand a few seconds until fat separates from meat juice. Skim fat from broth and discard.

4 Return broth to clean Dutch oven or saucepot; add canned chicken broth and remaining 2 teaspoons salt; heat to boiling over high heat. Stir in carrots and celery; heat to boiling. Reduce heat to low; cover and simmer 8 to 10 minutes, until vegetables are tender. Add meatballs and remaining ¼ cup Romano cheese; heat to boiling over high heat. Reduce heat to low; cover and simmer 15 minutes or until meatballs are cooked through. Stir in escarole and reserved chicken; heat through. Serve with grated Romano cheese to sprinkle over each serving. Makes about 16 cups or 14 first-course servings.

Each serving: About 235 calories, 18 g protein, 10 g carbohydrate, 13 g total fat (5 g saturated), 61 mg cholesterol, 760 mg sodium.

Country Beef & Veggie Soup

PREP: 25 MINUTES PLUS OVERNIGHT TO SOAK BEANS
COOK: 1 HOUR 45 MINUTES

This is so filling it can almost be considered a stew. Serve with our crusty Farmhouse White Bread (page 184) for a cozy Sunday supper.

8 ounces dry large lima beans (1¼ cups)
1 tablespoon vegetable oil
2 pounds beef shank cross cuts, each 1½ inches thick
2 medium onions, finely chopped
3 garlic cloves, minced
⅛ teaspoon ground cloves
4 large carrots, cut into ½-inch pieces
2 large celery stalks, cut into ½-inch pieces
8 ounces green cabbage (about ½ small head), cut into ½-inch pieces (about 5 cups)
1 can (13¾ to 14½ ounces) beef broth
2 teaspoons salt
½ teaspoon dried thyme
½ teaspoon coarsely ground black pepper
3 medium all-purpose potatoes (1 pound), peeled and cut into ¾-inch pieces
1 can (14½ ounces) diced tomatoes
1 cup frozen whole-kernel corn
1 cup frozen peas
¼ cup chopped fresh parsley leaves

Country Beef & Veggie Soup

1 Rinse beans with cold running water and discard any stones or shriveled beans. In large bowl, place beans and *enough water to cover* by 2 inches. Cover and let stand at room temperature overnight. (Or, in 4-quart saucepan, place beans and *enough water to cover* by 2 inches. Heat to boiling over high heat; cook 2 minutes. Remove from heat; cover and let stand 1 hour.) Drain and rinse beans.

2 In 8-quart Dutch oven, heat vegetable oil over medium-high heat until hot. Add beef shanks and cook until meat is well browned on all sides. Transfer beef shanks to plate.

3 Reduce heat to medium; add onions and cook, stirring occasionally, 5 minutes or until tender. Add garlic and ground cloves; cook 30 seconds, stirring. Return beef shanks to Dutch oven; stir in carrots, celery, cabbage, beef broth, salt, thyme, pepper, and *4½ cups water*. Heat to boiling over high heat. Reduce heat to low; cover and simmer 1 hour or until beef is tender.

4 Meanwhile, in 4-quart saucepan, heat beans and 5 *cups water* to boiling over high heat. Reduce heat to low; cover and simmer 30 minutes or until beans are tender. Drain beans.

5 When beef is tender, add potatoes and cooked beans to Dutch oven; heat to boiling over high heat. Reduce heat to low; cover and simmer 5 minutes. Stir in tomatoes with their juice; cover and simmer 10 minutes longer or until potatoes are tender.

6 With slotted spoon, remove beef shanks from soup. Cut beef into ½-inch pieces; discard bones and fat. Return beef to Dutch oven. Add frozen corn and peas; heat through. Sprinkle with parsley to serve. Makes about 14 cups or 8 main-dish servings.

Each serving: About 375 calories, 27 g protein, 44 g carbohydrate, 11 g total fat (4 g saturated), 38 mg cholesterol, 990 mg sodium.

Old-Fashioned Chicken Broth

PREP: 15 MINUTES PLUS OVERNIGHT TO CHILL
COOK: 4 HOURS 15 MINUTES

We made our broths without salt so they're versatile enough to use in a variety of recipes. If you want to serve the broth on its own, stir in 2 teaspoons salt (or to taste) after cooking.

1 whole chicken (about 3½ pounds)
2 carrots, peeled and cut into 2-inch pieces
1 celery stalk, cut into 2-inch pieces
1 medium onion, unpeeled and cut into quarters
5 parsley sprigs
1 garlic clove, unpeeled
½ teaspoon dried thyme
½ bay leaf

1 In 8-quart Dutch oven or saucepot, place whole chicken with its neck (refrigerate or freeze giblets for use another day), carrots, celery, onion, parsley, garlic, thyme, and bay leaf. Add 3 *quarts water*; heat to boiling over high heat. With slotted spoon, skim any foam from surface. Reduce heat to low; cover and simmer 1 hour, turning chicken once and skimming foam occasionally.

2 Remove Dutch oven from heat and transfer chicken to cutting board. When chicken is cool enough to handle, remove meat from bones (refrigerate or freeze meat for use another day). Return chicken bones, skin, and scraps to Dutch oven; heat to boiling over high heat. Reduce heat to low; simmer, uncovered, 3 hours.

3 Drain broth through colander into large bowl. Strain broth through sieve into another large bowl. Discard solids in sieve; cool broth slightly. Cover and refrigerate overnight.

4 When cold, discard fat from surface of broth. Makes about 5 cups broth.

PRESSURE-COOKER CHICKEN BROTH: In 6-quart pressure cooker, place all ingredients called for in Old-Fashioned Chicken Broth, but use only *4 cups water*. Following manufacturer's directions, cover pressure cooker and bring up to high pressure (15 pounds). Cook 15 minutes. Remove cooker from heat and allow pressure to drop for 5 minutes, then follow manufacturer's directions for quick release of pressure. Drain broth through colander into large bowl. Strain broth through sieve into another large bowl. Transfer chicken to cutting board; discard solids in sieve. When chicken is cool enough to handle, remove meat from bones (refrigerate or freeze meat for use another day); discard skin and bones. Skim fat from broth (or refrigerate overnight to make skimming easier). Makes about 5½ cups broth.

Each ½ cup: About 10 calories, 1 g protein, 1 g carbohydrate, 0 g total fat, 0 mg cholesterol, 30 mg sodium.

Chicken Soup with Rice

PREP: 10 MINUTES • COOK: 25 MINUTES

Everyone loves this old favorite—a specialty of grandmas everywhere, it's like comfort in a bowl.

⅔ cup regular long-grain rice
1 recipe Old-Fashioned Chicken Broth (at left)
3 medium carrots, cut into ¼-inch pieces
1 medium celery stalk, cut into ¼-inch pieces
2 cups bite-size pieces cooked chicken (reserved from making broth)
1½ teaspoons salt

1 In 1-quart saucepan, prepare rice as label directs.

2 Meanwhile, in 3-quart saucepan, heat chicken broth, carrots, and celery to boiling over high heat. Reduce heat to low; simmer, uncovered, 15 minutes or until vegetables are tender. Stir in chicken, salt, and rice; heat through. Makes about 8 cups or 4 main-dish servings.

Each serving: About 290 calories, 25 g protein, 32 g carbohydrate, 5 g total fat (1 g saturated), 58 mg cholesterol, 960 mg sodium.

POULTRY

Chicken with Asparagus & Mushrooms

PREP: 20 MINUTES • COOK: ABOUT 25 MINUTES

Serve alongside couscous flecked with chopped tomato.

4 medium skinless, boneless chicken-breast
    halves (about 1¼ pounds)
¼ teaspoon coarsely ground black pepper
¾ teaspoon salt
3 teaspoons olive oil
1 medium onion, chopped
¼ pound shiitake mushrooms, thinly sliced and
    stems discarded
¼ pound white mushrooms, thinly sliced
1½ pounds asparagus, trimmed and cut into
    2-inch pieces
½ cup half-and-half or light cream

1 Sprinkle chicken with pepper and ¼ teaspoon salt.

2 In nonstick 12-inch skillet, heat 1 teaspoon olive oil over medium-high heat until hot. Add chicken and cook 6 minutes. Reduce heat to medium; turn chicken over and cook 6 to 8 minutes longer, until juices run clear when thickest part of breast is pierced with tip of knife. Transfer chicken to platter; cover with foil to keep warm.

3 In same skillet, heat remaining 2 teaspoons olive oil over medium heat until hot. Add onion and mushrooms and cook until vegetables are tender and liquid evaporates, about 5 minutes, stirring frequently.

4 Add asparagus, *¼ cup water*, and remaining ½ teaspoon salt to mushroom mixture; heat to boiling. Cook until asparagus is tender-crisp, about 5 minutes, stirring often. Stir in half-and-half; heat through.

5 To serve, pour asparagus mixture over chicken. Makes 4 main-dish servings.

Each serving: About 270 calories, 38 g protein, 11 g carbohydrate, 9 g total fat (3 g saturated), 92 mg cholesterol, 510 mg sodium.

Tarragon & Grape Chicken

PREP: 15 MINUTES • COOK: ABOUT 20 MINUTES

Serve with steamed broccoli and orzo.

4 medium skinless, boneless chicken-breast
    halves (about 1¼ pounds)
¼ teaspoon coarsely ground black pepper
½ teaspoon salt
1 teaspoon olive oil
2 teaspoons margarine or butter
3 medium shallots, minced (about ⅓ cup)
¼ cup dry white wine
¼ cup chicken broth
¼ cup half-and-half or light cream
1 cup seedless red and/or green grapes, each
    cut in half
1 tablespoon chopped fresh tarragon

1 Sprinkle chicken with pepper and ¼ teaspoon salt.

2 In nonstick 12-inch skillet, heat olive oil over medium-high heat until hot. Add chicken and cook 6 minutes. Reduce heat to medium; turn chicken over and cook 6 to 8 minutes longer, until juices run clear when thickest part of breast is pierced with tip of knife. Transfer chicken to platter; cover with foil to keep warm.

3 In same skillet, melt margarine or butter over medium-low heat. Add shallots and remaining ¼ teaspoon salt and cook, stirring, 3 to 5 minutes, until tender and golden. Stir in wine; cook 30 seconds. Stir in chicken broth, half-and-half, grapes, and tarragon. Return chicken to skillet; heat through. Makes 4 main-dish servings.

Each serving: About 255 calories, 34 g protein, 10 g carbohydrate, 8 g total fat (2 g saturated), 87 mg cholesterol, 455 mg sodium.

Tarragon & Grape Chicken ➤

Chicken with Creamy Leek Sauce

PREP: 15 MINUTES • COOK: ABOUT 25 MINUTES

Serve with boiled red potatoes and steamed green beans.

1 small bunch leeks (about 1 pound)
4 medium skinless, boneless chicken-breast halves (about 1¼ pounds)
½ teaspoon salt
¼ teaspoon coarsely ground black pepper
1 teaspoon olive oil
1 tablespoon margarine or butter
½ cup chicken broth
¼ cup dry white wine
¼ cup heavy or whipping cream

1 Cut off roots from leeks. Cut each leek crosswise at point where light-green part meets dark-green top. Discard tops. Cut each leek bottom lengthwise into quarters, then crosswise into ¼-inch-wide slices. Rinse leeks in bowl of cold water; with hand, transfer leeks to colander. Repeat until all sand is removed. Drain well.

2 Sprinkle chicken with ¼ teaspoon salt and ⅛ teaspoon pepper.

3 In nonstick 12-inch skillet, heat olive oil over medium-high heat until hot. Add chicken and cook 6 minutes. Reduce heat to medium; turn chicken over and cook 6 to 8 minutes longer, until juices run clear when thickest part of breast is pierced with tip of knife. Transfer chicken to platter; cover with foil to keep warm.

4 In same skillet, melt margarine or butter over medium-low heat. Add leeks and cook, stirring frequently, 5 to 7 minutes, until tender and golden. Add chicken broth and wine; heat to boiling over medium-high heat. Boil 1 minute or until slightly reduced. Add cream, remaining ¼ teaspoon salt, and ⅛ teaspoon pepper; heat to boiling. Boil 1 to 2 minutes longer or until sauce thickens slightly.

5 To serve, pour sauce over chicken. Makes 4 main-dish servings.

Each serving: About 285 calories, 35 g protein, 9 g carbohydrate, 12 g total fat (5 g saturated), 103 mg cholesterol, 510 mg sodium.

Chicken Breasts with Cumin, Coriander & Lime

PREP: 10 MINUTES • COOK: 10 TO 12 MINUTES

Serve with: Rice and peas. An exotic blend of spices and lime juice adds instant flavor to boneless chicken breasts. For a quick side dish, cook rice as package directs, and stir in frozen peas during last 3 minutes of cooking time.

3 tablespoons fresh lime juice (about 2 limes)
1 teaspoon ground cumin
1 teaspoon ground coriander
1 teaspoon salt
1 teaspoon sugar
⅛ teaspoon ground red pepper (cayenne)
4 small skinless, boneless chicken-breast halves (about 1 pound)
Nonstick cooking spray
1 tablespoon chopped fresh cilantro leaves

1 In large bowl, mix lime juice, cumin, coriander, salt, sugar, and ground red pepper; add chicken, tossing to coat.

2 Spray grill pan or cast-iron skillet with nonstick cooking spray; heat over medium-high heat until hot but not smoking. Add chicken and cook 5 to 6 minutes per side or until juices run clear when thickest part of breast is pierced with tip of knife, turning once and brushing with any remaining cumin mixture halfway through cooking. Place chicken breasts on platter; sprinkle with cilantro. Makes 4 main-dish servings.

Each serving: About 150 calories, 27 g protein, 3 g carbohydrate, 3 g total fat (1 g saturated), 72 mg cholesterol, 600 mg sodium.

Mediterranean Chicken

PREP: 15 MINUTES • COOK: ABOUT 20 MINUTES

Serve with crusty whole-wheat peasant bread and a tossed green salad.

4 medium skinless, boneless chicken-breast
  halves (about 1¼ pounds)
¼ teaspoon salt
¼ teaspoon coarsely ground black pepper
3 teaspoons olive oil
1 small onion, finely chopped
4 medium plum tomatoes (about 12 ounces), cut
  into ¼-inch pieces
¼ cup Kalamata olives, pitted and chopped
1 tablespoon fresh lemon juice
½ cup crumbled feta cheese
2 tablespoons chopped fresh parsley

1 Sprinkle chicken with salt and ⅛ teaspoon pepper.

2 In nonstick 12-inch skillet, heat 1 teaspoon olive oil over medium-high heat until hot. Add chicken and cook 6 minutes. Reduce heat to medium; turn chicken over and cook 6 to 8 minutes longer, until juices run clear when thickest part of breast is pierced with tip of knife. Transfer chicken to platter; cover with foil to keep warm.

3 In same skillet, heat remaining 2 teaspoons olive oil over medium-low heat. Add onion and cook, stirring, about 5 minutes or until tender and golden. Add tomatoes, olives, lemon juice, ¼ *cup water*, and remaining ⅛ teaspoon pepper, and cook, stirring, 1 minute or until tomatoes release their juice. Stir in feta cheese and parsley.

4 To serve, pour tomato mixture over chicken. Makes 4 main-dish servings.

Each serving: About 275 calories, 36 g protein, 8 g carbohydrate, 11 g total fat (3 g saturated), 95 mg cholesterol, 525 mg sodium.

Mediterranean Chicken

Crispy Chicken with 3 Dipping Sauces

PREP: 30 MINUTES • BAKE: 30 TO 35 MINUTES

The baked chicken with 3 homemade sauces is delicious hot or cold—a perfect buffet dish for a crowd.

Olive-oil nonstick cooking spray
1¾ cups walnuts
1 cup plain dried bread crumbs
1½ teaspoons salt
¼ to ½ teaspoon ground red pepper (cayenne)
2 large eggs
8 medium chicken-breast halves (about
   3½ pounds), skin removed
8 medium chicken drumsticks (about
   1¾ pounds), skin removed
Blue-Cheese Sauce (below)
Honey-Mustard Sauce (at right)
Apricot-Balsamic Sauce (at right)

1 Preheat oven to 450°F. Spray two 15½" by 10½" jelly-roll pans with olive-oil cooking spray.

2 In food processor with knife blade attached, blend walnuts with ¼ cup bread crumbs until walnuts are finely ground. Place nut mixture, salt, ground red pepper, and remaining ¾ cup bread crumbs in medium bowl; mix well.

3 In pie plate, with fork, beat eggs. Cut each chicken-breast half crosswise into 2 pieces. One at a time, dip chicken-breast pieces and drumsticks in beaten egg, then into walnut mixture to coat; place in jelly-roll pans. Spray chicken pieces with olive-oil cooking spray.

4 Bake chicken, on 2 oven racks, 30 to 35 minutes, rotating pans between upper and lower racks halfway through cooking, until chicken is golden brown and juices run clear when chicken is pierced with a knife.

5 While chicken is cooking, prepare sauces. Cover and refrigerate sauces if not serving right away.

6 Serve chicken hot with dipping sauces. Or, cool chicken slightly; cover and refrigerate to serve cold later with sauces. Makes 16 main-dish servings.

BLUE-CHEESE SAUCE: In medium bowl, stir together *4 ounces blue cheese*, crumbled (1 cup), *½ cup mayonnaise, ½ cup plain low-fat yogurt, ½ teaspoon hot pepper sauce*, and *¼ teaspoon coarsely ground black pepper*. Makes about 1½ cups.

HONEY-MUSTARD SAUCE: In medium bowl, stir together *⅔ cup Dijon mustard, ¼ cup sour cream, ¼ cup honey*, and *¾ teaspoon Worcestershire sauce*. Makes about 1¼ cups.

APRICOT-BALSAMIC SAUCE: In medium bowl, stir together *one 12-ounce jar apricot preserves (1 cup), 2 tablespoons balsamic vinegar, 1 tablespoon soy sauce*, and *¼ teaspoon grated fresh orange peel*. Makes about 1¼ cups.

Each serving chicken without sauces: About 230 calories, 23 g protein, 7 g carbohydrate, 12 g total fat (2 g saturated), 84 mg cholesterol, 320 mg sodium.

Each tablespoon blue-cheese sauce: About 55 calories, 1 g protein, 0 g carbohydrate, 5 g total fat (2 g saturated), 6 mg cholesterol, 95 mg sodium.

Each tablespoon honey-mustard sauce: About 30 calories, 1 g protein, 4 g carbohydrate, 1 g total fat (0 g saturated), 1 mg cholesterol, 205 mg sodium.

Each tablespoon apricot-balsamic sauce: About 50 calories, 0 g protein, 12 g carbohydrate, 0 g total fat, 0 mg cholesterol, 55 mg sodium.

New Chicken Cordon Bleu

PREP: 10 MINUTES • COOK: ABOUT 15 MINUTES

These sautéed chicken breasts are topped with sliced ham and mozzarella and served on a bed of baby spinach.

1 tablespoon margarine or butter
4 small skinless, boneless chicken-breast halves
   (about 1 pound)
½ cup chicken broth
2 tablespoons balsamic vinegar
⅛ teaspoon coarsely ground black pepper
4 thin slices cooked ham (about 2 ounces)
4 thin slices part-skim mozzarella cheese (about
   2 ounces)
1 bag (5 to 6 ounces) prewashed baby spinach

1 In nonstick 12-inch skillet, melt margarine or butter over medium-high heat. Add chicken breasts and cook until golden brown, about 6 minutes. Turn breasts over; cover and reduce heat to medium. Cook chicken breasts about 6 minutes longer or until juices run clear when thickest part is pierced with tip of knife.

LAST-MINUTE CHICKEN DINNERS

Most supermarkets now sell hot, cooked rotisserie chickens and refrigerated brand-name roasted ones. We came up with 8 ways to make a great dinner for 4 to 6 people using the cooked, skinless meat (about 3 cups) from a 2½-pound bird:

Barbecued Chicken Sandwiches Pull meat into shreds and mix with your favorite bottled BBQ sauce; heat in microwave. Mound mixture and coleslaw on a sandwich bun.

Pasta with Chicken & Pesto Toss steaming pasta, such as corkscrew or fusilli, with store-bought pesto sauce and diced chicken.

Chicken Burritos In skillet, heat shredded chicken with chili powder and rinsed, drained canned black beans. Place mixture, cooked rice, shredded Monterey Jack, and salsa down center of warm flour tortillas; roll up each tortilla.

Chicken Cordon Bleu Sandwiches Pull chicken into shreds and place on bottom halves of hero rolls. Top with sliced smoked ham, Swiss cheese, and top halves of rolls. Bake until cheese melts.

Chicken Salad Mix diced chicken with mayonnaise, chopped celery, halved red or green grapes, and toasted pecans. Serve by the scoop on mixed greens with sliced tomatoes.

Chicken Stir-Fry Sauté sliced onions, peppers, and carrots until tender. Add diced chicken and bottled stir-fry sauce and heat through. Serve over cooked rice; sprinkle with sliced green onion.

Chili-Stuffed Baked Potatoes Stir diced chicken into warm canned vegetarian chili. Split tops of baked potatoes and fill with chili; sprinkle with shredded Cheddar. Serve sour cream on the side.

Mediterranean Chicken Couscous Toss cooked couscous with olive oil, lemon juice, diced chicken, tomato chunks, olives, and feta. Sprinkle with chopped basil or mint.

---

2 Increase heat to medium-high. Stir in chicken broth, vinegar, and pepper; cook, uncovered, 1 minute. Remove skillet from heat; top each chicken breast with a slice of ham, then a slice of cheese. Cover skillet until cheese melts, about 3 minutes.

3 Arrange spinach on large platter; top with chicken breasts and drizzle with balsamic mixture. Makes 4 main-dish servings.

Each serving: About 225 calories, 34 g protein, 5 g carbohydrate, 8 g total fat (3 g saturated), 82 mg cholesterol, 560 mg sodium.

Mock Buffalo Wings

PREP: 8 MINUTES • COOK: 8 MINUTES

Our version is remarkably similar to the popular red-hot deep-fried chicken wings that originated in Buffalo, New York—except it has less fat and can be whipped up in minutes! Serve with carrot and celery sticks and our tangy lower-fat blue-cheese dip.

1 package (about 1 pound) chicken tenders
½ cup reduced-fat sour cream
¼ cup crumbled blue cheese (1 ounce)
2 tablespoons light mayonnaise
2 tablespoons fat-free (skim) milk
½ teaspoon Worcestershire sauce
¼ teaspoon coarsely ground black pepper
¼ cup cayenne pepper sauce*
1 tablespoon lower-fat margarine (40% fat)
1 bag (12 ounces) precut carrot sticks
1 bag (12 ounces) precut celery sticks

1 Heat skillet over medium-high heat until hot. Add chicken tenders, and cook until chicken just loses its pink color throughout, about 8 minutes, stirring occasionally.

2 Meanwhile, in small bowl, with fork, mix sour cream, blue cheese, mayonnaise, milk, Worcestershire, and black pepper until blended.

3 Transfer tenders to small platter. Add cayenne pepper sauce and *1 tablespoon water* to skillet; heat to boiling. Remove skillet from heat; stir in margarine until blended. Pour sauce over chicken. Serve with carrot and celery sticks, and blue-cheese dip. Makes 4 main-dish servings.

*Cayenne pepper sauce is a milder variety of hot pepper sauce that adds tang and flavor, not just heat.

Each serving: About 270 calories, 31 g protein, 17 g carbohydrate, 8 g total fat (2 g saturated), 81 mg cholesterol, 1180 mg sodium.

Tortilla Chicken Tenders with Easy Southwest Salsa

PREP: 15 MINUTES • BAKE: 10 MINUTES

2 ounces baked tortilla chips
2 teaspoons chili powder
¼ teaspoon salt
Olive oil nonstick cooking spray
1 pound chicken tenders
2 ears corn, husks and silk removed
1 jar (11 to 12 ounces) mild salsa
¼ cup loosely packed fresh cilantro leaves,
  chopped
Lime wedges

1 Place tortilla chips in self-sealing plastic bag. Crush tortilla chips with rolling pin to fine crumbs (you should have about ½ cup crumbs). On sheet of waxed paper, mix tortilla-chip crumbs, chili powder, and salt; set aside.

2 Preheat oven to 450°F. Spray 15½" by 10½" jelly-roll pan with olive oil spray. Place chicken tenders in medium bowl; spray with olive oil spray, tossing to coat well. Roll chicken in tortilla crumbs; place in jelly-roll pan and spray again.

3 Bake chicken 10 minutes or until juices run clear when thickest part of chicken tender is pierced with tip of knife.

4 Meanwhile, cut corn kernels from cobs; place in small bowl. Stir in salsa and cilantro until blended.

5 Serve chicken with lime wedges. Makes 4 main-dish servings.

Each serving: About 245 calories, 30 g protein, 24 g carbohydrate, 3 g total fat (0 g saturated), 66 mg cholesterol, 685 mg sodium.

FOOD EDITOR'S TIP

Q Why is a simple item like skinless, boneless chicken breasts packaged so many ways? How do I know which kind to buy?

A The demand for chicken breasts has increased with consumers' growing commitment to cut back on fat. Now, companies market several variations on this popular choice. For example, skinless, boneless breast halves may be labeled exactly that, or as skinless, boneless split breasts, or portions. If the label doesn't indicate that the breast is cut into 2 pieces—the clues are halves, split, or portions—it could be whole, which takes longer to cook.

Companies also package tenderloins (the narrow pieces of chicken from the underside of the breast). These could be labeled tenders or fillets—any which way, they're boneless, very tender, and perfect for chicken fingers, stir-fries, and salads. (You may also find chicken breast that has been precut especially for stir-fries.) Thin-sliced chicken-breast cutlets are breast halves cut horizontally in half again for quicker cooking (about 5 minutes). They're great in place of pounded chicken breasts, or instead of veal in veal scalloppine. You can use them in our recipes too; just decrease the cooking time.

Spaghetti Squash with Smoked Mozzarella & Chicken

PREP: 15 MINUTES • MICROWAVE: 12 TO 14 MINUTES

We microwaved the squash to speed up the cooking time. While it cooks, sauté the onion and chicken.

1 medium spaghetti squash (about 2½ pounds)
1 tablespoon olive oil
1 large onion, thinly sliced
12 ounces chicken breast cut for stir-fry
½ teaspoon salt
¼ teaspoon coarsely ground black pepper
2 medium tomatoes, diced
2 ounces smoked mozzarella or smoked Gouda
  cheese
¼ cup loosely packed fresh basil leaves, thinly
  sliced

1 With tip of sharp knife, pierce squash in about 10 places. Microwave on High 6 to 7 minutes. Turn squash over and pierce in another 10 places; microwave 6 to 7 minutes longer or until squash is soft to the touch.

2 Meanwhile, in nonstick 12-inch skillet, heat olive oil over medium heat. Add onion and cook until tender and golden, about 8 minutes, stirring occasionally.

3 Add chicken, ¼ teaspoon salt, and ⅛ teaspoon pepper, and cook until chicken loses its pink color throughout, about 8 minutes, stirring occasionally.

4 When squash is done, cut lengthwise in half; discard seeds. With fork, gently scrape squash lengthwise and lift out pulp in strands as it becomes free; place in large bowl. Discard squash skin.

5 Mix tomatoes, cheese, and remaining ¼ teaspoon salt, and ⅛ teaspoon pepper with hot squash. Spoon squash mixture into 4 bowls; top with onion and chicken mixture. Sprinkle with basil. Makes 4 main-dish servings.

Each serving: About 260 calories, 25 g protein, 20 g carbohydrate, 9 g total fat (3 g saturated), 62 mg cholesterol, 585 mg sodium.

Chicken Caesar Salad

PREP: 20 MINUTES

You could also make this with cooked shrimp or deli roast beef (cut into ½-inch-wide strips).

2 small garlic cloves
1 tablespoon fresh lemon juice
1 teaspoon Worcestershire sauce
1 teaspoon Dijon mustard
½ teaspoon anchovy paste
½ teaspoon salt
¼ teaspoon coarsely ground black pepper
3 tablespoons olive oil
½ loaf French bread (4 ounces)
12 ounces skinless, boneless rotisserie chicken, cut into thin strips
12 cups loosely packed bite-size pieces romaine lettuce or other favorite lettuce (about 1 pound)
¼ cup grated Parmesan cheese

1 Into large salad bowl, crush 1 garlic clove with garlic press. With wire whisk, mix crushed garlic with lemon juice, Worcestershire, mustard, anchovy paste, salt, and pepper until blended. Slowly whisk in 2 tablespoons olive oil until dressing thickens slightly; set aside.

2 Preheat broiler. Cut bread horizontally in half. Brush cut surface with remaining 1 tablespoon olive oil. Place bread, cut side up, on rack in broiling pan. Place pan in broiler 5 to 7 inches from source of heat and broil bread 2 to 3 minutes, until lightly toasted.

3 Cut remaining garlic clove lengthwise in half. Rub cut sides of toasted bread lightly with garlic-clove halves; discard garlic. Cut bread into 1-inch cubes to make croutons; set aside.

4 To serve, add chicken to dressing; toss to coat. Add lettuce, garlic croutons, and grated Parmesan; toss again. Makes 4 main-dish servings.

Each serving: About 390 calories, 33 g protein, 20 g carbohydrate, 20 g total fat (5 g saturated), 82 mg cholesterol, 720 mg sodium.

Thai Salad

PREP: 20 MINUTES

A summery blend of Boston lettuce, fresh herbs, and shredded carrots, tossed with a tangy, spicy Asian dressing. Like Chicken Caesar Salad (at left), this salad is equally good with roast beef or shrimp.

12 cups loosely packed bite-size pieces Boston lettuce (about two 6-ounce heads)
½ cup loosely packed fresh cilantro leaves
½ cup loosely packed fresh mint leaves
1 bag (10 ounces) shredded carrots
3 green onions, cut into 1-inch pieces
¼ cup fresh lime juice
2 tablespoons Asian fish sauce*
2 tablespoons vegetable oil
1 jalapeño chile, seeded and minced
1 tablespoon grated, peeled fresh ginger
1 teaspoon sugar
12 ounces skinless, boneless rotisserie chicken, cut into thin strips

1 In large bowl, toss lettuce with cilantro, mint, carrots, and green onions.

2 In another large bowl, with wire whisk, mix lime juice, fish sauce, oil, jalapeño, ginger, and sugar until blended.

3 To serve, add chicken to dressing in bowl; toss to coat. Add lettuce mixture; toss again. Makes 4 main-dish servings.

*Available in the Asian sections of some supermarkets. For more information, see "Food Editor's Tip," page 114.

Each serving: About 285 calories, 27 g protein, 14 g carbohydrate, 14 g total fat (2 g saturated), 76 mg cholesterol, 755 mg sodium.

Chicken Gumbo Casserole

PREP: 45 MINUTES • BAKE: 45 MINUTES

Most gumbos—a Creole specialty from New Orleans—are a bit indulgent, but we created a lighter version and baked it, casserole-style.

¼ cup all-purpose flour
1 tablespoon vegetable oil
4 medium skinless chicken thighs (about 1¼ pounds with bones)
2 ounces low-fat kielbasa (smoked Polish sausage), diced (½ cup)
1 can (14½ ounces) chicken broth
1 can (14½ ounces) diced tomatoes
¼ cup tomato paste
1 medium red pepper, chopped
1 medium onion, thinly sliced
1 large celery stalk, sliced
1 garlic clove, minced
1 bay leaf
½ teaspoon salt
¼ teaspoon dried thyme
¼ teaspoon ground red pepper (cayenne)
¼ teaspoon ground allspice
1 package (10 ounces) frozen cut okra
1 cup regular long-grain rice

1 Preheat oven to 375°F. In 5-quart Dutch oven, toast flour over low heat until pale golden, 10 to 15 minutes, stirring frequently. Transfer flour to cup; set aside.

2 In same Dutch oven, heat vegetable oil over medium-high heat. Add chicken thighs and cook about 10 minutes or until golden, turning once; transfer chicken to plate. Reduce heat to medium; add kielbasa and cook 1 minute or until lightly browned, stirring. With slotted spoon, transfer kielbasa to plate with chicken. Stir ¼ cup chicken broth into flour in cup until blended; add to Dutch oven and cook 1 minute, stirring. Gradually stir in remaining chicken broth.

3 Return chicken thighs and kielbasa to Dutch oven. Stir in tomatoes, tomato paste, red pepper, onion, celery, garlic, bay leaf, salt, thyme, ground red pepper, and allspice; heat to boiling over high heat. Add okra; cover Dutch oven and bake 45 minutes or until chicken is cooked through and vegetables are tender.

4 Meanwhile, in 2-quart saucepan, prepare rice as label directs, but do not add salt, margarine, or butter.

5 Discard bay leaf and serve gumbo over rice. Makes about 7 cups or 4 main-dish servings.

Each serving: About 435 calories, 25 g protein, 61 g carbohydrate, 10 g total fat (1 g saturated), 57 mg cholesterol, 845 mg sodium.

Greek Salad

PREP: 20 MINUTES

This salad is a pretty combination of summer tomatoes, chunks of feta cheese, and garden mint.

¼ cup fresh lemon juice
3 tablespoons olive oil
½ teaspoon sugar
¼ teaspoon salt
⅛ teaspoon coarsely ground black pepper
1 small garlic clove, crushed with garlic press
12 ounces skinless, boneless rotisserie chicken, cut into thin strips
3 ripe medium tomatoes (about 1 pound), each cut into 8 wedges
1 large seedless (English) cucumber, cut into ½-inch chunks
1 small red onion, cut in half and thinly sliced
½ cup loosely packed fresh mint leaves, chopped
¼ cup Kalamata olives, pitted and halved
12 cups loosely packed bite-size pieces salad greens, such as arugula, spinach, or romaine lettuce
2 ounces feta cheese, crumbled (½ cup)

1 In large bowl, with wire whisk or fork, mix lemon juice, olive oil, sugar, salt, pepper, and crushed garlic until blended; set dressing aside.

2 Add chicken to dressing in bowl; toss to coat. Add tomatoes, cucumber, red onion, mint, and olives; toss well.

3 To serve, line large platter with greens. Spoon tomato mixture over greens; top with crumbled feta cheese. Toss salad before serving. Makes 4 main-dish servings.

Each serving: About 380 calories, 31 g protein, 16 g carbohydrate, 23 g total fat (6 g saturated), 88 mg cholesterol, 520 mg sodium.

◄ *Greek Salad*

Chicken Potpie with Corn-Bread Crust

PREP: 45 MINUTES • BAKE: 35 MINUTES

Our healthy down-home potpie is made with low-fat milk, extra veggies, and a tender country-style topping instead of the usual pastry crust. To reduce prep time, buy a rotisserie chicken at your market to shred (without skin) for the filling.

CHICKEN FILLING:
1 tablespoon margarine or butter
2 medium carrots, cut into ½-inch pieces
1 medium onion, cut into ¼-inch pieces
1 can (14½ ounces) chicken broth
¾ teaspoon salt
¼ teaspoon coarsely ground black pepper
¼ teaspoon dried thyme
3 tablespoons cornstarch
1½ cups low-fat (1%) milk
3 cups (12 ounces) shredded cooked chicken, without skin
1 package (10 ounces) frozen whole-kernel corn, thawed
1 package (10 ounces) frozen lima beans, thawed

CORN-BREAD CRUST:
½ cup all-purpose flour
½ cup yellow cornmeal
1 tablespoon sugar
1½ teaspoons baking powder
½ teaspoon salt
2 tablespoons cold margarine or butter
¾ cup low-fat (1%) milk

1 Preheat oven to 375°F. Prepare Chicken Filling: In 3-quart saucepan, melt margarine or butter over medium-low heat. Add carrots and onion, and cook 5 minutes, stirring occasionally. Add chicken broth, salt, pepper, and thyme; heat to boiling over high heat. Reduce heat to low; cover and simmer 10 minutes or until vegetables are tender.

2 Meanwhile, in small bowl, with wire whisk, mix cornstarch and ½ cup milk until blended. Stir cornstarch mixture and remaining 1 cup milk into saucepan with carrots; heat to boiling over high heat. Boil 1 minute, stirring. Stir in chicken, corn, and lima beans. Transfer mixture to shallow 2½-quart casserole.

3 Prepare Corn-Bread Crust: In medium bowl, with fork, stir flour, cornmeal, sugar, baking powder, and salt. With pastry blender or two knives used scissor-fashion, cut in margarine or butter until mixture resembles coarse crumbs. Stir in milk until blended and mixture thickens slightly. Pour mixture over filling; spread to form an even layer. Bake casserole, uncovered, 35 minutes or until filling is bubbling and top is golden. Makes 6 main-dish servings.

Each serving: About 440 calories, 32 g protein, 51 g carbohydrate, 13 g total fat (3 g saturated), 67 mg cholesterol, 960 mg sodium.

Bisteeya

PREP: 1½ HOURS • BAKE: 45 MINUTES

Moroccan families traditionally eat this "pie" by tearing into the hot pastry with their fingers. Hygiene issues aside, this can be a painful mistake if you don't know what you're doing. We recommend a knife and fork.

CHICKEN FILLING:
4 pounds chicken-leg quarters
1 medium onion, finely chopped
⅓ cup loosely packed fresh cilantro leaves, chopped
1 cinnamon stick (3 inches long)
1 teaspoon coarsely ground black pepper
¾ teaspoon ground ginger
½ teaspoon salt
¼ teaspoon ground turmeric
Pinch saffron threads

ALMOND FILLING:
8 ounces natural or blanched almonds, toasted
½ cup confectioners' sugar
2 teaspoons ground cinnamon
3 tablespoons unsalted butter, melted

EGG FILLING:
¼ cup fresh lemon juice
10 large eggs, lightly beaten
¼ teaspoon salt

PHYLLO LAYERS:
5 tablespoons unsalted butter, melted
8 sheets (about 16" by 12" each) fresh or frozen (thawed) phyllo (one-fourth 16-ounce package)

GARNISH:
2 teaspoons confectioners' sugar
1 teaspoon ground cinnamon

1 Prepare Chicken Filling: In 5-quart Dutch oven, combine chicken-leg quarters, onion, cilantro, cinnamon stick, pepper, ginger, salt, turmeric, saffron, and 3 *cups water*; heat to boiling over high heat. Reduce heat to low; cover and simmer 30 minutes or until chicken loses its pink color throughout. With slotted spoon, transfer chicken to large plate; cool until easy to handle. Skim fat and reserve broth. Discard cinnamon stick. Shred chicken into small pieces; discard skin and bones.

2 Meanwhile, prepare Almond Filling: In food processor with knife blade attached, pulse toasted almonds, confectioners' sugar, and cinnamon until finely ground; set aside. Transfer to small bowl and stir in melted butter; set aside.

3 Prepare Egg Filling: In same Dutch oven, heat

Top to bottom: Artichokes with Dill Sauce (page 162), Bisteeya (recipe at left), and Green Pepper & Tomato Salad (page 178)

reserved broth to boiling over high heat. Boil broth 20 to 30 minutes or until reduced to 2 cups. Reduce heat to low and stir in lemon juice. Pour beaten eggs into simmering broth, stirring frequently, until eggs are set. Pour egg mixture into colander to drain excess liquid. Transfer egg mixture to plate to cool; sprinkle with salt.

4 Prepare Phyllo Layers: Preheat oven to 400°F. Brush 13" by 9" metal baking pan with some melted butter. Remove phyllo from package; keep covered with plastic wrap to prevent drying out. On waxed paper, lightly brush 1 phyllo sheet with some melted butter. Place sheet crosswise in one half of pan, allowing phyllo to drape over sides and one end of pan. Place a second phyllo sheet crosswise in other end of pan. Top each sheet with 1 more phyllo sheet, but do not brush with butter, to make 2 layers, 4 sheets in all.

5 Place cooled shredded chicken pieces over phyllo; top with cooled egg mixture, and sprinkle with almond mixture. Fold overhanging edges of phyllo over filling. Place 1 phyllo sheet lengthwise over filling, tucking edges in to fit top; but do not brush with butter. Repeat with another phyllo sheet but lightly brush with butter. Repeat layering to make 4 sheets in all.

6 Bake pie 25 minutes or until lightly golden. Remove pan from oven; cover with large baking sheet and invert hot pie onto baking sheet. Bake pie 20 minutes longer or until golden.

7 To garnish pie, if you like, cut 1-inch- wide strips waxed paper. Place waxed-paper strips, 1 inch apart, on top of pie. In cup, mix confectioners' sugar and cinnamon. Sprinkle spaces between paper with some cinnamon-sugar mixture. Carefully remove waxed-paper strips and place at right angles to first set of lines and repeat sprinkling. Remove waxed paper and discard. Makes 8 main-dish or 16 first-course servings.

Each main-dish serving: About 620 calories, 42 g protein, 26 g carbohydrate, 40 g total fat (12 g saturated), 386 mg cholesterol, 350 mg sodium.

Roast Turkey Breast with Caramelized Shallots

PREP: 40 MINUTES • ROAST: 2½ TO 3 HOURS

1 tablespoon olive oil
8 ounces shallots or red onion, peeled and thinly sliced (2 cups)
4 garlic cloves, peeled and thinly sliced

2 tablespoons brown sugar
1 tablespoon balsamic vinegar
½ teaspoon salt
¼ teaspoon coarsely ground black pepper
1 bone-in turkey breast (about 7 pounds)
½ cup dry red wine
1 cup chicken broth
1 tablespoon cornstarch

1 In nonstick 10-inch skillet, heat olive oil over medium heat. Add shallots and cook 8 minutes, stirring occasionally until tender and golden. Add garlic and cook 1 minute. Stir in brown sugar, vinegar, salt, pep-

---

LOW-STRESS MAKE-AHEAD GRAVY

Hate making gravy at the last minute, while hungry guests are waiting to eat? Try this homestyle version, which gets its flavor from inexpensive turkey wings. All you have to do before dinner is reheat the gravy in the microwave or on the stove top. (Note: If you hate to waste turkey drippings on Thanksgiving Day, combine them with this do-ahead gravy. Remove the turkey from the roasting pan, skim and discard fat from drippings, pour in the premade gravy, and bring the mixture to a boil while scraping up the brown bits on the bottom of the pan. Or, just stir a couple of spoonfuls of drippings into the premade gravy before reheating.)

PREP: 10 MINUTES • COOK: 1½ HOURS

2 tablespoons vegetable oil
2 turkey wings (about 1½ pounds), separated at joints
1 large onion, cut into 4 pieces
2 carrots, peeled and each cut into 4 pieces
2 celery stalks, each cut into 4 pieces
½ cup dry white wine
2 cans (14½ ounces each) chicken broth
1 garlic clove, sliced
¼ teaspoon dried thyme leaves
½ cup all-purpose flour

1 In 5-quart saucepot, heat vegetable oil over medium-high heat until hot. Add turkey wings and cook 10 minutes or until golden on all sides. Add onion, carrots, and celery and cook 8 to 10 minutes until vegetables and turkey wings are browned, but not burned, stirring frequently. Transfer turkey and vegetables to large bowl.

2 Add wine to saucepot and stir until brown bits are loosened; boil 1 minute. Return turkey and vegetables to saucepot; stir in chicken broth, garlic, thyme, and 3 cups water; heat to boiling over high heat. Reduce heat to low; simmer, uncovered, 45 minutes. Drain, reserving broth.

3 Let broth stand a few seconds until fat separates from meat juice. Spoon ¼ cup fat from broth into 2-quart saucepan; skim and discard any remaining fat.

4 Into fat in saucepan over medium heat, stir flour; cook, stirring, until flour turns golden brown. Gradually stir in reserved broth and cook, stirring, until gravy boils and thickens slightly. Pour gravy into medium bowl; place plastic wrap directly on surface of gravy and refrigerate up to 3 days.

5 To serve, reheat on stove top or in microwave. (If serving with a roast turkey or chicken, stir in some of the pan drippings.) Makes about 6 cups without pan drippings.

Each ¼ cup: About 50 calories, 1 g protein, 2 g carbohydrate, 4 g total fat (1 g saturated), 3 mg cholesterol, 115 mg sodium.

per, and *1 tablespoon water*; cook 1 minute. Transfer to bowl and cool to room temperature.

2 Preheat oven to 325°F. With fingertips, gently separate skin from meat on turkey breast. Spread cooled shallot mixture on meat under skin.

3 Place turkey breast, skin side up, on rack in medium roasting pan (about 14" by 10"). Insert meat thermometer into center of turkey breast being careful that pointed end of thermometer does not touch bone. Cover turkey breast with a loose tent of foil. Roast turkey 2½ to 3 hours or until temperature on meat thermometer reaches 170°F. Start checking for doneness during last 30 minutes of roasting.

4 To brown turkey breast, remove foil during last hour of roasting time and baste with pan drippings occasionally. Transfer turkey to carving board. Let stand 15 minutes to set juices for easier slicing.

5 Meanwhile, prepare sauce: Remove rack from roasting pan. Skim and discard fat from drippings in pan. In 2-quart saucepan, heat red wine to boiling over high heat; boil for 2 minutes. Stir in chicken broth, *½ cup water*, and pan drippings; heat to boiling. In cup, dissolve cornstarch in *1 tablespoon water*; whisk into boiling sauce, and boil 1 minute. Pour sauce through coarse sieve into bowl. Serve sauce with turkey breast. Makes 10 main-dish servings.

Each serving with sauce: About 445 calories, 60 g protein, 10 g carbohydrate, 17 g total fat (5 g saturated), 152 mg cholesterol, 320 mg sodium.

Roast Turkey with Pan Gravy

PREP: 45 MINUTES • ROAST: ABOUT 3¾ HOURS

1 fresh or frozen (thawed) turkey (14 pounds)
1½ teaspoons salt
½ teaspoon coarsely ground black pepper
Pan Gravy (at right)

1 Preheat oven to 325°F. Remove giblets and neck from turkey; reserve for making Pan Gravy. Rinse turkey with cold running water and drain well.

2 Fasten neck skin to back with 1 or 2 skewers. With turkey breast side up, fold wings under back of turkey so they stay in place. Depending on brand of turkey, with string, tie legs and tail together, or push drumsticks under band of skin, or use stuffing clamp.

3 Place turkey, breast side up, on rack in large roasting pan. Rub turkey all over with salt and pepper. Cover turkey with a loose tent of foil. Insert meat thermometer through foil into thickest part of thigh next to body, being careful that pointed end of thermometer does not touch bone. Roast turkey about 3¾ hours; start checking for doneness during last hour of roasting.

4 While turkey is roasting, cook giblets and neck as directed below for Pan Gravy.

5 To brown turkey, remove foil during last 1 hour of roasting time and baste occasionally with pan drippings. Turkey is done when thigh temperature on meat thermometer reaches 180° to 185°F. and drumstick feels soft when pressed with fingers protected by paper towels. (Breast temperature should be 170° to 175°F.)

6 When turkey is done, place on warm large platter; keep warm. Prepare Pan Gravy.

7 Serve with gravy. Remove skin from turkey before eating, if you like. Makes 14 main-dish servings.

PAN GRAVY: In 3-quart saucepan over high heat, heat gizzard, heart, neck, and *enough water to cover* to boiling. Reduce heat to low; cover and simmer 45 minutes. Add liver and cook 15 minutes longer. Drain, reserving broth. Pull meat from neck; discard bones. Coarsely chop neck meat and giblets. Cover and refrigerate meat and broth separately.

To make gravy, remove rack from roasting pan. Pour pan drippings through sieve into 4-cup measure or medium bowl. Add 1 cup giblet broth to roasting pan and stir until brown bits are loosened; add to drippings in measuring cup. Let stand a few seconds, until fat separates from meat juice. Spoon 2 tablespoons fat from drippings into 2-quart saucepan; skim and discard any remaining fat. Add remaining giblet broth and *enough water* to meat juice in cup to equal 3 cups.

Into fat in saucepan over medium heat, stir *2 tablespoons all-purpose flour* and *½ teaspoon salt*; cook, stirring, until flour turns golden brown. Gradually stir in meat-juice mixture and cook, stirring, until gravy boils and thickens slightly. Stir in reserved giblets and neck meat; heat through. Pour gravy into gravy boat.

Each serving of turkey without skin or gravy: About 330 calories, 57 g protein, 0 g carbohydrate, 10 g total fat (3 g saturated), 149 mg cholesterol, 250 mg sodium.

Each ¼ cup gravy: About 65 calories, 7 g protein, 2 g carbohydrate, 4 g total fat (1 g saturated), 63 mg cholesterol, 110 mg sodium.

Corn-Bread Stuffing

PREP: 15 MINUTES PLUS COOLING
BAKE: ABOUT 55 MINUTES

A hand-me-down recipe from South Carolinian Fannie Pressley, the great-grandmother of Good Housekeeping Institute Assistant Theresa Washington. Pressley passed the recipe on to Washington's mother and her mother's two sisters, who make the stuffing every Thanksgiving along with collard greens, ham, macaroni and cheese, and all the traditional fare.

CORN BREAD:
1½ cups yellow cornmeal
1½ cups all-purpose flour
3 tablespoons sugar
1 tablespoon baking powder
½ teaspoon salt
1¼ cups milk
3 tablespoons margarine or butter, melted and
   cooled
1 large egg

VEGETABLE MIXTURE:
5 tablespoons margarine or butter
2 large celery stalks, diced
1 medium green pepper, diced
1 medium onion, diced
½ teaspoon salt
¼ teaspoon coarsely ground black pepper
1 cup chicken broth
1 large egg, lightly beaten

1 Prepare Corn Bread: Preheat oven to 400°F. Grease 9" by 9" metal baking pan.

2 In medium bowl, combine cornmeal, flour, sugar, baking powder, and salt. With fork, beat milk, melted margarine or butter, and egg into cornmeal mixture just until blended. Spoon batter into baking pan; spread evenly.

3 Bake corn bread 20 minutes or until toothpick inserted in center comes out clean. Cool in pan on wire rack 10 minutes. Invert Corn Bread; break into large pieces and cool completely. (If not making stuffing right away, cover and reserve pieces up to 2 days.)

4 Prepare Vegetable Mixture: In 12-inch skillet, melt margarine or butter over medium-high heat. Add celery, green pepper, onion, salt, and black pepper, and cook 15 minutes or until tender and golden, stirring occasionally. Add chicken broth; heat to boiling. Boil 1 minute.

5 Into large bowl, crumble Corn-Bread pieces. Stir in cooked vegetables and egg; toss gently to mix well. Spoon stuffing into 13" by 9" glass baking dish; bake in preheated 325°F. oven 30 minutes or until heated through. Makes about 8 cups.

Each ½ cup: About 180 calories, 4 g protein, 24 g carbohydrate, 7 g total fat (2 g saturated), 29 mg cholesterol, 350 mg sodium.

New England Apple-Nut Stuffing

PREP: 45 MINUTES • BAKE: 45 MINUTES

This is the only dish that Editorial Assistant Catheryn Keegan's father, Robert, makes, and he's been doing it so well for the past 30 years that it's become a custom to have it at all family holiday gatherings, especially Thanksgiving. Thanks, Mr. Keegan, for sharing your stuffing secret!

½ cup margarine or butter (1 stick)
3 large celery stalks, diced
1 large onion, chopped
3 medium Golden Delicious apples (about
   1 pound), peeled, cored, and diced
1½ loaves (16 ounces each) sliced firm white
   bread, cut into ¾-inch cubes and lightly
   toasted
1 can (14½ ounces) chicken broth
½ cup pecans, toasted and chopped
½ cup walnuts, toasted and chopped
2 tablespoons sesame seeds, toasted
½ teaspoon poultry seasoning
¼ teaspoon dried oregano
¼ teaspoon coarsely ground black pepper

1 In 12-inch skillet, melt margarine or butter over medium heat. Add celery and onion and cook 10 minutes or until tender, stirring occasionally. Add apples and cook 5 minutes longer.

2 In large bowl, combine celery mixture with toasted bread cubes and remaining ingredients; toss to mix well. Spoon stuffing into greased 13" by 9" glass baking dish; cover with foil and bake in preheated 325°F. oven 45 minutes or until heated through. Makes about 12 cups.

Each ½ cup: About 155 calories, 3 g protein, 18 g carbohydrate, 8 g total fat (1 g saturated), 0 mg cholesterol, 255 mg sodium.

TURKEY'S CLASSIC COMPANIONS

Here are three different spins on that most all-American of condiments, cranberry sauce.

Our Southwestern-style sauce comes from Lifestyle Director Donna Bulseco who moved with her husband to New York City from Southern California in 1979, leaving behind her family. At one of her first Thanksgiving get-togethers with other "holiday refugees" who stayed in town, Bulseco couldn't get enough of this tart, spicy sauce, brought by friend Loren Weinberger. The jalapeño in the recipe appeals to her yen for spicy flavors and brings her a little taste of home as well.

The second recipe—an intriguing blend of orange juice, raspberries, and cranberries—comes from Lauri Lappin, a research associate, who started making this dish quite by accident about 8 years ago. Inspired by her Aunt Susie, who's a wonderful cook, Lauri decided to make a cheesecake with a cranberry topping. The cheesecake didn't quite work out, but the topping was so tasty that Lappin decided to serve it on its own at Thanksgiving.

Our last sauce is actually a fresh relish and comes from Editorial Assistant Heather Harlan who raves about what a great cook her grandma, Lorraine, is—and this delicious, no-cook relish is proof of her talent.

Southwestern Cranberry Sauce

PREP: 10 MINUTES PLUS CHILLING • COOK: 5 MINUTES

1 medium lemon
1 bag (12 ounces) cranberries (3 cups)
½ cup honey
¼ cup cider vinegar
1 teaspoon mustard seeds
½ teaspoon salt
½ teaspoon coarsely ground black pepper
1 pickled jalapeño chile, minced

1 With vegetable peeler, remove peel from lemon in 1-inch-wide strips. Cut strips crosswise into very thin slivers. Wrap and refrigerate lemon for use another day.

2 In 2-quart saucepan, heat all ingredients to boiling over high heat. Reduce heat to medium-low and simmer, covered, until most of the cranberries pop and mixture thickens slightly, about 5 minutes, stir-

ring occasionally. Spoon into serving bowl; cover and refrigerate until well chilled, about 3 hours. Or, spoon into an airtight container and refrigerate up to 4 days. Makes about 2 cups.

Each ¼ cup: About 85 calories, 0 g protein, 23 g carbohydrate, 0 g total fat, 0 mg cholesterol, 160 mg sodium.

Cranberry-Orange Sauce

PREP: 10 MINUTES PLUS CHILLING
COOK: ABOUT 8 MINUTES

1 large orange or 2 tangerines
1 bag (12 ounces) cranberries (3 cups)
1 package (10 ounces) frozen raspberries in syrup
½ cup sugar
2 tablespoons fresh lemon juice
3 tablespoons orange-flavor liqueur

1 From orange or tangerines, grate 1 teaspoon peel and squeeze ½ cup juice.

2 In 3-quart saucepan, heat all ingredients except liqueur to boiling over high heat. Reduce heat to medium and cook, uncovered, until most of the cranberries pop and mixture thickens slightly, about 5 minutes, stirring occasionally. Remove saucepan from heat; stir in liqueur. Spoon into serving bowl; cover and refrigerate until well chilled, about 3 hours. Or, spoon into airtight container and refrigerate up to 4 days. Makes about 3½ cups.

Each ¼ cup: About 75 calories, 0 g protein, 18 g carbohydrate, 0 g total fat, 0 mg cholesterol, 1 mg sodium.

Grandma's Fresh Cranberry Relish

PREP: 10 MINUTES PLUS CHILLING

1 bag (12 ounces) cranberries (3 cups)
1 medium Granny Smith apple, peeled, cored, and cut up
1 medium Gala apple, peeled, cored, and cut up
1 small navel orange, unpeeled and cut up
⅔ cup sugar

In food processor with knife blade attached, pulse all ingredients until coarsely chopped. Spoon into serving bowl; cover and refrigerate until well chilled, about 3 hours or up to 4 days. Makes about 4 cups.

Each ¼ cup: About 55 calories, 0 g protein, 15 g carbohydrate, 0 g total fat, 0 mg cholesterol, 1 mg sodium.

Italian Sausage Stuffing

PREP: 25 MINUTES • BAKE: 30 MINUTES

When GH Art Director Scott Yardley was a teenager, he would make the sausage for this stuffing while working at his uncle's butcher shop. Now that Yardley's no longer an apprentice butcher, his mom, Rita Yardley, makes the stuffing with store-bought sausage—but, like the pasta she always serves as a first course, this is still an integral part of their Italian-American Thanksgiving meal.

1 pound sweet Italian-sausage links, casings removed
1 package (14 to 16 ounces) herb-seasoned stuffing mix
½ cup margarine or butter (1 stick)
2 large celery stalks, diced
1 medium onion, diced

1 Heat 10-inch skillet over medium-high heat until hot. Add sausage and cook until browned, about 10 minutes, stirring frequently to break up sausage. With slotted spoon, transfer sausage to large bowl; stir in stuffing mix.

2 To drippings in skillet, add margarine or butter; heat until melted. Add celery and onion and cook, stirring occasionally, until vegetables are tender and golden, about 10 minutes. Transfer celery mixture to bowl with sausage.

3 Pour 2½ cups hot water over stuffing mixture; toss to mix well. Spoon stuffing into 13" by 9" glass baking dish; cover with foil and bake in preheated 325°F. oven 30 minutes or until stuffing is heated through. Makes about 12 cups.

Each ½ cup: About 175 calories, 4 g protein, 16 g carbohydrate, 10 g total fat (3 g saturated), 15 mg cholesterol, 480 mg sodium.

Turkey Cutlets à l'Orange

PREP: 10 MINUTES • COOK: ABOUT 6 MINUTES

After quickly browning the cutlets, add a spicy mix of orange marmalade, ginger, and vinegar to the skillet to make the simple sauce. Serve the turkey atop our Bulgur with Dried Cranberries.

2 teaspoons olive oil
1 pound turkey cutlets
½ teaspoon salt
¼ teaspoon coarsely ground black pepper
⅓ cup orange marmalade
2 tablespoons red wine vinegar
1 tablespoon grated, peeled fresh ginger
1 small navel orange, cut into wedges, and parsley sprig for garnish

1 In nonstick 12-inch skillet, heat oil over medium-high heat until hot. Add turkey cutlets; sprinkle with salt and pepper. Cook cutlets until they are lightly

Turkey Cutlets à l'Orange on a bed of Bulgur with Dried Cranberries (page 142)

browned on the outside and just lose their pink color on the inside, about 2 minutes per side, turning once.

2 Meanwhile, in small bowl, combine marmalade, vinegar, and ginger.

3 Add mixture to turkey cutlets in skillet; heat to boiling. Garnish with orange wedges and parsley to serve. Makes 4 main-dish servings.

Each serving: About 220 calories, 27 g protein, 20 g carbohydrate, 4 g total fat (1 g saturated), 68 mg cholesterol, 340 mg sodium.

Turkey Burgers

PREP: 10 MINUTES • COOK: 20 MINUTES

Serve with: Sweet & Tangy Coleslaw (page 177), hamburger buns, and ketchup. Moist, juicy, and mildly spiced, these are also great cold—for lunch-box sandwiches.

3 teaspoons olive oil
1 small onion, finely chopped
1 garlic clove, crushed with garlic press
1 pound ground turkey breast
1 large egg
1 slice firm white bread, crumbled
3 tablespoons mango chutney, chopped
2 tablespoons milk
½ teaspoon salt
¼ teaspoon rubbed sage

1 In nonstick 12-inch skillet, heat 1 teaspoon olive oil over medium heat until hot. Add onion and garlic and cook, stirring often, 5 minutes or until onion is tender. Transfer mixture to large bowl; set skillet aside.

2 Add ground turkey, egg, bread, chutney, milk, salt, and sage to onion mixture and mix well. With wet hands, shape mixture into four 1-inch-thick round patties.

3 In same skillet, heat remaining 2 teaspoons olive oil over medium heat until hot. Add patties and cook about 12 minutes, turning once, until browned on both sides and cooked through. Makes 4 main-dish servings.

Each serving: About 235 calories, 28 g protein, 13 g carbohydrate, 7 g total fat (2 g saturated), 113 mg cholesterol, 375 mg sodium.

Spicy Turkey Chili

PREP: 5 MINUTES • COOK: 15 MINUTES

Serve this winter-white chili (no tomato!) with fluffy rice, salad, and Italian bread.

1 teaspoon olive oil
1 pound ground turkey breast
1 small onion, diced
1 teaspoon ground coriander
1 teaspoon ground cumin
¼ teaspoon salt
2 cans (15 to 16 ounces each) no-salt-added navy or small white beans, rinsed and drained
1 can (14½ ounces) reduced-sodium chicken broth
1 package (10 ounces) frozen whole-kernel corn (thawed)
1 can (4 to 4½ ounces) chopped mild green chiles, drained
2 tablespoons cayenne pepper sauce*
1 cup chopped fresh cilantro leaves

1 In nonstick 12-inch skillet, heat olive oil over medium-high heat until hot. Add ground turkey and onion; cook, stirring and breaking up meat with side of spoon, 10 minutes or until meat loses its pink color and all liquid evaporates. Add coriander, cumin, and salt; cook 1 minute, stirring to combine.

2 Meanwhile, in small bowl, mash half of beans; set aside.

3 Add mashed and unmashed beans, chicken broth, corn, and green chiles to turkey mixture. Heat to boiling over medium-high heat; stir in pepper sauce. Sprinkle chili with cilantro. Makes about 6 cups or 6 main-dish servings.

*Cayenne pepper sauce is a milder variety of hot pepper sauce that adds tang and flavor, not just heat.

Each serving: About 270 calories, 28 g protein, 33 g carbohydrate, 3 g total fat (1 g saturated), 45 mg cholesterol, 825 mg sodium.

Crispy Citrus Goose

PREP: 30 MINUTES • ROAST: ABOUT 4½ HOURS

1 fresh or frozen (thawed) goose (about
   12 pounds)
1 bunch fresh thyme
4 bay leaves
5 medium oranges, each cut in half
½ teaspoon coarsely ground black pepper
½ teaspoon dried thyme
1¼ teaspoons salt
2 tablespoons cornstarch
3 tablespoons orange-flavor liqueur
½ cup orange marmalade
Orange wedges and fresh thyme for garnish

1 Preheat oven to 400°F. Remove giblets and neck from goose; refrigerate or freeze for use another day. Discard fat from body cavity and any excess skin. Rinse goose with cold running water and drain well.

GOOSE-ROASTING TIPS

• Order goose from your butcher or supermarket meat manager at least 1 week ahead to get the proper-size bird.

• Most geese sold in the United States are frozen, so allow time for thawing. A 12-pound goose takes at least 2 days to thaw in the refrigerator. You can also thaw the goose in cold water in about 5 hours: Place the bird (in its original wrapping) in a sink with *enough cold water to cover*, changing the water every half hour. When thawed, cook or refrigerate immediately.

• Before roasting, pierce the skin all over, using a fork. This will allow the fat to drain during roasting and help crisp the skin. If necessary, spoon off fat from roasting pan occasionally during cooking to avoid splatters and spillovers.

• To carve the goose: Remove wings from the body. Cut through the leg joints to remove legs. Separate thighs from drumsticks. Cut down on 1 side of breastbone, continuing to cut along the bone toward the wing joint. With a fork in the breast meat, gradually cut meat away from breastbone and rib cage. Repeat on the other side. Slice the breast meat on cutting board.

2 With goose breast side up, fold wings under back of goose so they stay in place. Place thyme sprigs, bay leaves, and 6 orange halves in body cavity. With string, tie legs and tail together. Fold neck skin over back.

3 Place goose, breast side up, on rack in large roasting pan (about 17" by 11½"). With fork, prick skin in many places. In cup, mix pepper, dried thyme, and 1 teaspoon salt; rub mixture over goose.

4 Insert meat thermometer into thickest part of meat between breast and thigh, being careful that pointed end of thermometer does not touch bone. Cover roasting pan with foil, and roast goose 1½ hours. Turn oven control to 325°F. and roast goose 2 hours longer.

5 Meanwhile, squeeze ¾ cup juice from remaining 4 orange halves. Stir in cornstarch, 1 tablespoon orange liqueur, and remaining ¼ teaspoon salt; set aside. In cup, mix orange marmalade with remaining 2 tablespoons orange-flavor liqueur.

6 Uncover goose, and roast 45 minutes longer. Remove goose from oven and turn oven control to 450°F. Brush orange-marmalade mixture over goose. Roast goose 10 minutes longer or until skin is golden and crisp. Goose is done when temperature on meat thermometer reaches 180° to 185°F. and juices run clear when thickest part of thigh is pierced with tip of knife.

7 Transfer goose to large platter; let stand 10 minutes for easier carving. Prepare sauce: Remove rack from roasting pan. Pour pan drippings through sieve into 8-cup glass measuring cup or large bowl. Let stand until fat separates from meat juice; pour off and discard fat (there should be about 5 cups fat and 1 cup meat juice; if necessary, add *enough water* to meat juice to equal 1 cup). Return meat juice to pan and add reserved orange-juice mixture. Heat sauce mixture to boiling over medium heat; boil 30 seconds.

8 To serve, garnish platter with orange wedges and fresh thyme. Pour orange-sauce mixture into gravy boat. Makes 10 main-dish servings.

Each serving of goose without skin: About 460 calories, 50 g protein, 12 g carbohydrate, 25 g total fat (8 g saturated), 170 mg cholesterol, 345 mg sodium.

Each tablespoon orange sauce: About 5 calories, 0 g protein, 1 g carbohydrate, 0 g total fat, 0 mg cholesterol, 20 mg sodium.

Crispy Citrus Goose ➤

Acadian Duck On Collard Greens

Panfry spicy duck breasts and serve with a sweet-and-sour blackberry sauce and garlicky greens. Much of the fat is rendered out of the duck skin during cooking, but if you prefer, remove skin first and add a little oil to skillet to prevent sticking.

COLLARD GREENS:
2 tablespoons vegetable oil
5 garlic cloves, minced
¼ teaspoon crushed red pepper
2 bunches collard greens (about 2½ pounds), trimmed and leaves cut crosswise into ½-inch-wide slices
1 cup chicken broth

BLACKBERRY SAUCE:
1¾ cups red wine vinegar
½ cup orange juice
½ cup sugar
2 medium jalapeño chiles, seeded and minced
¼ teaspoon ground nutmeg
½ cup seedless blackberry jam

Acadian Duck on Collard Greens

DUCK BREASTS:
4 large or 8 small boneless duck-breast halves with skin (about 8 ounces each), well trimmed
⅓ cup Cajun-spice seasoning blend
2 tablespoons grated fresh lemon peel
Blackberries and orange wedges for garnish

1 Prepare Collard Greens: In 5-quart Dutch oven, heat oil over medium heat. Add garlic and crushed red pepper and cook, stirring, 30 seconds. Add collard greens and cook, stirring frequently, until wilted. Add chicken broth and heat to boiling over high heat. Reduce heat to low; cover and simmer 20 minutes or until greens are tender. Keep warm.

2 While collards are simmering, prepare Blackberry Sauce: In 2-quart saucepan, heat vinegar, orange juice, sugar, jalapeños, and nutmeg to boiling over high heat, stirring. Reduce heat to low; simmer, uncovered, 20 minutes or until mixture is reduced by half (you should have about 1¼ cups). Remove saucepan from heat; stir in blackberry jam until blended. Cover and set sauce aside. Makes about 1¾ cups sauce.

3 Prepare Duck Breasts: Rinse breasts with cold running water and pat dry with paper towels. With sharp knife, cut 4 diagonal slashes about ¼ inch deep, across skin on each breast half.

4 Heat deep 12-inch skillet over medium heat until hot. Add breasts, skin side down, and cook until golden, about 7 minutes. Do not turn breasts over. Transfer breasts, skin side down, to paper towels to drain. Pour off fat from skillet, but do not wash skillet.

5 In cup, mix Cajun spice blend and lemon peel. Coat both sides of breasts with mixture. Heat same skillet over medium heat until hot. Return breasts to skillet skin side up and cook 10 minutes. Reduce heat to medium-low. Turn breasts over; cover and cook 10 minutes longer for medium-rare or until of desired doneness. Meanwhile, reheat Blackberry Sauce.

6 To serve, cut duck breasts into ¼-inch-thick slices. Place collards on platter and top with duck slices. Garnish with blackberries and orange wedges. Serve with sauce. Makes 8 main-dish servings.

Each serving collards and duck (with skin): About 240 calories, 23 g protein, 8 g carbohydrate, 13 g total fat (3 g saturated), 116 mg cholesterol, 985 mg sodium.

Each serving collards and duck (without skin): About 190 calories, 26 g protein, 8 g carbohydrate, 6 g total fat (1 g saturated), 110 mg cholesterol, 1005 mg sodium.

Each tablespoon sauce: About 30 calories, 0 g protein, 9 g carbohydrate, 0 g total fat, 0 mg cholesterol, 1 mg sodium.

MEAT

Pan-Seared Steak with White Bean Salad

PREP: 15 MINUTES • COOK: 12 TO 15 MINUTES

Serve this quick weeknight dish with steamed broccoli flowerets. To really streamline the meal, use precut broccoli.

4 teaspoons olive oil
1 beef flank steak (about 1¼ pounds), well
   trimmed
¾ teaspoon salt
¼ plus ⅛ teaspoon coarsely ground black
   pepper
1 can (15 to 19 ounces) white kidney beans
   (cannellini), rinsed and drained
½ cup loosely packed fresh basil leaves, coarsely
   chopped
1 small tomato, diced
1 small shallot, minced
1 teaspoon red wine vinegar

1 In heavy 12-inch skillet (preferably cast iron), heat 2 teaspoons olive oil over high heat until very hot.

2 Sprinkle flank steak with ½ teaspoon salt and ¼ teaspoon pepper. Add steak to hot skillet; reduce heat to medium-high and cook 12 to 15 minutes for medium-rare or until of desired doneness, turning once.

3 Meanwhile, in medium bowl, mix beans, basil, tomato, shallot, vinegar, remaining 2 teaspoons olive oil, ¼ teaspoon salt, and ⅛ teaspoon pepper until blended.

4 Thinly slice flank steak and serve with bean salad. Makes 4 main-dish servings.

Each serving: About 415 calories, 44 g protein, 23 g carbohydrate, 16 g total fat (5 g saturated), 62 mg cholesterol, 745 mg sodium.

Beef Pizzaiolo

PREP: 15 MINUTES • COOK: ABOUT 25 MINUTES

Serve with a loaf of fresh bread.

2 boneless beef top loin steaks, ¾ inch thick
   (10 ounces each), well trimmed
¼ teaspoon coarsely ground black pepper
½ teaspoon salt
1 tablespoon olive oil
1 jumbo onion (12 ounces), cut in half and sliced
1 small red pepper, cut into 1-inch pieces
1 small green pepper, cut into 1-inch pieces
2 garlic cloves, crushed with garlic press
½ cup chicken broth
2 tablespoons red wine vinegar
1 teaspoon sugar
8 cherry tomatoes, each cut in half
½ cup lightly packed fresh basil leaves, chopped
Basil sprigs for garnish

1 Pat steaks dry with paper towels. Sprinkle steaks with black pepper and ¼ teaspoon salt.

2 Heat nonstick 12-inch skillet over medium-high heat until hot. Add steaks and cook 4 minutes; turn steaks over and cook 4 to 5 minutes longer for medium-rare or until of desired doneness. Transfer steaks to platter; cover with foil to keep warm.

3 In same skillet, heat olive oil over medium heat until hot. Add onion, red and green peppers, garlic, and remaining ¼ teaspoon salt, and cook until vegetables are tender and golden, about 10 minutes, stirring often.

4 Increase heat to medium-high. Stir in chicken broth, vinegar, sugar, and tomatoes; heat to boiling. Cook 1 minute. Remove skillet from heat and stir in basil.

5 To serve, slice steaks and arrange on 4 dinner plates; top with pepper mixture. Garnish with basil. Makes 4 main-dish servings.

Each serving: About 315 calories, 32 g protein, 16 g carbohydrate, 13 g total fat (4 g saturated), 88 mg cholesterol, 450 mg sodium.

Beef Pizzaiolo ➤

Marinated Peppercorn Beef Tenderloin

PREP: 20 MINUTES PLUS MARINATING
ROAST: 45 MINUTES

Tenderloin is expensive but a perfect cut of meat for entertaining. Here, an easy marinade and a spicy peppercorn crust add flavor with minimal fuss. Prepare the quick no-cook sauce while the meat roasts.

MARINADE:
2 cups dry red wine
1 medium onion, sliced
1 tablespoon chopped fresh rosemary leaves
2 tablespoons olive oil
2 garlic cloves, crushed with garlic press
2 bay leaves

1 whole beef tenderloin, trimmed (about
    4½ pounds)*
¼ cup cracked black peppercorns

HORSERADISH-TARRAGON SAUCE:
⅔ cup mayonnaise
½ cup sour cream
2 to 3 tablespoons chopped fresh tarragon
    leaves
2 tablespoons prepared white horseradish,
    drained
1 tablespoon Dijon mustard

1 Prepare Marinade: In jumbo self-sealing plastic bag (2 gallons), mix marinade ingredients. Add tenderloin, turning to coat meat. Seal bag, pressing out excess air. Place bag in shallow baking dish and refrigerate at least 4 hours or overnight, turning bag occasionally.

2 Preheat oven to 425°F. Remove meat from marinade; tuck thinner end under tenderloin to make meat an even thickness. With string, tie tenderloin at 2-inch intervals to help hold its shape. Place peppercorns on sheet of waxed paper. Press tenderloin into peppercorns on waxed paper, turning to coat.

3 Place tenderloin on rack in medium roasting pan (15½" by 10½"); roast 40 to 45 minutes, until meat thermometer reaches 140°F. The internal temperature of meat will rise to 145°F. (medium-rare) upon standing. Or, roast to desired doneness. Transfer tenderloin to large platter; let stand 10 minutes for easier slicing.

4 While tenderloin is roasting, prepare Horseradish-Tarragon Sauce: In small bowl, blend sauce ingredients; cover and refrigerate if not serving right away.

5 To serve, remove string from tenderloin. Cut tenderloin into slices; arrange on platter. Serve with Horseradish-Tarragon Sauce. Makes 10 main-dish servings.

*If you buy an untrimmed tenderloin, it should weigh 6 to 6½ pounds to yield 4½ pounds trimmed.

Each serving: About 495 calories, 44 g protein, 3 g carbohydrate, 34 g total fat (10 g saturated), 137 mg cholesterol, 250 mg sodium.

Herb-Crusted Rib Roast

PREP: 15 MINUTES • ROAST: ABOUT 2½ HOURS

This is an expensive choice, but worth it for a holiday splurge, especially since a 3-pound roast yields 10 servings.

One 3-rib beef rib roast (small end), about
    5½ pounds, well trimmed and with chine bone
    removed
1 teaspoon salt
½ teaspoon dried rosemary leaves, crushed
¼ teaspoon coarsely ground black pepper
1 medium lemon
1½ cups fresh bread crumbs (from about 3 slices
    white bread)
½ cup chopped fresh parsley leaves
1 tablespoon olive oil
2 garlic cloves, minced
2 tablespoons Dijon mustard

1 Preheat oven to 325°F. In medium roasting pan (about 14" by 10"), place beef rib roast, fat side up. Rub salt, rosemary, and pepper over roast. Insert meat thermometer into center of roast, being careful that pointed end of thermometer does not touch bone. Roast beef 1½ hours.

2 After beef has roasted 1½ hours, prepare coating: From lemon, grate ½ teaspoon peel and squeeze 1 tablespoon juice. In small bowl, combine lemon peel, lemon juice, bread crumbs, parsley, olive oil, and garlic. Remove roast from oven; evenly spread mustard on top. Press bread-crumb mixture onto mustard-coated roast.

3 Roast 1 hour longer or until coating is golden and meat thermometer reaches 140°F. Internal temperature of meat will rise to 145°F. (medium-rare) upon standing.

4 When roast is done, place on warm large platter, and let stand at room temperature 15 minutes to set juices for easier carving. Makes 10 main-dish servings.

Each serving: About 510 calories, 31 g protein, 4 g carbohydrate, 40 g total fat (15 g saturated), 114 mg cholesterol, 410 mg sodium.

Seared Rosemary Steak

PREP: 5 MINUTES • COOK: 12 TO 15 MINUTES

Our Warm Caesar Potato Salad (page 180) is the ideal accompaniment for this steak.

1 beef flank steak (about 1 pound), well trimmed
½ teaspoon salt
¾ teaspoon dried rosemary leaves, crushed
¼ teaspoon coarsely ground black pepper
4 cups loosely packed arugula

1 Heat 10-inch cast-iron skillet over high heat until hot.

2 Rub flank steak with salt, rosemary, and pepper. Add steak to hot skillet; reduce heat to medium-high,

and cook 12 to 15 minutes for medium-rare or until of desired doneness, turning once.

3 Thinly slice flank steak. Serve on bed of arugula. Makes 4 main-dish servings.

Each serving: About 200 calories, 28 g protein, 1 g carbohydrate, 9 g total fat (4 g saturated), 47 mg cholesterol, 330 mg sodium.

Tuscan Beef with Spinach

PREP: 15 MINUTES • COOK: ABOUT 15 MINUTES

2 boneless beef top loin steaks, ¾ inch thick (10 ounces each), well trimmed
½ teaspoon salt
1 tablespoon olive oil
2 garlic cloves, minced
1 can (15 to 19 ounces) white kidney beans (cannellini), rinsed and drained
½ teaspoon dried rosemary, crushed
¼ teaspoon crushed red pepper
½ cup chicken broth
1 pound fresh spinach, tough stems removed

1 Pat steaks dry with paper towels. Sprinkle steaks with ¼ teaspoon salt.

2 Heat nonstick 12-inch skillet over medium-high heat until hot. Add steaks and cook 4 minutes; turn steaks over and cook 4 to 5 minutes longer for medium-rare or until of desired doneness. Transfer steaks to platter; cover with foil to keep warm.

3 Reduce heat to low. To same skillet, add olive oil and garlic and cook, stirring, about 30 seconds. Stir in beans, rosemary, crushed red pepper, and remaining ¼ teaspoon salt; cook 1 minute. Add chicken broth; heat to boiling over medium-high heat. Gradually add spinach, stirring, until spinach just wilts, about 2 minutes longer.

4 To serve, slice steaks and arrange on 4 dinner plates; top with bean-and-spinach mixture. Makes 4 main-dish servings.

Each serving: About 380 calories, 40 g protein, 24 g carbohydrate, 14 g total fat (4 g saturated), 88 mg cholesterol, 800 mg sodium.

Margarita Steak

PREP: 10 MINUTES • COOK: ABOUT 25 MINUTES

Serve the steak on a bed of rice.

2 boneless beef top loin steaks, ¾ inch thick
   (10 ounces each), well trimmed
⅛ teaspoon ground red pepper (cayenne)
1¼ teaspoons ground cumin
¾ teaspoon salt
1 teaspoon olive oil
2 medium red onions, sliced
1 lime
2 tablespoons orange-flavor liqueur or orange
   juice
½ cup chicken broth
¼ cup packed fresh cilantro, chopped
1 medium avocado, sliced (optional)
Cilantro sprigs for garnish (optional)

1 Pat steaks dry with paper towels. In cup, mix ground red pepper, 1 teaspoon cumin, and ½ teaspoon salt. Rub steaks with spice mixture.

2 Heat nonstick 12-inch skillet over medium-high heat until hot. Add steaks and cook 4 minutes; turn steaks over and cook 4 to 5 minutes longer for medium-rare or until of desired doneness. Transfer steaks to platter; cover with foil to keep warm.

3 In same skillet, heat olive oil over medium heat until hot. Add onions; sprinkle with remaining ¼ teaspoon ground cumin and ¼ teaspoon salt and cook, stirring occasionally, 8 to 10 minutes, until onions are tender and golden.

4 Meanwhile, from lime, remove 3 strips of peel (2" by 1" each) and squeeze 2 tablespoons juice.

5 Add lime peel to skillet and cook 30 seconds. Stir in orange liqueur or orange juice and cook 30 seconds longer. Add chicken broth and lime juice. Heat to boiling over medium-high heat; boil 1 minute.

6 To serve, slice steaks and arrange on 4 dinner plates; top with sauce. Sprinkle with chopped cilantro. If you like, serve with avocado slices and cilantro sprigs. Makes 4 main-dish servings.

Each serving without avocado: About 265 calories, 31 g protein, 8 g carbohydrate, 11 g total fat (4 g saturated), 88 mg cholesterol, 580 mg sodium.

Margarita Steak

Philly Cheese Steaks

PREP: 10 MINUTES • COOK: 12 MINUTES

These sandwiches have all the flavor of the traditional Philadelphia treat, but take half the time; while the peppers and onion cook on the stove, the broiler is working too.

1 teaspoon olive oil
1 jumbo onion (12 ounces), thinly sliced
1 medium red pepper, thinly sliced
1 medium green pepper, thinly sliced
4 hero-style rolls (about 3 ounces each), each cut horizontally in half
8 ounces thinly sliced deli roast beef
4 ounces thinly sliced Provolone cheese

1 In nonstick 12-inch skillet, heat olive oil over medium-high heat until hot. Add onion and peppers, and cook about 12 minutes or until tender and golden, stirring occasionally.

2 Meanwhile, preheat broiler. Place rolls, cut sides up, on rack in broiling pan. Top each bottom half with one-fourth of roast beef and one-fourth of cheese. With broiling pan 5 to 7 inches from source of heat, broil 1 to 2 minutes, until cheese melts and bread is toasted.

3 Pile onion mixture on top of melted cheese; replace top halves of rolls. Makes 4 sandwiches.

Each sandwich: About 620 calories, 35 g protein, 60 g carbohydrate, 26 g total fat (12 g saturated), 94 mg cholesterol, 500 mg sodium.

Moussaka Light

PREP: 40 MINUTES • BAKE: 35 MINUTES

The classic Greek layered casserole can be laden with fat, but we slimmed it down considerably by baking the eggplant slices instead of frying them in oil, using less meat, and skipping the creamy sauce.

Olive oil nonstick cooking spray
2 small eggplants (about 1¼ pounds each), cut lengthwise into ½-inch-thick slices
1 cup regular long-grain rice
12 ounces lean ground beef
1 jumbo onion (1 pound), diced

A STEAK BY ANY OTHER NAME

Having a hard time finding the boneless beef top loin steaks called for in the recipe for Margarita Steak (at left)? That's not surprising. While that is the beef industry's official name for this tender cut of beef, it also goes by several other labels, which vary by region. Among them: strip steak, shell steak, Delmonico steak, New York strip steak, Kansas City steak, hotel-style steak, boneless club steak, and ambassador steak.

---

4 garlic cloves, crushed with garlic press
1½ teaspoons salt
1 teaspoon ground cumin
½ teaspoon ground cinnamon
1 can (28 ounces) tomatoes in puree
⅓ cup grated Parmesan cheese

1 Preheat oven to 450°F. Spray large cookie sheet with olive oil cooking spray. Place eggplant slices on cookie sheet, overlapping slightly if necessary, and spray top side of slices. Bake eggplant 25 to 30 minutes, until soft and browned. Remove eggplant from oven; turn oven control to 375°F.

2 While eggplant is cooking, prepare rice as label directs, but do not add salt, margarine, or butter.

3 Heat nonstick 12-inch skillet over medium-high heat. Add ground beef, onion, and garlic, and cook until meat is browned, about 15 minutes. Stir in salt, cumin, and cinnamon; cook 2 minutes longer. Remove skillet from heat; stir in tomatoes with their puree, breaking up tomatoes with side of spoon. Transfer meat mixture to large bowl; stir in cooked rice.

4 In shallow 2½-quart casserole or glass baking dish, arrange half of eggplant slices, overlapping slices to fit if necessary. Top with half of meat mixture. Repeat with remaining eggplant slices and meat mixture.

5 Cover casserole and bake 15 minutes. Uncover casserole; sprinkle with Parmesan cheese and bake, uncovered, 20 minutes longer or until filling is hot in the center and bubbling around the edges. Makes 8 main-dish servings.

Each serving: About 300 calories, 14 g protein, 37 g carbohydrate, 11 g total fat (4 g saturated), 35 mg cholesterol, 840 mg sodium.

Glazed Pork
with Pear Chutney

PREP: 10 MINUTES • BROIL: ABOUT 20 MINUTES

PORK TENDERLOINS:
¼ cup packed brown sugar
1 tablespoon cider vinegar
1 teaspoon Dijon mustard
2 pork tenderloins (about 1½ pounds)
¼ teaspoon salt
¼ teaspoon coarsely ground black pepper

PEAR CHUTNEY:
1 can (28 ounces) pear halves in heavy syrup
⅓ cup pickled sweet red peppers, drained and chopped
¼ cup dark seedless raisins
2 teaspoons cider vinegar
1 teaspoon brown sugar
¼ teaspoon ground ginger
¼ teaspoon salt
⅛ teaspoon coarsely ground black pepper
1 green onion, chopped

1 Prepare Pork Tenderloins: Preheat broiler. In small bowl, mix brown sugar, vinegar, and mustard; set aside. Rub tenderloins with salt and black pepper; place on rack in broiling pan. With broiling pan 5 to 7 inches from source of heat, broil tenderloins 8 minutes. Brush with some brown-sugar glaze and broil 2 minutes longer. Turn tenderloins and broil 8 minutes. Brush with remaining brown-sugar glaze and broil 2 minutes longer or until tenderloins are still slightly pink in center (internal temperature of meat should be 160°F. on meat thermometer).

2 Meanwhile, prepare Pear Chutney: Drain all but ½ cup syrup from canned pears; cut pears into ½-inch chunks. In 2-quart saucepan, heat red peppers, raisins, vinegar, brown sugar, ginger, salt, black pepper, and reserved pear syrup to boiling over high heat. Reduce heat to medium and cook 5 minutes. Reduce heat to low; stir in pears and green onion and cook, covered, 5 minutes longer. Makes about 2½ cups chutney.

3 Place tenderloins on cutting board. Holding knife at an angle, thinly slice tenderloins. Spoon warm

◄ *Glazed Pork with Pear Chutney*

chutney over pork slices to serve. Makes 6 main-dish servings.

Each serving: About 350 calories, 28 g protein, 39 g carbohydrate, 10 g total fat (3 g saturated), 70 mg cholesterol, 410 mg sodium.

Moussaka Stacks

PREP: 15 MINUTES • BAKE: 20 MINUTES

Here's another take on moussaka. Instead of the usual baked, layered casserole, we made individual stacks using baked eggplant slices—just as tasty as the traditional version, and ready in less than half the time.

1 medium eggplant (about 1½ pounds)
1 tablespoon olive oil
½ teaspoon salt
1 pound lean ground beef
1 small onion, finely chopped
1 garlic clove, crushed with garlic press
½ teaspoon dried oregano
¼ teaspoon ground cinnamon
¼ teaspoon coarsely ground black pepper
1 can (15 ounces) tomato sauce
¼ cup coarsely shredded Parmesan cheese

1 Preheat oven to 450°F. Cut ends from eggplant and discard. Cut eggplant crosswise into 4 equal rounds. Brush cut sides of eggplant slices with olive oil; sprinkle with ¼ teaspoon salt and place on cookie sheet.

2 Bake eggplant slices 20 minutes or until tender and golden, turning slices over halfway through cooking.

3 Meanwhile, in nonstick 12-inch skillet, cook ground beef, onion, and garlic over medium-high heat 10 minutes or until beef begins to brown, stirring frequently. Spoon off fat, if any.

4 Stir in oregano, cinnamon, pepper, and remaining ¼ teaspoon salt; cook 1 minute. Stir in tomato sauce; heat to boiling. Reduce heat to low; simmer, uncovered, 5 minutes or until mixture thickens slightly, stirring occasionally.

5 Place eggplant slices on 4 dinner plates; top with beef mixture. Sprinkle with Parmesan cheese. Makes 4 main-dish servings.

Each serving: About 360 calories, 26 g protein, 20 g carbohydrate, 21 g total fat (8 g saturated), 75 mg cholesterol, 1025 mg sodium.

Pork Crown Roast with Apple Stuffing

PREP: 30 MINUTES • ROAST: ABOUT 2 HOURS

1 pork rib crown roast (about 7 pounds), well trimmed
2¼ teaspoons salt
½ plus ⅛ teaspoon coarsely ground black pepper
6 tablespoons margarine or butter (¾ stick)
4 medium celery stalks, diced
1 large onion, diced
3 large Golden Delicious apples (about 1½ pounds), peeled, cored, and diced
12 slices firm white bread, cut into ½-inch pieces (about 8 cups)
½ cup apple juice
1 teaspoon poultry seasoning
1 large egg
¼ cup applejack brandy, Calvados, or apple juice
3 tablespoons all-purpose flour
1 can (14½ ounces) chicken broth

1 Preheat oven to 325°F. Rub inside and outside of pork roast with 1 teaspoon salt and ¼ teaspoon pepper. Place pork, rib ends down, in large roasting pan (about 17" by 11½"). Roast pork 1 hour.

2 Meanwhile, in 5-quart Dutch oven, melt margarine or butter over medium heat. Add celery and onion and cook until tender, about 10 minutes, stirring often. Add apples and cook 6 to 8 minutes longer, until softened. Remove from heat; stir in bread pieces, apple juice, poultry seasoning, egg, 1 teaspoon salt, and ¼ teaspoon pepper.

3 When pork has roasted 1 hour, remove from oven and turn rib ends up. Spoon about 4 cups stuffing into center. (Place remaining stuffing in greased 1½-quart casserole; cook, uncovered, during last 30 minutes of pork roasting time.)

4 Insert meat thermometer between 2 ribs into thickest part of meat, being careful that pointed end of thermometer does not touch bone. Return pork to oven and continue roasting about 1 hour or until meat thermometer reaches 155°F. Internal temperature of meat will rise to 160°F. upon standing. If stuffing browns too quickly, cover it loosely with foil.

5 When roast is done, place on warm platter; let stand 15 minutes to set juices for easier carving.

6 Meanwhile, prepare gravy: Pour pan drippings into 2-cup measuring cup or medium bowl; set pan aside. Let stand a few seconds until fat separates from meat juice. Skim 3 tablespoons fat from drippings (add enough melted margarine or butter, if necessary, to equal 3 tablespoons) into 2-quart saucepan; skim and discard any remaining fat. Add applejack to roasting pan. Stir until brown bits are loosened; add to meat juices in measuring cup.

7 Into fat in saucepan over medium heat, stir flour, ¼ teaspoon salt, and ⅛ teaspoon pepper; cook, stirring, 1 minute. Stir in meat-juice mixture and chicken broth and cook, stirring, until gravy boils and thickens. Makes about 2½ cups.

8 Serve pork with gravy and stuffing. Makes 14 main-dish servings.

Each serving of pork with stuffing: About 480 calories, 35 g protein, 18 g carbohydrate, 30 g total fat (10 g saturated), 95 mg cholesterol, 565 mg sodium.

Each tablespoon gravy: About 15 calories, 0 g protein, 1 g carbohydrate, 1 g total fat (0 g saturated), 1 mg cholesterol, 50 mg sodium.

PORK CROWN ROAST TIPS

• Order your roast a few days ahead so the butcher has enough time to prepare it.

• A 7-pound pork rib crown roast has 14 to 16 ribs. When preparing it, your butcher will "french" or scrape the meat from the ends of the ribs or chops to expose part of the bones. Ask your butcher to grind this meat for you; it can be added to meat loaf or meatballs.

• Request that the decorative paper or aluminum "frills" be placed in a separate bag, rather than on the tops of the raw rib bones. This way, you can use the clean "frills" on your finished roast for serving if you like.

• To carve the crown roast, make centered cuts between ribs so there is an equal portion of meat on both sides of the chop. Spoon stuffing over chops after each rib is cut away.

Pork Loin with Mango-Chutney Sauce

PREP: 10 MINUTES • ROAST: ABOUT 1½ HOURS

This recipe is a keeper for dinner parties because it's so simple to prepare.

½ cup plain dried bread crumbs
1 teaspoon salt
½ teaspoon coarsely ground black pepper
¼ cup plus 2 tablespoons Dijon mustard with seeds
1 boneless pork loin roast (3 pounds), well trimmed
½ cup mango chutney, chopped
Parsley sprigs for garnish

1 Preheat oven to 350°F. In small bowl, combine bread crumbs, salt, pepper, and ¼ cup mustard.

2 Pat pork roast dry with paper towels. With hand, pat bread-crumb mixture onto pork. Place pork on rack in small roasting pan (about 14" by 10") and roast 1 hour and 30 minutes or until temperature on meat thermometer reaches 155°F. (internal temperature will rise to 160°F. upon standing). Transfer pork to cutting board; let stand 10 minutes.

3 In 1-quart saucepan, heat mango chutney, remaining 2 tablespoons mustard, and ⅓ *cup water* over medium heat, stirring constantly, until heated through, about 1 minute.

4 To serve, slice pork. Arrange pork on platter with parsley sprigs. Serve with sauce. Makes 8 main-dish servings.

Each serving: About 375 calories, 38 g protein, 15 g carbohydrate, 16 g total fat (5 g saturated), 80 mg cholesterol, 700 mg sodium

Brazilian Pork

PREP: 15 MINUTES • COOK: ABOUT 15 MINUTES

Serve with a mixed green salad.

4 boneless pork loin chops, ¾ inch thick (5 ounces each), well trimmed
½ teaspoon ground cumin
½ teaspoon ground coriander
¼ teaspoon dried thyme
⅛ teaspoon ground allspice
½ teaspoon salt
1 teaspoon olive oil
1 medium onion, chopped
3 garlic cloves, crushed with garlic press
1 can (15 to 19 ounces) black beans, rinsed and drained
½ cup chicken broth
1 tablespoon fresh lime juice
¼ teaspoon coarsely ground black pepper
¼ cup packed fresh cilantro, chopped
Fresh orange wedges (optional)

1 Pat pork chops dry with paper towels. In cup, mix cumin, coriander, thyme, allspice, and ¼ teaspoon salt. Rub pork chops with spice mixture.

2 Heat nonstick 12-inch skillet over medium-high heat until hot. Add pork chops and cook 4 minutes; turn pork over and cook 3 to 4 minutes longer, until lightly browned on the outside and still slightly pink on the inside. Transfer pork to platter; cover with foil to keep warm.

3 In same skillet, heat olive oil over medium heat. Add onion and cook, stirring frequently, 5 minutes or until golden. Add garlic and cook 1 minute longer, stirring.

4 Add beans, chicken broth, lime juice, pepper, and remaining ¼ teaspoon salt; heat through.

5 To serve, spoon bean mixture over pork; sprinkle with cilantro. Serve with orange wedges if you like. Makes 4 main-dish servings.

Each serving: About 340 calories, 42 g protein, 25 g carbohydrate, 11 g total fat (3 g saturated), 76 mg cholesterol, 760 mg sodium

Spicy Peanut Pork

Serve with steamed rice.

4 boneless pork loin chops, ¾ inch thick
    (5 ounces each), well trimmed
¼ teaspoon coarsely ground black pepper
½ teaspoon salt
4 medium green onions, cut into 1-inch diagonal
    slices
8 ounces snow peas, strings removed
1 tablespoon minced, peeled fresh ginger
3 garlic cloves, crushed with garlic press
¼ cup creamy peanut butter
1 tablespoon sugar
1 tablespoon soy sauce
⅛ teaspoon ground red pepper (cayenne)

1 Pat pork chops dry with paper towels. Sprinkle pork chops with pepper and ¼ teaspoon salt.

2 Heat nonstick 12-inch skillet over medium-high heat until hot. Add pork chops and cook 4 minutes; turn pork over and cook 3 to 4 minutes longer, until lightly browned on the outside and still slightly pink on the inside. Transfer pork to platter; cover with foil to keep warm.

3 To same skillet, add green onions, snow peas, and remaining ¼ teaspoon salt, and cook over medium heat 4 minutes, stirring frequently. Stir in ginger and garlic; cook 1 minute. Return pork to skillet.

4 Meanwhile, in small bowl, stir peanut butter, sugar, soy sauce, ground red pepper, and ¾ *cup water* until blended.

5 Pour peanut-butter mixture into same skillet; heat to boiling over medium-high heat. Reduce heat to low; simmer 1 minute. Makes 4 main-dish servings.

Each serving: About 350 calories, 37 g protein, 13 g carbohydrate, 17 g total fat (5 g saturated), 76 mg cholesterol, 685 mg sodium.

Latin American Pork Stew

Pork, black beans, cilantro, and sweet potatoes give this dish authentic Latino flavor.

2 teaspoons olive oil
2 pounds boneless pork loin, cut into 1-inch
    pieces
1 large onion, chopped
4 garlic cloves, minced
1 can (14½ ounces) diced tomatoes
1 cup loosely packed fresh cilantro leaves and
    stems, chopped
1 teaspoon ground cumin
¾ teaspoon salt
½ teaspoon ground coriander
¼ teaspoon ground red pepper (cayenne)
3 medium sweet potatoes (1½ pounds), peeled
    and cut into ½-inch chunks
2 cans (15 to 19 ounces each) black beans,
    rinsed and drained

1 Preheat oven to 350°F. In nonstick 5-quart Dutch oven, heat olive oil over medium-high heat. Add pork in batches and cook until lightly browned, about 5 minutes per batch. Transfer pork to medium bowl.

2 Reduce heat to medium. In drippings in Dutch oven, cook onion until tender, about 10 minutes, stirring frequently. Add garlic and cook 1 minute longer.

3 Add tomatoes with their juice, cilantro, cumin, salt, coriander, ground red pepper, and 2 *cups water*; heat to boiling over high heat. Stir in pork; cover Dutch oven and bake 30 minutes.

4 Stir in sweet potatoes; cover and bake 40 minutes longer or until meat and potatoes are very tender. Stir in black beans; cover and bake 15 minutes longer or until heated through. Makes about 10 cups or 8 main-dish servings.

Each serving: About 340 calories, 36 g protein, 36 g carbohydrate, 9 g total fat (3 g saturated), 58 mg cholesterol, 735 mg sodium.

Pork with Lemon & Capers

Pork with Lemon & Capers

PREP: 10 MINUTES • COOK: 10 MINUTES

Serve with steamed green and yellow baby squashes and a crispy baguette.

4 boneless pork loin chops, ¾ inch thick
   (5 ounces each), well trimmed
¼ teaspoon salt
¼ teaspoon coarsely ground black pepper
1 lemon
½ cup chicken broth
2 garlic cloves, crushed with garlic press
1 tablespoon capers, drained
½ cup lightly packed fresh parsley leaves,
   chopped
1 tablespoon margarine or butter
Lemon-peel strips for garnish

1 Pat pork chops dry with paper towels. Sprinkle pork chops with salt and pepper.

2 Heat nonstick 12-inch skillet over medium-high heat until hot. Add pork chops and cook 4 minutes; turn pork over and cook 3 to 4 minutes longer, until lightly browned on the outside and still slightly pink on the inside. Transfer pork to platter; cover with foil to keep warm.

3 Meanwhile, from lemon, grate ½ teaspoon peel and squeeze 1 tablespoon juice; set aside.

4 To same skillet, add chicken broth, garlic, capers, lemon peel and juice; heat to boiling. Cook 1 minute, stirring often. Remove skillet from heat; stir in parsley and margarine or butter.

5 To serve, pour sauce over pork. Garnish with lemon-peel strips. Makes 4 main-dish servings.

Each serving: About 245 calories, 32 g protein, 1 g carbohydrate, 12 g total fat (4 g saturated), 76 mg cholesterol, 435 mg sodium.

Boneless BBQ "Ribs"

PREP: 10 MINUTES • COOK: ABOUT 7 MINUTES

All the great flavors of a summertime barbecue—
without the work of heating up a grill. We like
these with Zesty Stovetop Beans (page 165), which
can heat while the pork cooks and—if you have
time—a crisp salad with ranch dressing.

3 tablespoons chili sauce
1 tablespoon mild molasses
2 teaspoons brown sugar
2 teaspoons minced, peeled fresh ginger
2 teaspoons Worcestershire sauce
2 teaspoons cider vinegar
1 teaspoon cornstarch
⅛ teaspoon salt
1 pound boneless pork "ribs"*

1 In small bowl, stir together all ingredients except
pork. Add *1 tablespoon water* to sauce mixture; set
aside.

2 Heat nonstick 12-inch skillet over medium-high
heat until hot. Add pork ribs and cook until they are
lightly browned on the outside and just lose their pink
color on the inside, about 5 minutes, turning once.

3 Reduce heat to low; add sauce to pork, and cook
30 seconds to 1 minute, until sauce bubbles and
thickens. Makes 4 main-dish servings.

*If you can't find boneless pork ribs at the market, fol-
low our easy instructions (below) for cutting a
1-pound boneless pork loin roast into "ribs."

Each serving: About 205 calories, 25 g protein, 10 g carbohydrate, 7 g total fat (2 g saturated), 58 mg cholesterol, 290 mg
sodium.

Apple-Sauce Pork

PREP: 10 MINUTES • COOK: ABOUT 20 MINUTES

4 boneless pork loin chops, ¾ inch thick
    (5 ounces each), well trimmed
¼ teaspoon coarsely ground black pepper
½ teaspoon salt
1 tablespoon margarine or butter
2 large Golden Delicious apples (about
    1 pound), peeled, cored, and each cut into
    12 wedges
1 medium onion, chopped
½ cup pitted prunes, chopped
¾ cup apple juice
1 tablespoon cider vinegar

1 Pat pork chops dry with paper towels. Sprinkle pork
chops with pepper and ¼ teaspoon salt.

2 Heat nonstick 12-inch skillet over medium-high
heat until hot. Add pork chops and cook 4 minutes;
turn pork over and cook 3 to 4 minutes longer, until
lightly browned on the outside and still slightly pink

HOW TO MAKE BONELESS "RIBS" FROM A PORK LOIN ROAST

*Holding sharp chef's knife parallel to work surface,
cut a well-trimmed 1-pound boneless pork loin roast
horizontally in half.*

*Cut each half crosswise into 8 strips (or 10 strips if
thinner "ribs" are desired).*

on the inside. Transfer pork to platter; cover with foil to keep warm.

3 In same skillet, melt margarine or butter over medium heat. Add apples, onion, prunes, and remaining ¼ teaspoon salt. Cook, covered, until apples and onion are tender and golden, about 10 minutes, stirring occasionally.

4 Remove cover. Add apple juice and vinegar; heat to boiling.

5 To serve, spoon apple mixture over pork chops. Makes 4 main-dish servings.

Each serving: About 365 calories, 32 g protein, 33 g carbohydrate, 12 g total fat (4 g saturated), 76 mg cholesterol, 390 mg sodium.

Asian Pork & Baby Peas

PREP: 10 MINUTES • COOK: 10 MINUTES

Pair with our refreshing Cucumber Salad (page 178)—it can be prepared while the pork browns—and an aromatic grain such as basmati rice, which cooks in 20 minutes.

2 teaspoons vegetable oil
1 pork tenderloin (about 1 pound), cut into
   ¼-inch-thick slices
2 garlic cloves, crushed with garlic press
1 package (10 ounces) frozen baby peas
3 tablespoons reduced-sodium soy sauce
2 tablespoons seasoned rice vinegar
1 tablespoon grated, peeled fresh ginger
1 tablespoon mild molasses
¼ teaspoon crushed red pepper

1 In nonstick 12-inch skillet, heat vegetable oil over medium-high heat until hot. Add pork slices and garlic and cook until they are browned on the outside and just lose their pink color on the inside, about 6 minutes, stirring occasionally. Transfer pork to plate.

2 To same skillet, add frozen peas, soy sauce, rice vinegar, ginger, molasses, and crushed red pepper; cook until peas are heated through, about 4 minutes. Return pork to skillet; toss to coat. Makes 4 main-dish servings.

Each serving: About 230 calories, 28 g protein, 19 g carbohydrate, 6 g total fat (1 g saturated), 64 mg cholesterol, 840 mg sodium.

Pork & Posole Stew

PREP: 45 MINUTES • BAKE: 1 HOUR 45 MINUTES

Posole is usually made with hominy—dried white or yellow corn kernels with the hull and germ removed. Our version uses canned hominy, which has already been reconstituted.

2 medium red peppers
3 pounds boneless pork shoulder, well trimmed
   and cut into 1½-inch pieces
1 jumbo onion (1 pound), chopped
4 garlic cloves, minced
3 jalapeño chiles, seeded and minced
1 cup loosely packed fresh cilantro leaves and
   stems, chopped
2 teaspoons ground cumin
1½ teaspoons salt
½ teaspoon dried oregano
¼ teaspoon ground red pepper (cayenne)
1 can (29 ounces) hominy, rinsed and drained
Lime wedges, radishes, and chopped cilantro
   leaves for garnish

1 Preheat broiler. Line broiling pan (without rack) with foil. Cut each red pepper lengthwise in half; discard stem and seeds. Arrange peppers, cut side down, in broiling pan. Place pan in broiler 5 to 6 inches from source of heat and broil peppers until charred and blistered, about 6 to 8 minutes. Wrap foil around peppers and allow to steam at room temperature 15 minutes or until cool enough to handle. Turn oven control to 325°F.

2 Remove peppers from foil; peel off skin and discard. Cut peppers into 1-inch pieces.

3 In 5-quart Dutch oven, combine roasted peppers and remaining ingredients except hominy and garnishes; stir in *1 cup water*; heat to boiling over high heat. Cover Dutch oven and bake 1½ hours or until pork is very tender.

4 Remove from oven; skim and discard fat. Stir in hominy; cover and bake 15 minutes longer or until heated through. Garnish with lime wedges, radishes, and chopped cilantro. Makes about 10 cups or 10 main-dish servings.

Each serving: About 300 calories, 38 g protein, 14 g carbohydrate, 9 g total fat (3 g saturated), 83 mg cholesterol, 565 mg sodium.

Sausage & Cheese Frittata

Packed with flavor and hearty ingredients, this frittata is delicious for brunch or dinner. Make the extra effort to buy freshly made mozzarella at an Italian market or specialty-food store—it really makes a difference. Complete your menu with a salad of baby greens and cherry-tomato halves.

6 ounces sweet Italian-sausage links, casings removed
2 medium yellow peppers, cut into 2" by ¼" strips
1 large red onion, thinly sliced
8 large eggs
¼ cup minced fresh parsley or basil leaves
¾ teaspoon salt
¼ teaspoon coarsely ground black pepper
4 ounces mozzarella cheese, shredded (1 cup)

1 Preheat oven to 350°F. Heat nonstick 10-inch skillet with oven-safe handle (or cover handle with heavy-duty foil for baking in oven later) over medium heat. Add sausage and cook until browned, about 5 minutes, stirring frequently to break up sausage. With slotted spoon, transfer sausage to paper towels to drain.

2 Discard all but 1 tablespoon of drippings from skillet. To skillet, add peppers, onion, and ½ *cup water*, and cook, stirring occasionally, until vegetables are tender, about 12 minutes.

3 Meanwhile, in large bowl, with wire whisk or fork, beat eggs with parsley, salt, and pepper until blended; stir in mozzarella.

4 Pour egg mixture over vegetables in skillet; stir in sausage. Cook 3 minutes, without stirring, or until egg mixture begins to set around edge. Place skillet in oven; bake 12 minutes or until frittata is set.

5 To serve, place a cutting board or platter over top of skillet; invert. Remove skillet and cut frittata into wedges. Makes 6 main-dish servings.

Each serving: About 265 calories, 17 g protein, 8 g carbohydrate, 18 g total fat (7 g saturated), 317 mg cholesterol, 615 mg sodium.

Polenta with Sausage & Peppers

Polenta with Sausage & Peppers

We used ready-to-slice polenta from the refrigerated section at the supermarket. While you cook the onion and pepper, open a package of your favorite prewashed greens and whip up a simple vinaigrette.

12 ounces hot and/or sweet Italian-sausage links, casings removed
Nonstick cooking spray
1 package (24 ounces) precooked polenta, cut into 16 slices
1 tablespoon olive oil
1 medium onion, thinly sliced
1 medium red pepper, thinly sliced
1 garlic clove, crushed with garlic press
½ cup chicken broth

1 Preheat broiler. Heat nonstick 12-inch skillet over medium-high heat until hot. Add sausage and cook until browned, about 10 minutes, stirring occasionally and breaking up sausage with side of spoon. With slotted spoon, transfer sausage to medium bowl; wipe skillet clean with paper towels.

2 Spray 15½" by 10½" jelly-roll pan with nonstick cooking spray. Place polenta slices in pan; spray to coat. With pan at closest position to source of heat, broil polenta 10 minutes, turning slices over halfway through cooking.

3 Meanwhile, in same skillet, heat olive oil over medium-high heat until hot. Add onion and pepper and cook until tender and lightly browned, 8 to 10 minutes, stirring occasionally. Add garlic and sausage; cook 1 minute, stirring. Add chicken broth and heat to boiling. Return mixture to bowl; keep warm.

4 Serve polenta topped with sausage mixture. Makes 4 main-dish servings.

Each serving: About 360 calories, 12 g protein, 31 g carbohydrate, 21 g total fat (6 g saturated), 45 mg cholesterol, 1150 mg sodium.

Ham & Cheese Grits Casserole

PREP: 25 MINUTES • BAKE: 45 TO 50 MINUTES

This is perfect for brunch or an easy weeknight supper.

3½ cups nonfat (skim) milk
1 teaspoon salt
1¼ cups quick-cooking grits
4 ounces cooked ham, diced (¾ cup)
3 ounces low-fat Monterey Jack cheese, shredded (¾ cup)
2 tablespoons grated Parmesan cheese
1 pickled jalapeño chile, minced
2 large eggs
3 large egg whites

1 Preheat oven to 325°F. Grease shallow 2-quart casserole. In heavy 3-quart saucepan, heat 1½ cups milk, 2¼ cups water, and salt to boiling over medium-high heat. Gradually stir in grits, beating constantly with wire whisk. Cover and simmer over low heat 5 minutes, stirring occasionally. Remove from heat; stir in ham, cheeses, and jalapeño.

2 In large bowl, with whisk, beat whole eggs, egg whites, and remaining 2 cups milk. Gradually add grits to egg mixture (mixture will be lumpy).

3 Pour mixture into casserole. Bake, uncovered, 45 to 50 minutes, until top is set and edges are lightly golden. Remove from oven; let stand 10 minutes. Makes 6 main-dish servings.

Each serving: About 300 calories, 19 g protein, 34 g carbohydrate, 9 g total fat (5 g saturated), 98 mg cholesterol, 870 mg sodium.

Lamb with Green Beans

PREP: 25 MINUTES • COOK: ABOUT 1 HOUR 20 MINUTES

This traditional Arab lamb stew combines fragrant nutmeg and allspice with tomatoes and green beans. Serve with warm pita bread or hot fluffy rice to soak up the delicious broth.

2 tablespoons olive oil
2 pounds boneless lamb for stew, well trimmed and cut into 1½-inch pieces
1 large onion, chopped
1 teaspoon salt
½ teaspoon coarsely ground black pepper
½ teaspoon ground allspice
¼ teaspoon ground nutmeg
1 can (28 ounces) tomatoes
2 pounds green beans, stem ends trimmed, and cut into 2-inch pieces

1 In 6-quart Dutch oven, heat 1 tablespoon olive oil over medium-high heat until hot. Add half the lamb and cook until browned on all sides, about 5 minutes, stirring occasionally. With slotted spoon, transfer meat to bowl; set aside. Repeat with remaining lamb.

2 In same Dutch oven, heat remaining 1 tablespoon olive oil until hot. Add onion, salt, pepper, allspice, and nutmeg; cook 5 minutes. Add tomatoes with their juice; heat to boiling, breaking up tomatoes with side of spoon.

3 Return lamb and any accumulated meat juices to Dutch oven; add green beans and heat to boiling. Reduce heat to low; cover and simmer 1 hour or until meat is tender. Makes about 10 cups or 8 main-dish servings.

Each serving: About 245 calories, 26 g protein, 14 g carbohydrate, 10 g total fat (3 g saturated), 80 mg cholesterol, 485 mg sodium.

Brown Sugar & Ginger Glazed Ham with Two Sauces

PREP: 45 MINUTES • ROAST: ABOUT 3½ HOURS

HAM & GLAZE:
1 fully cooked smoked whole ham (about 14 pounds)
½ cup packed brown sugar
½ cup honey
1 teaspoon ground ginger

MUSTARD SAUCE:
1 cup sour cream
¾ cup mayonnaise
1 jar (8 ounces) Dijon mustard with seeds
1 teaspoon Worcestershire sauce
½ teaspoon coarsely ground black pepper

CRANBERRY-CHERRY SAUCE:
1 large orange
1 can (21 ounces) cherry-pie filling
1 bag (12 ounces) cranberries (3 cups)
¼ cup sugar
¼ teaspoon ground allspice

1 Prepare Ham: Preheat oven to 325°F. Remove skin and trim some fat from whole ham, leaving about ¼ inch fat.

2 Place ham on rack in large roasting pan (about 17" by 11½"). Insert meat thermometer into center of ham, being careful that pointed end of thermometer does not touch bone. Roast ham 2½ hours.

3 After ham has roasted 2½ hours, prepare glaze: In 1-quart saucepan, mix brown sugar, honey, and ginger; heat to boiling over medium-high heat. Boil 1 minute. When bubbling subsides, brush ham with some glaze. Roast ham 30 minutes to 1 hour longer, brushing occasionally with remaining glaze until thermometer reaches 140°F.

4 Meanwhile, prepare Mustard Sauce: In medium bowl, stir together sour cream, mayonnaise, mustard, Worcestershire, and pepper. Cover and refrigerate until ready to serve. Makes about 2½ cups.

5 When ham is done, place on large cutting board; let stand 20 minutes for easier slicing.

6 Meanwhile, prepare Cranberry-Cherry Sauce: From orange, grate ½ teaspoon peel and squeeze ½ cup juice. In 3-quart saucepan, heat orange peel, juice, cherry-pie filling, cranberries, sugar, and allspice to boiling over high heat, stirring occasionally. Reduce heat to low; simmer 10 minutes, stirring occasionally, until most of cranberries pop. Makes about 3½ cups.

7 Serve ham with the two sauces. Makes 24 main-dish servings.

Each serving of ham without sauces: About 325 calories, 36 g protein, 10 g carbohydrate, 15 g total fat (5 g saturated), 95 mg cholesterol, 2400 mg sodium.

Each tablespoon mustard sauce: About 50 calories, 1 g protein, 1 g carbohydrate, 5 g total fat (1 g saturated), 4 mg cholesterol, 170 mg sodium.

Each tablespoon cranberry-cherry sauce: About 20 calories, 0 g protein, 5 g carbohydrate, 0 g total fat, 0 mg cholesterol, 1 mg sodium.

HAM ROASTING TIPS

• When shopping for ham, look for "fully cooked" on the label. This means it's ready to serve. To improve the flavor and texture, heat ham to an internal temperature of 130° to 140°F. If the label says "cook before eating," the meat must be cooked to 160°F.

• To carve a whole, bone-in ham: Place ham on cutting board. Using carving fork to steady ham, cut a few slices from the thin side to form a level base. Turn ham onto cut surface. Starting at the shank end, slice down to the bone and cut out a small wedge of meat. Continue slicing, perpendicular to bone, cutting thin slices until you reach the bone at the other end. Then, cut meat along the leg bone to release slices. For more servings, turn ham to its original position and cut slices to bone.

• Try to use leftovers within 3 or 4 days to avoid the need to freeze them—freezing changes the flavor and texture of smoked-pork products. Use frozen ham within 1 month.

FISH & SHELLFISH

Tarragon Salmon with Caper Sauce

PREP: 20 MINUTES • ROAST: ABOUT 40 MINUTES

Some helpful tips when roasting a whole salmon: To estimate cooking time for a whole fish, use the 10-minute rule. Allow 10 minutes per inch of thickness, measuring at the plumpest part—near the base of the head. To test for doneness, use a small knife and peel at the backbone to see if the flesh is opaque. For easier serving, peel off the top skin with a fork and knife. Slide the knife under the front section of the fillet and using a pancake turner, transfer the top fillet to a platter. Slide the knife under the backbone and lift it away from the bottom fillet. Slide the knife between the bottom skin and fillet and transfer the bottom fillet to the platter.

CAPER SAUCE:
¾ cup sour cream
½ cup mayonnaise
¼ cup milk
3 tablespoons capers, drained and chopped
2 tablespoons chopped fresh tarragon leaves
½ teaspoon grated lemon peel
⅛ teaspoon coarsely ground black pepper

SALMON:
2 large lemons, thinly sliced
1 whole salmon (about 5½ pounds), dressed, with head and tail removed
2 tablespoons olive oil
½ teaspoon salt
½ teaspoon coarsely ground black pepper
1 large bunch fresh tarragon
1 small bunch fresh Italian parsley
Lemon wedges and tarragon sprigs for garnish

1 Prepare Caper Sauce: In medium bowl, mix all sauce ingredients until blended. Cover and refrigerate up to 2 days or until ready to serve. Makes about 1⅓ cups.

2 Prepare Salmon: Preheat oven to 450°F. Line 15½" by 10½" jelly-roll pan with foil.

3 Place one-third of lemon slices in a row down center of pan. Rub outside of salmon with olive oil. Place salmon on top of lemon slices. Sprinkle cavity with salt and pepper. Place tarragon and parsley sprigs inside cavity with half of remaining lemon slices. Place remaining lemon slices on top of fish.

4 Roast salmon 40 minutes or until fish turns opaque throughout and flakes easily when tested with a fork. Remove lemon slices and skin from top of salmon; discard. Transfer salmon to large platter. Garnish with lemon wedges and tarragon sprigs if you like. Serve with Caper Sauce. Makes 10 main-dish servings.

Each serving of fish without sauce: About 180 calories, 25 g protein, 0 g carbohydrate, 8 g total fat (2 g saturated), 45 mg cholesterol, 160 mg sodium.

Each tablespoon of sauce: About 60 calories, 0 g protein, 1 g carbohydrate, 6 g total fat (2 g saturated), 6 mg cholesterol, 80 mg sodium.

Seafood Stew

PREP: 10 MINUTES • COOK: 20 MINUTES

1¼ pounds all-purpose potatoes, peeled and cut into ½-inch pieces
1 can (14½ ounces) chunky tomatoes with olive oil, garlic, and spices
1 can (14½ ounces) chicken broth
⅓ cup dry white wine
16 large mussels, scrubbed and debearded
16 large shrimp, shelled and deveined, with tail part of shell left on
1 piece cod fillet (12 ounces), cut into 2-inch pieces
1 tablespoon chopped fresh parsley leaves

1 In 2-quart saucepan, heat potatoes and *enough water to cover* to boiling over high heat. Reduce heat to low; cover and simmer 5 to 8 minutes, until potatoes are tender; drain.

2 Meanwhile, in 5-quart Dutch oven, heat tomatoes with their liquid, chicken broth, and wine to boiling over high heat. Add mussels; reduce heat to medium. Cover and cook mussels 3 to 5 minutes, transferring mussels to bowl as shells open.

3 Add shrimp and cod to Dutch oven; cover and cook 3 to 5 minutes, until shrimp and cod turn opaque throughout. Add potatoes and mussels; heat through. Sprinkle with parsley. Makes 4 main-dish servings.

Each serving: About 305 calories, 35 g protein, 28 g carbohydrate, 5 g total fat (0 g saturated), 136 mg cholesterol, 965 mg sodium.

Seafood Stew ➤

Five-Spice Salmon

PREP: 5 MINUTES • COOK: 10 MINUTES

2 teaspoons Chinese five-spice powder
1 teaspoon all-purpose flour
½ teaspoon salt
¼ teaspoon cracked black pepper
4 salmon fillets (about 4 ounces each), skin removed
2 teaspoons light corn-oil spread

1 On waxed paper, mix Chinese five-spice powder, flour, salt, and pepper. Coat salmon fillets with spice mixture.

2 In nonstick 10-inch skillet over medium heat, heat corn-oil spread. Add salmon; cook 8 to 10 minutes, until fish flakes easily when tested with a fork, turning fillets once halfway through cooking time. Makes 4 main-dish servings.

Each serving: About 175 calories, 22 g protein, 1 g carbohydrate, 8 g total fat (1 g saturated), 61 mg cholesterol, 330 mg sodium.

Mustard-Dill Salmon with Herbed Potatoes

PREP: 20 MINUTES • BROIL: 8 TO 10 MINUTES

A light and creamy sauce adds piquant flavor to succulent salmon. After you make the sauce, sauté snow peas in a nonstick skillet with a teaspoon of vegetable oil for a healthy side dish.

¾ pound small red potatoes, cut into 1-inch chunks
¾ pound small white potatoes, cut into 1-inch chunks
1½ teaspoons salt
3 tablespoons chopped fresh dill
½ teaspoon coarsely ground black pepper
4 pieces salmon fillet (about 6 ounces each)
2 tablespoons light mayonnaise
1 tablespoon white wine vinegar
2 teaspoons Dijon mustard
¾ teaspoon sugar

1 In 3-quart saucepan, place potatoes, 1 teaspoon salt, and *enough water to cover*; heat to boiling over high heat. Reduce heat to low; cover and simmer 15 minutes or until potatoes are fork-tender. Drain potatoes and toss with 1 tablespoon dill, ¼ teaspoon salt, and ¼ teaspoon coarsely ground black pepper; keep the potatoes warm.

2 Meanwhile, preheat broiler. Grease rack in broiling pan. Place salmon on rack; sprinkle with ⅛ teaspoon salt and ⅛ teaspoon coarsely ground black pepper. Broil salmon at closest position to source of heat 8 to 10 minutes, until fish flakes easily.

3 While salmon is broiling, prepare sauce: In small bowl, mix mayonnaise, vinegar, mustard, sugar, remaining 2 tablespoons dill, ⅛ teaspoon salt, and ⅛ teaspoon black pepper.

4 Serve salmon with sauce and potatoes. Makes 4 main-dish servings.

Each serving: About 335 calories, 37 g protein, 31 g carbohydrate, 7 g total fat (1 g saturated), 86 mg cholesterol, 655 mg sodium.

Salmon Cakes

PREP: 8 MINUTES • COOK: 10 MINUTES

Serve these tender cakes with our Cucumber Salad (page 178); prepare it while the cakes cook.

1 can (14¾ ounces) red or pink salmon, drained and flaked
1 green onion, sliced
3 tablespoons prepared white horseradish
2 tablespoons plain dried bread crumbs
1 teaspoon soy sauce
¼ teaspoon coarsely ground black pepper
Nonstick cooking spray
4 sandwich buns, split
Lettuce leaves

1 In medium bowl, with fork, lightly mix all ingredients except cooking spray, buns, and lettuce leaves. Shape mixture into four 3-inch round patties. Spray both sides of patties with nonstick cooking spray.

2 Heat skillet over medium heat until hot. Add salmon cakes, and cook about 5 minutes per side or until golden and hot. Serve on buns with lettuce. Makes 4 main-dish servings.

Each serving: About 255 calories, 19 g protein, 26 g carbohydrate, 9 g total fat (2 g saturated), 50 mg cholesterol, 815 mg sodium.

Tunisian Snapper

PREP: 5 MINUTES • COOK: 5 TO 8 MINUTES

4 red-snapper fillets (about 6 ounces each)
½ teaspoon salt
¼ teaspoon cumin seeds, crushed
¼ teaspoon coriander seeds, crushed
¼ teaspoon fennel seeds, crushed
¼ teaspoon crushed red pepper
2 teaspoons vegetable oil
Lime wedges

1 With tweezers, remove any small bones from snapper fillets.

2 On waxed paper, combine salt, cumin seeds, coriander seeds, fennel seeds, and crushed red pepper. Rub mixture on flesh side of fillets.

3 In nonstick 12-inch skillet, heat vegetable oil over medium-high heat until hot. Add fillets and cook 5 to 8 minutes, turning once, until fish flakes easily when tested with a fork. Serve with lime wedges. Makes 4 main-dish servings.

Each serving: About 190 calories, 35 g protein, 0 g carbohydrate, 5 g total fat (1 g saturated), 62 mg cholesterol, 340 mg sodium.

Romesco Sauce

PREP: 10 MINUTES • COOK: 15 MINUTES

This bold red-pepper-and-almond sauce originated in Spain, where fishermen cooked lesser-quality catches with it. Try it with our Quick Poached Salmon (at right).

¼ cup whole blanched almonds
½ slice firm white bread, torn into pieces
2 small garlic cloves, crushed and peeled
1 tablespoon olive oil
1 medium red pepper, thinly sliced
1 small onion, cut in half and thinly sliced
1 teaspoon paprika
2 teaspoons red wine vinegar
½ teaspoon salt
¼ teaspoon coarsely ground black pepper
1 small tomato, cut into eighths

1 In nonstick 12-inch skillet, cook almonds, bread, and garlic cloves over medium heat until almonds are golden, 5 to 6 minutes, stirring often. Transfer almonds and bread to small bowl, leaving garlic in skillet.

2 Increase heat to medium-high. Add olive oil, red pepper, and onion, and cook 8 minutes or until vegetables are lightly browned. Add paprika, vinegar, salt, black pepper, and tomato, and cook, stirring often, 2 minutes longer.

3 Transfer almond mixture and pepper mixture to blender; add *¼ cup water*. Process mixture in blender, occasionally scraping down sides of blender with rubber spatula, until sauce is almost smooth but still thick. If not using right away, cover and refrigerate up to 2 days; let sauce come to room temperature before serving. Makes about 1¼ cups.

Each tablespoon: About 20 calories, 1 g protein, 2 g carbohydrate, 1 g total fat (0 g saturated), 0 mg cholesterol, 60 mg sodium.

QUICK POACHED SALMON

A microwave, the ultimate kitchen convenience tool, cooks fish in mere minutes. The method couldn't be easier: Simply place *4 pieces (6 ounces each) center-cut salmon fillet* in 8" by 8" glass baking dish; sprinkle with *¼ teaspoon salt*. Add *¼ cup water* to dish. Cover and cook in microwave on High 8 minutes or until fish just turns opaque throughout and flakes easily when tested with a fork. With slotted wide metal spatula, remove salmon from baking dish, and drain over paper towels. Place salmon on platter; keep warm. Makes 4 main-dish servings.

Each serving: About 315 calories, 47 g protein, 0 g carbohydrate, 13 g total fat (2 g saturated), 84 mg cholesterol, 235 mg sodium.

Editor's tip This cooking method can be adapted for other varieties of fish, from cod to red snapper. Just bear in mind that the size and thickness of the fish will have an effect on the final cooking time. For an added hint of flavor, add parsley leaves, celery leaves, lemon slices, whole peppercorns, or carrot slices to the poaching liquid.

Roasted Scrod with Tomato Relish

PREP: 10 MINUTES • COOK: 20 MINUTES

1 can (28 ounces) plum tomatoes
3 teaspoons vegetable oil
1 small onion, diced
¼ cup red wine vinegar
2 tablespoons brown sugar
½ teaspoon salt
4 pieces scrod fillet (about 6 ounces each)
¼ teaspoon coarsely ground black pepper

1 Preheat oven to 450°F. Drain juice from tomatoes; reserve for use another day. Cut each tomato into quarters.

2 In 2-quart saucepan, heat 2 teaspoons vegetable oil over medium heat until hot. Add onion with 2 *tablespoons water* and cook until tender and golden, about 10 minutes. Stir in tomatoes, vinegar, brown sugar, and ¼ teaspoon salt; heat to boiling over high heat. Continue cooking over high heat, 10 to 15 minutes, stirring frequently, until relish thickens.

3 Meanwhile, place scrod in 9" by 9" glass baking dish; sprinkle with pepper, remaining 1 teaspoon vegetable oil, and ¼ teaspoon salt. Roast, uncovered, 12 to 15 minutes or until fish flakes easily when tested with a fork. Serve tomato relish over scrod. Makes 4 main-dish servings.

Each serving: About 230 calories, 32 g protein, 15 g carbohydrate, 5 g total fat (1 g saturated), 73 mg cholesterol, 590 mg sodium.

Lemon-Thyme Cod

PREP: 5 MINUTES • COOK: 10 MINUTES

We tossed lemon peel and thyme with a little flour and used the mixture to coat the cod in one easy step. Quickly sauté the fish in butter and serve with a squeeze of fresh lemon juice.

2 large lemons
2 tablespoons all-purpose flour
2 teaspoons chopped fresh thyme leaves, or
    ½ teaspoon dried thyme
½ teaspoon salt
¼ teaspoon coarsely ground black pepper

1 cod fillet (about 1¼ pounds), cut into 4 pieces
2 tablespoons margarine or butter

1 Grate peel from 1 lemon; cut remaining lemon into wedges.

2 On waxed paper, combine flour, thyme, grated lemon peel, salt, and pepper. Dip each piece of cod in flour mixture to coat.

3 In nonstick 12-inch skillet, heat margarine or butter over medium-high heat. Add cod and cook 10 minutes, turning once, until fish flakes easily when tested with a fork. Serve cod with lemon wedges. Makes 4 main-dish servings.

Each serving: About 190 calories, 26 g protein, 6 g carbohydrate, 7 g total fat (1 g saturated), 61 mg cholesterol, 430 mg sodium.

Chinese-Style Scrod Fillets

PREP: 5 MINUTES • BAKE: ABOUT 15 MINUTES

The fish is baked in a flavorful ginger-soy sauce that goes nicely over red-skinned potatoes.

4 pieces fresh or frozen (thawed) scrod fillet
    (6 ounces each)
3 tablespoons reduced-sodium soy sauce
2 tablespoons seasoned rice vinegar
1 tablespoon grated, peeled fresh ginger
2 green onions, sliced

1 Preheat oven to 450°F. With tweezers, remove any small bones from scrod.

2 In 8" by 8" glass baking dish or shallow 1½-quart casserole, combine soy sauce, rice vinegar, ginger, and green onions. Add scrod, turning to coat with mixture.

3 Cover baking dish with foil and bake scrod about 15 minutes or until it flakes easily when tested with a fork. Makes 4 main-dish servings.

Each serving: About 155 calories, 31 g protein, 5 g carbohydrate, 1 g total fat (0 g saturated), 73 mg cholesterol, 760 mg sodium.

Toasted Macadamia Mahi-Mahi

Toasted Macadamia Mahi-Mahi

PREP: 10 MINUTES PLUS MARINATING • BROIL: 8 MINUTES

The fish is marinated in a mixture of yogurt, pineapple, and rum, then broiled. If you can't find mahi-mahi, use ¾-inch-thick halibut steaks instead.

1 can (8 ounces) crushed pineapple in
   unsweetened pineapple juice
1 container (8 ounces) plain low-fat yogurt
3 tablespoons dark rum
2 pounds mahi-mahi fillets, cut into 8 pieces
⅓ cup macadamia nuts, chopped
¼ cup sweetened flaked coconut
½ teaspoon salt
Fresh pineapple leaves for garnish

1 In 13" by 9" glass baking dish, mix pineapple with its juice, yogurt, and rum. Add mahi-mahi to dish and turn to coat with pineapple marinade. Cover and refrigerate up to 1 hour.

2 Meanwhile, in small skillet, toast macadamia nuts and coconut over medium-low heat until golden, about 5 minutes, stirring; set aside.

3 Preheat broiler. Remove fish from marinade and place on greased rack in broiling pan; sprinkle with salt. With broiling pan 5 to 7 inches from source of heat, broil fish 4 minutes; do not turn over. Spoon some reserved marinade on top of fish and broil 4 minutes longer or until fish flakes easily when tested with a fork. Discard remaining marinade. Transfer fish to platter and sprinkle with coconut and macadamia nuts; garnish with pineapple leaves. Makes 4 main-course or 8 first-course servings.

Each main-course serving: About 420 calories, 46 g protein, 12 g carbohydrate, 20 g total fat (6 g saturated), 88 mg cholesterol, 530 mg sodium.

Lentils & Cod

The fennel and orange in this recipe bring home the flavors of Provence.

8 ounces dried lentils (1 cup)
1 tablespoon olive oil
2 medium carrots, diced
1 medium onion, diced
1 large celery stalk, diced
½ teaspoon herbes de Provence*
¼ teaspoon fennel seeds
3 strips orange peel (3" by 1" each)
3 garlic cloves, crushed with garlic press

1 can (14½ ounces) reduced-sodium chicken broth
¾ teaspoon salt
½ teaspoon coarsely ground black pepper
1 can (14½ ounces) tomatoes in puree
4 pieces cod fillet (6 ounces each)

1 Rinse lentils with cold running water and discard any stones or shriveled lentils. Set aside.

2 In 4-quart saucepan, heat olive oil over medium-high heat. Add carrots, onion, and celery, and cook until lightly browned, about 10 minutes, stirring occasionally.

3 Add herbes de Provence, fennel seeds, orange peel, and garlic; cook, stirring, 2 minutes.

BEST TUNA SALAD

Top to bottom: Mediterranean Tuna Salad, Curried Tuna Salad, Southwestern Tuna Salad

PREP: 15 MINUTES

Enjoy this simple family favorite in a sandwich with lettuce and tomato or on a bed of greens. For a change of pace, try one of our 3 new variations.

1 can (6 ounces) chunk-light tuna packed in water, drained
¼ cup finely chopped celery
3 tablespoons light mayonnaise
2 teaspoons fresh lemon juice
Baguette or other favorite bread

In small bowl, with fork, combine all ingredients except baguette. Cover and refrigerate if not serving right away. Serve on a baguette if you like. Makes about 1¼ cups or 2 main-dish servings.

Each serving without bread: About 170 calories, 19 g protein, 1 g carbohydrate, 11 g total fat (3 g saturated), 30 mg cholesterol, 415 mg sodium.

Curried Tuna Prepare Best Tuna Salad as above. Stir in *½ cup finely chopped Granny Smith apple* and *1 teaspoon curry powder.* Serve on raisin-walnut or sourdough bread if you like. Makes about 1½ cups or 2 main-dish servings. Each serving without bread: About 190 calories, 20 g protein, 7 g carbohydrate, 11 g total fat (3 g saturated), 30 mg cholesterol, 415 mg sodium.

Mediterranean Tuna Prepare Best Tuna Salad as above. Stir in *2 tablespoons capers*, chopped, and *¼ teaspoon freshly grated lemon peel.* Serve on Italian bread if you like. Makes about 1¼ cups or 2 main-dish servings. Each serving without bread: About 170 calories, 19 g protein, 2 g carbohydrate, 11 g total fat (3 g saturated), 30 mg cholesterol, 730 mg sodium.

Southwestern Tuna Prepare Best Tuna Salad as above. Stir in *2 tablespoons chopped fresh cilantro leaves* and *1 pickled jalapeño chile*, finely chopped. Serve rolled up in warm flour tortillas if you like. Makes about 1¼ cups or 2 main-dish servings. Each serving without tortilla: About 170 calories, 19 g protein, 2 g carbohydrate, 11 g total fat (3 g saturated), 30 mg cholesterol, 510 mg sodium.

4 Add lentils, chicken broth, and *2 cups water*; heat to boiling over high heat. Reduce heat to low; cover and simmer 20 minutes, stirring occasionally. Add ½ teaspoon salt, ¼ teaspoon pepper, and tomatoes with their puree, stirring and breaking up tomatoes with side of spoon. Heat to boiling over high heat. Reduce heat to low; cover and simmer 5 minutes longer.

5 Preheat oven to 400°F. Transfer lentil mixture to shallow 2½-quart casserole. Place cod fillets on top of lentil mixture; sprinkle cod with remaining ¼ teaspoon salt and ¼ teaspoon pepper. Cover casserole and bake 20 to 25 minutes, until fish flakes easily when tested with a fork and lentil mixture is heated through. Discard cooked orange peel. Makes 6 main-dish servings.

*If you can't find herbes de Provence, substitute ¼ teaspoon each dried thyme and rosemary, crushed, and increase fennel seeds to ½ teaspoon.

Each serving: About 325 calories, 32 g protein, 40 g carbohydrate, 4 g total fat (1 g saturated), 49 mg cholesterol, 760 mg sodium.

Pan-Fried Scrod with Wheat-Germ Crust

PREP: 10 MINUTES • COOK: ABOUT 8 TO 10 MINUTES

We dipped scrod fillets in a wheat-germ and bread-crumb coating, and pan-fried them until crisp and golden with hardly any fat!

¼ cup toasted wheat germ
¼ cup plain dried bread crumbs
½ teaspoon salt
¼ teaspoon ground red pepper (cayenne)
4 pieces scrod fillet (6 ounces each)
1 tablespoon Dijon mustard
Nonstick cooking spray
Chopped fresh parsley leaves for garnish

1 On waxed paper, combine wheat germ, bread crumbs, salt, and ground red pepper.

2 With tweezers, remove any bones from scrod fillets. Lightly brush 1 side of each fillet with mustard. Dip mustard-coated side of each fillet into wheat-germ mixture. Turn over and lightly brush other side with mustard; dip into wheat-germ mixture to coat.

3 Spray nonstick 12-inch skillet with nonstick cooking spray. Heat skillet over medium-high heat until

hot. Add scrod fillets and cook about 5 minutes per side or until fish flakes easily when tested with a fork and coating is golden brown. Garnish with parsley. Makes 4 main-dish servings.

Each serving: About 200 calories, 33 g protein, 9 g carbohydrate, 3 g total fat (1 g saturated), 73 mg cholesterol, 525 mg sodium.

Asian-Style Flounder Packets

PREP: 10 MINUTES • BAKE: 8 MINUTES

For flavorful fish—with no added fat—bake these fillets in foil (or parchment) packets. Serve with crusty dinner rolls.

2 large green onions
2 tablespoons soy sauce
2 tablespoons seasoned rice vinegar
4 flounder fillets (about 6 ounces each)
2 teaspoons grated, peeled fresh ginger

1 Cut tops of green onions crosswise into 2-inch pieces, then cut each piece lengthwise into thin strips; reserve for garnish. Thinly slice white part of green onions.

2 In small bowl, mix soy sauce and rice vinegar.

3 Preheat oven to 425°F. From roll of foil or cooking parchment, cut four 15" by 12" sheets.

4 Arrange 1 flounder fillet on half of each piece of foil; spread each with ½ teaspoon ginger. Spoon 1 tablespoon soy-sauce mixture over each flounder fillet; top with sliced green onions. Fold other half of foil over fish. To create sealed packets, fold edges of foil over about ½ inch all around, overlapping folds. Place packets in 15½" by 10½" jelly-roll pan. Bake packets 8 minutes.

5 To serve, with kitchen shears, cut an X in top of each packet to let steam escape before serving. (When packets are open, check that fish flakes easily when tested with a fork.) Garnish fish with reserved green-onion strips. Makes 4 main-dish servings.

Each serving: About 175 calories, 33 g protein, 5 g carbohydrate, 2 g total fat (1 g saturated), 90 mg cholesterol, 855 mg sodium.

Shrimp Paella

PREP: 45 MINUTES • BAKE: 30 MINUTES

The word *paella* refers to the large, two-handled, shallow pan that this traditional saffron-flavored Spanish dish is cooked in. It is typically made with medium-grain rice (try Spanish, Asian, or arborio), but regular long-grain rice may be substituted.

1 tablespoon olive oil
1 medium onion, finely chopped
1 medium red pepper, finely chopped
2 garlic cloves, minced
¼ teaspoon ground red pepper (cayenne)
1 can (14½ ounces) tomatoes in puree
½ cup dry white wine
1 ounce fully cooked chorizo sausage or
   pepperoni, diced (¼ cup)
2 bottles (8 ounces each) clam juice
2 cups medium-grain rice
1 teaspoon salt
⅛ teaspoon loosely packed saffron threads,
   crumbled
⅛ teaspoon dried thyme
1 bay leaf
1 package (10 ounces) frozen baby peas
1 pound large shrimp, shelled, deveined, and cut
   lengthwise in half
¼ cup chopped fresh parsley leaves
Lemon wedges

1 Preheat oven to 350°F. In deep 12-inch skillet with heat-safe handle, heat olive oil over medium heat. Add onion and red pepper, and cook until vegetables are tender, about 10 minutes, stirring occasionally. Stir in garlic and ground red pepper, and cook 30 seconds. Add tomatoes with their puree and white wine; cook, stirring frequently, until mixture is very dry, breaking up tomatoes with side of spoon.

2 Stir chorizo, clam juice, rice, salt, saffron, thyme, bay leaf, and 2¼ *cups water* into tomato mixture; heat to boiling over high heat. Cover skillet and bake 15 minutes.

3 Stir in frozen peas. Tuck shrimp into rice mixture; cover and bake 10 to 15 minutes longer, until shrimp turn opaque. Remove skillet from oven and let stand

5 minutes. Discard bay leaf. Sprinkle paella with parsley and serve with lemon wedges. Makes 6 main-dish servings.

Each serving: About 400 calories, 22 g protein, 64 g carbohydrate, 5 g total fat (1 g saturated), 101 mg cholesterol, 975 mg sodium.

Shrimp Curry & Rice

PREP: 10 MINUTES • COOK: ABOUT 20 MINUTES

This tastes as good as classic slow-cooking curry, but is ready in a flash. Serve with crisp flatbreads such as pappadams.

1 cup regular long-grain rice
2 teaspoons olive oil
1 medium onion, diced
1 tablespoon curry powder
1 teaspoon mustard seeds
1 pound shelled and deveined fresh or frozen
   (thawed) large shrimp with tail part of shell left
   on if you like
½ cup light coconut milk (not cream of coconut)
¾ cup frozen peas, thawed
1 cup frozen whole baby carrots, thawed
½ teaspoon salt
Chopped fresh cilantro leaves (optional)

1 Prepare rice as label directs but do not add margarine or butter.

2 Meanwhile, in nonstick 12-inch skillet, heat 1 teaspoon olive oil over medium-high heat until hot. Reduce heat to medium; add onion and cook 8 minutes or until tender. Add curry powder and cook 1 minute, stirring. Transfer onion mixture to medium bowl.

3 Increase heat to medium-high. In same skillet, heat remaining 1 teaspoon olive oil until hot. Add mustard seeds; cook 30 seconds, stirring. Add shrimp and cook 4 minutes or until opaque throughout, stirring frequently.

4 Return onion mixture to skillet; stir in coconut milk, peas, carrots, and salt; heat through. Serve over rice. Sprinkle with cilantro if you like. Makes 4 main-dish servings.

Each serving: About 390 calories, 30 g protein, 49 g carbohydrate, 8 g total fat (2 g saturated), 175 mg cholesterol, 490 mg sodium.

◄ *Curried Shrimp & Rice*

Scrambled Egg Foo Yong

This Chinese-American dish is traditionally made with eggs, vegetables, and chicken, pork, or ham, and cooked like a pancake. We prepared our easy version scrambled egg-style, and added fresh shrimp.

6 large eggs
2 teaspoons Asian sesame oil
1 teaspoon sugar
¾ teaspoon salt
1 tablespoon vegetable oil
1 medium celery stalk, cut lengthwise in half and thinly sliced
1 package (8 ounces) mushrooms, thinly sliced
3 green onions, thinly sliced
2 tablespoons grated, peeled fresh ginger
8 ounces medium shrimp, shelled and deveined, and each cut crosswise in half
Soy sauce (optional)

1 In large bowl, with wire whisk, mix eggs, sesame oil, sugar, and salt until blended; set aside.

2 In nonstick 10-inch skillet, heat vegetable oil over medium-high heat. Add celery and cook 2 minutes, stirring occasionally. Add mushrooms, green onions, and ginger, and cook until mushrooms are light brown, about 10 minutes. Stir in shrimp and cook 1 minute.

3 Pour egg mixture into skillet. Reduce heat to low and cook, stirring occasionally, about 4 minutes, or until shrimp turn opaque throughout and eggs are just set. Serve with soy sauce if you like. Makes 4 main-dish servings.

Each serving: About 240 calories, 20 g protein, 7 g carbohydrate, 14 g total fat (3 g saturated), 390 mg cholesterol, 575 mg sodium.

Lobster Newburg

Here is a lighter take on the classic 1950's-style Lobster Newburg. We cut out 1 cup heavy cream, 3 egg yolks, and 3 tablespoons margarine or butter, but it still tastes heavenly.

3 tablespoons margarine or butter
1 package (10 ounces) medium mushrooms, each cut into quarters
¼ teaspoon salt
2 tablespoons all-purpose flour
¼ teaspoon paprika
Pinch ground nutmeg
3 tablespoons dry sherry
1 cup chicken broth
1 cup heavy or whipping cream
¾ pound cooked lobster meat, cut into small chunks*
8 slices white bread, toasted and each cut diagonally in half
2 tablespoons fresh parsley leaves, chopped

1 In 12-inch skillet, melt 1 tablespoon margarine or butter over medium-high heat. Add mushrooms and ⅛ teaspoon salt, and cook 10 minutes or until mushrooms are golden, stirring occasionally. Transfer mushrooms to small bowl.

2 In same skillet, melt remaining 2 tablespoons margarine or butter. Reduce heat to low; add flour, paprika, and nutmeg, and cook 1 minute, stirring. Add sherry and cook 30 seconds. Increase heat to medium; gradually stir in broth and cream, and cook, stirring, until mixture boils and thickens slightly. Stir in cooked lobster, mushrooms, and remaining ⅛ teaspoon salt, and heat through.

3 To serve, arrange toast on 8 small plates. Spoon lobster mixture over toast; sprinkle with parsley. Makes 8 first-course servings.

*We cooked 2½ pounds frozen lobster tails, which yielded ¾ pound of meat. Or, you can buy fresh or frozen cooked lobster meat from your fish store or supermarket.

Each serving: About 270 calories, 12 g protein, 17 g carbohydrate, 17 g total fat (8 g saturated), 69 mg cholesterol, 505 mg sodium.

GRILLING

Grilled Flatbread

PREP: 15 MINUTES PLUS RISING
GRILL: ABOUT 5 MINUTES PER FLATBREAD

Cooking this bread on the grill gives it a unique look and imparts a rustic flavor. Serve simply with herb-infused olive oil and fresh herbs, or top with our chopped salad (at right) or *zahtar* spice blend (see Flatbread with Zahtar, page 110).

1 package active dry yeast
1 teaspoon sugar
About 4 cups all-purpose flour
About 3 tablespoons olive oil
2 teaspoons salt

1 In large bowl, combine yeast, sugar, and ¼ *cup warm water* (105° to 115°F.). Let stand until yeast mixture foams, about 5 minutes. With wooden spoon, stir in 1½ cups flour, 2 tablespoons olive oil, salt, and *1 cup warm water* until combined. With spoon, gradually stir in 2 cups flour. With floured hand, knead mixture in bowl to combine.

2 Turn dough onto lightly floured surface and knead until smooth and elastic, about 10 minutes, working in more flour (about ½ cup) while kneading.

3 Shape dough into a ball and place in greased large bowl, turning dough over to grease top. Cover and let rise in warm place (80° to 85°F.) until doubled, about 1 hour. (After dough has risen, if not using dough right away, punch down and leave in bowl, covered loosely with greased plastic wrap. Refrigerate until ready to use, up to 24 hours. When ready to use, follow directions below.)

4 Punch down dough. Turn dough onto lightly floured surface. Cover and let rest 15 minutes.

5 Shape dough into 4 balls. On lightly floured surface, with floured rolling pin, roll 1 dough ball at a time into a 12-inch round about ⅛ inch thick. (The diameter or shape of the round is not as important as an even thickness.) Place rounds on greased large cookie sheets; lightly brush tops with some remaining olive oil.

6 With hands, place 1 round at a time, greased side down, on grill over medium heat. Grill 2 to 3 minutes until grill marks appear on underside and dough stiffens (dough may puff slightly). Brush top with some olive oil. With tongs, turn bread over and grill 2 to 3 minutes longer, until grill marks appear on underside and bread is cooked through. Transfer flatbread to tray; keep warm.

7 Repeat as above with remaining dough rounds. Makes 4 flatbreads or 12 accompaniment servings.

Each serving: About 185 calories, 5 g protein, 32 g carbohydrate, 4 g total fat (1 g saturated), 0 mg cholesterol, 355 mg sodium.

Flatbread with Salad

PREP: 20 MINUTES PLUS TIME TO PREPARE FLATBREADS

Try this salad "pizza" as an alternative to the usual tomato-and-cheese kind. It's especially good because it starts with our crusty Grilled Flatbread (at left).

Grilled Flatbread (at left)
2 tablespoons extravirgin olive oil
2 tablespoons red wine vinegar
1 teaspoon sugar
1 teaspoon Dijon mustard
¼ teaspoon salt
⅛ teaspoon coarsely ground black pepper
6 cups salad greens, such as radicchio, endive, and arugula, cut into ½-inch pieces
2 ripe medium tomatoes, cut into ½-inch pieces
1 small cucumber, peeled and cut into ½-inch pieces

1 Prepare Grilled Flatbread through step 5.

2 About 10 minutes before grilling flatbread, prepare salad topping: In large bowl, with wire whisk, mix olive oil, vinegar, sugar, mustard, salt, and pepper until dressing is blended.

3 Add salad greens, tomatoes, and cucumber to dressing in bowl; toss to coat well. Set salad aside.

4 Grill flatbreads as in step 6 of flatbread recipe.

5 To serve, top each flatbread with about 2 cups salad. Cut each round into quarters. Makes 8 first-course or 4 main-dish servings.

Each first-course serving: About 310 calories, 8 g protein, 53 g carbohydrate, 7 g total fat (1 g saturated), 0 mg cholesterol, 625 mg sodium.

Flatbread with Salad ➤

Flatbread with Zahtar

PREP: 30 MINUTES PLUS TIME TO PREPARE FLATBREADS

Top our home-grilled flatbread with this popular Middle Eastern spice blend.

Grilled Flatbread (page 108)
2 large lemons
½ cup sesame seeds, toasted
⅓ cup olive oil
3 tablespoons chopped fresh parsley leaves
2 teaspoons dried thyme
½ teaspoon salt
Pinch ground red pepper (cayenne)
1 garlic clove, crushed with garlic press

1 Prepare Grilled Flatbread recipe through step 4.

2 While flatbread dough is resting, prepare topping: From both lemons, grate 1 tablespoon peel. From 1 lemon, squeeze 2 tablespoons juice. In small bowl, mix lemon juice and lemon peel with remaining ingredients until combined. Set *zahtar* mixture aside.

3 Roll dough as in step 5 of flatbread recipe.

4 Grill flatbreads as in step 6 of flatbread recipe, except after turning each round over, do not brush with oil. With small metal spatula or spoon, spread a scant ¼ cup *zahtar* mixture on top of each flatbread. Grill 2 to 3 minutes longer, until grill marks appear on underside and bread is cooked through. Repeat with remaining dough and *zahtar* mixture.

5 To serve, cut each flatbread into 6 wedges. Makes 12 appetizer servings.

Each serving: About 265 calories, 6 g protein, 34 g carbohydrate, 12 g total fat (2 g saturated), 0 mg cholesterol, 445 mg sodium.

Glazed Japanese Eggplant

PREP: 15 MINUTES • GRILL: ABOUT 10 MINUTES

Make sure to buy Japanese eggplants for this recipe—they're purple and usually long and slender.

EVERYBODY LOVES A COOKOUT

Nothing compares to the taste of food roasted in the open air—that's why grilling is a favorite sport (and way of life) from Argentina to Portugal. In America, traditions range from pulled pork on a bun (North Carolina) to barbecued brisket with a tomato-based sauce (Texas). Here, a look at different styles beyond our shores:

• *Afghanistan* Meat is usually marinated for hours in yogurt with onion, garlic, chiles, red pepper flakes, and cumin before roasting. Common accompaniments: pickles and lavash (flatbread).

• *Argentina* At a traditional midday *asado* (meat roast), the fire is lit by dawn, and suckling pigs and sides of ribs are cooked on stakes around the fire. Argentine cooks also brown sausages, innards, and steaks over a *parrilla*, a grill set over coals.

• *Brazil* Cooking to perfection over a fire is big business here; the method is called *churrasco*. At Brazilian *churrascarias*, waiters circulate with swordlike spits of meat to serve tableside.

• *France* The French rarely grill at restaurants, but they're avid about it at home. Many use grapevines for the fire to impart a light, sweet flavor. One French farmhouse favorite: thinly sliced lamb grilled until golden outside, rare inside.

• *Indonesia* Satés, cubed meat on sticks, are served everywhere. They're made with meat, fish, or poultry, and eaten as a snack or a full meal, often with a peanut-based dipping sauce.

• *Jamaica* Jerk, Jamaican barbecue, is prepared by marinating beef, pork, goat, or chicken in a spicy mixture and roasting it until brown and crusty.

• *Japan* Yakitori parlors—publike barbecue places with charcoal grills—offer a wide selection, from chicken and mushrooms to quail eggs. Japanese grilling is on the healthy side: Meats are served in moderate portions, with broth-based sauces.

• *Morocco* Most Moroccans feast on grilled food when they're in a hurry or on a budget. Cooked in public squares, markets, and waterfront restaurants, lamb and seafood are popular.

• *Portugal* Fishermen char fresh catches like tuna and sardines right on the beach.

6 medium Japanese eggplants (about 5 ounces each), each cut lengthwise in half
1 tablespoon dark brown sugar
1 tablespoon minced, peeled fresh ginger
3 tablespoons soy sauce
1 tablespoon seasoned rice vinegar
½ teaspoon Asian sesame oil
¼ teaspoon cornstarch
3 garlic cloves, crushed with garlic press
4 teaspoons vegetable oil

1 With knife, score cut side of each eggplant half with several ¼-inch-deep parallel slits, being careful not to cut all the way through to skin. Repeat with a second set of slits diagonal to the first.

2 In small bowl, with fork, mix brown sugar, ginger, soy sauce, vinegar, sesame oil, cornstarch, garlic, and 3 *tablespoons water*.

3 Brush cut side of eggplant halves with vegetable oil. With tongs, place eggplant halves on grill, cut side down, over medium heat. Grill eggplant 5 minutes, or until lightly browned.

4 Fold 34" by 18" sheet of heavy-duty foil crosswise in half. Place eggplant halves on double thickness of foil. Pour soy-sauce mixture over eggplant halves, and bring long sides of foil up and fold several times to seal well. Fold over ends to seal in juices.

5 Place foil packet on grill over medium heat, and cook 5 minutes or until eggplant is soft. Makes 6 accompaniment servings.

Each serving: About 90 calories, 2 g protein, 14 g carbohydrate, 4 g total fat (0 g saturated), 0 mg cholesterol, 585 mg sodium.

Grilled Eggplant Parmesan

PREP: 25 MINUTES • GRILL: 9 TO 12 MINUTES

1 medium-large eggplant (about 1½ pounds), cut lengthwise into 4 slices
1 tablespoon plus 1 teaspoon olive oil
½ teaspoon salt
¼ teaspoon coarsely ground black pepper
4 ounces mozzarella cheese, shredded (1 cup)
¼ cup grated Parmesan cheese
½ cup loosely packed fresh basil leaves, sliced
2 medium tomatoes, each cut into 4 slices

1 Lightly brush eggplant slices with oil and sprinkle with salt and pepper. In small bowl, mix mozzarella cheese, Parmesan cheese, and basil; set aside.

2 Place eggplant slices on grill over medium heat. Cook 8 to 10 minutes, until tender and lightly browned, turning once. Top eggplant slices with tomato slices and cheese mixture. Cover grill and cook 1 to 2 minutes, until cheese melts and tomato slices are warm. Makes 4 main-dish servings.

Each serving: About 205 calories, 10 g protein, 14 g carbohydrate, 13 g total fat (6 g saturated), 27 mg cholesterol, 500 mg sodium.

Charred-Corn & Bean Salad

PREP: 25 MINUTES • GRILL: 10 TO 15 MINUTES

A fresh mix of sweet corn, red onion, and pinto beans tossed with a zesty vinaigrette.

3 medium ears corn, husks and silk removed
1 small red onion, cut into 4 slices
1 can (15 to 19 ounces) pinto or small pink beans, rinsed and drained
1 jalapeño chile, seeded and minced
½ cup loosely packed fresh cilantro leaves, chopped
3 tablespoons fresh lime juice
1 tablespoon olive oil
¾ teaspoon salt
¼ teaspoon coarsely ground black pepper

1 Place corn and onion slices on grill over medium-high heat. Cook corn 10 to 15 minutes, turning occasionally, until golden. Cook onion 10 minutes, turning once, until tender and golden. Transfer grilled vegetables to cutting board.

2 Cut corn kernels from cobs and dice onion. In large bowl, mix corn and onion with remaining ingredients. Cover and refrigerate if not serving right away. Makes about 4 cups or 6 accompaniment servings.

Each serving: About 140 calories, 6 g protein, 25 g carbohydrate, 3 g total fat (0 g saturated), 0 mg cholesterol, 500 mg sodium.

Chiles Relleños

PREP: 20 MINUTES • GRILL: ABOUT 25 MINUTES

If you prefer hotter flavor: After grilling and before filling chiles, remove seeds and veins but don't rinse the insides. Serve chiles with salsa if you like.

6 medium poblano chiles (about 4 ounces each)
6 ounces Monterey Jack cheese, shredded
   (1½ cups)
1 cup corn kernels (cut from 2 medium ears of
   corn)
½ cup loosely packed fresh cilantro leaves,
   chopped

1 Place whole poblano chiles on grill over medium heat and cook, turning occasionally, until blistered and blackened on all sides, 10 to 15 minutes.

2 Transfer chiles to large sheet of foil. Wrap foil around chiles and allow to steam at room temperature 15 minutes or until cool enough to handle.

3 While chiles are steaming, in medium bowl, combine cheese, corn, and cilantro.

4 Remove chiles from foil. Cut 2-inch lengthwise slit in side of each chile, being careful not to cut through top or bottom. Under running cold water, gently peel off skin. Remove seeds and veins from opening; rinse with running water for a milder flavor. Pat chiles dry with paper towels.

5 With spoon, fill each chile with about ½ cup cheese mixture. Gently reshape chiles to close opening. Place 3 filled chiles in single layer on each of two 18" by 18" sheets of heavy-duty foil. Bring 2 sides of foil up and fold several times to seal well. Fold over ends to seal in juices. (Recipe can be prepared to this point and refrigerated up to 6 hours before grilling.)

6 Place foil packet on grill over medium heat and cook 10 minutes to heat chiles and melt cheese. Makes 6 accompaniment servings.

Each serving: About 175 calories, 10 g protein, 16 g carbohydrate, 9 g total fat (6 g saturated), 25 mg cholesterol, 165 mg sodium.

Veggie Kabobs

PREP: 15 MINUTES • GRILL: 15 TO 20 MINUTES

Balsamic vinaigrette adds zip to an assortment of colorful vegetables.

3 small zucchini (about 6 ounces each), cut
   diagonally into 1-inch chunks
3 small yellow summer squash (about 6 ounces
   each), cut diagonally into 1-inch chunks
6 plum tomatoes (about 1¼ pounds), each cut
   lengthwise in half
1 tablespoon brown sugar
1 tablespoon balsamic vinegar
½ teaspoon salt
⅛ teaspoon coarsely ground black pepper
⅛ teaspoon ground cinnamon
3 tablespoons olive oil
¾ cup loosely packed fresh basil leaves, thinly
   sliced

1 Onto 6 long metal skewers, alternately thread zucchini chunks, yellow-squash chunks, and tomato halves, leaving about ⅛ inch space between each

Veggie Kabobs

vegetable piece to allow even cooking. (Threading zucchini and squash through skin side gives vegetables more stability on skewers.)

2 In cup, combine brown sugar, vinegar, salt, pepper, cinnamon, and 2 tablespoons olive oil. Brush kabobs with remaining 1 tablespoon olive oil.

3 Place kabobs on grill over medium heat; cook 15 to 20 minutes, until vegetables are browned and tender. Turn kabobs occasionally and brush vegetables with some vinaigrette during last 3 minutes of cooking.

4 To serve, arrange kabobs on large platter; drizzle with any remaining vinaigrette and sprinkle with basil. Makes 6 accompaniment servings.

Each serving: About 120 calories, 3 g protein, 13 g carbohydrate, 7 g total fat (1 g saturated), 0 mg cholesterol, 190 mg sodium.

Potato Packet with Herbs

PREP: 15 MINUTES • GRILL: 30 MINUTES

Toss red-potato chunks in a parsley and lemon-butter sauce, then wrap in foil and cook until fork-tender.

2 tablespoons margarine or butter
1 tablespoon minced fresh parsley leaves
½ teaspoon salt
½ teaspoon freshly grated lemon peel
⅛ teaspoon coarsely ground black pepper
1½ pounds small red potatoes, each cut in half,
   or into quarters if large

1 In 3-quart saucepan, melt margarine or butter with parsley, salt, lemon peel, and pepper. Remove saucepan from heat; add potatoes and toss to coat.

2 Fold 30" by 18" sheet of heavy-duty foil crosswise in half. Place potato mixture on double thickness of foil and bring long sides of foil up and fold several times to seal well. Fold over ends to seal in juices.

3 Place foil packet on grill over medium heat and cook 30 minutes or until potatoes are fork-tender. Makes about 4 cups or 6 accompaniment servings.

Each serving: About 120 calories, 3 g protein, 19 g carbohydrate, 4 g total fat (1 g saturated), 0 mg cholesterol, 235 mg sodium.

Grilled Polenta with Fontina

PREP: 10 MINUTES • GRILL: ABOUT 10 MINUTES

This easy side dish begins with slices of precooked polenta from the supermarket. We added melted cheese and diced tomatoes for a tasty topping.

2 ripe medium tomatoes, diced
2 tablespoons chopped fresh parsley leaves
¼ teaspoon salt
⅛ teaspoon coarsely ground black pepper
1 package (24 ounces) precooked polenta, cut
   into 12 slices
1 tablespoon olive oil
2 ounces Fontina cheese, shredded (½ cup)

1 In small bowl, combine tomatoes, parsley, salt, and pepper; set aside.

2 Brush both sides of polenta slices with olive oil. Place polenta on grill over medium heat and cook 5 minutes or until underside is golden. Turn slices over and top with Fontina cheese. Cook polenta about 5 minutes longer or just until cheese melts.

3 Transfer polenta slices to platter and top with tomato mixture. Makes 6 accompaniment servings.

Each serving: About 145 calories, 5 g protein, 19 g carbohydrate, 5 g total fat (2 g saturated), 11 mg cholesterol, 520 mg sodium.

Five-Spice Shrimp & Scallops

An intriguing mix of sweet and spicy flavors.

1 tablespoon brown sugar
1 tablespoon soy sauce
1 tablespoon vegetable oil
2 teaspoons Chinese five-spice powder
1¼ teaspoons salt
¼ teaspoon coarsely ground black pepper
1 pound large shrimp, shelled and deveined
¾ pound sea scallops

1 In large bowl, mix brown sugar, soy sauce, vegetable oil, Chinese five-spice powder, salt, and pepper; add shrimp and scallops, tossing to coat.

2 Onto 6 long metal skewers, alternately thread shrimp and scallops. Place skewers on grill over medium heat; cook 10 to 12 minutes, until shrimp and scallops turn opaque throughout, turning skewers occasionally and brushing shrimp and scallops with any remaining spice mixture halfway through cooking. Makes 6 main-dish servings.

Each serving: About 155 calories, 26 g protein, 4 g carbohydrate, 4 g total fat (0 g saturated), 150 mg cholesterol, 905 mg sodium.

FOOD EDITOR'S TIP

Q So many of the recipes I come across use Asian fish sauce. What exactly is it, and how long will it keep?

A Although somewhat new to American palates, fish sauce (*nuoc nam* or *nam pla*) has been around since the Roman Empire. A transparent brownish liquid, it's made from salted, fermented fish and has a pungent odor that mellows when mixed with other ingredients, leaving a sweetish aftertaste. Basically used as a condiment and flavoring, like soy sauce, it's a key ingredient in Thai and Vietnamese dishes. It's sold in large bottles, but keeps almost indefinitely without refrigeration (store in a cool place)—so you'll have plenty of time to use it in recipes, including our Thai Snapper (at right) and Thai Salad (page 63).

Thai Snapper

Tender fillets seasoned with lime and ginger and cooked in a foil packet.

3 tablespoons fresh lime juice
1 tablespoon Asian fish sauce
1 tablespoon olive oil
1 teaspoon grated, peeled fresh ginger
½ teaspoon sugar
½ teaspoon minced garlic
4 red snapper fillets (6 ounces each)
1 large carrot, cut into 2¼-inch-long matchstick-thin strips
1 large green onion, thinly sliced
¼ cup packed fresh cilantro leaves

1 In small bowl, mix lime juice, fish sauce, olive oil, ginger, sugar, and garlic.

2 From roll of foil, cut four 16" by 12" sheets. Fold each sheet crosswise in half and open up again.

3 Place 1 red snapper fillet, skin side down, on half of each piece of foil. Top with carrot, green onion, then cilantro leaves. Spoon the lime-juice mixture over the snapper and vegetables. Fold other half of foil over fish. Fold and crimp foil edges all around to create 4 sealed packets.

4 Place packets on grill over medium heat; cook 8 minutes.

5 To serve: With kitchen shears, cut an X in top of each packet so steam can escape. (When packets are open, check that fish flakes when tested with a fork.) Makes 4 main-dish servings.

Each serving: About 220 calories, 36 g protein, 5 g carbohydrate, 6 g total fat (1 g saturated), 62 mg cholesterol, 445 mg sodium.

Grilled Salmon with Roasted-Tomato Relish

PREP: 30 MINUTES PLUS OVERNIGHT TO DRY TOMATOES
ROAST: 2 HOURS 40 MINUTES • GRILL/BROIL: 10 MINUTES

Spoon the delicious relish—made with homemade oven-dried tomatoes, roasted garlic, olives, and lemon peel—over tender salmon fillets.

1 large head garlic
1 teaspoon sugar
1 teaspoon dried thyme
½ teaspoon salt
2 tablespoons plus 1½ teaspoons extravirgin olive oil
12 plum tomatoes (3 pounds), each cut lengthwise in half and seeded
½ cup oil-cured olives, pitted and coarsely chopped
2 tablespoons chopped fresh parsley leaves
1 tablespoon balsamic vinegar
½ teaspoon grated fresh lemon peel
8 pieces (6 ounces each) salmon fillet
Lemon-peel strips for garnish

1 Preheat oven to 250°F. Remove 2 garlic cloves from head of garlic and mince; reserve remaining head to roast next day. Line large cookie sheet with kitchen parchment or waxed paper. In cup, mix sugar, thyme, salt, minced garlic, and 2 tablespoons olive oil. Arrange tomatoes, cut side up, on cookie sheet and brush tomatoes with olive-oil mixture. Roast 2 hours. Turn off oven and leave tomatoes in oven overnight to dry.

2 The following day, remove tomatoes from oven. Preheat oven to 425°F. Remove any loose papery skin from head of garlic, leaving head intact. Cut top from head, just to tip of cloves (do not cut into cloves). Place head on sheet of heavy-duty foil; drizzle with ½ teaspoon olive oil. Loosely wrap foil around garlic, being careful that seam is folded to seal in oil. Roast garlic 40 minutes or until tender. Transfer package from oven to plate. Cool slightly.

3 While garlic is roasting, cut tomatoes into ¼-inch-thick slices; place in medium bowl.

4 When garlic is cool enough to handle, with tip of knife, remove garlic cloves from skins and place in bowl with tomato slices. Add olives, parsley, vinegar, and grated lemon peel; mix well. Set tomato relish aside.

5 With tweezers, remove any small bones from salmon; brush skinless side only with remaining 1 teaspoon olive oil. Place salmon, skin side down, on grill over medium heat; cook 8 to 10 minutes, without turning, until just opaque throughout.

6 To serve, spoon tomato relish over salmon. Garnish with lemon-peel strips. Makes 8 main-dish servings.

Each serving: About 290 calories, 36 g protein, 8 g carbohydrate, 13 g total fat (2 g saturated), 90 mg cholesterol, 520 mg sodium.

Spiced Salmon Steaks

PREP: 10 MINUTES • GRILL: 8 MINUTES

Juicy summer-ripe red and yellow tomatoes are a cool and easy go-along for this entrée.

1 tablespoon chili powder
2 teaspoons light brown sugar
1 teaspoon ground cumin
1 teaspoon dried thyme
1 teaspoon salt
2 teaspoons olive oil
4 salmon steaks, ¾ inch thick (about 8 ounces each)
Lemon wedges (optional)

1 In cup, mix chili powder, brown sugar, cumin, thyme, salt, and olive oil.

2 With tweezers, remove any small bones from salmon steaks.

3 With hands, rub spice mixture over both sides of salmon steaks. Place salmon on grill over medium heat. Cook about 8 minutes or until salmon flakes easily when tested with a fork, turning once. Serve with lemon wedges if you like. Makes 4 main-dish servings.

Each serving: About 295 calories, 36 g protein, 4 g carbohydrate, 14 g total fat (2 g saturated), 100 mg cholesterol, 635 mg sodium.

Honey-Lime Salmon

PREP: 10 MINUTES • GRILL: ABOUT 10 MINUTES

Rich salmon fillets stand up to an assertively spiced rub. On the side, serve coleslaw dressed with a vinaigrette.

3 tablespoons honey
1 teaspoon ground cumin
1 teaspoon ground coriander
¾ teaspoon salt
¾ teaspoon grated fresh lime peel
¼ teaspoon coarsely ground black pepper
4 pieces salmon fillet, ¾ inch thick (about
    6 ounces each), skin removed
3 tablespoons chopped fresh cilantro leaves
Lime wedges

1 In cup, mix honey, cumin, coriander, salt, lime peel, pepper, and *1 teaspoon very hot water* until blended.

2 With tweezers, remove any bones from salmon. With hands, rub honey-spice mixture all over salmon pieces.

3 Place salmon on grill over medium heat and cook 4 minutes. With wide metal spatula, carefully turn salmon over; cook 4 to 5 minutes longer, just until salmon turns opaque throughout and flakes easily when tested with a fork.

4 Sprinkle salmon with cilantro and serve with lime wedges. Makes 4 main-dish servings.

Each serving: About 330 calories, 30 g protein, 13 g carbohydrate, 17 g total fat (3 g saturated), 86 mg cholesterol, 485 mg sodium.

Grilled Salmon with Mustard-Dill Sauce

PREP: 15 MINUTES • GRILL: ABOUT 8 MINUTES

We brought the flavors of Swedish gravlax to the grill. Traditional gravlax is made by marinating raw salmon in a savory mixture of fresh dill, sugar, and salt, then serving it with a sweet mustard sauce.

GRILLED SALMON:
2 tablespoons sugar
1 tablespoon chopped fresh dill
2 tablespoons white wine vinegar
¾ teaspoon salt
¼ teaspoon coarsely ground black pepper
4 salmon steaks, ¾ inch thick (about 6 ounces
    each)

MUSTARD-DILL SAUCE:
3 tablespoons chopped fresh dill
3 tablespoons Dijon mustard
3 tablespoons light mayonnaise
2 teaspoons sugar
4 teaspoons white wine vinegar
¼ teaspoon coarsely ground black pepper

1 Prepare Grilled Salmon: In medium bowl, mix sugar, dill, vinegar, salt, and pepper.

2 With tweezers, remove any bones from salmon. Add salmon to bowl with sugar mixture, turning to coat; let stand 10 minutes.

3 Meanwhile, prepare Mustard-Dill Sauce: In small bowl, mix all sauce ingredients.

4 Place salmon on grill over medium heat and cook 4 minutes. With wide metal spatula, carefully turn salmon over; cook 4 to 5 minutes longer, just until salmon turns opaque throughout and flakes easily when tested with a fork. Serve with mustard sauce. Makes 4 main-dish servings.

Each serving: About 270 calories, 30 g protein, 13 g carbohydrate, 11 g total fat (1 g saturated), 80 mg cholesterol, 850 mg sodium.

◄ *Honey-Lime Salmon*

Asian Tuna Burgers

PREP: 15 MINUTES • GRILL: 6 TO 7 MINUTES

Finely chop fish by hand for a light texture; using a food processor will make the patties dense and dry. Serve with pickled ginger, with or without a bun.

1 tuna steak (about 1 pound)
1 green onion, thinly sliced
2 tablespoons reduced-sodium soy sauce
1 teaspoon grated, peeled fresh ginger
¼ teaspoon coarsely ground black pepper
¼ cup plain dried bread crumbs
2 tablespoons sesame seeds
Nonstick cooking spray

1 With large chef's knife, finely chop tuna. Place tuna in medium bowl and mix in green onion, soy sauce, ginger, and pepper until combined.

2 Shape tuna mixture into four 3-inch round patties (mixture will be very soft and moist).

3 On waxed paper, combine bread crumbs and sesame seeds. With hands, carefully press patties, 1 at a time, into bread-crumb mixture, turning to coat both sides. Spray both sides of tuna patties with nonstick spray.

GAS VS. CHARCOAL: WHICH COOKS BETTER?

Most food experts—including the 8 GH editors who participated in this blind taste panel—assume that meat and chicken come out better grilled over charcoal than flipped over gas. The thinking is that charcoal imparts a smoky flavor that you just can't get from a gas-generated flame.

But surprise: When our pros sampled hamburgers and skinless, boneless chicken breasts cooked to the same degree of doneness on both a charcoal grill and a gas one, they couldn't detect a difference in flavor. The thick sirloin steaks were another story; the charcoal method won unanimously. The reason? The steaks took twice as long to cook, so they had more time to pick up the fiery flavor. The charbroiled steak was crustier outside, more tender inside, and just plain tasted more like real barbecue to our pros. So while a charcoal fire may take longer to coax than a gas one, if you're a steak lover, it's time well spent.

4 Place tuna patties on grill over medium heat and cook 6 to 7 minutes, until browned on the outside and still slightly pink in the center for medium-rare or until of desired doneness, turning patties over once. Makes 4 main-dish servings.

Each serving: About 220 calories, 29 g protein, 7 g carbohydrate, 9 g total fat (2 g saturated), 45 mg cholesterol, 415 mg sodium.

Turkey on the Grill

PREP: 15 MINUTES • GRILL: 2¼ TO 3 HOURS

This easy method yields tender meat, crispy skin, and a smoky flavor. There's no turning or basting, and little fuss. (Note: When turkey is cooked on a covered grill, there may be a narrow rosy-pink band of meat just under the skin. This doesn't mean the meat is undercooked—it's a result of charcoal combustion reacting with the pigment in the meat.)

1 fresh or frozen (thawed) turkey (12 pounds)
2 tablespoons vegetable oil
2 teaspoons dried sage leaves
2 teaspoons dried thyme
2 teaspoons salt
½ teaspoon coarsely ground black pepper

1 To prepare coals: In bottom of covered charcoal grill, with vents open and grill uncovered, ignite 60 charcoal briquettes (not self-starting). Allow briquettes to burn 30 minutes or until all coals are covered with a thin coating of gray ash. Push hot briquettes to 2 sides of grill; place sturdy disposable foil pan (about 13" by 9" by 2") between coals.

2 Meanwhile, remove giblets and neck from turkey; refrigerate for soup another day. Rinse turkey with cold running water and drain well. Fasten neck skin to back with 1 or 2 skewers. With turkey breast side up, fold wings under back of turkey so they stay in place. Depending on brand of turkey, with string, tie legs and tail together, or push drumsticks under band of skin, or use stuffing clamp. In cup, mix vegetable oil, sage, thyme, salt, and pepper; rub mixture all over turkey.

3 To grill: Place turkey, breast side up, on cooking grate directly over foil pan (to catch drips). Cover grill and roast turkey 2¼ to 3 hours (about 11 to 13 minutes per pound for unstuffed bird), adding 8 to 9 more briquettes to each side of pan every hour to maintain a grill temperature of 325°F. on oven or grill thermometer. Turkey is done when thigh temperature reaches 180° to 185°F. on meat thermometer and juices run clear when thickest part of thigh is pierced with tip of knife.

4 When turkey is done, place on warm platter; let stand 15 minutes to set juices for easier carving. Carefully remove drip pan from grill. If you like, skim fat from drippings and serve drippings along with turkey. Makes 12 main-dish servings.

Each serving of turkey without skin or drippings: About 330 calories, 57 g protein, 0 g carbohydrate, 10 g total fat (3 g saturated), 149 mg cholesterol, 250 mg sodium.

Mediterranean Chicken Sandwiches

PREP: 25 MINUTES • GRILL: 10 TO 12 MINUTES

1 teaspoon fennel seeds
½ teaspoon dried thyme
½ teaspoon salt
¼ teaspoon coarsely ground black pepper
4 medium skinless, boneless chicken-breast halves (about 1¼ pounds)
¼ cup Kalamata olives, pitted and minced
2 tablespoons mayonnaise
1 loaf (8 ounces) Italian bread
2 small tomatoes, each cut into 4 slices

1 In mortar with pestle, crush fennel seeds with thyme, salt, and pepper. Rub both sides of chicken breasts with fennel-seed mixture; set aside.

2 In small bowl, mix olives and mayonnaise. Cut bread crosswise into 4 equal pieces, then cut each piece horizontally in half. Spread olive mixture evenly on cut sides of bread; set aside.

3 Place chicken on grill over medium heat and cook 10 to 12 minutes, turning once, until juices run clear when thickest part is pierced with tip of knife. Transfer chicken to cutting board.

4 To assemble sandwiches, slice chicken breasts crosswise into ¼-inch-thick slices. On bottom halves of bread, layer sliced chicken and tomatoes. Replace top halves of bread. Makes 4 sandwiches.

Each sandwich: About 425 calories, 41 g protein, 32 g carbohydrate, 15 g total fat (3 g saturated), 99 mg cholesterol, 850 mg sodium.

Grilled Chicken with Red-Potato Salad

PREP: 20 MINUTES • GRILL: ABOUT 8 MINUTES

Boneless breasts are dipped in lime-teriyaki sauce and quickly grilled, then paired with guilt-free potato salad.

1½ pounds medium red potatoes
2 tablespoons light mayonnaise
2 tablespoons low-fat (1%) milk
1 tablespoon distilled white vinegar
1 teaspoon Dijon mustard
1 teaspoon salt
½ teaspoon coarsely ground black pepper
1 medium tomato, seeded and diced
1 medium yellow pepper, thinly sliced
1 green onion, thinly sliced
2 tablespoons fresh lime juice
1 tablespoon teriyaki sauce
4 small skinless, boneless chicken-breast halves (about 1 pound)
Boston lettuce leaves for garnish

1 Cut potatoes into 2-inch chunks. In 3-quart saucepan, place potatoes and *enough water to cover*; heat to boiling over high heat. Reduce heat to low; cover and simmer 10 to 15 minutes, until potatoes are fork-tender; drain. Set aside to cool.

2 Meanwhile, in large bowl, mix mayonnaise, milk, vinegar, mustard, ¾ teaspoon salt, and ¼ teaspoon black pepper.

3 To mayonnaise mixture, add potatoes, tomato, yellow pepper, and green onion; toss to mix well.

4 In another bowl, mix lime juice, teriyaki sauce, remaining ¼ teaspoon salt, and ¼ teaspoon pepper; add chicken and toss to coat.

5 Place chicken on grill over medium heat and cook about 8 minutes or until juices run clear when pierced with knife, spooning teriyaki mixture in bowl over chicken halfway through cooking. Serve chicken with potato salad. Garnish with lettuce. Makes 4 main-dish servings.

Each serving: About 315 calories, 30 g protein, 35 g carbohydrate, 6 g total fat (1 g saturated), 69 mg cholesterol, 855 mg sodium.

Chicken with Gremolata Salsa

PREP: 15 MINUTES • GRILL: ABOUT 40 MINUTES

Tomatoes from the garden make this fresh salsa extratasty.

4 ripe medium tomatoes, diced
2 tablespoons finely chopped fresh parsley
  leaves
1 teaspoon grated lemon peel
1 small garlic clove, minced
1 teaspoon plus optional 1 tablespoon olive oil
1 teaspoon salt
½ teaspoon coarsely ground black pepper
1 chicken (about 3½ pounds), cut into quarters,
  skin removed if you like
Grilled green onions for garnish (optional)

1 In small bowl, stir tomatoes, parsley, lemon peel, garlic, 1 teaspoon olive oil, ½ teaspoon salt, and ¼ teaspoon pepper. Set salsa aside. Makes about 3 cups.

2 Sprinkle chicken quarters with remaining ½ teaspoon salt and ¼ teaspoon pepper. (If skin has been removed from chicken, brush quarters with 1 tablespoon olive oil.)

3 Place chicken on grill over medium heat and cook 20 minutes. Turn chicken over and cook 20 to 25 minutes longer, until juices run clear when thickest part of thigh is pierced with tip of knife.

4 Serve chicken with salsa. Garnish each serving with a grilled green onion if you like. Makes 4 main-dish servings.

Each serving without skin: About 335 calories, 42 g protein, 6 g carbohydrate, 15 g total fat (4 g saturated), 125 mg cholesterol, 665 mg sodium.

Each serving with skin: About 410 calories, 44 g protein, 6 g carbohydrate, 23 g total fat (6 g saturated), 170 mg cholesterol, 670 mg sodium.

Chicken with Gremolata Salsa

Cornish Hens with Ginger-Plum Glaze

PREP: 25 MINUTES • GRILL: ABOUT 30 MINUTES

The hens are cut in half for fast, even cooking, then brushed with gingery plum jam. Glazed plum halves are grilled right alongside.

⅔ cup plum jam or preserves
3 teaspoons grated, peeled fresh ginger
4 large plums, each cut in half
2 Cornish hens (about 1¾ pounds each)
2 tablespoons soy sauce
1 teaspoon Chinese five-spice powder
¾ teaspoon salt
¼ teaspoon coarsely ground black pepper
2 small garlic cloves, crushed with garlic press

1 In 1-quart saucepan, heat plum jam and 1 teaspoon ginger over low heat, stirring, 1 to 2 minutes, until jam melts. Spoon 2 tablespoons plum glaze into medium bowl; add plums and toss to coat. Set glaze aside.

2 Remove giblets and necks from hens; freeze to use in soup another day. With kitchen shears, cut each hen in half. Pat hens dry.

3 In small bowl, mix remaining 2 teaspoons ginger with soy sauce, Chinese five-spice powder, salt, pepper, and garlic. Brush mixture on hen halves.

4 Place hen halves, skin side down, on grill over medium heat and cook 15 minutes, turning once. Brush skin side of hens with plum glaze from saucepan; turn hens over and cook 5 minutes. Brush hens with remaining glaze; turn over and cook 10 minutes longer or until juices run clear when thickest part of thigh is pierced with tip of knife and hens are golden.

5 Just before hens are done, place plums on grill and cook about 6 minutes or until plums are hot and lightly browned, turning once. Makes 4 main-dish servings.

Each serving: About 435 calories, 29 g protein, 49 g carbohydrate, 15 g total fat (1 g saturated), 52 mg cholesterol, 985 mg sodium.

Stuffed Veal Chops

PREP: 15 MINUTES • GRILL: 10 TO 12 MINUTES

Serve on a bed of arugula or other favorite greens.

VEAL CHOPS:
4 veal rib chops, 1 inch thick (about 10 ounces each)
¼ cup drained and chopped (one-third 7-ounce jar) roasted red peppers
2 tablespoons chopped fresh basil leaves
2 ounces Fontina cheese, sliced
½ teaspoon salt
½ teaspoon coarsely ground black pepper

ARUGULA SALAD:
1 tablespoon olive oil
1 tablespoon balsamic vinegar
1 tablespoon chopped fresh basil leaves
½ teaspoon Dijon mustard
⅛ teaspoon salt
⅛ teaspoon coarsely ground black pepper
4 ounces arugula, watercress, or baby spinach, tough stems removed

1 Prepare Veal Chops: With knife, cut each veal chop from meat side parallel to the surface of the chop to form a deep pocket with as small an opening as possible.

2 In small bowl, mix roasted red peppers and basil. Place Fontina cheese slices in veal pockets; spread red-pepper mixture over cheese. Sprinkle veal chops with salt and pepper.

3 Place chops on grill over medium-high heat and cook 10 to 12 minutes, until chops are lightly browned on both sides and chops just lose their pink color throughout, turning chops over once.

4 Prepare Arugula Salad: In medium bowl, with wire whisk, mix olive oil, vinegar, basil, mustard, salt, and pepper; add arugula, tossing to coat.

5 To serve, spoon arugula mixture onto platter; arrange chops on top. Makes 4 main-dish servings.

Each serving: About 435 calories, 40 g protein, 3 g carbohydrate, 29 g total fat (11 g saturated), 180 mg cholesterol, 635 mg sodium.

Korean Steak

PREP: 40 MINUTES PLUS MARINATING
GRILL: ABOUT 15 MINUTES

½ cup reduced-sodium soy sauce
2 tablespoons sugar
2 tablespoons minced, peeled fresh ginger
2 tablespoons seasoned rice vinegar
1 tablespoon Asian sesame oil
¼ teaspoon ground red pepper (cayenne)
3 garlic cloves, crushed with garlic press
1 beef top round steak, 1 inch thick (about
   1½ pounds)
1 cup regular long-grain rice
3 green onions, thinly sliced
1 tablespoon sesame seeds, toasted
1 head romaine lettuce, separated into leaves

1 In large self-sealing plastic bag, combine soy sauce, sugar, ginger, vinegar, sesame oil, ground red pepper, and garlic; add steak, turning to coat. Seal bag, pressing out excess air. Place bag on plate; refrigerate steak 1 to 4 hours to marinate, turning once.

2 Just before grilling steak, prepare rice as label directs; keep warm.

Korean Steak

3 Remove steak from bag; reserve marinade. Place steak on grill over medium heat and cook 14 to 15 minutes for medium-rare or until of desired doneness, turning steak over once. Transfer steak to cutting board; let stand 10 minutes to allow juices to set for easier slicing.

4 In 1-quart saucepan, heat reserved marinade and ¼ *cup water* to boiling over high heat; boil 2 minutes.

5 To serve, thinly slice steak. Let each person place some steak slices, rice, green onions, and sesame seeds on a lettuce leaf, then drizzle with some cooked marinade. Fold sides of lettuce leaf over filling to make a package to eat out of hand. Makes 6 main-dish servings.

Each serving: About 345 calories, 30 g protein, 37 g carbohydrate, 8 g total fat (2 g saturated), 56 mg cholesterol, 1165 mg sodium.

Chili-Crusted Flank Steak

PREP: 10 MINUTES • GRILL: ABOUT 20 MINUTES

2 tablespoons chili powder
1 tablespoon brown sugar
¼ teaspoon salt
2 tablespoons fresh lime juice
1 large garlic clove, crushed with garlic press
1 beef flank steak (about 1½ pounds)
3 large red onions (about 8 ounces each), each
   cut into 6 wedges
1 tablespoon olive oil

1 In cup, mix chili powder, brown sugar, salt, lime juice, and garlic. Rub both sides of steak with chili-powder mixture. In medium bowl, toss red onions with olive oil.

2 Place steak and onions on grill over medium heat. Cook steak 15 to 20 minutes for medium-rare or until of desired doneness, turning steak once. Cook onions about 15 minutes or until browned and just tender, turning occasionally.

3 Transfer onions and steak to cutting board. Let steak stand 10 minutes to allow juices to set for easier slicing. Thinly slice steak and serve with grilled onions. Makes 6 main-dish servings.

Each serving: About 255 calories, 24 g protein, 10 g carbohydrate, 14 g total fat (5 g saturated), 58 mg cholesterol, 185 mg sodium.

Bourbon-Marinated Steak

PREP: 20 MINUTES PLUS MARINATING
GRILL/BROIL: ABOUT 20 MINUTES

A sweetly spiced marinade adds flavor and tenderness to classic grilled flank steak.

½ cup packed brown sugar
½ cup bourbon whiskey
⅓ cup soy sauce
2 tablespoons fresh lemon juice
1 tablespoon Worcestershire sauce
1 teaspoon coarsely ground black pepper
¼ teaspoon hot pepper sauce
2 flank steaks (about 1½ pounds each), well trimmed*

1 In jumbo self-sealing plastic bag (2 gallons), combine brown sugar, bourbon, soy sauce, lemon juice, Worcestershire, black pepper, hot pepper sauce, and *1 cup water*. Add steaks, turning to coat. Seal bag, pressing out excess air. Place bag in shallow glass baking dish and refrigerate at least 4 hours or overnight, turning bag occasionally.

2 Remove steaks from marinade. Discard marinade. Place steaks on grill over medium heat and cook 15 to 20 minutes for medium-rare or until of desired doneness, turning once.

3 Transfer steaks to warm large platter; let stand 10 minutes for easier slicing. To serve, cut into thin slices. Makes 12 main-dish servings.

*Or, use 2 beef top round steaks, about 1½ inches thick (about 1½ pounds each). Follow recipe for flank steaks, but grill 25 to 30 minutes for medium-rare or until of desired doneness.

Each serving: About 215 calories, 27 g protein, 4 g carbohydrate, 9 g total fat (4 g saturated), 47 mg cholesterol, 235 mg sodium.

Spiced Pork Tenderloin with Mango Salsa

PREP: 20 MINUTES • GRILL: 6 TO 7 MINUTES

A tasty blend of seasonings lends exotic flavor to lean and tender pork "cutlets." The salsa adds a tropical taste.

MANGO SALSA:
2 ripe medium mangoes, peeled and coarsely chopped
2 medium kiwifruit, peeled and coarsely chopped
3 tablespoons seasoned rice vinegar
1 tablespoon grated, peeled fresh ginger
1 tablespoon minced fresh cilantro leaves

PORK:
2 pork tenderloins (about 1 pound each)
3 tablespoons all-purpose flour
1 teaspoon salt
1 teaspoon ground cumin
1 teaspoon ground coriander
½ teaspoon ground cinnamon
½ teaspoon ground ginger

1 Prepare Mango Salsa: In medium bowl, mix all salsa ingredients. Cover and refrigerate if not serving right away. Makes about 4 cups salsa.

2 Prepare Pork: Cut each pork tenderloin lengthwise almost in half, being careful not to cut all the way through. Open and spread flat. Place each tenderloin between 2 sheets of plastic wrap; with meat mallet or rolling pin, pound to ¼-inch thickness. Cut each tenderloin into 4 pieces.

3 On waxed paper, mix flour, salt, cumin, coriander, cinnamon, and ginger; use to coat pork.

4 Place pork on grill over medium heat and cook 6 to 7 minutes, turning pork over once, until lightly browned on both sides and pork just loses its pink color throughout. Serve with Mango Salsa. Makes 8 main-dish servings.

Each serving pork without salsa: About 210 calories, 27 g protein, 3 g carbohydrate, 10 g total fat (3 g saturated), 70 mg cholesterol, 330 mg sodium.

Each ¼ cup salsa: About 30 calories, 0 g protein, 7 g carbohydrate, 0 g total fat, 0 mg cholesterol, 75 mg sodium.

Secret-Recipe BBQ Sauce

PREP: 25 MINUTES • COOK: 40 MINUTES

Brush this over anything—from hamburgers to chicken. The recipe makes almost 5 cups, so you'll have enough for several dishes.

1 tablespoon olive oil
1 jumbo onion (12 ounces), chopped
2 tablespoons chopped, peeled fresh ginger
3 tablespoons chili powder
3 garlic cloves, crushed with garlic press
1 can (8 ounces) crushed pineapple in juice
1 can (28 ounces) crushed tomatoes in puree
⅓ cup ketchup

¼ cup cider vinegar
3 tablespoons dark brown sugar
3 tablespoons mild molasses
2 teaspoons dry mustard
1 teaspoon salt

1 In 5- to 6-quart saucepot, heat olive oil over medium heat until hot. (Do not use a smaller pan; sauce bubbles up and splatters during cooking—the deeper the pan, the better.) Add onion and ginger, and cook 10 minutes or until onion is tender and golden. Add chili powder and cook 1 minute, stirring. Add garlic and crushed pineapple with its juice, and cook 1 minute longer.

2 Remove saucepot from heat. Stir in tomatoes with their puree and remaining ingredients.

3 Spoon one-fourth of sauce into blender. At low speed, blend sauce until smooth. Pour sauce into

RIB RULES

Ribs are the quintessential grill food—part splurge, part fun, part finger-licking flavor. The different kinds are interchangeable (what rib doesn't taste good brushed with BBQ sauce and grilled?), but here's a guide to the basics:

Beef

Back ribs are the large bones left when a standing rib roast is cut to make a boneless rib-eye roast. The ribs are trimmed and divided into single-rib portions.

Short ribs, cut from the shoulder, are rectangular. They contain a cross section of rib bones with alternating layers of lean meat and fat.

Flanken-style ribs are similar to short ribs (they're from the same area of the cow) but are cut lengthwise rather than between the ribs.

Pork

Spareribs, cut from the underbelly, are most widely available. They're the least meaty and most fatty of all pork ribs, containing long rib bones with a thin covering of meat on the outside and between the ribs.

Back ribs, also known as loin back ribs and baby back ribs (when small), are short, easy to hold, and meatier than spareribs because they contain loin meat. We love baby back ribs on the grill (see Ribs Supreme, opposite page).

Ribs Supreme with Secret-Recipe BBQ Sauce

Country-style ribs are cut from the shoulder end of the loin and have the highest meat-to-bone ratio, with the least fat. They're sometimes mistaken for pork chops—because you usually need a knife and fork to eat them.

Lamb

Riblets are cut from the breast and contain long and narrow ribs with meat and fat layers.

bowl; repeat with remaining sauce. Return sauce to saucepot; heat to boiling over high heat. Reduce heat to medium-low and cook, partially covered, 25 minutes or until reduced to about 4¾ cups, stirring occasionally.

4 Cover and refrigerate sauce if not using right away. Sauce will keep up to 1 week in refrigerator or up to 2 months in freezer. Makes about 4¾ cups.

Each ¼ cup: About 60 calories, 1 g protein, 12 g carbohydrate, 1 g total fat (0 g saturated), 0 mg cholesterol, 310 mg sodium.

Ribs Supreme

PREP: 15 MINUTES PLUS TIME TO PREPARE BBQ SAUCE
COOK/GRILL: 1 HOUR 15 MINUTES

Only 15 minutes of grilling time! The trick: Steam the ribs for an hour in the oven up to 2 days before barbecuing.

4 teaspoons grated, peeled fresh ginger
2 teaspoons grated fresh lemon peel
¾ teaspoon salt
2 garlic cloves, crushed with garlic press
4 racks pork baby back ribs (about 1 pound each)
2 cups Secret-Recipe BBQ Sauce (at left)

1 Preheat oven to 350°F. In cup, mix ginger, lemon peel, salt, and garlic until combined. Rub ginger mixture all over ribs.

2 Place ribs in large roasting pan (15½" by 11½"), overlapping slightly. Pour 2 *cups boiling water* into roasting pan. Cover pan tightly with foil. Steam ribs 1 hour.

3 Carefully remove foil from roasting pan (escaping steam is very hot). Remove ribs from roasting pan; discard water. Ribs may be grilled immediately, or refrigerated up to 2 days before grilling.

4 Place ribs, meat side up, on grill over medium heat; cook 5 minutes, turning once. Turn ribs over; brush with some BBQ sauce and grill 5 minutes. Turn ribs over again, brush with more BBQ sauce, and grill 5 minutes longer. Cut racks into 2-rib portions; serve with remaining sauce. Makes 6 main-dish servings.

Each serving: About 490 calories, 28 g protein, 17 g carbohydrate, 34 g total fat (12 g saturated), 77 mg cholesterol, 655 mg sodium.

Southern Peach Pork Chops

PREP: 15 MINUTES • GRILL: ABOUT 15 MINUTES

Juicy July peaches hot off the grill are perfect with tender seared meat.

1 tablespoon curry powder
1 tablespoon brown sugar
1 tablespoon olive oil
½ teaspoon salt
¼ teaspoon ground cinnamon
Pinch coarsely ground black pepper
1 garlic clove, crushed with garlic press
4 pork loin chops, each ¾ inch thick (about 5 ounces each)
4 large peaches, each cut in half
½ cup peach or apricot jam or preserves
Arugula for garnish

1 In cup, stir curry powder, brown sugar, olive oil, salt, cinnamon, pepper, and garlic.

2 With hands, rub both sides of pork chops with curry mixture.

3 Brush cut side of peach halves and one side of chops with some jam. Place peaches, brushed side down, and chops, brushed side up, on grill over medium heat; cook 5 minutes.

4 Turn chops and peaches over and brush grilled side of chops with some jam; cook 5 minutes longer. Remove peaches from grill when browned and placed on platter. Turn chops and brush with remaining jam; cook 2 to 3 minutes longer, until chops are browned on the outside and still slightly pink on the inside. Place chops on platter with peaches; garnish with arugula. Makes 4 main-dish servings.

Each serving: About 475 calories, 23 g protein, 42 g carbohydrate, 24 g total fat (8 g saturated), 58 mg cholesterol, 325 mg sodium.

Backyard BLTs

PREP: 15 MINUTES • GRILL: ABOUT 5 MINUTES

1 medium lemon
⅓ cup light mayonnaise
1 tablespoon chopped fresh parsley leaves
½ teaspoon chopped fresh thyme leaves
⅛ teaspoon coarsely ground black pepper
3 ripe medium tomatoes (about 1 pound), cut into ¼-inch-thick slices
⅛ teaspoon salt
8 slices (each ½ inch thick) sourdough bread
8 ounces thinly sliced Canadian bacon (about 24 slices)
8 small romaine lettuce leaves

1 From lemon, grate ¼ teaspoon peel and squeeze 1 teaspoon juice. In small bowl, mix lemon peel and lemon juice with mayonnaise, parsley, thyme, and pepper until blended; set aside. Place tomato slices on sheet of waxed paper and sprinkle with salt.

2 With tongs, place bread slices on grill over medium heat and cook just until grill marks appear on bottom side of bread. Remove bread slices from grill; set aside.

3 With tongs, place bacon slices on grill over medium heat and cook 2 minutes, just until grill marks appear on bacon (do not overcook; bacon will dry out and toughen).

4 To assemble, spread mayonnaise mixture on ungrilled side of bread slices. Top half of bread slices with half of bacon slices, all of tomato slices, remaining bacon slices, then lettuce leaves. Place remaining bread slices, grilled side up, on top. Cut each sandwich in half to serve. Makes 4 sandwiches.

Each sandwich: About 315 calories, 17 g protein, 32 g carbohydrate, 14 g total fat (2 g saturated), 35 mg cholesterol, 1195 mg sodium.

Sausage & Pepper Grill

....

PREP: 15 MINUTES • GRILL: 15 TO 20 MINUTES

⅓ cup balsamic vinegar
1 teaspoon brown sugar
½ teaspoon salt
¼ teaspoon coarsely ground black pepper
2 medium red peppers, cut into 1½-inch-wide strips
2 medium green peppers, cut into 1½-inch-wide strips
2 large red onions (about 8 ounces), each cut into 6 wedges
1 tablespoon olive oil
¾ pound sweet Italian-sausage links
¾ pound hot Italian-sausage links

1 In cup, mix balsamic vinegar, brown sugar, salt, and black pepper. In large bowl, toss red and green peppers and onions with olive oil to coat.

2 Place sausages and vegetables on grill over medium heat. Cook sausages 15 to 20 minutes, turning occasionally, until golden brown and cooked through. Cook vegetables, about 15 minutes or until tender, turning occasionally and brushing with some balsamic mixture during last 3 minutes of cooking. Transfer vegetables and sausages to platter as they finish cooking.

3 To serve, cut sausages into 2-inch diagonal slices. Drizzle any remaining balsamic mixture over vegetables. Makes 4 main-dish servings.

Each serving: About 450 calories, 22 g protein, 24 g carbohydrate, 30 g total fat (10 g saturated), 78 mg cholesterol, 1200 mg sodium.

Pork Tenderloins with Oregano

PREP: 10 MINUTES PLUS MARINATING
GRILL: ABOUT 20 MINUTES

A quick 20-minute marination in lemon juice and herbs gives this lean cut of pork fresh flavor.

¼ cup fresh lemon juice
2 tablespoons chopped fresh oregano leaves
2 tablespoons chopped fresh parsley leaves
2 pork tenderloins (about ¾ pound each)
1 tablespoon olive oil
½ teaspoon salt
¼ teaspoon coarsely ground black pepper

1 In large self-sealing plastic bag, combine lemon juice with 1 tablespoon each oregano and parsley. Add tenderloins, turning to coat. Seal bag, pressing out excess air. Place bag on plate; refrigerate tenderloins 20 minutes to marinate, turning once.

2 Remove tenderloins from bag; discard marinade. In cup, mix olive oil, salt, pepper, and remaining oregano and parsley; rub mixture all over tenderloins.

3 Place tenderloins on grill over medium heat and cook about 20 minutes or until they're browned on the outside and still slightly pink in the center, turning occasionally (internal temperature of meat should be 160°F. on meat thermometer). Thinly slice tenderloins to serve. Makes 6 main-dish servings.

Each serving: About 225 calories, 27 g protein, 1 g carbohydrate, 12 g total fat (4 g saturated), 71 mg cholesterol, 245 mg sodium.

Spiced Butterflied Lamb

PREP: 10 MINUTES PLUS MARINATING
GRILL: 20 TO 35 MINUTES

Place a few slices of bread on the grill when the lamb is almost finished cooking for a crisp accompaniment.

1 cup plain low-fat yogurt
8 garlic cloves, peeled
1 piece fresh ginger (about 2 inches), peeled and coarsely chopped
1 tablespoon ground coriander
1 tablespoon ground cumin
2 tablespoons fresh lemon juice
2 teaspoons salt
¼ to ½ teaspoon ground red pepper (cayenne)
3 pounds boneless butterflied lamb leg*

1 In blender, combine yogurt, garlic, ginger, coriander, cumin, lemon juice, salt, and ground red pepper, and blend until smooth. Pour yogurt mixture into large self-sealing plastic bag; add lamb, turning to coat. Seal bag, pressing out excess air. Place bag on plate; refrigerate lamb 1 hour, turning occasionally. (Do not marinate more than 2 hours or texture of meat will change.)

2 Remove lamb from bag. Pour marinade into small bowl and reserve.

3 Place lamb on grill over medium heat; cook 15 minutes, turning once. Brush both sides of lamb with reserved marinade and cook 10 to 20 minutes longer for medium-rare or until of desired doneness, turning lamb occasionally. Thickness of butterflied lamb will vary throughout; cut off sections of lamb as they are cooked and place on cutting board. Makes 10 main-dish servings.

*Ask butcher to bone a 4-pound lamb leg shank half and slit the meat lengthwise to spread open like a thick steak.

Each serving: About 255 calories, 29 g protein, 4 g carbohydrate, 13 g total fat (6 g saturated), 94 mg cholesterol, 510 mg sodium.

Hot Fruit Salad

PREP: 15 MINUTES • GRILL: 10 TO 15 MINUTES

A few turns on the grill transform fresh fruit into a sumptuous finale.

½ cup honey
1 tablespoon fresh lemon juice
¼ cup loosely packed fresh mint leaves, thinly
   sliced
1 medium pineapple, cut lengthwise into
   6 wedges, with leaves attached
2 large bananas, each cut diagonally into thirds
3 medium plums, each cut in half
2 medium nectarines or peaches, each cut into
   quarters

1 In cup, stir together honey, lemon juice, and 1 tablespoon mint leaves.

2 With tongs, place all fruit pieces on grill over medium heat. Grill fruit 10 to 15 minutes, until browned

Hot Fruit Salad

and tender, turning fruit occasionally. Brush fruit with some honey mixture during last 3 minutes of cooking.

3 To serve, arrange grilled fruit on large platter; drizzle with any remaining honey mixture. Sprinkle grilled fruit with remaining mint. Makes 6 servings.

Each serving: About 215 calories, 2 g protein, 55 g carbohydrate, 1 g total fat (0 g saturated), 0 mg cholesterol, 5 mg sodium.

Toasted Angel Cake

PREP: 10 MINUTES • GRILL: ABOUT 1 MINUTE

Serve golden wedges of cake with sun-ripened berries and brown-sugar whipped cream. Try with grilled pound cake slices too!

1 pint strawberries, hulled and each cut into
   quarters
1 cup blueberries
3 tablespoons brown sugar
½ cup heavy or whipping cream
1 teaspoon vanilla extract
1 store-bought angel food cake (12 ounces)

1 In medium bowl, stir strawberries and blueberries with 1 tablespoon brown sugar to coat; set aside.

2 In small bowl, with mixer at medium speed, beat cream and vanilla until soft peaks form. Gradually add remaining 2 tablespoons brown sugar and beat until stiff peaks form. Cover and refrigerate.

3 Cut angel food cake into 6 wedges. Place cake on grill over medium heat and cook about 1 minute or until golden on both sides, turning once.

4 To serve, place cake on 6 dessert plates; top each wedge with berry mixture, then a dollop of whipped cream. Makes 6 servings.

Each serving: About 270 calories, 4 g protein, 47 g carbohydrate, 8 g total fat (5 g saturated), 27 mg cholesterol, 435 mg sodium.

PASTA & GRAINS

Light Sesame Noodles

PREP: 10 MINUTES • COOK: 10 MINUTES

The orange vinaigrette is made with Asian sesame oil for delectable flavor.

1 package (9 ounces) refrigerated angel-hair pasta
2 cups packaged shredded carrots
2 teaspoons vegetable oil
12 ounces skinless, boneless chicken breasts or tenders, thinly sliced
2 garlic cloves, crushed with garlic press
1 medium orange
3 tablespoons seasoned rice vinegar
3 tablespoons soy sauce
1 teaspoon sugar
2 teaspoons Asian sesame oil
1 teaspoon grated, peeled fresh ginger
1/8 teaspoon ground red pepper (cayenne)
4 large radishes, each cut in half and thinly sliced
2 green onions, thinly sliced diagonally
2 tablespoons toasted sesame seeds

1 In large saucepot, prepare pasta in *boiling water* as label directs but do not add salt. Place shredded carrots in colander; drain pasta over carrots to soften them slightly. Transfer mixture to large bowl and set aside.

2 In nonstick 12-inch skillet, heat vegetable oil over medium-high heat until hot. Add sliced chicken and garlic; cook 4 to 5 minutes, stirring constantly, until chicken loses its pink color throughout. Transfer chicken to bowl with pasta.

3 To prepare vinaigrette, from orange, grate 1 teaspoon peel and squeeze 1/4 cup juice. In small bowl, with wire whisk or fork, mix orange peel, orange juice, vinegar, soy sauce, sugar, sesame oil, ginger, and ground red pepper until combined.

4 Toss pasta mixture in bowl with vinaigrette, radish slices, and green onions; sprinkle with sesame seeds. Serve warm or refrigerate until ready to serve. Makes 4 main-dish servings.

Each serving: About 415 calories, 30 g protein, 51 g carbohydrate, 10 g total fat (2 g saturated), 121 mg cholesterol, 1170 mg sodium.

Broccoli Pesto Spaghetti

PREP: 8 MINUTES • COOK: ABOUT 12 MINUTES

The pesto is best made in a food processor; a blender makes the mixture too creamy. Serve with breadsticks and a green salad splashed with balsamic vinegar.

1 package (16 ounces) spaghetti or thin spaghetti
Salt
1 bag (16 ounces) frozen chopped broccoli
1 cup chicken broth
1/4 cup grated Parmesan cheese
2 tablespoons olive oil
1 small garlic clove
Coarsely ground black pepper

1 In saucepot, prepare pasta in *boiling salted water* as label directs. In saucepan, prepare broccoli as label directs.

2 In food processor with knife blade attached, blend cooked broccoli, chicken broth, Parmesan, olive oil, garlic, and 1/4 teaspoon salt until smooth, stopping processor occasionally to scrape down side.

3 Drain pasta; toss with broccoli pesto. Sprinkle with coarsely ground black pepper to serve. Makes about 8 cups or 4 main-dish servings.

Each serving: About 550 calories, 22 g protein, 91 g carbohydrate, 11 g total fat (3 g saturated), 5 mg cholesterol, 615 mg sodium.

Broccoli Pesto Spaghetti ➤

Cheese Tortellini with Pesto

PREP: 15 MINUTES • COOK: 10 MINUTES

Toss refrigerated pasta with a homemade basil sauce, cherry tomatoes, and grated Parmesan for a terrific impromptu meal.

2 packages (9 ounces each) refrigerated cheese tortellini
2 cups loosely packed fresh basil leaves
¼ cup pine nuts (pignoli), toasted
¼ cup grated Parmesan cheese
1 tablespoon olive oil
¼ teaspoon salt
¼ teaspoon coarsely ground black pepper
1 small garlic clove, crushed with garlic press
½ pint cherry tomatoes, each cut in half or into quarters if large

1 In saucepot, prepare tortellini in *boiling water* as label directs. Drain tortellini, reserving *½ cup pasta cooking water*. Return tortellini to saucepot.

2 In blender, combine basil, pine nuts, Parmesan cheese, olive oil, salt, pepper, garlic, and reserved pasta cooking water and blend until mixture is smooth, stopping blender occasionally and scraping down sides with rubber spatula.

3 Add basil mixture and tomatoes to tortellini; toss until evenly mixed. Makes 6 main-dish servings.

Each serving: About 330 calories, 16 g protein, 42 g carbohydrate, 12 g total fat (4 g saturated), 43 mg cholesterol, 480 mg sodium.

Linguine with No-Cook Puttanesca Sauce

PREP: 12 MINUTES • COOK: ABOUT 5 MINUTES

We found a way to make spicy puttanesca sauce without turning on the stove!

2 packages (9 ounces each) refrigerated linguine
Salt
6 ripe medium tomatoes (2 pounds), chopped
½ cup salad olives or coarsely chopped pimiento-stuffed olives
3 tablespoons capers, drained
2 tablespoons extravirgin olive oil
1 tablespoon balsamic vinegar
1 teaspoon sugar
¼ teaspoon ground red pepper (cayenne)
1 garlic clove, crushed with garlic press
1 cup loosely packed fresh basil leaves, thinly sliced

DRIED VS. FRESH PASTA

Dried pasta is made with semolina, a flour milled from durum wheat, high in gluten, which gives it the strength to withstand the mechanical pasta-making process and hold its shape when cooked. Dried pasta has a slightly rough surface to which a sauce can cling. The long shapes, from fine angel's hair to thick *bucatini*, are best with oil-based and tomato sauces that coat each strand. Short shapes are best served with chunky meat or vegetable sauces—their hollows and grooves hold the sauce well. Stored in a cool dry place, dried pasta will stay fresh for up to 2 years.

Fresh pasta, which you'll find in a refrigerated case at your market, is usually made with white flour and eggs. The term "fresh" doesn't imply superior quality; it simply means that the dough was made recently and must be kept refrigerated. The pasta has a soft, porous texture and is best paired with light sauces containing cream, butter, and cheese. Wrapped airtight, it will keep for a week refrigerated, or a month in the freezer.

Note A pound of fresh pasta makes fewer servings than a pound of dried pasta because the fresh pasta absorbs less water during cooking. On package labels, a serving size for dried pasta is 2 ounces, while a serving size for fresh pasta is 3 ounces; both yield 1 cup cooked.

1 Prepare linguine in *boiling salted water* as label directs.

2 Meanwhile, in large bowl, stir tomatoes with remaining ingredients except basil. Taste and add additional salt if desired.

3 Drain linguine. Add linguine and basil to tomato mixture; toss well. Makes 4 main-dish servings.

Each serving: About 495 calories, 15 g protein, 83 g carbohydrate, 14 g total fat (2 g saturated), 0 mg cholesterol, 1100 mg sodium.

Potato Gnocchi au Gratin

PREP: 20 MINUTES • COOK: 35 MINUTES

1½ pounds potatoes, peeled and cut into 2-inch chunks
1 tablespoon light corn-oil spread
1 small onion, chopped
1 can (28 ounces) Italian plum tomatoes
1 teaspoon sugar
1 teaspoon dried basil
1½ teaspoons salt
1 container (8 ounces) part-skim ricotta cheese
1¼ cups all-purpose flour
2 ounces part-skim mozzarella cheese, thinly sliced

1 In 3-quart saucepan, heat potatoes and *enough water to cover* to boiling over high heat. Reduce heat to low; cover and simmer 15 to 20 minutes, until potatoes are fork-tender; drain. Return potatoes to saucepan.

2 Meanwhile, in nonstick 12-inch skillet, melt light corn-oil spread over medium heat. Add onion and 2 *tablespoons water* and cook until liquid evaporates and onion is tender and golden. Stir in tomatoes with their liquid, sugar, basil, and ¼ teaspoon salt; heat to boiling over high heat. Reduce heat to low; simmer, uncovered, 15 minutes. Keep sauce warm.

3 With potato masher, mash potatoes until smooth. Add ricotta cheese and remaining 1¼ teaspoons salt; mash until smooth. With spoon, stir in flour to make a soft dough.

4 Turn gnocchi dough onto floured surface; divide into 2 pieces. Shape each piece into an 8" by 2" log. Cut each log into ½-inch-thick slices.

5 Preheat broiler. In 5-quart Dutch oven, heat *4 quarts water* to boiling over high heat. Gently drop gnocchi, 1 at a time, into water. With slotted spoon, carefully remove gnocchi to jelly-roll pan as soon as they start to float.

6 Spoon all but 1 cup sauce into shallow 2½-quart glass or ceramic baking dish. Arrange gnocchi, slightly overlapping, over sauce. Spoon remaining sauce randomly over gnocchi; top with mozzarella cheese. Broil gnocchi 1 to 2 minutes until cheese is browned and bubbly. Makes 6 main-dish servings.

Each serving: About 315 calories, 13 g protein, 52 g carbohydrate, 7 g total fat (3 g saturated), 17 mg cholesterol, 880 mg sodium.

Bow Ties with Tomatoes, Herbs & Lemon

PREP: 15 MINUTES • COOK: 15 MINUTES

The easy late-summer sauce "cooks" from the heat of the drained pasta. While the pasta boils, slice and warm a loaf of semolina bread for a simple go-along.

6 medium tomatoes (about 2 pounds), chopped
¼ cup loosely packed fresh mint leaves, chopped
¼ cup loosely packed fresh basil leaves, chopped
2 tablespoons olive oil
1 teaspoon grated fresh lemon peel
¼ teaspoon coarsely ground black pepper
1 garlic clove, crushed with garlic press
Salt
1 package (16 ounces) bow-tie or ziti pasta

1 In large serving bowl, stir tomatoes, mint, basil, olive oil, lemon peel, pepper, garlic, and 1 teaspoon salt. Set tomato mixture aside to allow flavors to develop.

2 Meanwhile, in large saucepot, cook pasta in *boiling salted water* as label directs. Drain well.

3 Add hot pasta to tomato mixture in bowl; toss well. Makes about 11 cups or 4 main-dish servings.

Each serving: About 530 calories, 17 g protein, 96 g carbohydrate, 9 g total fat (1 g saturated), 0 mg cholesterol, 695 mg sodium.

Potato Dumplings with Cabbage & Apples

Pierogi, Polish-style comfort food, are usually filled with meat, seafood, cheese, potatoes, or mushrooms. They can be quite time-consuming to prepare from scratch, but fortunately, excellent frozen varieties are available. Serve with sliced-tomato salad and pumpernickel-raisin rolls. Slice the tomatoes and warm the rolls while the cabbage cooks.

1 package (16 to 19 ounces) frozen potato-and-
   onion pierogi
Salt
1 tablespoon margarine or butter

1 small onion, thinly sliced
1½ pounds green cabbage (1 small head),
   sliced, with tough ribs discarded
½ cup chicken broth
2 medium McIntosh apples (about 12 ounces)
2 teaspoons cider vinegar
1 tablespoon chopped fresh dill

1 In large saucepot, prepare pierogi in *boiling salted water* as label directs.

2 Meanwhile, in nonstick 12-inch skillet, melt margarine or butter over medium-low heat. Add onion and cook, stirring occasionally, 7 minutes or until onion is tender and lightly browned.

3 Increase heat to medium-high; add cabbage, chicken broth, and ½ teaspoon salt and cook until cabbage is tender, about 10 minutes. While cabbage is cooking, core and cut apples into ¼-inch-thick wedges.

4 Add apples and vinegar to skillet with cabbage and cook until apples soften, about 5 minutes.

Potato Dumplings with Cabbage & Apples

5 Drain pierogi; toss with cabbage mixture and chopped dill. Makes 4 main-dish servings.

Each serving: About 355 calories, 9 g protein, 64 g carbohydrate, 7 g total fat (2 g saturated), 0 mg cholesterol, 950 mg sodium.

Cavatelli with Ricotta & Fresh Tomato Sauce

PREP: 5 MINUTES • COOK: 25 MINUTES

We used frozen cavatelli—a short, curled, rippled pasta. If you can't find it, substitute frozen gnocchi. Just before serving, toss mixed Italian salad greens with olive oil and a squeeze of lemon juice. Serve with breadsticks.

1 bag (16 ounces) frozen cavatelli
Salt
1 tablespoon olive oil
1 garlic clove, crushed with garlic press
4 medium tomatoes (about 1½ pounds), diced
¼ teaspoon coarsely ground black pepper
¾ cup part-skim ricotta cheese
¼ cup grated Pecorino Romano or Parmesan cheese

1 In large saucepot, prepare cavatelli in *boiling salted water* as label directs.

2 Meanwhile, in nonstick 10-inch skillet, heat olive oil over medium heat. Add garlic and cook 1 minute, stirring. Stir in tomatoes, pepper, and ½ teaspoon salt and cook, stirring occasionally, 5 minutes or until tomatoes break up slightly.

3 Drain cavatelli; transfer to serving bowl. Stir in ricotta and Romano. Pour tomato mixture on top; toss before serving. Makes 4 main-dish servings.

Each serving: About 455 calories, 20 g protein, 71 g carbohydrate, 11 g total fat (5 g saturated), 40 mg cholesterol, 560 mg sodium.

Couscous Paella

PREP: 10 MINUTES • COOK: 10 MINUTES

A box of couscous makes paella quick enough for a weeknight. Serve with a salad blend from the supermarket and our Spicy Tomato Dressing (page 177).

1 can (14½ ounces) chicken broth
1 package (10 ounces) couscous (1½ cups)
1 package (10 ounces) frozen peas
2 teaspoons olive oil
1 red or green pepper, diced
2 ounces low-fat kielbasa (smoked Polish sausage), sliced
12 ounces skinless, boneless chicken breast, cut into 1-inch pieces
1 garlic clove, crushed with garlic press
½ teaspoon salt
¼ teaspoon dried thyme
¼ teaspoon coarsely ground black pepper
1½ cups cherry tomatoes, each cut in half

1 In 3-quart saucepan, heat chicken broth and ¼ *cup water* to boiling over high heat. Remove saucepan from heat; stir in couscous and frozen peas. Cover saucepan and let stand 5 minutes or until ready to use.

2 Meanwhile, in nonstick 12-inch skillet, heat olive oil over medium-high heat until hot. Add red or green pepper and kielbasa and cook 5 minutes, stirring occasionally. Add chicken, garlic, salt, thyme, and black pepper, and cook until chicken loses its pink color throughout, about 5 minutes, stirring occasionally. Remove skillet from heat, and stir in cherry-tomato halves.

3 Fluff couscous with fork; add to chicken mixture in skillet, and toss gently until combined. Makes 4 main-dish servings.

Each serving: About 520 calories, 38 g protein, 73 g carbohydrate, 8 g total fat (1 g saturated), 50 mg cholesterol, 725 mg sodium.

Pad Thai

PREP: 25 MINUTES • COOK: 5 MINUTES

Thailand's best-known dish is a delicious mix of rice noodles, shrimp, peanuts, garlic, and eggs. This dish cooks so quickly, it's essential to have everything in place before you start.

1 package (7 or 8 ounces) flat rice stick noodles,* broken in half, or 8 ounces angel hair pasta
½ pound medium shrimp, shelled and deveined
¼ cup fresh lime juice
¼ cup Asian fish sauce†
2 tablespoons sugar
1 tablespoon vegetable oil
2 garlic cloves, crushed with garlic press
¼ teaspoon crushed red pepper
2 large eggs, lightly beaten
6 ounces fresh bean sprouts (about 2 cups), rinsed
2 tablespoons unsalted roasted peanuts, coarsely chopped
3 green onions, thinly sliced
½ cup loosely packed cilantro leaves
Lime wedges

1 In large bowl, soak rice stick noodles in *hot tap water to cover* 20 minutes. (Or, break angel hair pasta in half; cook as label directs and rinse with cold running water.)

2 Meanwhile, cut each shrimp horizontally in half. In small bowl, combine lime juice, fish sauce, and sugar. Assemble all remaining ingredients before beginning to cook.

3 Drain noodles. In nonstick wok or 12-inch skillet, heat vegetable oil over high heat until hot but not smoking. Add shrimp, garlic, and crushed red pepper and cook, stirring, 1 minute. Add eggs and cook, stirring, 20 seconds or until just set. Add noodles and cook, stirring, 2 minutes. Add lime-juice mixture, half of bean sprouts, half of peanuts, and half of green onions; cook, stirring, 1 minute.

4 Transfer Pad Thai to platter; top with remaining bean sprouts, peanuts, and green onions. Sprinkle with cilantro leaves. Serve with lime wedges. Makes 4 main-dish servings.

*Rice stick noodles are available in Asian groceries.

†Asian fish sauce is available in the Asian sections of some supermarkets. For more information, see "Food Editor's Tip," page 114.

Each serving: About 395 calories, 19 g protein, 59 g carbohydrate, 9 g total fat (2 g saturated), 172 mg cholesterol, 1400 mg sodium.

Shells with Tuna & Capers

PREP: 5 MINUTES • COOK: ABOUT 15 MINUTES

This pasta dish is sure to become a dinner standby. Try it with a little good-quality extravirgin olive oil drizzled over each serving. While the pasta cooks, whip up 1 of our low-fat salad dressings to toss with fresh greens.

1 package (16 ounces) medium shell pasta
Salt
1 medium lemon
2 tablespoons olive oil
2 garlic cloves, crushed with garlic press
¼ teaspoon crushed red pepper
2 cans (6 ounces each) tuna in water, drained and flaked
¼ cup capers, drained and chopped
1 cup packed fresh Italian parsley leaves, chopped

1 In saucepot, prepare pasta in *boiling salted water* as label directs.

2 Meanwhile, from lemon, grate 1 teaspoon peel, and squeeze 2 tablespoons juice. In 10-inch skillet, heat olive oil over medium heat. Add garlic and crushed red pepper, and cook, stirring, 30 seconds. Add tuna, capers, lemon juice, lemon peel, and ¼ teaspoon salt, and cook 2 minutes.

3 When pasta has cooked to desired doneness, remove ½ *cup pasta cooking water*. Drain pasta and return to saucepot. Add parsley, tuna mixture, and reserved pasta cooking water; toss well. Makes 6 main-dish servings.

Each serving: About 395 calories, 26 g protein, 58 g carbohydrate, 6 g total fat (1 g saturated), 0 mg cholesterol, 590 mg sodium.

◄ *Pad Thai*

Tubetti Macaroni Salad

PREP: 15 MINUTES • COOK: 15 MINUTES

Carrots and celery add crunch to this lemony fresh salad. If it seems dry after chilling, stir in a touch of milk to moisten.

1 package (16 ounces) tubetti or ditalini pasta
Salt
4 medium carrots, cut into 2" by ¼" sticks
1 lemon
⅔ cup light mayonnaise
⅓ cup milk
¾ teaspoon salt
2 medium celery stalks, cut into 2" by ¼" sticks
2 green onions, thinly sliced

1 Prepare pasta as label directs in *boiling salted water*. After pasta has cooked 10 minutes, add carrot sticks to pasta cooking water and cook 1 to 2 minutes longer, until carrots are just tender-crisp and pasta is done.

2 Meanwhile, from lemon, grate 1 teaspoon peel and squeeze 3 tablespoons juice. In large bowl, with wire whisk, mix lemon peel, lemon juice, mayonnaise, milk, and salt.

3 Drain pasta and carrots well. Add to mayonnaise mixture with celery and green onions; toss well. Serve at room temperature or cover and refrigerate until ready to serve. Makes 12 accompaniment servings.

Each serving: About 180 calories, 5 g protein, 35 g carbohydrate, 2 g total fat (0 g saturated), 1 mg cholesterol, 320 mg sodium.

Apricot Couscous

PREP: 5 MINUTES • COOK: 5 MINUTES

A low-maintenance side dish that cooks in 5 minutes. Stir in parsley or cilantro, depending on flavorings in main dish.

1 cup chicken broth
3 strips orange peel (3" by 1" each)
½ cup dried apricot halves, cut into thin strips
1 cup couscous (Moroccan pasta)
⅓ cup chopped fresh parsley or cilantro leaves

1 In 2-quart saucepan, heat chicken broth, orange peel, apricots, and ¼ *cup water* to boiling over high heat. Remove saucepan from heat; stir in couscous.

2 Cover saucepan and let stand 5 minutes or until ready to serve. Remove orange-peel strips. Fluff couscous with fork; stir in chopped parsley or cilantro. Makes 4 accompaniment servings.

Each serving: About 225 calories, 8 g protein, 46 g carbohydrate, 1 g total fat (0 g saturated), 0 mg cholesterol, 205 mg sodium.

Bow Ties with Shrimp & Fennel

PREP: 10 MINUTES • COOK: ABOUT 15 MINUTES

The secrets to success here are a bag of frozen shrimp and a mixture of garlic and fennel seeds. If you don't have a mortar and pestle, crush garlic with a press and place the seeds in a sealed plastic bag, then mash with a rolling pin.

1 package (16 ounces) bow-tie pasta
Salt
1 bag (16 ounces) frozen uncooked, shelled, and deveined extralarge shrimp
1 cup frozen peas
1 small garlic clove
1 teaspoon fennel seeds
½ teaspoon salt
¼ teaspoon coarsely ground black pepper
4 ripe medium tomatoes, diced
2 tablespoons olive oil
2 ounces feta cheese, crumbled (½ cup)

1 In large saucepot, prepare pasta in *boiling salted water* as label directs. After pasta has cooked 12 minutes, add frozen shrimp and peas to pasta cooking water, and continue cooking 3 minutes or until pasta is done and shrimp turn opaque throughout.

2 Meanwhile, in mortar with pestle, crush garlic with fennel seeds, salt, and pepper. Transfer mixture to medium bowl and stir in tomatoes and olive oil.

3 Drain pasta and shrimp; return to saucepot. Add tomato mixture and feta cheese; toss well. Makes 6 main-dish servings.

Each serving: About 465 calories, 29 g protein, 66 g carbohydrate, 9 g total fat (3 g saturated), 125 mg cholesterol, 520 mg sodium.

Couscous & Smoked-Turkey Salad

Couscous & Smoked-Turkey Salad

PREP: 10 MINUTES • COOK: 5 MINUTES

If you see plums, peaches, or apricots at the farmer's market, try using them instead of the nectarines.

1 teaspoon ground cumin
1 package (10 ounces) couscous (Moroccan pasta)
⅓ cup dried tart cherries
3 tablespoons fresh lemon juice
2 tablespoons olive oil
1 tablespoon Dijon mustard
¾ teaspoon salt
¼ teaspoon coarsely ground black pepper
3 ripe medium nectarines, diced

4 ounces smoked turkey breast (in 1 piece), cut into ¼-inch pieces
Boston lettuce leaves

1 In 3-quart saucepan, heat cumin over medium-high heat until fragrant, 1 to 3 minutes. In saucepan with cumin, prepare couscous as label directs, adding cherries but no salt or butter.

2 In large bowl, with wire whisk or fork, mix lemon juice, olive oil, mustard, salt, and pepper until dressing is blended.

3 Toss warm couscous mixture, diced nectarines, and turkey with dressing.

4 Spoon couscous onto large platter lined with Boston lettuce leaves. Makes about 7½ cups or 6 main-dish servings.

Each serving: About 300 calories, 11 g protein, 51 g carbohydrate, 6 g total fat (1 g saturated), 3 mg cholesterol, 470 mg sodium.

Spiced Couscous with Vegetables

PREP: 15 MINUTES • COOK: 15 MINUTES

A blend of cumin, curry powder, and paprika complements this tasty Moroccan-style side dish.

1 package (10 ounces) couscous (Moroccan pasta)
¼ teaspoon coarsely ground black pepper
2 tablespoons olive oil
1 teaspoon salt
2 medium carrots, cut into ¼-inch dice
1 medium red onion, cut into ¼-inch dice
1 medium zucchini, cut into ¼-inch dice
3 medium tomatoes, cut into ¼-inch dice
1 tablespoon ground cumin
2 teaspoons curry powder
2 teaspoons paprika
¼ cup pine nuts (pignoli), toasted
¼ cup fresh parsley leaves, chopped
¼ cup pitted prunes, cut into slivers

1 Prepare couscous as label directs, but instead of the amount of salt or butter called for, stir in pepper, 1 tablespoon olive oil, and ½ teaspoon salt; cover and keep warm.

2 Meanwhile, in nonstick 12-inch skillet, heat remaining 1 tablespoon olive oil over medium heat until hot. Add carrots and onion, and cook 5 minutes, stirring occasionally. Add zucchini and cook 5 minutes longer or until vegetables are tender. Stir in tomatoes, cumin, curry, paprika, and remaining ½ teaspoon salt, and cook 2 minutes longer.

3 Stir vegetable mixture into couscous; sprinkle with pine nuts, parsley, and prunes. Makes about 8 cups or 8 accompaniment servings.

Each serving: About 230 calories, 7 g protein, 38 g carbohydrate, 6 g total fat (1 g saturated), 0 mg cholesterol, 285 mg sodium.

Spinach Spaetzle

PREP: 15 MINUTES • COOK: 15 MINUTES

Spaetzle, which means "little sparrow" in German, is a pasta side dish made by pushing an egg-pasta dough through a colander with large holes to form little noodles. You can actually buy a specialty gadget called a spaetzle maker, but a colander or a box grater works nicely.

2½ cups all-purpose flour

PASTA SIDE DISHES

PREP: 10 MINUTES • COOK: 15 MINUTES

Start with 6 ounces orzo or mini bow-tie macaroni, cooked as label directs but without adding salt, to make any of the delicious side dishes below.

Peas & Onion Pasta In nonstick 10-inch skillet over medium heat, melt *2 teaspoons light corn-oil spread.* Add *1 small onion, chopped,* and *2 tablespoons water* and cook until onion is tender and golden, about 10 minutes. Stir in *1 cup thawed frozen peas* and cooked orzo; heat through. Makes 4 accompaniment servings. Each serving: About 210 calories, 8 g protein, 39 g carbohydrate, 2 g total fat (0 g saturated), 0 mg cholesterol, 450 mg sodium.

Orange-Fennel Pasta In nonstick 10-inch skillet over medium heat, melt *2 teaspoons light corn-oil spread.* Add *1 garlic clove, crushed with garlic press,* *¾ teaspoon salt,* and *¼ teaspoon coarsely ground*

black pepper and cook 30 seconds. Stir in *1 teaspoon grated fresh orange peel* and *½ teaspoon fennel seeds, crushed.* Add cooked orzo and *2 tablespoons chopped fresh parsley leaves;* heat through. Makes 4 accompaniment servings. Each serving: About 170 calories, 6 g protein, 32 g carbohydrate, 2 g total fat (0 g saturated), 0 mg cholesterol, 415 mg sodium.

Confetti Pasta In nonstick 10-inch skillet, melt *2 teaspoons light corn-oil spread* over medium heat. Add *2 medium carrots, shredded, 1 medium zucchini (8 ounces), shredded, 1 garlic clove, crushed with garlic press, ¾ teaspoon salt,* and *¼ teaspoon coarsely ground black pepper* and cook 5 minutes. Stir in cooked orzo; heat through. Makes 4 accompaniment servings. Each serving: About 180 calories, 6 g protein, 35 g carbohydrate, 2 g total fat (0 g saturated), 0 mg cholesterol, 405 mg sodium.

1 package (10 ounces) frozen chopped spinach, thawed and squeezed dry
2 large eggs
½ cup milk
¼ teaspoon ground nutmeg
1 teaspoon salt
2 tablespoons margarine or butter (¼ stick)
2 tablespoons grated Parmesan cheese
¼ teaspoon ground black pepper

1 In 6-quart saucepot, heat *4 quarts water* to boiling over high heat. Meanwhile, in medium bowl, with spoon, beat flour, spinach, eggs, milk, nutmeg, ½ teaspoon salt, and *½ cup water* until smooth.

2 Reduce heat to medium; over simmering water, with rubber spatula, press mixture through spaetzle maker (or colander or grater with large holes). Cook spaetzle 2 to 3 minutes until tender but firm, stirring gently so spaetzle doesn't stick together; drain well in colander.

3 In nonstick 12-inch skillet, heat margarine or butter over medium-high heat. Add Parmesan, pepper, and remaining ½ teaspoon salt and stir until margarine melts. Stir in spaetzle; heat through. Makes 6 accompaniment servings.

Each serving: About 285 calories, 11 g protein, 44 g carbohydrate, 7 g total fat (2 g saturated), 75 mg cholesterol, 515 mg sodium.

Bulgur Pilaf

PREP: 2 MINUTES • COOK: 10 TO 15 MINUTES

1 can (14½ ounces) chicken broth
¼ teaspoon dried thyme
Pinch ground nutmeg
1 cup bulgur

1 In 2-cup glass measuring cup, combine chicken broth and *enough water to equal 2 cups.*

2 In 2-quart saucepan, heat broth mixture, thyme, and nutmeg to boiling over high heat. Add bulgur; reduce heat to medium-low. Cover and simmer 10 to 15 minutes, until liquid is absorbed. Makes 4 accompaniment servings.

Each serving: About 135 calories, 6 g protein, 27 g carbohydrate, 1 g total fat (0 g saturated), 0 mg cholesterol, 335 mg sodium.

Wild Rice & Orzo Pilaf

PREP: 25 MINUTES • COOK: 45 MINUTES

You can prepare this and refrigerate it for up to 2 days, then bake just before serving.

1¼ cups orzo pasta (about 8 ounces)
1 cup wild rice (about 6 ounces)
3 tablespoons margarine or butter
1 small onion, diced
1 medium celery stalk, diced
1 pound medium mushrooms, sliced
2 teaspoons chopped fresh thyme leaves
1 teaspoon salt
¼ teaspoon coarsely ground black pepper

1 Prepare orzo and wild rice, separately, as labels direct.

2 Meanwhile, in 12-inch skillet, melt margarine or butter over medium heat. Add onion and celery, and cook until tender, about 10 minutes, stirring occasionally. Add mushrooms, thyme, salt, and pepper, and cook 10 minutes longer, stirring occasionally, until mushrooms are tender and liquid evaporates.

3 Preheat oven to 350°F. In shallow 2½-quart baking dish, stir orzo, rice, and mushroom mixture until blended.

4 Bake orzo-wild rice mixture, covered, 35 minutes or until hot. Makes about 9 cups or 12 accompaniment servings.

Each serving: About 155 calories, 5 g protein, 26 g carbohydrate, 3 g total fat (1 g saturated), 0 mg cholesterol, 220 mg sodium.

Confetti Rice Pilaf

PREP: 10 MINUTES • COOK: 25 MINUTES
BAKE: 30 MINUTES

Tender rice with peas, carrots, and green onions—this colorful side dish goes well with a simple roast chicken or pork.

3 tablespoons margarine or butter
2 medium carrots, diced
2 cups regular long-grain rice
1 can (14½ ounces) chicken broth
1 small bay leaf
½ teaspoon salt
¼ teaspoon coarsely ground black pepper
1 package (10 ounces) frozen peas
2 medium green onions, sliced

1 In 3-quart saucepan, melt margarine or butter over medium heat. Add carrots and cook 2 to 3 minutes, until slightly softened, stirring occasionally. Add rice and cook 1 minute, stirring, until grains are coated. Stir in chicken broth, bay leaf, salt, pepper, and 2 *cups water*; heat to boiling over high heat. Reduce heat to low; cover and simmer 15 to 20 minutes, until all liquid is absorbed and rice is tender.

2 Preheat oven to 350°F. Discard bay leaf from rice; stir in peas and green onions. Transfer mixture to shallow 2½-quart baking dish.

3 Bake pilaf, covered, 30 minutes or until hot. Makes about 8 cups or 12 accompaniment servings.

Each serving: About 165 calories, 4 g protein, 29 g carbohydrate, 3 g total fat (1 g saturated), 0 mg cholesterol, 260 mg sodium.

Bulgur with Dried Cranberries

PREP: 5 MINUTES • COOK: 10 TO 15 MINUTES

Bulgur, a nutritious Middle Eastern staple made from wheat kernels that have been steamed, dried, and crushed, has a nice earthy flavor. We added chewy berries and lemon peel for a delicious sweet-tart accent.

1 can (14½ ounces) reduced-sodium chicken broth
1 cup bulgur (cracked wheat)
⅓ cup dried cranberries
1 teaspoon grated fresh lemon peel
¼ teaspoon salt
⅛ teaspoon coarsely ground black pepper

In 2-quart saucepan, heat all ingredients to boiling over high heat. Reduce heat to low; cover and simmer 10 to 15 minutes, until liquid is absorbed and bulgur is plump and soft. Makes about 3 cups or 4 accompaniment servings.

Each serving: About 160 calories, 6 g protein, 35 g carbohydrate, 1 g total fat (0 g saturated), 0 mg cholesterol, 420 mg sodium.

10 SPEEDY STIR-INS FOR RICE

To flavor rice without loading on the fat, start with 1 cup of raw rice; when cooked, stir in:

• 3 green onions, chopped, and ¼ cup chopped fresh basil, mint, or parsley

• 1 teaspoon curry powder and 1 unpeeled Granny Smith apple, diced

• 1 garlic clove, minced, 3 tablespoons chopped parsley, and 2 teaspoons grated lemon peel

• 2 carrots, shredded, and 2 teaspoons chopped fresh thyme leaves

• 1 zucchini, shredded, and 1 teaspoon chopped fresh rosemary leaves

• ¼ cup grated Parmesan cheese and 2 tablespoons chopped fresh basil leaves

• ⅓ cup dark seedless raisins, 1 teaspoon grated fresh orange peel, and ¼ cup chopped mango chutney

• 2 teaspoons soy sauce, 1 teaspoon grated, peeled fresh ginger, and ½ teaspoon Asian sesame oil

• 1 tablespoon chopped fresh mint leaves and ¼ cup crumbled feta cheese

• ⅓ cup bottled salsa and 2 tablespoons chopped fresh cilantro leaves

MEATLESS MAIN DISHES

Skillet Vegetable Curry

PREP: 15 MINUTES • COOK: ABOUT 20 MINUTES

A package of precut cauliflower shortens prep time. As vegetables simmer, toast some pita bread to serve alongside.

¾ pound cauliflower flowerets
1 large all-purpose potato (about 8 ounces), peeled and cut into 1-inch chunks
1 large sweet potato (about 12 ounces), peeled and cut into 1-inch chunks
2 tablespoons lightly packed sweetened flaked coconut
2 teaspoons olive oil
1 medium onion, finely chopped
1 teaspoon mustard seeds
1½ teaspoons ground cumin
1½ teaspoons ground coriander
⅛ teaspoon ground red pepper (cayenne)
2 medium tomatoes, diced
1 cup frozen peas, thawed
1¼ teaspoons salt
½ cup loosely packed fresh cilantro leaves, chopped

1 In 4-quart saucepan, place cauliflower, potato, sweet potato, and *enough water to cover*; heat to boiling over high heat. Reduce heat to low; cover and simmer 8 to 10 minutes, until vegetables are tender; drain well, reserving ¾ *cup cooking water.*

2 Meanwhile, in nonstick 12-inch skillet, cook coconut over medium heat until lightly browned, about 3 minutes, stirring constantly; transfer to small bowl.

3 In same skillet, heat olive oil over medium heat until hot; add onion and cook 5 minutes. Add mustard seeds, cumin, coriander, and ground red pepper; cover and cook 5 minutes longer or until onion is tender and lightly browned and seeds start to pop, shaking skillet frequently.

4 Spoon cauliflower mixture into skillet; add tomatoes, peas, salt, reserved cooking water, and toasted coconut; heat through. Sprinkle with cilantro to serve. Makes about 8 cups or 4 main-dish servings.

Each serving: About 230 calories, 8 g protein, 43 g carbohydrate, 4 g total fat (1 g saturated), 0 mg cholesterol, 735 mg sodium.

Vegetarian Tortilla Pie

PREP: 8 MINUTES • BAKE: 10 TO 12 MINUTES

This dish can be assembled in a jiffy, thanks to its no-cook filling of canned black beans and corn, prepared salsa, and pre-shredded Jack cheese. A wedge of iceberg lettuce on the side with our Spicy Tomato Dressing (page 177) adds the missing crunch.

1 jar (11 to 12 ounces) medium salsa
1 can (8 ounces) no-salt-added tomato sauce
1 can (15 to 16 ounces) no-salt-added black beans, rinsed and drained
1 can (15¼ ounces) no-salt-added whole-kernel corn, drained
½ cup packed fresh cilantro leaves
4 (10-inch diameter) low-fat flour tortillas
6 ounces shredded reduced-fat Monterey Jack cheese (1½ cups)
Reduced-fat sour cream (optional)

1 Preheat oven to 500°F. Spray 15½" by 10½" jelly-roll pan with nonstick cooking spray.

2 In small bowl, mix salsa and tomato sauce. In medium bowl, mix black beans, corn, and cilantro.

3 Place 1 tortilla in jelly-roll pan. Spread one-third of salsa mixture over tortilla. Top with one-third of bean mixture and one-third of cheese. Repeat layering 2 more times, ending with last tortilla.

4 Bake pie 10 to 12 minutes, until cheese melts and filling is hot. Serve with reduced-fat sour cream if you like. Makes 4 main-dish servings.

Each serving without sour cream: About 440 calories, 25 g protein, 65 g carbohydrate, 11 g total fat (5 g saturated), 30 mg cholesterol, 820 mg sodium.

Vegetarian Tortilla Pie ➤

Cabbage & Bulgur Casserole

PREP: 45 MINUTES • BAKE: 40 MINUTES

We layered Napa cabbage with a filling that is healthy and tastes good too.

1½ cups bulgur (cracked wheat)
1 tablespoon vegetable oil
2 medium carrots, diced
2 medium celery stalks, diced
1 medium red pepper, diced
½ small head Napa (Chinese cabbage), about
    1¾ pounds, cut crosswise into 2-inch pieces to
    equal about 12 cups leafy tops and 2 cups
    crunchy stems
3 garlic cloves, crushed with garlic press
3 green onions, sliced
2 tablespoons minced, peeled fresh ginger
2 tablespoons plus 1 teaspoon soy sauce
2 tablespoons seasoned rice vinegar
1 can (14½ ounces) diced tomatoes
2 tablespoons brown sugar
2 tablespoons chopped fresh parsley leaves for
    garnish

1 Preheat oven to 350°F. In 2-quart saucepan, heat *1½ cups water* to boiling over high heat; stir in bulgur. Remove saucepan from heat; cover and set aside.

2 In 5-quart Dutch oven, heat vegetable oil over medium-high heat. Add carrots, celery, and red pepper; cook 5 minutes. Add cabbage stems, and cook 7 minutes longer or until vegetables are tender.

3 Reduce heat to low; add garlic, green onions, and ginger, and cook 1 minute longer, stirring. Add ½ *cup water*; heat to boiling over high heat. Reduce heat to low; simmer 1 minute, stirring. Remove Dutch oven from heat; stir in 2 tablespoons soy sauce, 1 tablespoon rice vinegar, and cooked bulgur.

4 In small bowl, combine tomatoes with their juice, brown sugar, remaining 1 tablespoon rice vinegar, and 1 teaspoon soy sauce.

5 In 3-quart casserole, place half of cabbage leaves; top with bulgur mixture, then remaining cabbage leaves. Spoon tomato mixture over top. Cover casserole and bake 40 minutes or until hot in the center and top layer of cabbage leaves is wilted. Sprinkle with chopped parsley before serving. Makes 6 main-dish servings.

Each serving: About 220 calories, 7 g protein, 43 g carbohydrate, 3 g total fat (0 g saturated), 0 mg cholesterol, 800 mg sodium.

Cabbage & Bulgur Casserole

Vegetarian Black Bean Burritos

PREP: 10 MINUTES • COOK: 15 MINUTES

A deceptively rich and tasty combination of fat-free bean chili, rice, fresh corn, and spicy cheese all wrapped up in warm flour tortillas.

½ cup regular long-grain rice
4 (10-inch diameter) low-fat flour tortillas
1¼ cups fresh corn kernels (about 2 large ears
    corn)
1 can (15 ounces) spicy fat-free black bean chili
1 can (8 ounces) tomato sauce
¼ cup shredded Monterey Jack cheese with
    jalapeño chiles (1 ounce)
⅓ cup packed fresh cilantro leaves, chopped

1 Preheat oven to 300°F. In 2-quart saucepan, prepare rice as label directs but do not add salt or margarine or butter.

2 Meanwhile, wrap tortillas in foil; heat in oven until warm, about 15 minutes.

3 When rice is done, stir in corn, black bean chili, and tomato sauce. Heat to boiling over medium-high heat; boil 1 minute.

4 Spoon about 1 cup chili mixture down center of each tortilla; sprinkle with cheese and cilantro. Fold sides of tortillas over filling. Place burritos seam-side down on platter. Makes 4 main-dish servings.

Each serving: About 430 calories, 15 g protein, 75 g carbohydrate, 8 g total fat (2 g saturated), 8 mg cholesterol, 910 mg sodium.

2 Place vegetables, oiled side down, on grill over medium heat, and cook 15 to 20 minutes, turning once, until tender and golden. Transfer vegetables to plate as they finish cooking.

3 Arrange one-fourth of grilled vegetables down center of each tortilla; sprinkle with Cheddar and Monterey Jack cheeses. Place open burritos on grill. Cover grill and cook 1 minute, or until cheeses melt.

4 Transfer burritos to plate; sprinkle cilantro over cheese. Fold sides of tortillas over filling. Serve with salsa if you like. Makes 4 main-dish servings.

Each serving: About 395 calories, 15 g protein, 45 g carbohydrate, 18 g total fat (7 g saturated), 28 mg cholesterol, 715 mg sodium.

Grilled Vegetable Burritos

PREP: 25 MINUTES • GRILL: ABOUT 20 MINUTES

Onion, peppers, and zucchini are grilled and rolled in tortillas with shredded cheeses for an all-in-one entrée.

1 tablespoon plus 1 teaspoon vegetable oil
1 teaspoon chili powder
1 teaspoon ground cumin
½ teaspoon salt
¼ teaspoon coarsely ground black pepper
2 medium zucchini (about 10 ounces each), cut lengthwise into ¼-inch-thick slices
1 large onion, cut into ½-inch-thick slices
1 medium red pepper, cut into quarters, stem and seeds discarded
1 medium green pepper, cut into quarters, stem and seeds discarded
4 burrito-size flour tortillas (10-inch diameter)
½ cup shredded sharp Cheddar cheese (2 ounces)
½ cup shredded Monterey Jack cheese with jalapeño chiles (2 ounces)
½ cup loosely packed fresh cilantro leaves
Bottled salsa (optional)

1 In small bowl, mix vegetable oil, chili powder, cumin, salt, and black pepper. Brush 1 side of zucchini slices, onion slices, and pepper pieces with oil mixture.

Rice Salad with Black Beans

PREP: 10 MINUTES • COOK: 20 MINUTES

A satisfying meal in one, packed with the zesty flavors of citrus, salsa, and cilantro.

¾ cup regular long-grain rice
2 large limes
2 cans (15 to 19 ounces each) black beans, rinsed and drained
1 bunch watercress, tough stems removed
½ cup bottled salsa
1 cup fresh corn kernels (about 2 medium ears corn)
¼ cup packed fresh cilantro leaves, chopped
1 tablespoon olive oil
½ teaspoon salt
¼ teaspoon coarsely ground black pepper

1 Prepare rice as label directs. Meanwhile, from limes, grate ½ teaspoon peel and squeeze 3 tablespoons juice.

2 In large bowl, mix all ingredients, tossing well. Cover and refrigerate if not serving right away. Makes about 7 cups or 4 main-dish servings.

Each serving: About 405 calories, 24 g protein, 81 g carbohydrate, 6 g total fat (1 g saturated), 0 mg cholesterol, 1125 mg sodium.

Meatless Chili

PREP: 30 MINUTES PLUS OVERNIGHT TO SOAK BEANS
BAKE: 1 HOUR 30 MINUTES

1½ pounds mixed dried beans, such as red
    kidney, white kidney (cannellini), and black
    (3 cups total)
1 tablespoon vegetable oil
3 medium carrots, cut into ¼-inch slices
2 medium onions, finely chopped
1 celery stalk, finely chopped
1 medium red pepper, finely chopped
3 garlic cloves, minced
1 jalapeño chile, minced, with seeds
2 teaspoons ground cumin
½ teaspoon ground coriander
1 can (28 ounces) tomatoes in puree
1 chipotle chile, canned in adobo sauce, minced
2 teaspoons salt
¼ teaspoon dried oregano
1 package (10 ounces) frozen whole-kernel corn
1¼ cups loosely packed fresh cilantro leaves and
    stems, chopped

1 Rinse beans with cold running water and discard any stones or shriveled beans. In large bowl, place beans and enough water to cover by 2 inches. Let stand at room temperature overnight. (Or, in 5-quart Dutch oven or saucepot, place beans and enough water to cover by 2 inches. Heat to boiling over high heat; boil 2 minutes. Remove Dutch oven from heat; cover and let stand 1 hour.) Drain and rinse beans.

2 Preheat oven to 375°F. In 5-quart Dutch oven, place beans and 8 cups water; heat to boiling over high heat. Cover Dutch oven and bake 1 hour or until beans are tender, stirring occasionally. Drain beans and return to Dutch oven.

3 Meanwhile, in 10-inch skillet, heat vegetable oil over medium heat. Add carrots, onions, celery, and red pepper, and cook until vegetables are tender, about 10 minutes, stirring frequently. Stir in garlic, jalapeño, cumin, and coriander; cook 30 seconds, stirring. Stir in tomatoes with their puree, chipotle chile, salt, and oregano, breaking up tomatoes with side of spoon; heat to boiling over high heat. Reduce heat to low; simmer, uncovered, 10 minutes.

4 Stir tomato mixture, corn, and *2 cups water* into beans. Cover Dutch oven and bake 30 minutes longer. Remove from oven; stir in cilantro. Makes about 12½ cups or 6 main-dish servings.

Each serving: About 360 calories, 20 g protein, 66 g carbohydrate, 4 g total fat (0 g saturated), 0 mg cholesterol, 1195 mg sodium.

GH INSTITUTE REPORT

DOES RINSING CANNED BEANS REDUCE SODIUM?

Canned beans can't be beat when it comes to low cost and high speed—whether you make three-bean salad, chili, our Falafel Sandwiches (page 152) or Black-Bean Soup (page 40). But if you're tracking your sodium, a canful of beans may be off-limits, packing more than 450 milligrams of sodium per half-cup—about as much as a 2½-ounce bag of potato chips.

Still, many people think that rinsing beans will significantly cut their saltiness. Are they full of beans? We wanted proof, so the Good Housekeeping Institute's Chemistry Department drained and rinsed 3 varieties by Goya and Progresso—red kidney, white kidney, and black—and then analyzed the amount of sodium remaining.

The surprise: Sodium was reduced in comparison to label claims, but results varied, with reductions generally between 16 and 30 percent. (For example, Progresso Red Kidney Beans started out with 340 mg sodium per serving and had 271 mg after draining and rinsing.) So if you want to rinse beans for a fresher taste (as we do in our test kitchens), keep it up. But don't count on this as a major salt-reducing step. If you're on a strict low-sodium diet, switch to dried beans—cooked without salt—or buy low-salt canned beans.

Asparagus Quiche

PREP: 45 MINUTES • BAKE: 40 TO 45 MINUTES

We made the delicate custard filling with half-and-half instead of heavy cream to save fat and calories.

1¼ cups all-purpose flour
¾ teaspoon salt
4 tablespoons margarine or butter
2 tablespoons shortening
1 pound asparagus, trimmed and cut into ¾-inch pieces
4 large eggs
2 cups half-and-half or light cream
⅛ teaspoon coarsely ground black pepper
Pinch ground nutmeg
4 ounces Gruyère or Swiss cheese, coarsely shredded (1 cup)

1 In medium bowl, with fork, stir flour and ¼ teaspoon salt. With pastry blender or two knives used scissor-fashion, cut in margarine or butter with shortening until mixture resembles coarse crumbs. Sprinkle about *4 tablespoons cold water*, 1 tablespoon at a time, into flour mixture, mixing lightly with fork after each addition, until dough is just moist enough to hold together. Shape dough into a disk; wrap with plastic wrap and refrigerate 30 minutes or until firm enough to roll.

2 Meanwhile, in 2-quart saucepan, heat *4 cups water* to boiling over high heat. Add asparagus and cook 6 to 8 minutes until tender. Drain asparagus and rinse with cold running water. Drain and set aside.

3 Preheat oven to 425°F. On lightly floured surface, with floured rolling pin, roll dough into a round 1½ inches larger in diameter than inverted 9-inch pie plate. Gently ease dough into pie plate; trim edge, leaving 1-inch overhang. Fold overhang under; bring up over pie-plate rim. Pinch dough to form decorative edge. With fork, prick dough at 1-inch intervals.

4 Line pie shell with foil and fill with pie weights, dried beans, or uncooked rice. Bake pie shell 15 minutes; remove foil with weights and bake 10 minutes longer or until crust is golden. (If crust puffs up during baking, gently press it to pie plate with back of spoon.) Turn oven control to 350°F.

5 Meanwhile, in medium bowl, with wire whisk or fork, mix eggs, half-and-half, pepper, nutmeg, and remaining ½ teaspoon salt until well blended.

6 Sprinkle asparagus and cheese into pie crust. Pour half-and-half mixture over asparagus and cheese.

7 Place sheet of foil underneath pie plate; crimp foil edges to form a rim to catch any drips during baking. Bake quiche 40 to 45 minutes, until knife inserted in center comes out clean. Serve quiche hot, or cool on wire rack to serve at room temperature later. Makes 8 main-dish servings.

Each serving: About 325 calories, 12 g protein, 19 g carbohydrate, 22 g total fat (9 g saturated), 141 mg cholesterol, 380 mg sodium.

Spinach Strata

PREP: 15 MINUTES PLUS REFRIGERATING • BAKE: 1 HOUR

You can assemble this a day ahead, then pop it in the oven—right from the refrigerator—just 1 hour before serving.

8 slices firm white bread
4 ounces mozzarella cheese, shredded (1 cup)
1 package (10 ounces) frozen chopped spinach, thawed and squeezed dry
1 tablespoon margarine or butter, softened
2 cups milk
6 large eggs
½ cup loosely packed fresh basil leaves, chopped
½ teaspoon salt
¼ teaspoon coarsely ground black pepper

1 Grease 8" by 8" glass baking dish. Place 4 slices bread in dish; top with ½ cup cheese, all spinach, then remaining cheese. Spread margarine or butter on 1 side of remaining bread slices; place in dish, buttered side up.

2 In medium bowl, with wire whisk or fork, beat milk, eggs, basil, salt, and pepper until blended. Slowly pour mixture over bread slices. Prick bread with fork and press slices down to absorb egg mixture.

3 Cover baking dish with plastic wrap and refrigerate at least 30 minutes or overnight.

4 To bake, preheat oven to 350°F. Uncover baking dish and bake strata 1 hour or until knife inserted in center comes out clean. Remove strata from oven and let stand 5 minutes. Makes 6 main-dish servings.

Each serving: About 290 calories, 17 g protein, 22 g carbohydrate, 15 g total fat (6 g saturated), 240 mg cholesterol, 575 mg sodium.

Veggie Enchiladas

PREP: 25 MINUTES • BAKE: 20 MINUTES

2 teaspoons olive oil
1 small zucchini (8 ounces), cut into ½-inch
    pieces
1 medium onion, chopped
1 medium red pepper, chopped
2 cans (15 to 19 ounces each) no-salt-added
    white kidney beans (cannellini), rinsed and
    drained
½ cup vegetable broth or chicken broth
2 garlic cloves, minced
1 can (15¼ ounces) no-salt-added whole-kernel
    corn, drained
2 pickled jalapeño chiles, minced, with seeds
1 cup loosely packed fresh cilantro leaves and
    stems, chopped
6 flour tortillas (8-inch diameter)
1 jar (15½ ounces) mild salsa
⅓ cup shredded Monterey Jack cheese
Lime wedges for garnish

1 In nonstick 12-inch skillet, heat olive oil over medium heat. Add zucchini, onion, and red pepper, and cook until vegetables are tender and golden, 10 to 15 minutes, stirring frequently.

2 Meanwhile, in food processor with knife blade attached or in blender at medium speed, blend half of white kidney beans with broth until almost smooth. Transfer bean mixture to large bowl; stir in remaining beans and set aside.

3 To vegetables in skillet, add garlic and cook 1 minute longer. Stir in corn and jalapeños; cook 2 minutes longer. Transfer vegetable mixture to bowl with beans; stir in cilantro until mixed.

4 Preheat oven to 375°F. Spoon about ¾ cup bean mixture along center of each tortilla. Fold sides of tortilla over filling, overlapping slightly.

5 Spoon ½ cup salsa into bottom of 13" by 9" glass or ceramic baking dish. Place enchiladas, seam side down, on top of salsa. Spoon remaining salsa over enchiladas; sprinkle with cheese. Bake 20 minutes. Serve with lime wedges. Makes 6 main-dish servings.

Each serving: About 415 calories, 17 g protein, 70 g carbohydrate, 8 g total fat (2 g saturated), 6 mg cholesterol, 700 mg sodium.

Polenta Lasagna

PREP: 45 MINUTES • BAKE: 30 MINUTES

This stress-free dish is perfect for a last-minute dinner party; serve with a salad of mixed baby greens.

1 tablespoon olive oil
1 small onion, finely chopped
1 garlic clove, minced
1 can (28 ounces) tomatoes in juice
2 tablespoons tomato paste
2 tablespoons chopped fresh basil
1 teaspoon salt
1 package (10 ounces) frozen chopped spinach,
    thawed and squeezed dry
1 cup part-skim ricotta cheese
2 tablespoons grated Parmesan cheese
¼ teaspoon coarsely ground black pepper
1 package (24 ounces) precooked polenta, cut
    into 16 slices
4 ounces part-skim mozzarella cheese, shredded
    (1 cup)

1 In 3-quart saucepan, heat olive oil over medium heat. Add onion and cook until tender, about 8 minutes, stirring occasionally. Add garlic and cook 30 seconds longer. Stir in tomatoes with their juice, tomato paste, basil, and ½ teaspoon salt, breaking up tomatoes with side of spoon; heat to boiling over high heat. Reduce heat to low and simmer, uncovered, 20 minutes, stirring occasionally. Set sauce aside.

2 Meanwhile, in medium bowl, mix spinach, ricotta, Parmesan, pepper, and remaining ½ teaspoon salt until blended.

3 Preheat oven to 350°F. Grease 8" by 8" glass baking dish.

4 Arrange half of polenta slices, overlapping slightly, in baking dish. Drop half of spinach mixture, by rounded tablespoons, on top of polenta (mixture will not completely cover slices). Pour half of sauce over spinach mixture; spread to form an even layer. Sprinkle with half of mozzarella. Repeat layering.

5 Bake casserole, uncovered, 30 minutes or until hot and bubbling. Let stand 10 minutes for easier serving. Makes 6 main-dish servings.

Each serving: About 270 calories, 16 g protein, 30 g carbohydrate, 10 g total fat (5 g saturated), 28 mg cholesterol, 1210 mg sodium.

Falafel Sandwiches

PREP: 10 MINUTES • COOK: 8 MINUTES PER BATCH

Serve these small, flat bean patties in pita pockets with lettuce, tomatoes, cucumbers, and tangy plain low-fat yogurt.

4 green onions, cut into 1-inch pieces
2 garlic cloves, each cut in half
½ cup packed fresh Italian parsley leaves
2 teaspoons dried mint
1 can (15 to 19 ounces) garbanzo beans, rinsed and drained
½ cup plain dried bread crumbs
1 teaspoon ground coriander
1 teaspoon ground cumin
1 teaspoon baking powder
½ teaspoon salt
¼ teaspoon ground red pepper (cayenne)
¼ teaspoon ground allspice
Olive oil nonstick cooking spray
4 pitas (6- to 7-inch diameter)

Accompaniments: sliced romaine lettuce, sliced tomatoes, sliced cucumber, sliced red onion, plain low-fat yogurt

1 In food processor with knife blade attached, finely chop green onions, garlic, parsley, and mint. Add garbanzo beans, bread crumbs, coriander, cumin, baking powder, salt, ground red pepper, and allspice, and blend until a coarse puree forms.

2 Shape bean mixture, by scant ½ cups, into eight 3-inch round patties and place on sheet of waxed paper. Spray both sides of patties with olive oil spray.

3 Heat nonstick 10-inch skillet over medium-high heat until hot. Add half of patties and cook 8 minutes or until dark golden brown, turning once. Transfer patties to paper towels to drain. Repeat with remaining patties.

4 Cut off top third of each pita to form a pocket. Place warm patties in pitas. Serve with choice of accompaniments. Makes 4 sandwiches.

Each sandwich without accompaniments: About 365 calories, 14 g protein, 68 g carbohydrate, 5 g total fat (1 g saturated), 0 mg cholesterol, 1015 mg sodium.

Falafel Sandwiches

Southwestern Black-Bean Burgers

PREP: 10 MINUTES • COOK: ABOUT 6 MINUTES

For an even easier weeknight meal, make a double batch and freeze uncooked burgers. Defrost 10 minutes, then cook until heated through, about 12 minutes, turning once. To make a fast meal with our Warm Caesar Potato Salad (page 180), start cooking the potatoes first, then concentrate on the burgers.

1 can (15 to 19 ounces) black beans, rinsed and
   drained
2 tablespoons light mayonnaise
¼ cup packed fresh cilantro leaves, chopped
1 tablespoon plain dried bread crumbs
½ teaspoon ground cumin
½ teaspoon hot pepper sauce
Nonstick cooking spray
1 cup loosely packed sliced lettuce
4 mini whole wheat pitas (4-inch diameter),
   warmed
½ cup mild salsa

1 In large bowl, with potato masher or fork, mash beans with mayonnaise until almost smooth (some lumps of beans should remain). Stir in cilantro, bread crumbs, cumin, and pepper sauce until combined. With lightly floured hands, shape bean mixture into four 3-inch round patties. Spray both sides of each patty lightly with nonstick cooking spray.

2 Heat skillet over medium heat until hot. Add patties and cook until lightly browned, about 3 minutes. With pancake turner, turn patties over, and cook 3 minutes longer or until heated through.

3 Arrange lettuce on pitas; top with burgers then salsa. Makes 4 main-dish servings.

Each serving: About 210 calories, 13 g protein, 42 g carbohydrate, 3 g total fat (0 g saturated), 0 mg cholesterol, 715 mg sodium.

Fresh Mozzarella & Tomato Sandwiches

PREP: 15 MINUTES

The essence of summer—with garden tomatoes and our fresh herb sauce.

½ cup Salsa Verde (below)
8 slices (½ inch thick each) Tuscan bread
2 ripe medium tomatoes, each cut into 4 slices
8 ounces fresh mozzarella cheese, cut into
   8 slices

Spread about 1 tablespoon Salsa Verde on 1 side of each bread slice. Place 2 tomato slices and 2 mozzarella slices on each of 4 bread slices. Place remaining bread slices, sauce side down, on top. Cut each sandwich in half to serve. Makes 4 sandwiches.

Each sandwich: About 455 calories, 17 g protein, 38 g carbohydrate, 26 g total fat (9 g saturated), 44 mg cholesterol, 690 mg sodium.

Salsa Verde

PREP: 15 MINUTES

Our recipe for Italian green sauce makes a terrific spread for Fresh Mozzarella & Tomato Sandwiches (above).

1 garlic clove, cut in half
¼ teaspoon salt
2 cups packed fresh Italian parsley leaves (about
   3 bunches)
⅓ cup olive oil
3 tablespoons capers, drained
3 tablespoons fresh lemon juice
1 teaspoon Dijon mustard
⅛ teaspoon coarsely ground black pepper

In food processor with knife blade attached or in blender, combine all ingredients and blend until finely chopped. If not using sauce right away, cover and refrigerate up to 3 days. Makes about ¾ cup.

Each tablespoon: About 60 calories, 0 g protein, 1 g carbohydrate, 6 g total fat (1 g saturated), 0 mg cholesterol, 140 mg sodium.

Capellini Frittata

PREP: 14 MINUTES • BAKE: ABOUT 6 MINUTES

A satisfying meal made with sautéed onion and red pepper baked in an egg-and-pasta custard. If you have leftover spaghetti in the fridge, use 1 cup of it instead of the cooked capellini. Serve with a green salad, our Spicy Tomato Dressing (page 177), and a chunk of hearty peasant bread.

2 ounces capellini or angel hair pasta, broken
   into pieces (about ½ cup)
2 teaspoons olive oil
1 small onion, thinly sliced
1 small red pepper, diced
6 large egg whites*
2 large eggs
⅓ cup grated Parmesan cheese
¼ cup fat-free (skim) milk
½ teaspoon salt
¼ teaspoon hot pepper sauce

1 In 2-quart saucepan, heat 3 *cups water* to boiling over high heat. Add pasta and cook 2 minutes or just until tender. Drain and set aside.

2 Meanwhile, preheat oven to 425°F. In nonstick 10-inch skillet with oven-safe handle (or cover handle with heavy-duty foil for baking in oven later), heat olive oil over medium heat. Add onion and red pepper, and cook, stirring frequently, until vegetables are tender, about 7 minutes.

3 In large bowl, with wire whisk or fork, beat egg whites, whole eggs, Parmesan, milk, salt, and hot pepper sauce; stir in pasta. Pour egg mixture over onion mixture; cover and cook 3 minutes or until set around the edge. Uncover skillet and place in oven. Bake 6 minutes longer or until frittata is set in center.

4 To serve, invert frittata onto cutting board and cut into wedges. Makes 4 main-dish servings.

*Or, use powdered egg whites, reconstituted following package directions. Powdered egg whites are available in the baking section of most supermarkets.

Each serving: About 190 calories, 15 g protein, 15 g carbohydrate, 8 g total fat (3 g saturated), 113 mg cholesterol, 545 mg sodium.

Mexican Potato Frittata

PREP: 5 MINUTES • COOK: 20 MINUTES

This flat, baked omelet combines a jar of salsa with a bit of sharp Cheddar cheese. While the frittata bakes, toss a package of prewashed baby spinach with sliced red onions, sliced fresh pears, and bottled salad dressing for a superquick salad to go with.

1 teaspoon olive oil
12 ounces red-skinned potatoes, cut into ½-inch
   cubes
6 large eggs
1 jar (11 to 12 ounces) medium-hot salsa
½ teaspoon salt
¼ teaspoon coarsely ground black pepper
¼ cup shredded sharp Cheddar cheese
   (1 ounce)
1 medium tomato, diced

1 Preheat oven to 425°F. In nonstick 10-inch skillet with oven-safe handle (or cover handle with heavy-duty foil for baking in oven later), heat olive oil over medium-high heat; add potatoes and cook, covered, until potatoes are tender and golden brown, about 10 minutes, stirring occasionally.

2 Meanwhile, in medium bowl, with wire whisk or fork, beat eggs with ¼ cup salsa (chopped, if necessary), salt, and pepper. Stir in cheese; set aside. Stir diced tomato into remaining salsa.

3 Stir egg mixture into potatoes in skillet and cook over medium heat, covered, 3 minutes or until egg mixture begins to set around edge. Remove cover and place skillet in oven; bake 4 to 6 minutes, until frittata is set.

4 To serve, invert frittata onto cutting board. Cut into wedges and top with salsa mixture. Makes 4 main-dish servings.

Each serving: About 235 calories, 14 g protein, 20 g carbohydrate, 11 g total fat (4 g saturated), 327 mg cholesterol, 795 mg sodium.

Mexican Potato Frittata ➤

Spinach Soufflé

PREP: 20 MINUTES • BAKE: 20 MINUTES

Even though this recipe requires about 40 minutes total, only 20 minutes is active prep. During the remaining 20 minutes, while the soufflé bakes, you can relax!

Nonstick cooking spray
3 tablespoons plain dried bread crumbs
1½ cups low-fat (1%) milk
⅓ cup cornstarch
2 large eggs, separated
1 package (10 ounces) frozen chopped spinach, thawed and squeezed dry
3 tablespoons grated Parmesan cheese
½ teaspoon salt
¼ teaspoon coarsely ground black pepper
½ teaspoon cream of tartar
4 large egg whites*

1 Preheat oven to 425°F. Spray 10-inch quiche dish or shallow 2-quart casserole with cooking spray; sprinkle with bread crumbs to coat. Set aside.

2 In 2-quart saucepan, with wire whisk, beat milk with cornstarch until blended. Heat milk mixture over medium-high heat until mixture thickens and boils, stirring constantly. Boil 1 minute. Remove saucepan from heat.

3 In large bowl, with rubber spatula, mix egg yolks, spinach, Parmesan, salt, and pepper until blended; stir in warm milk mixture. Cool slightly (if spinach mixture is too warm, it will deflate beaten egg whites).

4 In another large bowl, with mixer at high speed, beat cream of tartar and 6 egg whites until stiff peaks form. Gently fold egg-white mixture, one-third at a time, into spinach mixture.

5 Spoon soufflé mixture into quiche dish. Bake soufflé 20 minutes or until top is golden and puffed. Serve immediately. Makes 4 main-dish servings.

*Or, use powdered egg whites, reconstituted following package directions. Powdered egg whites are available in the baking section of most supermarkets.

Each serving: About 195 calories, 15 g protein, 23 g carbohydrate, 5 g total fat (2 g saturated), 114 mg cholesterol, 590 mg sodium.

Asparagus Omelets

PREP: 10 MINUTES • COOK: ABOUT 5 MINUTES

If you don't have pale yellow, nutty-flavored Gruyère cheese, substitute the same amount of shredded Swiss or Jarlsberg, or a few shavings of fresh Parmesan.

FILLING:
1 pound asparagus, trimmed
1/8 teaspoon coarsely ground black pepper
4 ounces Gruyère cheese, shredded (1 cup)

OMELETS:
8 large eggs*
1/2 teaspoon salt
4 teaspoons margarine or butter
Parsley sprigs for garnish

1 Prepare Filling: In deep 12-inch skillet, in *1 inch boiling water*, heat asparagus to boiling over high heat. Reduce heat to medium-low; simmer, uncovered, just until tender. Drain asparagus; rinse with cold running water to stop cooking. Sprinkle pepper over cheese.

2 To make Omelets: In medium bowl, with wire whisk, beat eggs, salt, and *1/2 cup cold water*. For each omelet, in nonstick 8-inch skillet, melt 1 teaspoon margarine or butter over medium-high heat. Pour in 1/2 cup egg mixture; cook until set (about 1 minute), gently lifting edge. Sprinkle one-fourth of cheese mixture on half of omelet; top with one-fourth of asparagus spears. Fold over other half of omelet; slide onto plate. Repeat to make 4 omelets in all. Garnish each omelet with a parsley sprig. Makes 4 main-dish servings.

*For lighter omelets, substitute 4 large eggs and 8 large egg whites.

Each serving: About 310 calories, 23 g protein, 3 g carbohydrate, 23 g total fat (9 g saturated), 457 mg cholesterol, 540 mg sodium.

Huevos Rancheros

PREP: 10 MINUTES • COOK: 20 MINUTES

Serve this hearty Mexican dish with any or all of the following: sliced avocado, black beans, mixed salad greens, and sour cream.

1 tablespoon plus 2 teaspoons vegetable oil
1 medium onion, coarsely chopped
1 small garlic clove, minced
1 jalapeño chile, seeded and minced
1 can (14½ ounces) tomatoes
1/4 teaspoon salt
8 large eggs
8 flour or corn tortillas (6-inch diameter), warmed
1 tablespoon chopped fresh cilantro leaves

1 In 2-quart saucepan, heat 1 tablespoon vegetable oil over medium-high heat until hot. Add onion, garlic, and jalapeño, and cook until onion is tender, stirring occasionally, about 8 minutes. Stir in tomatoes with their juice and salt; heat to boiling over high heat, breaking up tomatoes with side of spoon. Reduce heat to low; cover and simmer 5 minutes, stirring occasionally.

2 In nonstick 10-inch skillet, heat 1 teaspoon vegetable oil over medium heat. One at a time, break 4 eggs into a saucer, then slip into skillet. Reduce heat to low; cook eggs slowly until whites are completely set and yolks begin to thicken but are not hard; turn eggs over if you like. Transfer eggs to warm plate; keep warm. Repeat with remaining oil and eggs.

3 Arrange tortillas on 4 dinner plates. Place 1 fried egg on each tortilla. Spoon 2 tablespoons tomato sauce over each egg; sprinkle with cilantro. Serve with remaining tomato sauce. Makes 4 main-dish servings.

Each serving: About 395 calories, 18 g protein, 37 g carbohydrate, 20 g total fat (4 g saturated), 426 mg cholesterol, 665 mg sodium.

Stir-Fried Tofu with Vegetables

PREP: 10 MINUTES • COOK: 10 MINUTES

2 teaspoons vegetable oil
1 package (16 ounces) extrafirm tofu, patted dry
   and cut into 1" by ½" pieces
3 green onions
1 cup vegetable or chicken broth
1 tablespoon dark brown sugar
1 tablespoon soy sauce
2 teaspoons cornstarch
1 bag (10 ounces) shredded carrots
1 medium red pepper, thinly sliced
2 garlic cloves, crushed with garlic press
1 tablespoon grated, peeled fresh ginger
½ teaspoon salt

1 In nonstick 12-inch skillet, heat 1 teaspoon oil over medium-high heat until hot. Add tofu and cook about 4 minutes, gently tossing until heated through and lightly golden. Transfer to plate; set aside.

2 Meanwhile, thinly slice green onions, separating white parts from green tops. In 2-cup measuring cup, mix broth, brown sugar, soy sauce, and cornstarch.

FOOD EDITOR'S TIP

Q I'd like to eat more tofu, but I'm confused about which type to buy and how to use it.

A I hear this a lot, as more and more people are counting on tofu (soybean curd) as a good protein source. In general, there are two different kinds: regular and silken. Regular tofu is similar in texture to compressed cottage cheese; silken tofu has a smooth consistency. Both types come in extrafirm, firm, and soft varieties, and lite (lower-fat) versions made with soybeans and powdered soy protein. Extrafirm is densest, with the least water content (and the most protein, fat, vitamins, and minerals). It can be sliced or diced, and stir-fried, grilled, or broiled. Firm tofu contains more water than extrafirm and, as a result, is lighter in texture; it's easily sliced, diced, crumbled, or pureed to make thick spreads, dips, and creamy soups. Soft tofu contains the most water and is perfect in smooth dressings, sauces, or shakes. Be sure to use the type of tofu called for in a recipe, since the texture can make a tremendous difference in the dish.

3 In same skillet, heat remaining 1 teaspoon vegetable oil. Add white parts of green onions, carrots, red pepper, garlic, ginger, and salt; cook 5 minutes, stirring frequently.

4 Return tofu to skillet. Stir broth mixture, and add to skillet; heat to boiling. Boil 30 seconds, gently stirring. Spoon over rice to serve; sprinkle with remaining green onions. Makes 4 main-dish servings.

Each serving without rice: About 160 calories, 9 g protein, 20 g carbohydrate, 6 g total fat (1 g saturated), 0 mg cholesterol, 610 mg sodium.

Shortcut Niçoise Salad

PREP: 15 MINUTES • COOK: 15 MINUTES

2 large eggs
½ pound green beans, trimmed
2 tablespoons white wine vinegar
1 tablespoon minced shallot
1 teaspoon Dijon mustard
½ teaspoon salt
¼ teaspoon coarsely ground black pepper
¼ teaspoon sugar
3 tablespoons olive oil
1 bag (10 ounces) European-blend salad greens
1 can (15½ ounces to 19 ounces) white kidney
   beans (cannellini), rinsed and drained
⅓ cup Kalamata olives (about 2 ounces), pitted

1 In small saucepan, hard-cook eggs.

2 Meanwhile, in 10-inch skillet, heat *1 inch water* to boiling over high heat. Add green beans; heat to boiling. Reduce heat to low; simmer 5 to 8 minutes, until beans are tender. Drain beans; immediately rinse with cold running water to stop cooking.

3 In small bowl, with wire whisk, combine vinegar, shallot, mustard, salt, pepper, and sugar. Slowly whisk in olive oil until dressing thickens slightly.

4 Remove shells from hard-cooked eggs. Cut each egg lengthwise into quarters.

5 To serve, into medium bowl, pour half of dressing. Add salad greens; toss to coat. Line large platter with dressed salad greens. Arrange green beans, white kidney beans, olives, and egg quarters in separate piles on top of lettuce. Drizzle remaining dressing over salad. Makes 4 main-dish servings.

Each serving: About 300 calories, 12 g protein, 29 g carbohydrate, 16 g total fat (3 g saturated), 107 mg cholesterol, 795 mg sodium.

Vegetables
& Side Salads

Broccoli & Cauliflower with Gremolata Crumbs

PREP: 15 MINUTES • COOK: 15 TO 17 MINUTES
BAKE: 25 TO 30 MINUTES

We combined classic gremolata—a mixture of lemon, parsley, and garlic—with a toasted crumb topping to give steamed veggies a burst of flavor.

1 large head cauliflower (about 2¼ pounds), trimmed and cut into 2-inch flowerets
1 large bunch broccoli (about 1½ pounds), cut into 2-inch flowerets, with stems peeled and sliced into ¼-inch-thick rounds
8 slices firm white bread, torn into ¼-inch pieces (about 4 cups)
2 large lemons
3 tablespoons margarine or butter
2 tablespoons olive oil
1 large garlic clove, minced
½ teaspoon salt
¼ teaspoon coarsely ground black pepper
1 cup fresh parsley leaves, chopped

1 Place steamer basket in 6- to 8-quart saucepot with *1 inch water*. Heat water to boiling over high heat. Add cauliflower and broccoli; reduce heat to medium. Cover and cook until vegetables are just tender, 5 to 7 minutes. Remove vegetables and rinse under cold running water to stop cooking; drain well.

2 Preheat oven to 350°F. Place bread pieces in 15½" by 10½" jelly-roll pan. Toast bread pieces until light golden, about 10 minutes.

3 Preheat oven to 400°F. From lemons, grate 1 tablespoon peel and squeeze 3 tablespoons juice. In 2-quart saucepan, melt margarine or butter with olive oil over medium-low heat. Add garlic, salt, pepper, lemon peel, and 1 tablespoon lemon juice. Reduce heat to low; cook 1 minute to blend flavors.

4 Place vegetables in large bowl; toss with half of margarine mixture. Transfer vegetables to 13" by 9" glass baking dish. Cover and bake vegetables 20 minutes or until heated through.

5 Meanwhile, in same large bowl, toss toasted bread pieces with half of parsley, remaining margarine mixture, and 2 tablespoons lemon juice. Uncover vegetables; top with seasoned bread mixture and bake,

uncovered, 5 to 7 minutes longer, until bread topping is crisp and browned. Sprinkle with remaining parsley. Makes 12 accompaniment servings.

Each serving: About 110 calories, 4 g protein, 12 g carbohydrate, 6 g total fat (1 g saturated), 0 mg cholesterol, 225 mg sodium.

Brussels Sprouts & Peas in Brown Butter

PREP: 20 MINUTES • COOK: 20 MINUTES

Cathy Lo, GH food assistant, likes this savory side dish because it can be put together without too much fuss. It also proves to the doubters in her family that Brussels sprouts—a much maligned vegetable—can be delicious.

2 containers (10 ounces each) Brussels sprouts
1 medium lemon
4 tablespoons margarine or butter
1 package (10 ounces) frozen peas, thawed
½ teaspoon salt
¼ teaspoon coarsely ground black pepper

1 Trim off stem and any yellow leaves from each Brussels sprout. Slice sprouts vertically into ¼-inch-thick slices. From lemon, grate 1 teaspoon peel and squeeze 1 tablespoon juice.

2 In 12-inch skillet, melt margarine or butter over medium-high heat; cook 2 minutes or until light golden brown, stirring. Add sliced Brussels sprouts and stir to coat with browned margarine or butter. Add ¼ *cup water* and cook, stirring occasionally, 10 minutes.

3 Reduce heat to low; add lemon peel, peas, salt, pepper, and ¼ *cup water* and cook, stirring occasionally, 5 minutes or until sprouts are tender. Stir in lemon juice. Makes 8 accompaniment servings.

Each serving: About 105 calories, 4 g protein, 11 g carbohydrate, 6 g total fat (1 g saturated), 0 mg cholesterol, 255 mg sodium.

Brussels Sprouts & Peas in Brown Butter ➤

Artichokes with Dill Sauce

PREP: 20 MINUTES • COOK: ABOUT 40 MINUTES

This unusual method of cooking the artichokes yields a luscious lemony sauce.

4 medium artichokes
2 tablespoons olive oil
1 medium onion, finely chopped
½ cup fresh lemon juice (about 3 medium lemons)
¼ cup all-purpose flour
¼ cup fresh dill, chopped
½ teaspoon salt

1 Remove tough outer leaves from artichokes. With serrated knife, cut about 1 inch across top of each artichoke; remove and discard stems. Trim thorny tops of leaves with kitchen shears. Cut each artichoke lengthwise in half; set artichokes aside.

2 In 8-quart Dutch oven or saucepot, heat olive oil over medium heat until hot. Add onion and cook until tender, about 5 minutes.

3 Meanwhile, in small bowl, stir lemon juice, flour, dill, and 1½ *cups water* until blended. When onion is tender, reduce heat to low and stir lemon-juice mixture into Dutch oven. Add artichokes and heat to boiling over high heat. Reduce heat to low; cover and simmer 20 minutes. Turn artichokes over. Cover and simmer 25 minutes longer or until knife inserted in center of artichoke heart goes through easily.

4 To serve, transfer artichokes to deep platter. Stir salt into sauce and pour sauce over artichokes. Serve artichokes hot or cool slightly to serve warm. Makes 8 accompaniment servings.

Each serving: About 85 calories, 3 g protein, 12 g carbohydrate, 4 g total fat (1 g saturated), 0 mg cholesterol, 190 mg sodium.

Pickled Eggs & Beets

PREP: 15 MINUTES PLUS COOLING AND CHILLING OVERNIGHT • COOK: 20 TO 25 MINUTES

It's a Pennsylvania-Dutch tradition to serve a balance of sweets and sours at the family meal. This recipe covers both flavors, and is a favorite of Entertainment Editor Joanna Powell. It was originally a picnic food, but Powell's mom, Florence Hoskinson, adapted it to serve for winter holiday meals.

6 large eggs
5 medium beets (about 1½ pounds, including tops)
1 cup cider vinegar
⅓ cup sugar

1 In 2-quart saucepan, place eggs and *enough cold water to cover* eggs by at least 1 inch; heat to boiling over high heat. Immediately, remove saucepan from heat and cover tightly; let stand 15 minutes. Pour off hot water and run cold water over eggs to cool. Remove shells from eggs; set eggs aside to cool.

2 Meanwhile, trim tops from beets, leaving about 1 inch of stems attached. Scrub beets well under cold running water. In 3-quart saucepan, place whole beets and *enough water to cover*; heat to boiling over high heat. Reduce heat to medium-low; cover and simmer 20 to 25 minutes, until beets are tender. Reserve 1 cup beet cooking liquid; drain beets. Immediately, remove beet skins under cold running water. Slice beets.

3 Place whole eggs in medium bowl or 1½-quart wide-mouth jar and layer sliced beets on top of eggs. In 1-quart saucepan, combine vinegar, sugar, and reserved beet cooking liquid; heat to boiling over high heat. Pour vinegar mixture over eggs and beets. With spoon, gently turn eggs occasionally for even color, until egg and beet mixture is cool. Cover and refrigerate at least 24 hours. Makes 12 first-course servings.

Each serving: About 55 calories, 4 g protein, 5 g carbohydrate, 3 g total fat (1 g saturated), 107 mg cholesterol, 50 mg sodium.

FLAVORED BUTTERS

PREP: 30 MINUTES PLUS CHILLING OR FREEZING

Any of these blended butters steps up the flavor of plain steamed beans or asparagus. Prepare all 4 varieties and freeze up to 2 months. Just before serving, choose 1 butter log, slice off a piece, and heat in skillet with cooked vegetables. Use about one-eighth of the butter log for every 8-ounce serving of beans or asparagus.

Tarragon Butter

½ cup margarine or butter (1 stick), softened
2 tablespoons finely chopped fresh tarragon
¼ teaspoon grated fresh lemon peel
⅛ teaspoon coarsely ground black pepper

In bowl, with spoon, mix margarine or butter with tarragon, lemon peel, and pepper until blended. Spoon mixture into a 6-inch-long strip across the width of sheet of plastic wrap or waxed paper. Freeze until slightly firm, about 20 minutes. Roll mixture, covered with plastic wrap or waxed paper, back and forth, to make a 6-inch-long log. Wrap well and refrigerate up to 2 days, or freeze up to 2 months. Makes 8 accompaniment servings.

Each serving: About 100 calories, 0 g protein, 0 g carbohydrate, 12 g total fat (2 g saturated), 0 mg cholesterol, 135 mg sodium.

Hazelnut Butter

½ cup hazelnuts (filberts)
½ cup margarine or butter (1 stick), softened
2 teaspoons grated lemon peel
¼ teaspoon ground black pepper

1 Preheat oven to 375°F. Place hazelnuts in 8" by 8" metal baking pan. Bake 10 to 15 minutes, until lightly toasted. To remove skins, wrap hot hazelnuts in clean cloth towel. With hands, roll hazelnuts back and forth until most of skins come off. Discard skins; let nuts cool. In food processor, with knife blade attached, finely grind nuts.

2 In bowl, with spoon, mix margarine or butter with ground nuts, lemon peel, and pepper until blended. Spoon mixture into a 6-inch-long strip across the width of sheet of plastic wrap or waxed paper. Freeze until slightly firm, about 20 minutes. Roll mixture, covered with plastic wrap or waxed paper, back and forth, to make a 6-inch-long log. Wrap well and refrigerate up to 2 days, or freeze up to 2 months. Makes 8 accompaniment servings.

Each serving: About 145 calories, 1 g protein, 1 g carbohydrate, 16 g total fat (3 g saturated), 0 mg cholesterol, 135 mg sodium.

Honey-Pecan Butter

½ cup pecans
½ cup margarine or butter (1 stick), softened
2 tablespoons honey
½ teaspoon coarsely ground black pepper

1 Preheat oven to 375°F. Place nuts in 8" by 8" metal baking pan. Bake pecans about 8 to 10 minutes, until lightly toasted. Cool completely. In food processor with knife blade attached, process pecans until finely ground.

2 In bowl, with spoon, mix margarine or butter with honey, pepper, and ground pecans until blended. Spoon mixture into a 6-inch-long strip across the width of sheet of plastic wrap or waxed paper. Freeze until slightly firm, about 20 minutes. Roll mixture, covered with plastic wrap or waxed paper, back and forth, to make a 6-inch-long log. Wrap well and refrigerate up to 2 days, or freeze up to 2 months. Makes 8 accompaniment servings.

Each serving: About 165 calories, 0 g protein, 6 g carbohydrate, 16 g total fat (3 g saturated), 0 mg cholesterol, 135 mg sodium.

Orange-Chive Butter

½ cup margarine or butter (1 stick), softened
2 tablespoons minced chives
1 teaspoon grated orange peel

In bowl, with spoon, mix margarine or butter with chives and orange peel until blended. Spoon mixture into a 6-inch-long strip across the width of sheet of plastic wrap or waxed paper. Freeze until slightly firm, about 20 minutes. Roll mixture, covered with plastic wrap or waxed paper, back and forth, to make a 6-inch-long log. Wrap well and refrigerate up to 2 days, or freeze up to 2 months. Makes 8 accompaniment servings.

Each serving: About 100 calories, 0 g protein, 0 g carbohydrate, 12 g total fat (2 g saturated), 0 mg cholesterol, 135 mg sodium.

Breaded Cauliflower

PREP: 30 MINUTES • COOK: ABOUT 40 MINUTES

On Thanksgiving Day, when Deputy Editor Diane Salvatore was a little girl, all of her relatives would pitch in to make this deliciously addictive side dish, taking turns breading and frying the cauliflower. Salvatore's grandfather, Leopold, who was born in Naples, taught everyone the recipe. These days, Salvatore's mom always makes a double batch so that everyone can have leftovers.

2 medium heads cauliflower (about 3¼ pounds),
    separated into 3-inch flowerets
Vegetable oil for frying
4 large eggs
¼ cup milk
1½ cups seasoned dried bread crumbs
Salt to taste

1 Place steamer basket in 8-quart Dutch oven or saucepot with *1 inch water*. Heat water to boiling over high heat; add cauliflower flowerets and reduce heat to medium. Cover and cook flowerets just until tender, about 10 minutes.

Sautéed Mushrooms & Green Beans

2 Remove flowerets; rinse with cold running water to stop cooking; drain well. In 4-quart saucepan, heat 1 inch vegetable oil over medium heat until hot (350° to 375°F. on deep-frying thermometer).

3 Preheat oven to 200°F. In large bowl, with wire whisk, lightly beat eggs with milk. Place bread crumbs in another large bowl. With tongs, dip some flowerets in egg mixture, then in bread crumbs to coat. Fry flowerets in small batches until light golden, about 3 to 5 minutes, turning once. Place flowerets on paper towels to drain. Place drained flowerets on jelly-roll pan and keep warm in oven.

4 Repeat in small batches with remaining flowerets. Sprinkle flowerets with salt before serving if you like. Makes 12 accompaniment servings.

Each serving: About 125 calories, 6 g protein, 16 g carbo-hydrate, 5 g total fat (1 g saturated), 72 mg cholesterol, 435 mg sodium.

Sautéed Mushrooms & Green Beans

PREP: 25 MINUTES • COOK: 25 MINUTES

Stephanie Eiseman, assistant to the managing editor, loves her mom Gerry's creative recipes. The beans for this savory skillet side dish can be cooked ahead and reserved after cooling in step 1.

1 teaspoon salt
2 pounds green beans, trimmed
2 tablespoons margarine or butter
2 packages (10 ounces each) mushrooms, sliced
2 large shallots, minced
1 tablespoon all-purpose flour
¼ teaspoon coarsely ground black pepper
¾ cup half-and-half or light cream

1 In 12-inch skillet, heat *1 inch water* and ½ teaspoon salt to boiling over high heat. Add green beans; heat to boiling. Reduce heat to low; simmer, uncovered, 5 to 10 minutes, until beans are tender-crisp. Drain and rinse beans with cold running water to stop cooking; drain well. Wipe skillet dry.

2 In same skillet, melt margarine or butter over medium-high heat. Add mushrooms and shallots; cook until browned, about 15 minutes, stirring occasionally. Add flour, pepper, and remaining ½ teaspoon salt, and cook 1 minute longer, stirring. Reduce heat to low; stir in green beans and half-and-half and heat through. Makes 10 accompaniment servings.

Each serving: About 95 calories, 4 g protein, 12 g carbohydrate, 5 g total fat (2 g saturated), 6 mg cholesterol, 175 mg sodium.

Zesty Stovetop Beans

PREP: 5 MINUTES • COOK: 5 MINUTES

Convenient canned beans are delicious in this sweet and spicy sauce.

1 can (15 to 16 ounces) no-salt-added navy or small white beans, rinsed and drained
1 can (15 to 16 ounces) no-salt-added red kidney beans, rinsed and drained
½ cup ketchup
1 tablespoon prepared white horseradish, drained
1 teaspoon brown sugar
1 teaspoon Worcestershire sauce

In 2-quart saucepan, heat all ingredients to boiling over medium heat, stirring occasionally. Makes about 3 cups or 4 accompaniment servings.

Each serving: About 230 calories, 13 g protein, 45 g carbohydrate, 1 g total fat (0 g saturated), 0 mg cholesterol, 470 mg sodium.

Sautéed Cabbage with Peas

PREP: 10 MINUTES • COOK: ABOUT 25 MINUTES

Onion, sautéed until golden, adds wonderful nutty flavor to this simple side dish.

2 tablespoons margarine or butter
1 medium onion, thinly sliced
1 small head savoy cabbage (about 2 pounds), cored and cut into ½-inch-thick slices, with tough ribs discarded
¾ teaspoon salt
½ teaspoon sugar
¼ teaspoon coarsely ground black pepper

½ cup chicken broth
1 package (10 ounces) frozen baby peas
¼ cup chopped fresh dill

1 In 12-inch skillet, melt margarine or butter over medium heat. Add onion and cook, stirring often, until tender and golden, about 8 minutes.

2 Add cabbage, salt, sugar, and pepper, and cook until cabbage is tender-crisp, about 5 minutes, stirring often. Stir in broth, and cook 10 minutes or until cabbage is tender.

3 Add frozen peas and dill. Cook over medium heat, stirring frequently, about 5 minutes, until heated through. Makes about 6 cups or 8 accompaniment servings.

Each serving: About 90 calories, 4 g protein, 13 g carbohydrate, 3 g total fat (1 g saturated), 0 mg cholesterol, 345 mg sodium.

Sweet & Sour Cabbage

PREP: 20 MINUTES • COOK: 15 MINUTES

This Pennsylvania-Dutch favorite calls for fresh chopped apples.

2 tablespoons margarine or butter
2 Granny Smith apples, peeled, cored, and chopped
1 medium onion, finely chopped
1 medium head red cabbage (2 pounds), cut into quarters, cored, and coarsely chopped
3 tablespoons cider vinegar
1 teaspoon sugar
1 teaspoon salt
¼ teaspoon coarsely ground black pepper

1 In deep 12-inch skillet or 5-quart Dutch oven, melt margarine or butter over medium heat. Add apples and onion, and cook until soft, about 5 minutes, stirring occasionally.

2 Gradually stir in cabbage, vinegar, sugar, salt, and pepper. Cook 12 minutes, until cabbage is tender but still slightly crunchy, stirring occasionally. Makes about 8 cups or 8 accompaniment servings.

Each serving: About 75 calories, 1 g protein, 12 g carbohydrate, 3 g total fat (1 g saturated), 0 mg cholesterol, 315 mg sodium.

Leeks Vinaigrette

PREP: 20 MINUTES • COOK: 10 MINUTES

Look for small, fresh leeks; if you can find only larger ones, cook them longer, then split them lengthwise completely in half after cooking (use only 8). The leeks can be cooked a day ahead and refrigerated, covered, until serving time.

16 slender leeks (4½ to 5 pounds)
2¼ teaspoons salt
2 tablespoons red wine vinegar
2 teaspoons Dijon mustard
¼ teaspoon coarsely ground black pepper
¼ cup olive oil
2 tablespoons chopped fresh parsley leaves

1 In 8-quart Dutch oven, heat 5 *quarts water* to boiling over high heat. Meanwhile, cut root ends from leeks. Trim leeks to 6 inches; discard tops (or save to make soup another day). Cut leeks lengthwise almost in half down to beginning of white part, keeping bottom 2 to 3 inches intact. Remove any bruised or tough dark-green outer leaves. Rinse leeks thoroughly with cold running water to remove all sand, gently fanning cut part.

2 Add leeks and 2 teaspoons salt to Dutch oven; cook 10 minutes or until tender when pierced with knife. With slotted spoon, transfer leeks to colander to drain; rinse under cold running water. Drain again and pat dry with paper towels.

3 Coarsely chop any loose pieces of leek and spread on platter; arrange leeks in a row, in a single layer, on top.

4 In small bowl, with wire whisk, mix vinegar, mustard, pepper, and remaining ¼ teaspoon salt. Gradually whisk in olive oil.

5 Spoon vinaigrette evenly over leeks; sprinkle with parsley. Makes 8 accompaniment servings.

Each serving: About 105 calories, 1 g protein, 11 g carbohydrate, 7 g total fat (1 g saturated), 0 mg cholesterol, 180 mg sodium.

Apricot-Ginger Carrots

PREP: 10 MINUTES • COOK: ABOUT 20 MINUTES

Here's a great way to dress up prepeeled baby carrots.

2 bags (1 pound each) peeled baby carrots
2 tablespoons margarine or butter
2 green onions, minced
1 large garlic clove, minced
1 tablespoon minced, peeled fresh ginger
⅓ cup apricot jam
1 tablespoon balsamic vinegar
¼ teaspoon salt
Pinch ground red pepper (cayenne)

1 Place steamer basket in deep 12-inch skillet with *1 inch water*. Heat to boiling over high heat. Add carrots and reduce heat to medium. Cover and cook 10 to 12 minutes, just until carrots are tender. Remove carrots and rinse with cold running water to stop cooking; drain well.

2 In 12-inch skillet, melt margarine or butter over medium heat. Add green onions, garlic, and ginger, and cook until soft, about 3 minutes, stirring often. Add apricot jam, vinegar, salt, and ground red pepper, and cook 3 to 4 minutes longer, stirring often.

3 Add carrots to glaze in skillet, cook glaze and carrots 5 minutes over medium-high heat. Increase heat to high and cook 3 minutes, stirring occasionally, until carrots are well coated and heated through. Makes about 6½ cups or 8 accompaniment servings.

Each serving: About 115 calories, 1 g protein, 22 g carbohydrate, 3 g total fat (1 g saturated), 0 mg cholesterol, 145 mg sodium.

◀ *Leeks Vinaigrette and Wild Rice & Orzo Pilaf (page 141)*

West Texas Creamed Corn

PREP: 10 MINUTES • COOK: 20 MINUTES

Freelance Food Consultant Lynn Perry's grandmother, Tressie, used to can creamed corn in the summertime in Hermleigh, Texas, using homegrown corn, and serve it every year on Thanksgiving. We tested her recipe with supermarket canned corn, and it's delicious.

3 tablespoons margarine or butter
1 jumbo onion (12 ounces), chopped
1 jalapeño chile, seeded and minced
1 garlic clove, minced
2 tablespoons all-purpose flour
¾ teaspoon ground coriander
¾ teaspoon ground cumin
¼ teaspoon salt
⅛ teaspoon ground red pepper (cayenne)
1 cup milk
2 cans (15¼ ounces each) whole-kernel corn, drained
2 tablespoons chopped fresh cilantro
¾ cup shredded Monterey Jack cheese (3 ounces)

1 In 3-quart saucepan, melt margarine or butter over low heat. Add onion and jalapeño and cook until tender, 6 to 8 minutes, stirring occasionally. Add garlic; cook 1 minute longer. Stir in flour, coriander, cumin, salt, and ground red pepper, and cook, stirring, 1 minute.

2 Stir in milk; heat over medium heat until mixture thickens and boils, stirring frequently; boil 1 minute. Add corn and cook 5 minutes, stirring frequently. Remove saucepan from heat. Reserve 1 teaspoon chopped cilantro. Stir in cheese and remaining chopped cilantro until cheese melts. Sprinkle with reserved cilantro. Makes about 4 cups or 8 accompaniment servings.

Each serving: About 185 calories, 6 g protein, 21 g carbohydrate, 9 g total fat (4 g saturated), 14 mg cholesterol, 440 mg sodium.

Sautéed Mixed Mushrooms

PREP: 15 MINUTES • COOK: 20 MINUTES

This tempting trio of cultivated and wild mushrooms will add a sophisticated touch to any meal. To make this dish ahead, prepare the mushrooms through step 2. Cool the mixture slightly and spoon into a large self-sealing plastic bag; refrigerate until ready to serve. At serving time, reheat mushroom mixture in 12-inch skillet over high heat for about 10 minutes.

4 tablespoons margarine or butter
2 large shallots, minced (about ½ cup)
1 pound white mushrooms, each cut into quarters
8 ounces shiitake mushrooms, stems removed and cut into 1-inch wedges
8 ounces oyster mushrooms, each cut in half if large
¼ teaspoon dried thyme
¼ teaspoon salt
¼ teaspoon coarsely ground black pepper
1 garlic clove, crushed with garlic press
2 tablespoons chopped fresh parsley leaves

1 In 12-inch skillet, melt 2 tablespoons margarine or butter over medium-high heat. Add shallots and cook, stirring, 1 minute. Stir in white mushrooms, and cook, stirring often, until mushrooms are tender and liquid has evaporated, about 8 minutes. Transfer mushrooms to bowl. In same skillet, melt remaining 2 tablespoons margarine or butter. Add shiitake and oyster mushrooms, and cook, stirring often, until mushrooms are tender and liquid has evaporated, about 6 minutes.

2 Return white mushrooms to pan; stir in ¼ *cup water*, and cook until liquid evaporates. Stir in thyme, salt, pepper, and garlic, and cook 1 minute longer.

3 Sprinkle with parsley to serve. Makes 8 accompaniment servings.

Each serving: About 95 calories, 3 g protein, 9 g carbohydrate, 6 g total fat (1 g saturated), 0 mg cholesterol, 150 mg sodium.

Mrs. Mary's Marinated Mushrooms

PREP: 20 MINUTES PLUS CHILLING

Always on the Thanksgiving table are these piquant tidbits, made by Editorial Assistant Mary Saltalamacchia's mother (also named Mary, and known to Mary Jr.'s friends as Mrs. Mary). The family serves the mushrooms on an antipasto platter along with imported provolone and olives, roasted peppers, sliced pepperoni, fried artichoke hearts, sliced fennel…and that's just the start of the meal!

3 cups distilled white vinegar
2 pounds medium mushrooms
1 tablespoon extravirgin olive oil
¼ teaspoon dried oregano
¼ teaspoon salt
¼ teaspoon coarsely ground black pepper

1 In 4-quart saucepan, heat vinegar and 3 *cups water* to boiling over high heat. Add mushrooms and cook 3 minutes, stirring constantly to help keep mushrooms submerged in liquid.

2 Drain mushrooms, reserving *1 cup cooking liquid.* Place drained mushrooms and reserved cooking liquid in large bowl. Stir in olive oil, oregano, salt, and pepper. Cool slightly; cover and refrigerate 2 hours or overnight. Makes about 5 cups or 10 first-course servings.

Each serving: About 25 calories, 2 g protein, 5 g carbohydrate, 1 g total fat (0 g saturated), 0 mg cholesterol, 55 mg sodium.

FOOD EDITOR'S TIP

Q I've seen several recipes calling for shallots. Can I use onions instead? Aren't they in the same family?

A Shallots combine the characteristics of onions and garlic, but are more subtly flavored, with less of a bite. They do belong to the onion family, yet grow like garlic, with a head of several cloves—about the size of a large walnut—wrapped in a thin, papery skin. They're about 4 times pricier than onions, which can be used as a substitute. (To replace 1 shallot, use 2 tablespoons chopped onion.) Our recipes include the minced, chopped, or sliced yield of shallot to make the measurement as clear as possible.

Spicy Pearl Onions

PREP: 45 MINUTES • COOK: 17 TO 20 MINUTES

The brown-sugar glaze for these pearl onions is spiked with cayenne pepper and raspberry vinegar. If you want to reduce prep time, use small white onions instead of pearl onions—they will take less time to peel—and increase simmering time slightly in step 1.

3 containers (10 ounces each) pearl onions
3 tablespoons dark brown sugar
2 tablespoons margarine or butter
2 teaspoons raspberry vinegar
1 teaspoon tomato paste
¼ teaspoon salt
¼ teaspoon ground red pepper (cayenne) or
  1 teaspoon chipotle chile puree

1 In deep 12-inch skillet, heat *1 inch water* to boiling over high heat. Add onions; heat to boiling. Reduce heat to low; cover and simmer 5 to 10 minutes until onions are tender; drain well. Wipe skillet dry.

2 Peel onions, leaving a little of the root ends to help onions hold their shape during glazing.

3 In 12-inch skillet, heat brown sugar, margarine or butter, vinegar, tomato paste, salt, and ground red pepper over high heat until melted, stirring often. Add onions and cook until onions are browned and glazed, about 10 minutes, stirring occasionally. Makes about 3½ cups or 8 accompaniment servings.

Each serving: About 85 calories, 1 g protein, 14 g carbohydrate, 3 g total fat (1 g saturated), 0 mg cholesterol, 120 mg sodium.

Twice-Baked Potatoes

PREP: 35 MINUTES • BAKE: 1 HOUR 10 MINUTES

For this family favorite, you roast the garlic along with the potatoes. You can make the potatoes ahead: After stuffing the potatoes, cover the jelly-roll pan and refrigerate. Reheat in a preheated 350°F. oven for 30 minutes.

1 large whole head garlic
1 teaspoon olive oil
10 small baking potatoes (about 5 ounces each)*
1 tablespoon chopped fresh parsley leaves
½ teaspoon salt
¼ teaspoon coarsely ground black pepper
¼ cup plus 2 tablespoons grated Parmesan
   cheese
½ cup heavy or whipping cream

1 Preheat oven to 450°F. Remove any loose papery skin from head of garlic, leaving head intact. Cut top from head, just to tip of cloves (do not cut into cloves). Place head on sheet of heavy-duty foil; drizzle with olive oil. Loosely wrap foil around garlic, being careful that seam is folded to seal in oil.

2 Place potatoes and wrapped garlic on oven rack. Bake 45 minutes or until potatoes and garlic are fork-tender. Transfer to wire rack; cool slightly. Turn oven control to 350°F.

3 Open garlic package carefully and discard foil. Separate cloves from head and scrape or squeeze out pulp from each clove into a large mixing bowl. Slice each potato lengthwise in half. With spoon, carefully scoop out potato flesh into bowl with garlic, leaving potato-skin shells intact. Place the 12 prettiest potato shells in 15½" by 10½" jelly-roll pan. If you like, refrigerate remaining 8 shells for use another day.

4 With mixer at low speed, beat garlic and potatoes with parsley, salt, pepper, and ¼ cup Parmesan until garlic and potatoes are broken up. Add cream and beat until almost smooth, about 30 seconds (do not overbeat; potato mixture will become gummy).

5 Spoon mixture into potato shells on jelly-roll pan; sprinkle with remaining 2 tablespoons Parmesan.

6 Bake potatoes in jelly-roll pan until hot on the inside and golden on top, 20 to 30 minutes. Makes 12 accompaniment servings.

*It's easiest to find small baking potatoes in 5-pound bags.

Each serving: About 150 calories, 4 g protein, 23 g carbohydrate, 5 g total fat (3 g saturated), 16 mg cholesterol, 155 mg sodium.

Oven-Roasted Potato Balls

PREP: 45 MINUTES • COOK: ABOUT 1 HOUR

Known in Editorial Assistant Lori Conte's family as Nonna's Potatoes, these crisp golden morsels have an unusual history. Conte's grandmother, Maria Santonostaso, first made them for a small group of nuns when she worked as a cook in a convent in Providence, her first job after emigrating from Italy. Now an accompaniment to the roast capon that is the Conte family's Thanksgiving tradition, the potatoes are still made only by Nonna.

5 large baking potatoes (about 3 pounds),
   peeled
1 tablespoon olive oil
2 medium onions, thinly sliced
¾ teaspoon salt
¼ teaspoon coarsely ground black pepper

1 With 1¼-inch melon baller, scoop out balls from potatoes; place in bowl of cold water. (You will have about 12 ounces potato remaining. If you like, save for use another day.)

2 Preheat oven to 450°F. In 4-quart saucepan, heat about *10 cups water* to boiling over high heat; add potato balls and heat to boiling. Reduce heat to low; cover and simmer 2 minutes. Drain well.

3 In 15½" by 10 ½" jelly-roll pan, toss potato balls with olive oil, onion slices, salt, and pepper. Roast potato mixture 30 minutes; stir. Roast 20 minutes longer, stirring once, until golden. Makes 8 accompaniment servings.

Each serving: About 110 calories, 3 g protein, 22 g carbohydrate, 2 g total fat (0 g saturated), 0 mg cholesterol, 205 mg sodium.

Twice-Baked Potatoes ▶

Sauté of Potatoes, Tomatoes & Fresh Corn

PREP: 30 MINUTES • COOK: ABOUT 40 MINUTES

Accented with fresh tarragon and a lemony dressing, this simple side dish is perfect with steak.

4 tablespoons olive oil
2 pounds small red potatoes, cut into 1-inch chunks
2 pints cherry tomatoes
4 cups fresh corn kernels (from about 8 medium ears corn)
2 teaspoons chopped fresh tarragon leaves
2 tablespoons fresh lemon juice
¾ teaspoon salt
¼ teaspoon coarsely ground black pepper

1 In nonstick 12-inch skillet, heat 1 tablespoon olive oil over medium heat until hot. Add potato chunks and cook, stirring occasionally, until potatoes are browned on the outside and tender on the inside, about 35 minutes. Transfer potatoes to large bowl.

2 In same skillet, heat 1 more tablespoon oil; add whole cherry tomatoes and cook 2 minutes, stirring. Add corn and tarragon, and cook 2 minutes longer. Transfer tomato mixture to bowl with potatoes.

3 In cup, mix lemon juice, salt, pepper, and remaining 2 tablespoons olive oil; pour over potato mixture and toss to combine. Makes about 12 cups or 12 accompaniment servings.

Each serving: About 165 calories, 4 g protein, 28 g carbohydrate, 5 g total fat (1 g saturated), 0 mg cholesterol, 150 mg sodium.

Sauté of Potatoes, Tomatoes & Fresh Corn

Oven Fries

PREP: 10 MINUTES • BAKE: 20 TO 25 MINUTES

You won't miss the fat in these hand-cut "fries." They bake beautifully on a jelly-roll pan with a spritz of nonstick cooking spray and a sprinkle of salt and pepper.

Nonstick cooking spray
3 medium baking potatoes (about 1½ pounds)
½ teaspoon salt
¼ teaspoon coarsely ground black pepper

1 Preheat oven to 500°F. Spray two 15½" by 10½" jelly-roll pans or 2 large cookie sheets with nonstick cooking spray.

2 Scrub unpeeled potatoes well, but do not peel. Cut each potato lengthwise in half. With each potato half cut side down, cut lengthwise into ¼-inch-thick slices. Place potatoes in medium bowl and toss with salt and pepper.

3 Divide potato slices evenly between pans. Place pans on 2 oven racks and spray potatoes with nonstick cooking spray. Bake potatoes about 20 minutes or until tender and lightly browned. Makes 4 accompaniment servings.

Each serving: About 130 calories, 4 g protein, 28 g carbohydrate, 1 g total fat (0 g saturated), 0 mg cholesterol, 280 mg sodium.

Mashed Potatoes with Sauerkraut

PREP: 15 MINUTES • COOK: 40 TO 45 MINUTES

Although mashed potatoes are considered standard holiday fare, when they're spiced up with sauerkraut, they gain an added zing that's been a hit with Gina Davis's family ever since her grandmother, Mary Carson Hodges, started serving them years ago. Davis, GH's associate art director, says you can pass the sauerkraut separately, so guests can help themselves.

SAUERKRAUT TOPPING:
4 tablespoons margarine or butter
4 medium onions, thinly sliced
2 packages (16 ounces each) sauerkraut, rinsed
  and squeezed dry
1 can (14½ ounces) chicken broth
2 medium Golden Delicious apples, peeled,
  cored, and grated
½ teaspoon caraway seeds

MASHED POTATOES:
5 pounds all-purpose potatoes (about 15
  medium), peeled and cut into 1-inch chunks
1¼ teaspoons salt
1¼ cups milk, warmed
½ cup margarine or butter (1 stick)

1 Prepare Sauerkraut Topping: In 12-inch skillet, melt margarine or butter over medium heat. Add onions and cook until tender and lightly browned, about 15 minutes, stirring occasionally. Add sauerkraut, chicken broth, apples, and caraway seeds; heat to boiling over high heat. Reduce heat to low; cover and simmer 40 to 45 minutes, until sauerkraut is tender; keep warm.

2 Meanwhile, prepare Mashed Potatoes: In 8-quart Dutch oven, place potatoes and *enough water to cover*; heat to boiling over high heat. Reduce heat to low; cover and simmer 15 minutes or until potatoes are fork-tender; drain.

3 Return potatoes to Dutch oven. With potato masher, mash potatoes with salt. Add warmed milk and margarine or butter; mash until mixture is well blended. Spoon potatoes into serving bowl; top with sauerkraut. Makes 14 accompaniment servings.

Each serving: About 245 calories, 5 g protein, 34 g carbohydrate, 11 g total fat (2 g saturated), 3 mg cholesterol, 610 mg sodium.

Spinach & Potato Gratin

PREP: 40 MINUTES • BAKE: 1½ HOURS

Food Associate Lori Perlmutter's mom, Judy, says she'd like to experiment with a new side dish, but her family won't let her. They all claim it wouldn't be Thanksgiving without this heavenly casserole!

1 tablespoon margarine or butter
3 large shallots, thinly sliced
2 packages (10 ounces each) frozen chopped
  spinach, thawed and squeezed dry
⅛ teaspoon ground nutmeg
1 teaspoon salt
½ teaspoon coarsely ground black pepper
3 pounds all-purpose potatoes (about
  9 medium), peeled and cut into ¼-inch-thick
  slices
4 ounces Gruyère cheese, shredded (1 cup)
1½ cups milk
1 cup heavy or whipping cream
1 tablespoon cornstarch

1 Preheat oven to 350°F. Grease shallow 3-quart casserole.

2 In 10-inch skillet, melt margarine or butter over medium heat. Add shallots and cook 5 minutes or until tender, stirring occasionally. Remove skillet from heat; stir in spinach, nutmeg, ¼ teaspoon salt, and ¼ teaspoon pepper.

3 Arrange one-third of potato slices, overlapping, in casserole. Top with one-third of cheese and one-half of spinach mixture. Repeat layering with remaining ingredients, ending with cheese.

4 In large bowl, with wire whisk, mix milk, cream, cornstarch, remaining ¾ teaspoon salt, and ¼ teaspoon pepper until smooth. Pour milk mixture evenly over casserole.

5 Place sheet of foil underneath casserole; crimp foil edges to form a rim to catch any drips during baking. Cover casserole and bake 30 minutes. Remove cover and bake 1 hour longer or until center is hot and bubbly and top is golden. Makes 12 accompaniment servings.

Each serving: About 230 calories, 8 g protein, 24 g carbohydrate, 13 g total fat (7 g saturated), 42 mg cholesterol, 315 mg sodium.

Zucchini Halves with Couscous & Corn

PREP: 35 MINUTES • COOK: ABOUT 40 MINUTES

This calls for big Israeli couscous (see "Food Editor's Tips," below), but if you can't find it, use the regular kind.

5 teaspoons olive oil
4 medium zucchini (about 8 ounces each), stems trimmed and each cut lengthwise in half
¼ cup minced shallots (about 2 medium)
¼ teaspoon salt
1½ cups fresh corn kernels (about 3 medium ears corn)
¾ cup Israeli couscous*
¾ teaspoon ground cumin
1¼ cups chicken broth*
2 tablespoons chopped fresh parsley leaves
Diced tomato for garnish

1 Preheat oven to 425°F. Grease broiling pan with 2 teaspoons olive oil. With spoon, scoop out flesh from each zucchini half, leaving about ¼-inch shell. Reserve zucchini flesh. Place zucchini shells, cut side down, in broiling pan; set aside.

2 In nonstick 12-inch skillet, heat 2 teaspoons olive oil over medium heat until hot. Add shallots and cook 2 minutes, stirring. Coarsely chop reserved zucchini flesh. Increase heat to medium-high; add chopped zucchini and salt, and cook 8 minutes, or until liquid evaporates and zucchini begins to brown. Add corn to skillet and cook 2 minutes, stirring. Transfer mixture to small bowl.

3 To same skillet, add couscous and remaining 1 teaspoon olive oil. Reduce heat to low; cook 2 minutes, stirring. Add cumin and cook 1 minute longer, stirring. Add chicken broth and *½ cup water*; heat to boiling over medium-high heat. Reduce heat to low; cover and simmer 25 minutes or until liquid is absorbed and couscous is tender.

4 Meanwhile, place zucchini shells in oven and roast 15 minutes or until tender and edges are browned.

5 Return corn mixture to skillet with couscous; stir in chopped parsley and heat through. Place zucchini shells on platter; fill with couscous and corn mixture. Sprinkle with diced tomato. Makes 8 accompaniment servings.

*If using regular couscous, in Step 3 use only *¾ cup chicken broth* and *¼ cup water*; heat to boiling over medium-high heat. Cover; remove from heat and let stand 5 minutes or until liquid is absorbed.

Each serving: About 145 calories, 5 g protein, 25 g carbohydrate, 3 g total fat (1 g saturated), 0 mg cholesterol, 200 mg sodium.

▌FOOD EDITOR'S TIP▐

Q I now know what couscous is, and my family enjoys it. But lately I've seen mentions of Israeli couscous. What is it?

A Medium-grain couscous, made from semolina, is what most of us are used to buying—usually imported from France in the past, it's now produced in the United States, too, and is front and center on many supermarket shelves. Israeli couscous (sometimes labeled "toasted couscous") is sold in specialty stores and Middle Eastern groceries. It's coarse, and about 4 times bigger than medium couscous; it's comparable to *acini di pepe*, the tiny pasta. The Israeli kind—used in Zucchini Halves with Couscous & Corn, above—can be boiled, steamed, or combined with boiling water and covered until the water is absorbed. It's chewier than the regular kind and looks pretty in summer salads and side dishes made with vegetables.

Creamy Zucchini Casserole

PREP: 35 MINUTES • BAKE: 25 TO 30 MINUTES

About 20 years ago, a friend gave Pam Duffy's mother this Thanksgiving side-dish recipe, and now that neither Duffy (an advertising account manager for GH in Chicago) nor her siblings live at home any more, they have made a point of having the casserole at their own Thanksgiving gatherings. Duffy says she likes it even better than the turkey!

6 tablespoons margarine or butter (¾ stick)
1 small onion, diced
3 medium-large zucchini (about 10 ounces each), cut into ¼-inch-thick slices
2 medium carrots, peeled and shredded

1 can (10¾ ounces) cream of chicken soup
½ cup sour cream
1 bag (8 ounces) herb-seasoned stuffing mix,
   coarsely crushed

1 Preheat oven to 350°F. Grease 13" by 9" glass baking dish.

2 In 12-inch skillet, melt margarine or butter over medium heat. Add onion and cook until tender but not browned, about 5 minutes, stirring occasionally. Add zucchini and carrots and cook until zucchini is tender, about 8 minutes.

3 Remove skillet from heat; stir in undiluted cream of chicken soup and sour cream until evenly mixed.

4 Sprinkle half of stuffing mix in baking dish. Spoon zucchini mixture on top, then remaining stuffing mix. Bake 25 to 30 minutes until hot and bubbly. Makes 16 accompaniment servings.

Each serving: About 140 calories, 3 g protein, 16 g carbohydrate, 8 g total fat (2 g saturated), 5 mg cholesterol, 405 mg sodium.

Mashed
Root Vegetables

PREP: 15 MINUTES • COOK: 25 MINUTES
BAKE: ABOUT 30 MINUTES

2 pounds assorted root vegetables: carrots,
   celery root (celeriac), parsnips, white turnips,
   and/or rutabaga, peeled and cut into 1-inch
   pieces (about 5 cups)
1 pound all-purpose potatoes, peeled and cut
   into 1-inch pieces (about 2½ to 3 cups)
2½ teaspoons salt
3 tablespoons margarine or butter
¼ teaspoon coarsely ground black pepper
Pinch ground nutmeg

1 Combine root vegetables, potatoes, 2 teaspoons salt, and *enough water to cover* in 5- or 6-quart saucepot; heat to boiling over high heat. Reduce heat to medium, and cook 15 minutes or until vegetables and potatoes are tender. Drain.

2 Preheat oven to 350°F. Return vegetables to saucepot; add margarine or butter, pepper, and remaining ½ teaspoon salt, and mash with potato masher until smooth. Spoon mixture into 1½-quart casserole.

3 Bake casserole, covered, 20 to 30 minutes or until heated through. Sprinkle with nutmeg. Makes 8 accompaniment servings.

Each serving: About 150 calories, 3 g protein, 26 g carbohydrate, 5 g total fat (1 g saturated), 0 mg cholesterol, 305 mg sodium.

Mashed
Sweet Potatoes

PREP: 10 MINUTES • COOK: 25 MINUTES

On Thanksgiving, cookbook Editor Lisa Brainerd Burge's family used to have sweet potatoes topped with marshmallows, until one day someone discovered how good they were flavored just with orange peel.

3 pounds sweet potatoes (about 6 medium),
   peeled and cut into 1-inch chunks
4 tablespoons margarine or butter
2 tablespoons brown sugar
1 teaspoon salt
½ teaspoon grated fresh orange peel
¼ teaspoon coarsely ground black pepper
1 tablespoon bourbon or dark rum (optional)

1 In 4-quart saucepan, place potatoes and *enough water to cover*; heat to boiling over high heat. Reduce heat to low; cover and simmer 15 minutes or until potatoes are fork-tender; drain.

2 Return potatoes to saucepan. With potato masher, mash potatoes with margarine or butter, brown sugar, salt, orange peel, and pepper until mixture is well blended. Stir in bourbon or dark rum if you like. Spoon potatoes into serving bowl. Makes about 5 cups or 8 accompaniment servings.

Each serving: About 280 calories, 3 g protein, 53 g carbohydrate, 6 g total fat (1 g saturated), 0 mg cholesterol, 370 mg sodium.

Sweet Potato & Apple Gratin

PREP: 40 MINUTES • BAKE: 1 HOUR

The buttery pecan-crumb topping is hard to resist.

SWEET-POTATO LAYERS:
2 tablespoons margarine or butter
3 large Golden Delicious apples (about
    1¼ pounds), peeled, cored, and cut into
    ¼-inch-thick slices
1 jumbo onion (12 ounces), cut in half and thinly
    sliced
2 tablespoons applejack brandy or Calvados
6 medium sweet potatoes (about 2½ pounds)
¾ teaspoon salt
¼ teaspoon coarsely ground black pepper
¼ teaspoon ground nutmeg
1 cup apple cider or apple juice

PECAN-CRUMB TOPPING:
2 tablespoons margarine or butter
3 slices firm white bread, cut into ¼-inch pieces
    (about 1¾ cups)
½ cup pecans, coarsely chopped

1 Prepare Sweet-Potato Layers: Grease shallow 2½-quart casserole. In 12-inch skillet, melt margarine or butter over medium heat. Add apples and onion, and cook, stirring frequently, until tender and golden, about 25 minutes. Stir in applejack; cook 1 minute. Remove skillet from heat.

2 Meanwhile, peel and thinly slice sweet potatoes. In cup, mix salt, pepper, and nutmeg.

3 Preheat oven to 400°F. Arrange one-third of sweet-potato slices, overlapping, in casserole. Spoon one-third of apple mixture over potatoes. Sprinkle with one-third salt mixture. Repeat layering 2 more times. Pour apple cider over potato and apple layers. Bake casserole, covered, 1 hour.

4 Meanwhile, prepare Pecan-Crumb Topping: In nonstick 10-inch skillet, melt margarine or butter over medium heat. Cook bread pieces and pecans until bread and pecans are lightly toasted, about 5 to 6 minutes, stirring occasionally.

5 Remove foil from casserole and sprinkle with crumb topping just before serving. Makes 8 accompaniment servings.

Each serving: About 300 calories, 4 g protein, 50 g carbohydrate, 11 g total fat (2 g saturated), 0 mg cholesterol, 335 mg sodium.

Summer Greens with Golden Beets & Mustard Vinaigrette

PREP: 25 MINUTES • COOK: 45 TO 60 MINUTES

A beautiful summer salad—if chive blossoms are available, use them to garnish each plate.

12 medium golden beets with tops (about
    4 pounds, including tops)
3 tablespoons red wine vinegar
1 tablespoon Dijon mustard
1 small shallot, minced (1 tablespoon)
½ teaspoon salt
¼ teaspoon coarsely ground black pepper
⅓ cup extravirgin olive oil
12 cups loosely packed mixed salad greens

1 Trim tops from beets, leaving about 1 inch of stems attached. (Reserve tops for use another time, if you like.) Scrub beets well under cold running water.

2 In 8-quart Dutch oven or saucepot, place whole beets and *enough cold water to cover*; heat to boiling over high heat. Reduce heat to medium-low; cover and simmer 30 to 45 minutes, until beets are fork-tender (time depends on age as well as size of beets).

3 Meanwhile, in small bowl, with wire whisk, mix vinegar, mustard, shallot, salt, and pepper. Gradually whisk in olive oil until vinaigrette is blended.

4 Drain beets in colander; rinse with cold water until easy to handle. Remove beet skins under cold running water. Slice beets; place in medium bowl. Cover and refrigerate beets if not using right away.

5 Just before serving, toss beet slices with half of vinaigrette. In large salad bowl, toss mixed salad greens with remaining vinaigrette; top with beet slices. Makes 12 accompaniment servings.

Each serving: About 90 calories, 2 g protein, 8 g carbohydrate, 6 g total fat (1 g saturated), 0 mg cholesterol, 170 mg sodium.

Sweet & Tangy Coleslaw

PREP: 5 MINUTES

1 can (8 ounces) crushed pineapple in
   unsweetened juice
3 tablespoons chili sauce
½ teaspoon salt
⅛ teaspoon coarsely ground black pepper
1 bag (16 ounces) shredded cabbage mix for
   coleslaw

In large bowl, stir pineapple with its juice, chili
sauce, salt, and pepper until blended. Add cabbage
mix and toss to coat. Makes 4 accompaniment servings.

Each serving: About 75 calories, 2 g protein, 18 g carbohydrate,
0 g total fat, 0 mg cholesterol, 460 mg sodium.

SKINNY SALAD DRESSINGS

PREP: 3 MINUTES

You may have the best inten-
tions—piling your plate with
lettuce, carrots, tomatoes, and
more—but commercial dressings can pour on up to 90 calories and 10 grams of fat per
tablespoon. And let's face it,
many bottled fat-free and low-
fat dressings and salad sprays
leave a lot to be desired. Now
try these quick, flavor-packed
versions—they taste so good,
you'll forget that you're eating
low-fat. Note: The dressings
will keep in the fridge for up to
1 week.

Orange-Ginger Dressing

½ cup seasoned rice vinegar
½ cup orange juice
½ teaspoon grated, peeled fresh
   ginger
½ teaspoon soy sauce
⅛ teaspoon Asian sesame oil

Into small bowl or jar, measure
all ingredients. Mix with wire
whisk or fork (or cover jar and
shake) until blended. Cover and

Clockwise from left: Creamy Ranch,
Spicy Tomato, and Orange-Ginger

refrigerate. Stir or shake before
using. Makes about 1 cup.

Each tablespoon: About 10 calories, 0
g protein, 3 g carbohydrate, 0 g total
fat, 0 mg cholesterol, 110 mg sodium.

Creamy Ranch Dressing

¾ cup plain nonfat yogurt
¼ cup low-fat mayonnaise
1 tablespoon cider vinegar
2 teaspoons Dijon mustard
¼ teaspoon coarsely ground
   black pepper
¼ teaspoon dried thyme
1 green onion, minced

Into small bowl, measure all
ingredients. Mix with wire whisk
or fork until blended. Cover and
refrigerate. Stir before using.
Makes about 1 cup.

Each tablespoon: About 15 calories, 1
g protein, 2 g carbohydrate, 0 g total
fat, 0 mg cholesterol, 60 mg sodium.

Spicy Tomato Dressing

1 can (5 ounces) spicy hot
   vegetable juice
3 tablespoons red wine vinegar
1 tablespoon olive oil
1 garlic clove, crushed with garlic
   press
½ teaspoon sugar
½ teaspoon dry mustard

Into small bowl or jar, measure
all ingredients. Mix with wire
whisk or fork (or cover jar and
shake) until blended. Cover and
refrigerate. Stir or shake before
using. Makes about 1 cup.

Each tablespoon: About 15 calories, 0
g protein, 1 g carbohydrate, 1 g total
fat (0 g saturated), 0 mg cholesterol,
35 mg sodium.

Cucumber Salad

PREP: 6 MINUTES

This cool side dish is simple to fix and a nice change from everyday tossed greens.

2 tablespoons seasoned rice vinegar
¼ teaspoon salt
¼ teaspoon Asian sesame oil
1 English (seedless) cucumber (about 12 ounces), unpeeled and thinly sliced
½ small red onion, thinly sliced

In medium bowl, with wire whisk, mix vinegar, salt, and sesame oil until blended. Add cucumber and red onion, and toss to coat. Makes 4 accompaniment servings.

Each serving: About 30 calories, 1 g protein, 8 g carbohydrate, 0 g total fat, 0 mg cholesterol, 335 mg sodium.

Green Pepper & Tomato Salad

PREP: 30 MINUTES PLUS CHILLING
BROIL: 10 TO 12 MINUTES

Toss diced tomatoes and freshly roasted peppers with a spicy lemon dressing.

5 small green peppers
2 medium lemons
3½ pounds ripe tomatoes, diced
2 garlic cloves, minced
⅓ cup olive oil
1 teaspoon salt
1 teaspoon ground cumin
¼ teaspoon coarsely ground black pepper
⅛ teaspoon paprika
Pinch ground red pepper (cayenne)

1 Preheat broiler. Line broiling pan (without rack) with foil. Arrange peppers in broiling pan. Place pan in broiler 5 to 6 inches from source of heat and broil peppers until charred and blistered, turning peppers frequently, 10 to 12 minutes. Wrap foil around peppers and allow to steam at room temperature 15 minutes or until cool enough to handle.

2 Meanwhile, from lemons, grate ¼ teaspoon peel and squeeze ¼ cup juice.

3 Remove peppers from foil. Peel off skin and discard. Cut each pepper lengthwise in half; discard stem and seeds. Cut each pepper into 1-inch pieces; place in large bowl. Mix lemon peel, lemon juice, and remaining ingredients with peppers. Cover and refrigerate up to 4 hours. Makes about 8 cups or 12 accompaniment servings.

Each serving: About 90 calories, 2 g protein, 9 g carbohydrate, 7 g total fat (1 g saturated), 0 mg cholesterol, 190 mg sodium.

Grapefruit Salad

PREP: 30 MINUTES

A colorful, refreshing salad with red onion, orange zest, and watercress. The raw onion is soaked in water to help mellow its flavor.

1 medium red onion, thinly sliced into rings
3 large grapefruit
1 medium orange
¼ cup fresh lemon juice
1 garlic clove, crushed with garlic press

Grapefruit Salad

1 teaspoon Dijon mustard
½ teaspoon salt
¼ cup olive oil
¼ teaspoon coarsely ground black pepper
1 bunch watercress

1 Place onion slices in bowl of ice water; set aside.

2 Meanwhile, remove peel and white pith from each grapefruit. Cut each grapefruit crosswise into ¼-inch-thick slices. Cut each slice into quarters and place on platter.

3 With vegetable peeler, remove peel from orange in 1-inch-wide strips. Cut strips crosswise into very thin slivers. From orange, squeeze ¼ cup juice.

4 In small bowl, with wire whisk, mix orange juice, lemon juice, garlic, mustard, and salt. Gradually whisk in olive oil until blended.

5 Drain onion slices well and arrange over grapefruit; sprinkle with orange-peel slivers. Drizzle dressing over salad; sprinkle with pepper. Cover and refrigerate up to 4 hours.

6 To serve, add watercress to salad and toss gently. Makes 8 accompaniment servings.

Each serving: About 110 calories, 1 g protein, 13 g carbohydrate, 7 g total fat (1 g saturated), 0 mg cholesterol, 155 mg sodium.

Carrot Salad

PREP: 30 MINUTES PLUS CHILLING

This refreshing Israeli dish marries sweet carrots and orange juice with fresh ginger and crushed red pepper.

1 bag (16 ounces) carrots, peeled and coarsely grated
1 cup freshly squeezed orange juice (about 2 large oranges)
¼ cup golden raisins
1 tablespoon peeled, minced fresh ginger
1 teaspoon salt
¼ teaspoon crushed red pepper
2 medium avocados

1 In large bowl, combine carrots, orange juice, raisins, ginger, salt, and crushed red pepper, tossing to mix. Cover and refrigerate at least 1 hour or up to 8 hours.

2 To serve, remove seed and peel from avocados. Cut avocados into very thin slices. Place some carrot salad and avocado slices on each plate. Makes about 2 cups or 8 accompaniment servings.

Each serving: About 140 calories, 2 g protein, 20 g carbohydrate, 7 g total fat (1 g saturated), 0 mg cholesterol, 290 mg sodium.

Summer Corn Salad

PREP: 30 MINUTES • COOK: ABOUT 10 MINUTES

A colorful blend of fresh corn off the cob, green beans, red pepper, and sweet onion in an all-American apple-cider vinaigrette.

12 ears corn, husks and silk removed
¾ pound green beans, trimmed and cut into ¼-inch pieces
½ cup cider vinegar
¼ cup olive oil
¼ cup chopped fresh parsley leaves
1 teaspoon salt
½ teaspoon coarsely ground black pepper
1 medium red pepper, diced
1 small sweet onion (about 4 ounces), finely chopped

1 In 8-quart saucepot, in *2 inches boiling water*, heat corn to boiling over high heat. Reduce heat to low; cover and simmer 5 minutes. Drain corn; set aside to cool. When cool enough to handle, cut off kernels.

2 Meanwhile, cook green beans: In 2-quart saucepan, in *1 inch boiling water*, heat green beans to boiling over high heat. Reduce heat to low; simmer, uncovered, about 5 minutes or until beans are tender-crisp. Drain.

3 In large salad bowl, with fork or wire whisk, mix vinegar, olive oil, parsley, salt, and black pepper until blended.

4 To dressing in bowl, add corn kernels, green beans, red pepper, and onion; toss well. If not serving right away, cover and refrigerate. Makes 12 accompaniment servings.

Each serving: About 135 calories, 3 g protein, 23 g carbohydrate, 6 g total fat (1 g saturated), 0 mg cholesterol, 195 mg sodium.

Two Bean & Tomato Salad

PREP: 25 MINUTES • COOK: 5 MINUTES

¾ pound French green beans (haricots verts) or
  green beans, ends trimmed
2 tablespoons extravirgin olive oil
2 tablespoons fresh lemon juice
1 medium shallot, finely chopped
½ teaspoon Dijon mustard
¼ teaspoon salt
¼ teaspoon coarsely ground black pepper
2 ripe medium tomatoes (about ¾ pound), each
  cut into 12 wedges
1 can (15 to 19 ounces) Great Northern or
  cannellini (white kidney) beans, rinsed and
  drained

1 In 10-inch skillet, heat ¾ *inch water* to boiling over high heat. Add green beans; heat to boiling. Reduce heat to medium; cook, uncovered, 3 to 5 minutes, until beans are tender-crisp; drain. Rinse beans with cold water; drain well.

2 In large salad bowl, with fork or wire whisk, mix olive oil, lemon juice, shallot, mustard, salt, and pepper until blended. Add green beans, tomatoes, and white beans; with rubber spatula, gently toss to mix well. Makes 8 accompaniment servings.

Each serving: About 170 calories, 8 g protein, 27 g carbohydrate, 4 g fat (1 g saturated), 0 mg cholesterol, 105 mg sodium.

Warm Caesar Potato Salad

PREP: 5 MINUTES • COOK: 15 MINUTES

1¼ pounds red potatoes, cut into ¾-inch chunks
2 tablespoons light mayonnaise
1 tablespoon grated Parmesan cheese
2 teaspoons cider vinegar
1 teaspoon Dijon mustard
½ teaspoon salt
¼ teaspoon coarsely ground black pepper
⅛ teaspoon anchovy paste
1 green onion, sliced

1 In 3-quart saucepan, place potatoes and *enough water to cover*; heat to boiling over high heat. Cover, and reduce heat to low; simmer 15 minutes or until potatoes are fork-tender.

2 Meanwhile, in medium bowl, mix mayonnaise with remaining ingredients.

3 Drain potatoes; gently toss with dressing in bowl. Makes 4 accompaniment servings.

Each serving: About 125 calories, 4 g protein, 26 g carbohydrate, 1 g total fat (0 g saturated), 2 mg cholesterol, 415 mg sodium.

HOW SAFE IS PREWASHED SALAD?

Packaged greens seem like a perfect shortcut to a healthy meal—until you hear media reports linking them to high bacteria levels or even outbreaks of deadly food-borne illness. Can you really trust the greens without washing them?

Branded, prewashed salad blends sold in hermetically sealed, clear bags are processed with rinse water that contains sanitizing agents such as chlorine. Even this careful process doesn't remove all microorganisms, but the bacteria commonly found in bagged lettuce cause food spoilage, not illness. If the salad isn't refrigerated properly or is not eaten before its "use by" date, these bacteria will cause it to turn brown and slimy, alerting you to discard it—before any possible illness-causing bacteria have a chance to multiply to unsafe levels.

Although bagged blends have an excellent safety record, don't assume all are ready to eat. Always read the small print. Salads from large manufacturers say washed and ready-to-eat right on the package, but we found other greens—like watercress, spinach, and shredded cabbage—that had the word washed on the front of the bag, but stated "rinse before using" on the back of it.

When in doubt, rinse. If you buy lettuce in bulk (such as mesclun mix), which is usually displayed in open bins or boxes so customers can help themselves, always rinse it well under clean, running water. Mesclun can become contaminated at any point during its journey from the farm to your table, and has been linked to some outbreaks of the potentially deadly E. coli O157:H7, so don't take any chances.

BREADS
& PASTRIES

Whole Wheat Pitas

PREP: 1¾ HOURS PLUS CHILLING OVERNIGHT, RISING, AND COOLING • BAKE: 5 MINUTES PER BATCH

These bread pockets are made with mashed potatoes and yogurt for a delicious, tangy flavor. Make the dough the day before serving, then let it rise 1 hour when ready to bake. Shape, roll, and pop into oven—only 5 minutes baking time per batch!

1 large baking potato (about 10 ounces), peeled and cut into 1-inch chunks
1 tablespoon honey
1 package active dry yeast
1 container (8 ounces) plain low-fat yogurt
1¼ teaspoons salt
About ¾ cup whole wheat flour
About 3¼ cups all-purpose flour

1 In 2-quart saucepan, place potato chunks and *enough water to cover*; heat to boiling over high heat. Reduce heat to low; cover and simmer 15 minutes or until potato chunks are fork-tender. Drain potatoes. Return to saucepan; heat over medium heat, shaking pan constantly, until excess liquid evaporates, about 30 seconds. With potato masher, mash potatoes until smooth. Set aside until cool, about 20 minutes.

2 In small bowl, stir honey and yeast into *¼ cup warm water* (105° to 115°F.); let stand until yeast mixture foams, about 5 minutes.

3 In large bowl, with wooden spoon, stir cooled mashed potatoes, yeast mixture, yogurt, and salt until combined. Stir in whole wheat flour and about 2¼ cups all-purpose flour or enough to make a soft dough. With floured hands, mix dough in bowl and shape into a ball. Cover bowl with plastic wrap and refrigerate dough overnight.

4 When ready to bake, turn dough onto well-floured surface and knead until smooth and elastic, about 10 minutes, working in more all-purpose flour (about 1 cup) while kneading (dough will be sticky). Cut dough into 16 equal pieces; with floured hands, shape each into a ball and place in 15½" by 10½" jelly-roll pan. Cover pan and let dough rise in warm place (80° to 85°F.) until doubled, about 40 minutes.

5 Preheat oven to 450°F. Place oven rack in center of oven. On floured surface, with floured rolling pin, roll 1 piece of dough into a 6-inch round, being careful to keep thickness of dough even. (If dough is too

thick or too thin, pitas will not rise uniformly when baked.) Repeat with 3 more pieces of dough. With pastry brush, remove excess flour from pitas.

6 Heat large cookie sheet in oven 5 to 7 minutes. Place 4 pita rounds on preheated cookie sheet; bake 5 minutes or until golden and puffed (some pitas will puff more than others). Cool on wire rack. Repeat with remaining dough. Makes 16 pitas.

Each pita: About 130 calories, 4 g protein, 27 g carbohydrate, 1 g total fat (0 g saturated), 1 mg cholesterol, 145 mg sodium.

Ciabatta

PREP: 30 MINUTES PLUS RISING AND COOLING BAKE: 25 TO 30 MINUTES

Try this flat Italian bread with any hearty soup or stew. We also like it with a simple green salad.

1 package active dry yeast
1 teaspoon sugar
5 cups all-purpose flour
1 tablespoon salt
2 tablespoons milk
2 tablespoons extravirgin olive oil

1 In cup, combine yeast, sugar, and *¼ cup warm water* (105° to 115° F.); let stand until yeast mixture foams, about 5 minutes.

2 Into bowl of heavy-duty mixer, measure flour and salt. With wooden spoon, stir in milk, olive oil, yeast mixture, and *2 cups warm water* (105° to 115°F.) until blended. With dough hook, mix on medium speed 15 minutes or until dough becomes elastic. (Or, if you prefer to mix by hand, in very large bowl, combine ingredients as above and stir with wooden spoon 15 minutes or until dough becomes elastic.) This is a very sticky and moist dough; resist the urge to add more flour, and do not knead or stir for less than the suggested time.

3 Scrape dough into greased large bowl; with greased hand, pat top of dough to coat. Cover bowl with plastic wrap, and let dough rise in warm place (80° to 85°F.) until doubled, 1 to 1½ hours.

4 Flour large cookie sheet. With floured hands, punch down dough and divide it in half. Turn pieces of dough onto cookie sheet, about 3 inches apart; cover and let rest 15 minutes for easier shaping. With

THE "ALL-AMERICAN" BREAD BASKET

Here's what's hot and fresh at country stores, city bake shops, and some supermarkets:

Baguette a long, thin loaf with diagonal slashes in the top crust.

Bâtarde a medium-long loaf, wide in the center and tapered at the ends; also called a French loaf.

Boule a round loaf of white bread; the name is French for "ball."

Ciabatta a flat, chewy choice with lots of holes in the dough and a flour-coated crust; the Italian name means "old slipper."

Focaccia flat Italian bread with a pebbly, dimpled top; may be plain or made with herbs, onions, or olives.

Fougasse a low, lattice-cut loaf originally made in the south of France and sometimes studded with Mediterranean ingredients like anchovies or olives.

Semolina Bread usually made with unbleached all-purpose flour and finely ground, unbleached patent durum flour, which gives the bread its characteristic pale-yellow color. Coarsely ground semolina flour, which has the texture of cornmeal and is used in pasta making, is traditionally dusted on the bread pans to prevent loaves from sticking.

---

hands, pull 1 piece of dough into 14" by 4" oval. Repeat with remaining piece of dough, still keeping loaves 3 inches apart. With floured fingers, make deep indentations all over each loaf, making sure to press all the way down to cookie sheet. Sprinkle loaves lightly with flour. Cover and let rise in warm place until doubled, about 30 minutes.

5 Preheat oven to 425°F. Place 12 ice cubes in 13" by 9" metal baking pan. Place pan in bottom of oven. Bake loaves on middle rack 25 to 30 minutes until golden, using spray bottle to spritz loaves with water 3 times during first 10 minutes of baking. Cool loaves on wire rack. Makes 2 loaves, 12 servings per loaf.

Each serving: About 105 calories, 3 g protein, 20 g carbohydrate, 1 g total fat (0 g saturated), 0 mg cholesterol, 270 mg sodium.

Olive-Rosemary Bread

PREP: 30 MINUTES PLUS RISING AND COOLING
BAKE: 30 MINUTES

Kalamata olives and fresh rosemary flavor this robust peasant loaf. Using high-gluten bread flour enhances the structure of the bread.

2 packages active dry yeast
1 tablespoon sugar
4 tablespoons extravirgin olive oil
1 cup Kalamata or green olives, pitted and chopped
2 tablespoons finely chopped fresh rosemary
2 teaspoons salt
About 5 cups bread flour

1 In small bowl, combine yeast, sugar, 3 tablespoons olive oil, and ½ *cup warm water* (105° to 115°F.); let stand until yeast mixture foams, about 5 minutes.

2 Meanwhile, in large bowl, with wooden spoon, mix olives, rosemary, salt, and 4 cups flour. Add yeast mixture and *1 cup warm water* (105° to 115°F.); stir until combined.

3 Turn dough onto lightly floured surface and knead until smooth and elastic, about 8 minutes, working in more flour (½ to 1 cup) while kneading.

4 Shape dough into a ball; place in greased large bowl, turning dough over to grease top. Cover bowl with plastic wrap and let dough rise in warm place (80° to 85°F.), until doubled, about 1 hour.

5 Punch down dough. Turn dough onto lightly floured surface and cut in half; cover and let rest 15 minutes for easier shaping. Grease large cookie sheet.

6 Shape each half into a 7½" by 4" oval and place on cookie sheet, about 3 inches apart. Cover and let rise in warm place until doubled, about 1 hour.

7 Preheat oven to 400°F. Brush tops of loaves with remaining 1 tablespoon olive oil. With sharp knife, cut 3 diagonal slashes across top of each loaf. Bake loaves 30 minutes or until golden. Makes 2 loaves, 12 servings per loaf.

Each serving: About 140 calories, 4 g protein, 22 g carbohydrate, 4 g total fat (1 g saturated), 0 mg cholesterol, 265 mg sodium.

Semolina Focaccia

PREP: 20 MINUTES PLUS RISING AND COOLING
BAKE: ABOUT 20 MINUTES

If you like, make our recipe in a bread machine to effortlessly produce a loaf with the same savory flavor, if not the shape, of this beloved Italian-style classic. For the bread-machine version, add the ingredients to the pan in the order specified by your machine's instruction manual but use only 1½ cups patent durum or semolina flour, increase olive oil in dough to ¼ cup, and don't drizzle bread with oil.

1 package active dry yeast
6 tablespoons olive oil
1 teaspoon plus 2 tablespoons sugar
2 teaspoons salt
1½ cups plus 2 tablespoons patent durum or
   finely ground semolina flour*
About 1½ cups all-purpose flour
¾ cup golden raisins
1 tablespoon fennel seeds, crushed

1 In cup, mix yeast, 3 tablespoons olive oil, 1 teaspoon sugar, and *1 cup warm water* (105° to 115°F.); let stand until yeast mixture foams, about 5 minutes.

2 Meanwhile, in large bowl, combine remaining 2 tablespoons sugar, salt, 1½ cups patent durum or semolina flour, and 1½ cups all-purpose flour; stir to blend.

3 With wooden spoon, stir in yeast mixture. With floured hands, knead to combine. Turn dough onto lightly floured surface and knead until smooth and elastic, about 8 minutes, working in more all-purpose flour (about 3 tablespoons) while kneading if necessary. Knead in raisins and fennel seeds.

4 Shape dough into a ball; place in greased large bowl, turning dough over to grease top. Cover bowl with plastic wrap and let dough rise in warm place (80° to 85°F.) until doubled, about 40 minutes.

5 Grease 15½" by 10½" jelly-roll pan; sprinkle with remaining 2 tablespoons patent durum or semolina flour. With floured rolling pin, roll dough evenly in jelly-roll pan; press dough into corners with fingers. Cover and let rise in warm place until doubled, about 30 minutes.

6 Preheat oven to 425°F. With fingers, make deep indentations, about 1 inch apart, over surface of dough. Drizzle focaccia with remaining 3 tablespoons olive oil.

7 Bake focaccia 20 minutes or until golden. Remove focaccia from jelly-roll pan and place on wire rack to cool. Makes 1 loaf, 12 servings.

*Patent durum or semolina flour is a high-protein, high-gluten flour milled from durum wheat. It is available in Italian grocery stores.

Each serving: About 240 calories, 5 g protein, 40 g carbohydrate, 7 g total fat (1 g saturated), 0 mg cholesterol, 360 mg sodium.

Farmhouse White Bread

PREP: 1½ HOURS PLUS RISING AND COOLING
BAKE: ABOUT 25 MINUTES

This recipe yields 2 loaves of dense, crusty bread, perfect thickly sliced and topped with jam, or filled for sandwiches. First, prepare the sponge starter 15 to 24 hours before mixing the dough, then allow 5 to 17 hours of rising before the loaves go into the oven. Don't be put off by the total amount of time needed; most of it is for rising, not active work.

SPONGE STARTER:
3 cups all-purpose flour
½ teaspoon active dry yeast

DOUGH:
¾ teaspoon active dry yeast
¼ teaspoon sugar
1 tablespoon plus 1 teaspoon salt
About 3⅓ cups all-purpose flour

1 Prepare Sponge Starter: Into large bowl, measure flour, yeast, and *1⅓ cups warm water* (105° to 115°F.). With mixer at low speed, beat 3 minutes to develop a smooth, elastic batter. Scrape starter into large bowl; cover with plastic wrap and refrigerate between 15 and 24 hours. (Starter is ready to use when it has thinned out slightly, the volume has tripled, and small bubbles appear on the surface.)

2 When starter is ready, let stand, covered, 30 minutes at room temperature before using. Meanwhile, prepare Dough: Into very large bowl, measure *1 cup warm water* (105° to 115°F.); stir in yeast and sugar and let stand until yeast mixture foams slightly, about 10 minutes.

1 *Lemon-Pepper Crisps*   **2** *Olive-Rosemary Bread*   **3** *Whole Wheat Pitas*   **4** *Farmhouse White Bread*
5 *Semolina Focaccia*   **6** *Portuguese Peasant Bread*   **7** *Whole Wheat Sesame Biscuits*   **8** *Bread-Machine Multigrain Loaf*   **9** *Chocolate-Cherry Bread*   **10** *Ciabatta*

3 Add starter to yeast mixture in bowl, breaking up starter with hand (mixture will not be completely blended). Stir in salt and 3 cups flour. With floured hands, knead to combine in bowl.

4 Turn dough onto lightly floured surface and knead until smooth and elastic, about 10 to 12 minutes, working in more flour (about ⅓ cup) while kneading if necessary.

5 Shape dough into a ball and place in greased large bowl, turning dough over to grease top. Cover and let rise in warm place (80° to 85°F.) until doubled, about 1 hour.

6 Punch down dough. In same bowl, shape dough into a ball. Cover and let rise again until doubled, about 1 hour.

7 Turn dough onto floured surface and cut in half; cover and let rest 15 minutes for easier shaping. Sprinkle large cookie sheet with flour.

8 Shape each half of dough into 7-inch round loaf.

Place loaves, about 3 inches apart, in opposite corners on cookie sheet. Cover and let rise in refrigerator at least 3 hours, or up to 15 hours.

9 Preheat oven to 500°F. Remove loaves from refrigerator. Sprinkle loaves with flour. With sharp knife, cut 2 parallel lines, 1½ inches apart, on top of each loaf, then cut 2 more lines, perpendicular to first lines (pattern should resemble a tic-tac-toe board). Place 12 ice cubes in 13" by 9" metal baking pan. Place pan in bottom of oven. Bake loaves on middle rack 10 minutes. Turn oven control to 400°F. Bake 15 minutes longer or until loaves are golden brown. Cool loaves on wire rack. Makes 2 loaves, 12 servings per loaf.

Each serving: About 120 calories, 4 g protein, 25 g carbohydrate, 0 g total fat, 0 mg cholesterol, 355 mg sodium.

Portuguese Peasant Bread

PREP: 20 MINUTES PLUS RISING AND COOLING
BAKE: 35 MINUTES

This dense bread is called *broa* in Portugal. Our "secret" ingredient for its unusual flavor and texture: barley cereal for babies! The loaves are also sprayed with water during baking to help give them the characteristic crisp and chewy crust.

2 tablespoons sugar
2 packages active dry yeast
1 package (8 ounces) barley cereal (about 4½ cups),* uncooked
2½ cups stone-ground cornmeal, preferably white
4 teaspoons salt
About 4¾ cups all-purpose flour

1 In small bowl, stir sugar and yeast into *½ cup warm water* (105° to 115°F.); let stand until yeast mixture foams, about 5 minutes.

2 In large bowl, combine barley cereal, cornmeal, salt, and 4 cups flour. With wooden spoon, stir in yeast mixture and *2½ cups warm water* (105° to 115°F.) until combined. With floured hands, shape dough into a ball in bowl.

3 Cover bowl with plastic wrap and let rise in warm place (80° to 85°F.) until doubled, about 1 hour.

4 Punch down dough and turn onto well-floured surface. Knead dough until smooth, about 5 minutes, working in more flour (about ¾ cup) as necessary while kneading.

5 Grease large cookie sheet. Cut dough in half and shape each half into a 6-inch round. Coat each round with flour; place on cookie sheet. Cover loaves with towel and let rise in warm place until doubled, about 1 hour.

6 Preheat oven to 400°F. Bake loaves until golden brown, about 35 minutes, using spray bottle to spritz loaves with water after first 5 minutes of baking, and again 10 minutes later. Cool on wire racks. Makes 2 loaves, 12 servings per loaf.

*Barley cereal can be found in the baby-food section of supermarkets.

Each serving: About 170 calories, 5 g protein, 36 g carbohydrate, 1 g total fat (0 g saturated), 0 mg cholesterol, 360 mg sodium.

Chocolate-Cherry Bread

PREP: 20 MINUTES PLUS RISING AND COOLING
BAKE: ABOUT 20 MINUTES

A not-too-sweet favorite studded with bits of bittersweet chocolate and dried tart cherries. Using Dutch-process (rather than natural) cocoa yields a rich, dark-brown color.

1 package active dry yeast
3 teaspoons granulated sugar
⅓ cup unsweetened Dutch-process cocoa
⅓ cup packed dark brown sugar
1¾ teaspoons salt
About 3½ cups all-purpose flour
1 cup warm brewed coffee (105° to 115°F.)
4 tablespoons margarine or butter, softened
1 large egg, separated
¾ cup dried tart cherries
3 ounces bittersweet chocolate, coarsely chopped

1 In cup, mix yeast, 1 teaspoon granulated sugar, and *¼ cup warm water* (105° to 115°F.); let stand until yeast mixture foams, about 5 minutes.

2 Meanwhile, in large bowl, combine cocoa, brown sugar, salt, and 3 cups flour; stir to blend.

3 With wooden spoon, stir warm coffee, margarine or butter, egg yolk (cover and refrigerate egg white to use later), and yeast mixture into flour mixture. With floured hands, knead to combine.

4 Turn dough onto lightly floured surface and knead until smooth and elastic, about 10 minutes, working in more flour (about ½ cup) while kneading if necessary. Knead in cherries and chocolate.

5 Place dough in greased bowl, turning dough over to grease top. Cover bowl with plastic wrap and let dough rise in warm place (80° to 85°F.) until doubled, about 1½ hours.

6 Punch down dough. Turn dough onto lightly floured surface and cut in half; cover and let rest 15 minutes for easier shaping. Shape each half of dough into a 5-inch round loaf. Place loaves, about 3 inches apart, in opposite corners on ungreased large cookie sheet. Cover and let rise in warm place until doubled, about 1 hour.

7 Preheat oven to 400°F. In cup, mix egg white with *1 teaspoon water*; brush mixture on tops of loaves. Sprinkle loaves with remaining 2 teaspoons granulated sugar. With knife, cut shallow X on top of each loaf. Bake loaves 20 minutes or until crusty. Makes 2 loaves, 12 servings per loaf.

Each serving: About 135 calories, 3 g protein, 23 g carbohydrate, 4 g total fat (1 g saturated), 9 mg cholesterol, 30 mg sodium.

Golden Raisin & Dried Cranberry Soda Bread

PREP: 15 MINUTES • BAKE: 50 TO 55 MINUTES

To satisfy her craving for soda bread, Freelance Recipe Developer Marianne Marinelli created this wonderfully moist quick bread. Marinelli likes to use cranberries during the holiday season, but other dried fruits, such as chopped apricots or cherries, can be used. She can't decide which way she likes the bread better—fresh out of the oven, or sliced, toasted, and buttered the next day.

2½ cups all-purpose flour
½ cup whole wheat flour
2 teaspoons baking soda
¼ teaspoon salt
½ cup plus 2 teaspoons sugar
4 tablespoons cold margarine or butter, cut up
½ cup golden raisins
½ cup dried cranberries
1½ cups buttermilk

SUCCESS WITH A STAND MIXER

Most of our bread recipes call for hands-on kneading, but you can get equally good results with a stand mixer fitted with the dough-hook attachment(s). Just be sure to stop the mixer as soon as the dough looks smooth and elastic; overkneading can produce tough loaves. Although some mixers may take just as long as hand kneading, heavy-duty machines do the job in as little as 2 minutes. See News & Notes, page 9, for more information on stand mixers.

1 Preheat oven to 350°F. Grease 9" by 5" metal loaf pan.

2 In large bowl, combine all-purpose flour, whole-wheat flour, baking soda, salt, and ½ cup sugar. With pastry blender or two knives used scissor-fashion, cut in margarine or butter until mixture resembles fine crumbs. With spoon, stir in raisins and cranberries, then buttermilk just until batter is combined.

3 Spoon batter into loaf pan. Sprinkle top with remaining 2 teaspoons sugar. Bake 50 to 55 minutes, until toothpick inserted in center of loaf comes out clean. Cool loaf in pan on wire rack 10 minutes; remove from pan and finish cooling on wire rack. Makes 12 servings.

Each serving: About 230 calories, 5 g protein, 44 g carbohydrate, 5 g total fat (1 g saturated), 1 mg cholesterol, 340 mg sodium.

Bread-Machine Multigrain Loaf

PREP: 10 MINUTES
BAKE: PER BREAD MACHINE'S INSTRUCTIONS

Be sure to follow your machine's instructions for the order of adding ingredients. This recipe uses the setting for a 1½-pound whole wheat loaf. Do not use the "delay start" mode for this bread; it contains buttermilk, which should not be left at room temperature for an extended period of time.

2 cups whole wheat flour
1 cup all-purpose flour
¼ cup bulgur (cracked wheat)
¼ cup old-fashioned oats, uncooked
2 tablespoons toasted wheat germ
1½ teaspoons salt
1¼ cups buttermilk
¼ cup honey
3 tablespoons vegetable oil
1 package active dry yeast

Prepare recipe according to your bread machine's instructions. Makes 1 loaf, 16 servings.

Each serving: About 145 calories, 5 g protein, 25 g carbohydrate, 3 g total fat (1 g saturated), 1 mg cholesterol, 220 mg sodium.

5-MINUTE SKILLET JAMS

PREP: 5 MINUTES PLUS 6 HOURS TO CHILL • COOK: 10 MINUTES

What could be better on a thick slice of home-made bread than butter and fresh fruit jam? Here are three ultra-quick recipes. After cooking the jam, pour into two ½-pint jars with tight-fitting lids. Cover and refrigerate until jam is set and cold, about 6 hours. Keep jam refrigerated and use within 3 weeks. Makes about 2 cups.

Blueberry Skillet Jam In 12-inch skillet, heat *1 pint blueberries*, mashed, *2 tablespoons powdered fruit pectin*, and *½ teaspoon margarine or butter* over medium-high heat, stirring constantly until mixture boils. Stir in *1 cup sugar*; heat to boiling. Boil 1 minute; remove from heat. Each tablespoon: About 30 calories, 0 g protein, 8 g carbohydrate, 0 g total fat, 0 mg cholesterol, 3 mg sodium.

Peach Skillet Jam In 12-inch skillet, heat *1 pound peaches*, peeled, pitted, and mashed, *2 tablespoons powdered fruit pectin*, *2 teaspoons fresh lemon juice*, and *½ teaspoon margarine or butter* over medium-high heat, stirring constantly until mixture boils. Stir in *1 cup sugar*; heat to boiling. Boil 1 minute; remove from heat. Each tablespoon: About 30 calories, 0 g protein, 8 g carbohydrate, 0 g total fat, 0 mg cholesterol, 2 mg sodium.

Raspberry Skillet Jam Starting with *3 cups raspberries*, press half of berries through sieve to remove

Top to bottom: Blueberry, Peach, and Raspberry skillet jams

some seeds. Add to 12-inch skillet along with remaining raspberries, *1 tablespoon plus 1 teaspoon powdered fruit pectin*, *½ teaspoon margarine or butter*. Heat over medium-high heat, stirring constantly until mixture boils. Stir in *1½ cups sugar*; heat to boiling. Boil 1 minute; remove from heat. Each tablespoon: About 45 calories, 0 g protein, 11 g carbohydrate, 0 g total fat, 0 mg cholesterol, 2 mg sodium.

Southern-Style Biscuits

PREP: 10 MINUTES • BAKE: ABOUT 15 MINUTES

Nutrition Director Delia Hammock's mother, Alma, has a special "biscuit bowl" that is reserved only for this special task. Hammock remembers that as a girl in Dublin, Georgia, she'd watch her mother take out the bowl, add the ingredients without measuring, and then mix everything by hand. Although we were unable to duplicate Alma's special technique, Hammock assures us that our version is reminiscent of the biscuits from her childhood.

3 cups self-rising cake flour (unsifted)*
⅓ cup shortening
1 cup milk

1 Preheat oven to 450°F. Into large bowl, measure self-rising cake flour. With pastry blender or two knives used scissor-fashion, cut in shortening until evenly combined.

2 Stir milk into flour mixture just until ingredients are blended.

3 Scoop dough by scant ¼ cups onto ungreased large cookie sheet. If you like, with floured hands, lightly pat scoops of dough to smooth slightly.

4 Bake biscuits about 15 minutes, or until lightly browned. Serve biscuits warm. Or, cool on wire rack; reheat if desired. Makes 12 biscuits.

*If not using self-rising cake flour in step 1, substitute *1½ cups all-purpose flour*, *1½ cups cake flour* (not self-rising), *1 tablespoon baking powder*, and *1 teaspoon salt*; place in large bowl, then cut in shortening. Continue as in steps 2 through 4.

Each biscuit: About 175 calories, 4 g protein, 24 g carbohydrate, 7 g total fat (2 g saturated), 3 mg cholesterol, 405 mg sodium.

Whole Wheat Sesame Biscuits

PREP: 15 MINUTES • BAKE: 12 TO 15 MINUTES

We blended whole wheat flour with toasted sesame seeds to make these light golden rounds.

2 tablespoons sesame seeds
1 cup whole wheat flour
1 cup all-purpose flour
1 tablespoon baking powder
¾ teaspoon salt
4 tablespoons margarine or butter
¾ cup plus 3 tablespoons milk

1 In small skillet, toast sesame seeds over medium heat until lightly browned, about 5 minutes, stirring occasionally.

2 Preheat oven to 425°F. Lightly grease large cookie sheet. In large bowl, mix flours, baking powder, salt, and 5 teaspoons toasted sesame seeds. With pastry blender or two knives used scissor-fashion, cut in margarine or butter until mixture resembles coarse crumbs. Stir in ¾ cup plus 2 tablespoons milk, stirring just until mixture forms soft dough that leaves side of bowl.

3 Turn dough onto lightly floured surface; knead 8 to 10 strokes to mix thoroughly. With floured rolling pin, roll dough ½ inch thick.

4 With floured 2½-inch round biscuit cutter, cut out biscuits. Place biscuits, about 2 inches apart, on cookie sheet.

5 Press trimmings together; roll and cut as above. Brush tops of biscuits with remaining 1 tablespoon milk; sprinkle with remaining 1 teaspoon sesame seeds. Bake 12 to 15 minutes until golden. Makes 12 biscuits.

Each biscuit: About 125 calories, 3 g protein, 17 g carbohydrate, 6 g total fat (1 g saturated), 3 mg cholesterol, 285 mg sodium.

Lemon-Pepper Crisps

PREP: 50 MINUTES PLUS COOLING
BAKE: 15 TO 18 MINUTES PER BATCH

These paper-thin flatbreads are great on their own, with your favorite dip, or with our Thai Chicken & Coconut Soup (see page 50).

2¼ cups all-purpose flour
1 cup packed fresh parsley leaves, finely chopped
1 tablespoon grated fresh lemon peel
1½ teaspoons baking powder
¼ teaspoon coarsely ground black pepper
2½ teaspoons kosher salt
2 tablespoons olive oil

1 In medium bowl, stir flour, parsley, lemon peel, baking powder, pepper, and 2 teaspoons salt. Add ¾ *cup water*; stir until dough comes together in a ball. With hand, knead dough in bowl until smooth, about 2 minutes. Divide dough in half; cover each half with plastic wrap and let rest 10 minutes.

2 Preheat oven to 350°F. On floured surface, with floured rolling pin, roll half of dough into paper-thin rectangle, about 18" by 12" (don't worry if edges are irregular). With pizza wheel or sharp knife, cut dough lengthwise in half to form two 18" by 6" rectangles. Cut rectangles crosswise into 2-inch-wide strips.

3 Transfer strips to 2 ungreased large cookie sheets (it's all right if dough stretches a little); let rest 10 minutes. With pastry brush, brush strips lightly with 1 tablespoon olive oil; sprinkle with ¼ teaspoon salt.

4 Place cookie sheets on 2 oven racks. Bake strips 15 to 18 minutes until lightly browned, rotating cookie sheets between upper and lower racks halfway through baking time. Immediately remove crisps to wire racks to cool.

5 Repeat with remaining dough, oil, and salt. Store crisps in tightly covered container to use within 2 weeks. Makes 3 dozen crisps.

Each crisp: About 35 calories, 1 g protein, 6 g carbohydrate, 1 g total fat (0 g saturated), 0 mg cholesterol, 90 mg sodium.

Blueberry-Lemon Tea Bread

PREP: 20 MINUTES PLUS COOLING
BAKE: 1 HOUR 5 MINUTES

It's so easy; bake 2 loaves, 1 for right away, the other to slice, freeze, and enjoy after blueberry season.

½ cup margarine or butter (1 stick), softened
1⅓ cups sugar
2 cups all-purpose flour
2 teaspoons baking powder
½ teaspoon salt
2 large eggs
½ cup milk
1½ cups blueberries
¼ cup fresh lemon juice

1 Preheat oven to 350°F. Grease and flour 9" by 5" loaf pan.

2 In large bowl, with mixer at low speed, beat margarine or butter and 1 cup sugar just until blended. Increase speed to medium; beat until light and fluffy, about 5 minutes.

3 Meanwhile, in medium bowl, combine flour, baking powder, and salt.

4 Reduce speed to low; add eggs, 1 at a time, beating after each addition until well blended, occasionally scraping bowl with rubber spatula. Alternately add flour mixture and milk, mixing just until blended. Gently stir in blueberries. Spoon batter into loaf pan.

5 Bake loaf 1 hour and 5 minutes or until toothpick inserted in center comes out clean. Cool loaf in pan on wire rack 10 minutes; remove from pan.

6 With skewer, prick top and sides of warm cake in many places. In small bowl, mix lemon juice and remaining ⅓ cup sugar. With pastry brush, brush top and sides of warm cake with lemon glaze. Cool cake on wire rack. Makes 16 servings.

Each serving: About 195 calories, 3 g protein, 31 g carbohydrate, 7 g total fat (1 g saturated), 28 mg cholesterol, 200 mg sodium.

Raspberry-Walnut Sour Cream Cake

PREP: 30 MINUTES PLUS COOLING
BAKE: ABOUT 1 HOUR 10 MINUTES

A classic cake with a tunnel of red raspberry jam inside. We tested this recipe in both a 9- and a 10-inch tube pan with equal success, so take your pick!

3¾ cups all-purpose flour
2 teaspoons baking powder
1 teaspoon baking soda
¾ teaspoon salt
1¾ cups sugar
½ cup margarine or butter (1 stick), softened
3 large eggs
1 container (16 ounces) sour cream
2 teaspoons vanilla extract
½ cup seedless red raspberry jam
½ cup walnuts, toasted and chopped

1 Preheat oven to 350°F. Grease 9- or 10-inch tube pan with removable bottom; dust with flour. In medium bowl, combine flour, baking powder, baking soda, and salt; set aside.

2 In large bowl, with mixer at low speed, beat sugar with margarine or butter until blended, scraping bowl often with rubber spatula. Increase speed to high; beat until creamy, about 2 minutes, occasionally scraping bowl. Reduce speed to low; add eggs, 1 at a time, beating well after each addition.

3 With mixer at low speed, alternately add flour mixture and sour cream, beginning and ending with flour mixture, until batter is smooth, occasionally scraping bowl. Beat in vanilla.

4 Spoon three-fourths of batter into pan. Spread raspberry jam evenly over batter, then spread remaining batter evenly over jam. Sprinkle walnuts on top.

5 Bake coffee cake about 1 hour and 10 minutes or until toothpick inserted in center comes out clean. Cool cake in pan on wire rack 10 minutes. With small metal spatula, loosen cake from side of pan and remove sides. Invert cake onto plate; remove bottom of pan. Immediately invert walnut side up onto wire rack to cool completely. Makes 16 servings.

Each serving: About 370 calories, 6 g protein, 54 g carbohydrate, 15 g total fat (5 g saturated), 53 mg cholesterol, 330 mg sodium.

Raspberry-Walnut Sour Cream Cake ➤

Pumpkin Spice Cake

PREP: 25 MINUTES PLUS COOLING
BAKE: 55 TO 60 MINUTES

Pumpkin-pie lovers will adore this moist Bundt cake with its brown butter glaze.

CAKE:
3½ cups all-purpose flour
1 tablespoon pumpkin-pie spice
2 teaspoons baking powder
1 teaspoon baking soda
½ teaspoon salt
1¾ cups sugar
1 cup margarine or butter (2 sticks), softened
4 large eggs
1 can (16 ounces) solid-pack pumpkin (not pumpkin-pie mix)
¼ cup milk
2 teaspoons vanilla extract

BROWN BUTTER GLAZE:
6 tablespoons margarine or butter (¾ stick)
½ cup packed light brown sugar
2 tablespoons milk
1 teaspoon vanilla extract
1 cup confectioners' sugar

1 Prepare Cake: Preheat oven to 350°F. Grease 10-inch Bundt pan; dust with flour.

2 In medium bowl, mix flour, pumpkin-pie spice, baking powder, baking soda, and salt; set aside.

3 In large bowl, with mixer at low speed, beat sugar with margarine or butter until blended, scraping bowl often with rubber spatula. Increase speed to high; beat until creamy, about 2 minutes, occasionally scraping bowl. Reduce speed to low; add eggs, 1 at a time, beating well after each addition.

4 In small bowl, mix together pumpkin, milk, and vanilla. With mixer at low speed, alternately add flour mixture and pumpkin mixture, beginning and ending with flour mixture, until batter is smooth, occasionally scraping bowl with rubber spatula.

5 Pour batter into pan. Bake 55 to 60 minutes until toothpick inserted in center of cake comes out almost clean. Cool cake in pan on wire rack 15 minutes. With small metal spatula, loosen cake from side of pan; invert onto wire rack to cool completely.

6 When cake is cool, prepare Brown Butter Glaze: In 2-quart saucepan, heat margarine or butter over medium heat until melted and golden brown, about

3 to 5 minutes, stirring occasionally. Add brown sugar and milk and whisk over low heat until sugar dissolves, about 2 minutes. Remove saucepan from heat; whisk in vanilla. Gradually whisk in confectioners' sugar until smooth, about 3 minutes. Cool glaze until slightly thickened, about 5 minutes, whisking occasionally. Pour glaze over cooled cake, allowing glaze to drip down side of cake. Makes 20 servings.

Each serving: About 330 calories, 4 g protein, 48 g carbohydrate, 14 g total fat (3 g saturated), 43 mg cholesterol, 340 mg sodium.

Bee-Sting Cake

PREP: 40 MINUTES PLUS RISING AND COOLING
BAKE: 20 TO 25 MINUTES

This old-time German cake is usually baked in a round pan, but we used a jelly-roll pan to get a higher proportion of yummy honey-almond topping to cake.

CAKE:
1 package active dry yeast
1 teaspoon plus ⅓ cup sugar
6 tablespoons margarine or butter (¾ stick), softened
1 large egg
1 large egg yolk
⅓ cup milk
1 teaspoon vanilla extract
¼ teaspoon salt
About 3 cups all-purpose flour

GLAZE:
⅔ cup sugar
½ cup margarine or butter (1 stick)
½ cup honey
¼ cup heavy or whipping cream
2 teaspoons fresh lemon juice
1⅓ cups sliced natural almonds

1 Prepare Cake: In cup, stir yeast and 1 teaspoon sugar into ¼ *cup warm water* (105° to 115°F.); let stand until yeast mixture foams, about 5 minutes.

2 Meanwhile, in large bowl, with mixer at low speed, beat margarine or butter with remaining ⅓ cup sugar until blended, scraping bowl often with rubber spatula. Increase speed to high; beat until creamy, about 3 minutes, occasionally scraping bowl. Reduce speed to low; beat in whole egg and egg yolk (mixture may look curdled). Beat in yeast mixture, milk, vanilla, salt, and 2½ cups flour until blended.

3 Turn dough onto lightly floured surface and knead until smooth and elastic, about 5 minutes, working in more flour (about ½ cup) while kneading (dough will be slightly sticky).

4 Shape dough into a ball; place in greased large bowl, turning dough over to grease top. Cover and let rise in warm place (80° to 85°F.) until doubled, about 45 minutes.

5 Punch down dough; cover and let rest 15 minutes. Meanwhile, grease 15½" by 10½" jelly-roll pan. Line bottom and sides of pan with foil; grease foil.

6 Turn dough into pan. With hands, press dough evenly in pan, making sure to get into corners. Cover and let rise in warm place until doubled, about 45 minutes.

7 Preheat oven to 375°F. Prepare Glaze: In 2-quart saucepan, heat sugar, margarine or butter, honey, and heavy or whipping cream over medium heat until mixture boils, stirring frequently. Remove saucepan from heat; stir in lemon juice. Set aside 5 minutes to cool slightly.

8 Pour glaze over dough and scatter almonds over top. Place 2 sheets of foil underneath pan; crimp foil edges to form a rim to catch any drips during baking.

Bee-Sting Cake

Bake cake 20 to 25 minutes, until top is golden. Cool in pan on wire rack 15 minutes. Run small knife between foil and edge of pan to loosen, then invert cake onto large cookie sheet. Gently peel off foil and discard. Immediately invert cake almond side up onto wire rack to cool completely. Makes 16 servings.

Each serving: About 345 calories, 6 g protein, 42 g carbohydrate, 18 g total fat (3 g saturated), 32 mg cholesterol, 175 mg sodium.

Raspberry Corn Muffins

PREP: 15 MINUTES • BAKE: 20 TO 25 MINUTES

Enjoy summer's bounty with your choice of raspberries or blueberries baked into these delicious buttermilk corn muffins.

1 cup all-purpose flour
1 cup yellow cornmeal
½ cup sugar
2 teaspoons baking powder
1 teaspoon baking soda
½ teaspoon salt
1 cup buttermilk
¼ cup vegetable oil
2 teaspoons vanilla extract
1 large egg
1¼ cups raspberries or 1½ cups blueberries

1 Preheat oven to 400°F. Grease twelve 2½" by 1¼" muffin-pan cups.

2 In large bowl, mix flour, cornmeal, sugar, baking powder, baking soda, and salt. In small bowl, with wire whisk or fork, beat buttermilk, vegetable oil, vanilla, and egg until blended; stir into flour mixture just until flour is moistened (batter will be lumpy). Fold in berries.

3 Spoon batter into muffin cups. Bake muffins 20 to 25 minutes or until toothpick inserted in center of muffin comes out clean. Immediately remove muffins from pans; serve warm. Or cool on wire rack. Makes 12 muffins.

Each muffin: About 180 calories, 3 g protein, 29 g carbohydrate, 6 g total fat (1 g saturated), 19 mg cholesterol, 285 mg sodium.

Orange-Cornmeal Breakfast Cake

PREP: 25 MINUTES PLUS COOLING
BAKE: 30 TO 35 MINUTES

Make this dense cake—with a hint of orange flavor and chewy dried cranberries—in a 5½- to 6-cup ring mold if you don't have a small Bundt pan.

¾ cup yellow cornmeal
½ cup all-purpose flour
½ teaspoon baking powder
¼ teaspoon salt
4 large eggs, separated
⅔ cup sugar
6 tablespoons margarine or butter (¾ stick), softened
2 teaspoons grated fresh orange peel
1 teaspoon vanilla extract
½ cup dried cranberries, chopped

1 Preheat oven to 325°F. Grease 6-cup Bundt pan; dust with flour.

2 In medium bowl, combine cornmeal, flour, baking powder, and salt; set aside.

3 In small bowl, with mixer at high speed, beat egg whites until stiff peaks form; set aside.

4 In large bowl, with same beaters and with mixer at low speed, beat sugar with margarine or butter, orange peel, vanilla, and egg yolks until blended. Increase speed to high; beat until creamy, about 5 minutes.

5 Stir cornmeal mixture and half of beaten egg whites into egg-yolk mixture (batter will be dry). With rubber spatula, fold in chopped cranberries and remaining whites until evenly blended.

6 Spoon batter into pan. Bake 30 to 35 minutes, until toothpick inserted in center of cake comes out clean. Cool cake in pan on wire rack 10 minutes. With small metal spatula, loosen cake from side of pan; invert onto wire rack to cool completely. Makes 10 servings.

Each serving: About 225 calories, 4 g protein, 32 g carbohydrate, 9 g total fat (2 g saturated), 85 mg cholesterol, 190 mg sodium.

Java-Banana Snack Cake with Oatmeal Streusel

PREP: 25 MINUTES PLUS COOLING
BAKE: 40 TO 45 MINUTES

The old-fashioned buttery streusel topping will draw everyone back for a second helping.

STREUSEL:
¾ cup walnuts, chopped
½ cup old-fashioned or quick-cooking oats, uncooked
⅓ cup packed light brown sugar
¼ cup all-purpose flour
4 tablespoons margarine or butter (½ stick), softened

CAKE:
2 cups all-purpose flour
1 teaspoon baking powder
1 teaspoon baking soda
¼ teaspoon salt
⅔ cup sugar
6 tablespoons margarine or butter (¾ stick), softened
2 large eggs
2 tablespoons instant-coffee powder or granules
3 ripe medium bananas, peeled and mashed (1 cup)
¼ cup buttermilk
1 teaspoon vanilla extract

1 Prepare Streusel: In medium bowl, mix walnuts, oats, brown sugar, and flour until blended. With fingertips, work in margarine or butter until evenly distributed. Cover and refrigerate.

2 Prepare Cake: Preheat oven to 350°F. Grease 9" by 9" metal baking pan; dust with flour.

3 In medium bowl, combine flour, baking powder, baking soda, and salt; set aside.

4 In large bowl, with mixer at low speed, beat sugar and margarine or butter until blended, scraping bowl often with rubber spatula. Increase speed to high; beat until creamy, about 4 minutes, occasionally scraping bowl. Reduce speed to low; add eggs, 1 at a time, beating well after each addition.

5 In medium bowl, stir coffee powder with *1 tablespoon hot tap water* until dissolved. Stir in mashed bananas, buttermilk, and vanilla. With mixer at low speed, alternately add flour mixture and coffee mixture, beginning and ending with flour mixture, until batter is blended, occasionally scraping bowl with rubber spatula.

6 Spoon batter into pan. Press Streusel into chunks and scatter over batter. Bake 40 to 45 minutes, until toothpick inserted in center of cake comes out almost clean. Cool cake in pan on wire rack 30 minutes to serve warm, or cool completely in pan to serve later. Makes 12 servings.

Each serving: About 350 calories, 6 g protein, 48 g carbohydrate, 16 g total fat (3 g saturated), 36 mg cholesterol, 325 mg sodium.

SUGAR & SPICE & EVERYTHING NICE: A COFFEE-CAKE GLOSSARY

Around the world, there are as many definitions of what a coffee cake is as there are filling flavors. Technically, coffee cake is defined as a sweet, rich bread, often made with fruits, nuts, and spices, that is sometimes glazed after baking. Tender sticky buns, crumb-covered cakes, streusel-topped rings, and fancy filled braids all qualify. It doesn't have to contain yeast or be drizzled with sugar icing. But there is one requirement—it must go well with a steaming mug of coffee or tea (or a glass of cold milk) for breakfast, snack time, or dessert.

Bienenstich or Bee-Sting A yeast-raised cake with a nut-studded honey glaze (*bienenstich* is German for "bee sting"). Sometimes, the cake is cut horizontally and filled with pastry cream for an old-fashioned indulgence.

Cinnamon or "Sticky" Buns Tender yeast rolls that first rose to popularity more than 100 years ago in Philadelphia; the dough is usually rolled around a sweet cinnamon-raisin filling, cut in slices, baked on top of a sinfully rich butter-and-nut mixture, then inverted while hot.

Danish Light, flaky, filled pastries that originated in Denmark. They're made by folding raised dough over butter and rolling it out several times. Danish come in various shapes, with every kind of filling from cherry-cheese to almond.

Gubana, Putiza, and Presniz Yeast cakes with nut fillings, from the Friuli region of Italy; they're reminiscent of Austrian and Hungarian baked goods and occasionally served with a sprinkle of grappa (a grape eau-de-vie).

Kringle Danish yeast bread, traditionally flavored with cardamom and made with raisins, candied citrus peel, and almonds.

Kuchen A fruit- or cheese-filled yeast cake that got its start in Germany (the German word for coffee cake is *kaffeekuchen*).

Kugelhopf (or Gugelhopf) A popular golden Eastern European cake made in a fluted mold (called a kugelhopf). The recipe varies by country—in Poland, the cake is plain and unadorned; in Austria, it can be a marble pound cake with raisins.

Moravian Sugar Cake A favorite of immigrants who settled in Pennsylvania and North Carolina, this yeast cake is made with mashed potatoes for added moistness and baked in a jelly-roll pan. Before baking, the dough is sprinkled with brown sugar and cinnamon, dimpled with fingertips (like Italian focaccia), and drizzled with melted butter.

Old-Fashioned Crumb Buns Yeast buns, most likely derived from the German *streuselkuchen*. The dough is topped with chunks of buttery cinnamon streusel and baked in a large pan, so the buns can be pulled apart after baking.

Pan Dulce The words mean "sweet bread" in Spanish. These small Mexican buns are often iced before baking with a rich blend of lard, sugar, cream, cinnamon, and other ingredients.

Sandtorte This German butter cake, named for its sandy texture, is similar to pound cake, but is baked in a Kugelhopf mold and sprinkled with confectioners' sugar. The batter is sometimes spiced with cinnamon, ginger, and nutmeg.

Sour Cream Coffee Cake The kind of typical American cake our grandmas and great-aunts took pride in, with a sour cream-based batter and sometimes a middle layer and/or topping of brown sugar, nuts, cinnamon, dried fruit, chocolate chips, sliced fruit, and/or jam. It's baked in a fluted ring, or a Bundt, angel-food, or loaf pan.

Classic Crumb Cake

PREP: 40 MINUTES PLUS COOLING
BAKE: 40 TO 45 MINUTES

The thick, rich, cinnamony crumbs are irresistible. Since the recipe yields 2 cakes, serve 1 now, and freeze the other for later.

CRUMB TOPPING:
2 cups all-purpose flour
½ cup granulated sugar
½ cup packed light brown sugar
1½ teaspoons ground cinnamon
1 cup margarine or butter (2 sticks), softened

CAKE:
2¼ cups all-purpose flour
2¼ teaspoons baking powder
½ teaspoon salt
1¼ cups granulated sugar
½ cup margarine or butter (1 stick), softened
3 large eggs
¾ cup milk
2 teaspoons vanilla extract

1 Preheat oven to 350°F. Grease two 9-inch round cake pans; dust with flour.

2 Prepare Crumb Topping: In medium bowl, mix flour, granulated sugar, brown sugar, and cinnamon until well blended. With fingertips, work in margarine or butter until evenly distributed; set aside.

3 Prepare Cake: In another medium bowl, mix flour, baking powder, and salt; set aside.

4 In large bowl, with mixer at low speed, beat sugar with margarine or butter until blended, scraping bowl often with rubber spatula. Increase speed to medium; beat until well mixed, about 2 minutes, occasionally scraping bowl. Reduce speed to low; add eggs, 1 at a time, beating well after each addition.

5 In small bowl, combine milk and vanilla. With mixer at low speed, alternately add flour mixture and milk mixture, beginning and ending with flour mixture, until batter is smooth, occasionally scraping bowl.

6 Pour batter into pans. Press Crumb Topping into large chunks; evenly sprinkle over batter. Bake cakes 40 to 45 minutes, until toothpick inserted in centers of cakes comes out clean. Cool cakes in pans on wire

racks 15 minutes. With small metal spatula, loosen cakes from sides of pans. Invert onto plates, then immediately invert crumb side up onto wire racks to cool completely. Makes 2 coffee cakes, 10 servings per cake.

Each serving: About 325 calories, 4 g protein, 44 g carbohydrate, 15 g total fat (3 g saturated), 33 mg cholesterol, 295 mg sodium.

Pear & Ginger Coffee Cake

PREP: 25 MINUTES PLUS COOLING
BAKE: 55 TO 60 MINUTES

Slices of fresh Anjou pears are baked atop a tender butter cake batter spiced with crystallized ginger. (Look for this candied form of ginger in the spice section of your supermarket.)

2½ cups cake flour (not self-rising)
2 teaspoons baking powder
¼ teaspoon salt
1½ cups sugar
¾ cup margarine or butter (1½ sticks), softened
3 large eggs
1 cup milk
1 teaspoon vanilla extract
½ cup crystallized ginger (about 3 ounces), finely chopped
3 medium Anjou pears, peeled, cored, and thinly sliced
2 tablespoons brown sugar

1 Preheat oven to 350°F. Grease 13" by 9" metal baking pan; dust with flour. In medium bowl, combine flour, baking powder, and salt; set aside.

2 In large bowl, with mixer at low speed, beat sugar with margarine or butter until blended, scraping bowl often with rubber spatula. Increase speed to high; beat until creamy, about 2 minutes, occasionally scraping bowl. Reduce speed to low; add eggs, 1 at a time, beating well after each addition.

3 In small bowl, combine milk and vanilla. With mixer at low speed, alternately add flour mixture and milk mixture until batter is smooth, occasionally scraping bowl. With spoon, stir in chopped ginger.

4 Spread batter evenly in pan. Arrange pear slices, overlapping slightly, on top. Sprinkle brown sugar over batter and pears.

5 Bake cake 55 to 60 minutes, until toothpick inserted in center comes out clean. Cool cake in pan on wire rack 30 minutes to serve warm, or cool completely in pan to serve later. Makes 15 servings.

Each serving: About 300 calories, 3 g protein, 48 g carbohydrate, 11 g total fat (2 g saturated), 45 mg cholesterol, 230 mg sodium.

Caramelized Plum Cake

PREP: 1 HOUR PLUS COOLING
BAKE: 55 TO 60 MINUTES

A true comfort cake for a special afternoon with friends or family.

FRUIT TOPPING:
5 medium plums or 2 large Granny Smith apples
   (about 1 pound)
2 tablespoons margarine or butter
⅔ cup packed dark brown sugar

CAKE:
1½ cups cake flour (not self-rising)
1½ teaspoons baking powder
¼ teaspoon salt
6 tablespoons margarine or butter (¾ stick),
   softened
¾ cup granulated sugar
4 ounces almond paste (about half 7- to 8-ounce
   can or tube)
2 large eggs
1½ teaspoons vanilla extract
½ cup milk

1 Preheat oven to 350°F. Wrap outside of 10" by 3" springform pan with foil to prevent batter from leaking. Grease side of pan.

2 Prepare Fruit Topping: Cut each unpeeled plum into thin wedges (or peel, core, and thinly slice each apple). Place margarine or butter in springform pan and heat in oven until melted, about 4 minutes; remove from oven. In small bowl, with fork, stir brown sugar into melted margarine or butter until blended, spreading mixture to coat bottom of pan.

Arrange fruit on top of brown-sugar mixture, overlapping pieces slightly; set aside.

3 Prepare Cake: In medium bowl, combine cake flour, baking powder, and salt; set aside.

4 In large bowl, with mixer at low speed, beat margarine or butter, granulated sugar, and almond paste until blended, about 2 to 3 minutes, scraping bowl often with rubber spatula. Increase speed to medium; beat until well mixed, occasionally scraping bowl. Gradually beat in eggs and vanilla, just until blended.

5 With mixer at low speed, alternately add flour mixture and milk to almond-paste mixture, starting and ending with flour mixture; beat until just mixed. Pour batter over fruit in pan.

6 Bake 55 to 60 minutes, until toothpick inserted in center of cake comes out clean. Cool cake in pan on wire rack 10 minutes. With spatula, loosen cake from side of pan. Invert cake onto large plate; remove side and bottom of pan. Let cake cool at least 1 hour before serving. Makes 12 servings.

Each serving: About 295 calories, 4 g protein, 45 g carbohydrate, 12 g total fat (2 g saturated), 37 mg cholesterol, 215 mg sodium.

Caramelized Plum Cake

1 DOUGH = 3 COFFEE CAKES

PREP: 40 MINUTES PLUS RISING AND COOLING • BAKE: 30 TO 35 MINUTES

Use our sweet yeast dough to make twist, braid, or wreath cakes. Just remember, you'll need to allow about 4 hours total from start to finish. The good news is, only about 40 minutes of that is active prep time—the rest is rising and cooling!

2 packages active dry yeast
1 teaspoon plus ½ cup sugar
½ cup margarine or butter (1 stick), softened
1 large egg
½ teaspoon salt
About 3¼ cups all-purpose flour

1 In 2-cup glass measuring cup, stir yeast and 1 teaspoon sugar into *½ cup warm water* (105° to 115°F.); let stand until yeast mixture foams, about 5 minutes.

2 Meanwhile, in large bowl, with mixer at low speed, beat margarine or butter with remaining ½ cup sugar until blended. Increase speed to high; beat until creamy, about 2 minutes, occasionally scraping bowl with rubber spatula. Reduce speed to low; beat in egg until blended. Beat in yeast mixture, salt, and ½ cup flour (batter will look curdled) just until blended. With wooden spoon, stir

in 2½ cups flour until blended.

3 Turn dough onto lightly floured surface and knead until smooth and elastic, about 8 minutes, working in more flour (about ¼ cup) while kneading.

4 Shape dough into a ball; place in greased large bowl, turning dough over to grease top. Cover and let rise in warm place (80° to 85°F.), until doubled, about 1 hour. Follow directions for the cake shape of your choice: Coffee Cake Twist (at right), Coffee Cake Braid (at right), Coffee Cake Wreath (page 200).

Coffee Cake Braid

Left: With sharp knife, cut dough on both sides of filling crosswise into 1-inch-wide strips.

Right: Place strips at angle across filling, alternating sides for braided effect. Ends of strips should cover one another so they stay in place as dough rises.

Coffee Cake Twist

Left: Starting at one long side, roll up dough jelly-roll fashion. With sharp knife, cut roll lengthwise in half.

Right: Transfer two halves to cookie sheet and, keeping cut sides up to show pattern, twist strands together.

Coffee Cake Wreath

Left: Starting at one long side, roll up dough jelly-roll fashion.

Right: After shaping roll into ring, cut ring at 1½-inch intervals, up to but not through inside edge. Then gently pull and twist each cut piece to show spiral filling.

Coffee Cake Twist

PREP: 40 MINUTES PLUS RISING AND COOLING
BAKE: 30 TO 35 MINUTES

A spectacular rolled and twisted ring that looks like it came from a bakery. Fill with Sweet Almond or Lemon-Poppy Seed Filling.

Coffee Cake Dough (at left)
Choice of filling: Sweet Almond or Lemon-Poppy
  Seed (page 200)
1 large egg
Coffee Cake Glaze, optional (page 200)

1 Make the Coffee Cake Dough. Meanwhile, prepare the filling of choice.

2 Punch down dough. Turn dough onto lightly floured surface; cover and let rest 15 minutes. Meanwhile, grease large cookie sheet (17" by 14").

3 With floured rolling pin, roll dough into 18" by 12" rectangle. With metal spatula, spread filling over dough to within ½ inch of edges. In cup, lightly beat egg. Brush edges of dough with some beaten egg. Refrigerate remaining beaten egg to brush on coffee cake later.

4 Starting at one long side, roll up dough jelly-roll fashion. With sharp knife, cut roll lengthwise in half. On cookie sheet, keeping cut sides up, twist strands together. Shape into ring; tuck ends under to seal. Cover; let rise in warm place until dough has risen slightly, about 1 hour. (Dough will continue to rise during baking.)

5 Preheat oven to 350°F. Brush twist with some reserved egg. Bake 30 to 35 minutes, until golden. Transfer twist from cookie sheet to wire rack to cool. When cool, drizzle with Coffee Cake Glaze, if you like. Makes 1 coffee cake, 16 servings.

Each serving with sweet almond filling: About 250 calories, 6 g protein, 34 g carbohydrate, 11 g total fat (2 g saturated), 27 mg cholesterol, 160 mg sodium.

Each serving with lemon-poppy seed filling: About 265 calories, 5 g protein, 41 g carbohydrate, 9 g total fat (1 g saturated), 27 mg cholesterol, 170 mg sodium.

Coffee Cake Braid

PREP: 40 MINUTES PLUS RISING AND COOLING
BAKE: 30 TO 35 MINUTES

A delicious and simple lattice-top loaf. Fill with Chocolate-Walnut or Cherry-Cheese Filling.

Coffee Cake Dough (page at left)
Choice of filling: Chocolate-Walnut or Cherry-
  Cheese (page 200)
1 large egg
Coffee Cake Glaze, optional (page 200)

1 Make the Coffee Cake Dough. Meanwhile, prepare the filling of choice.

2 Punch down dough. Turn dough onto lightly floured surface; cover and let rest 15 minutes. Meanwhile, grease large cookie sheet (17" by 14").

3 Place dough on cookie sheet. With floured rolling pin, roll dough into a 14" by 10" rectangle (placing a damp towel under cookie sheet will help prevent it from moving when rolling out dough). With metal spatula, spread filling in 3-inch-wide strip lengthwise down center of dough rectangle, leaving 1-inch border at both ends. Sprinkle chopped walnuts over chocolate filling (or spoon cherries on top of cheese filling). With sharp knife, cut dough on both sides of filling crosswise into 1-inch-wide strips just to filling.

4 Place strips at an angle across filling, alternating sides for braided effect and making sure that end of each strip is covered by the next strip so strips stay in place as dough rises. Pinch both ends of braid to seal. Cover; let rise in warm place until dough has risen slightly, about 1 hour. (Dough will continue to rise during baking.)

5 Preheat oven to 350°F. In cup, lightly beat egg. Brush braid with beaten egg. Bake braid 30 to 35 minutes, until golden. Transfer braid from cookie sheet to wire rack to cool. When cool, drizzle with Coffee Cake Glaze, if you like. Makes 1 coffee cake, 16 servings.

Each serving with chocolate-walnut filling: About 285 calories, 6 g protein, 39 g carbohydrate, 12 g total fat (3 g saturated), 29 mg cholesterol, 165 mg sodium.

Each serving with cherry-cheese filling: About 255 calories, 6 g protein, 34 g carbohydrate, 10 g total fat (3 g saturated), 39 mg cholesterol, 200 mg sodium.

Coffee Cake Wreath

PREP: 40 MINUTES PLUS RISING AND COOLING
BAKE: 30 TO 35 MINUTES

A traditional coffee cake with your choice of two terrific new fillings: Prune-Date or Apricot-Orange.

Coffee Cake Dough (page 198)
Choice of filling: Prune-Date or Apricot-Orange (below)
Coffee Cake Glaze, optional (below)

1 Make the Coffee Cake Dough. Meanwhile, prepare the filling of choice.

2 Punch down dough. Turn dough onto lightly floured surface; cover and let rest 15 minutes. Meanwhile, grease large cookie sheet (17" by 14").

3 With floured rolling pin, roll dough into 18" by 12" rectangle. With metal spatula, spread filling over dough to within ½ inch of edges.

4 Starting at one long side, roll up dough jelly-roll fashion (see photo, page 198). Carefully lift roll and place seam side down on cookie sheet. Shape roll into a ring; press ends together to seal. With knife or kitchen shears, cut ring at 1½-inch intervals, up to but not through inside edge. Gently pull and twist each cut piece to show spiral filling (see photo, page 198). Cover; let rise in warm place until dough has risen slightly, about 1 hour. (Dough will continue to rise during baking.)

5 Preheat oven to 350°F. Bake 30 to 35 minutes, until golden. Transfer wreath from cookie sheet to wire rack to cool completely. When cool, drizzle with Coffee Cake Glaze, if you like. Makes 1 coffee cake, 16 servings.

Each serving with prune-date filling, without glaze: About 240 calories, 4 g protein, 44 g carbohydrate, 6 g total fat (1 g saturated), 13 mg cholesterol, 160 mg sodium.

Each serving with apricot-orange filling, without glaze: About 220 calories, 4 g protein, 39 g carbohydrate, 6 g total fat (1 g saturated), 13 mg cholesterol, 150 mg sodium.

SWEET COFFEE CAKE FILLINGS

Six ways to fill our tender, homespun coffee cakes, two for each shape—the hardest part is picking just one. The simple confectioners' sugar glaze can be drizzled on top after baking for a pretty finishing touch.

Sweet Almond Filling In food processor, with knife blade attached, blend *½ cup whole blanched almonds* with *¼ cup packed dark brown sugar* until almonds are finely ground. Add *4 ounces almond paste* (about half 7- to 8-ounce can or tube) and *2 large egg whites* and process until mixture is smooth. Makes about 1 cup.

Lemon-Poppy Seed Filling In small bowl, stir *1 can (12½ ounces) poppy seed filling* with *1 teaspoon grated fresh lemon peel*. Makes about 1 cup.

Chocolate-Walnut Filling In 1-quart saucepan, melt *3 squares (1 ounce each) semisweet chocolate* and *1 square (1 ounce) unsweetened chocolate* with *¾ cup low-fat sweetened condensed milk* over low heat until smooth. Cool to room temperature. Toast and chop *½ cup walnuts* and reserve for assembling braid. Makes about 1 cup.

Cherry-Cheese Filling Press *½ cup farmer cheese* (half 7½-ounce package) through coarse sieve set over small bowl. Stir in *1 package (3 ounces) cream cheese*, softened, *¼ cup confectioners' sugar*, and *1 tablespoon milk* until creamy. Cover and refrigerate until ready to use. Measure out *1 cup canned cherry-pie filling* and set aside for filling for assembling braid. Makes about 1¾ cups.

Prune-Date Filling In food processor with knife blade attached, blend *1 cup prune butter (lekvar)* with *1 cup pitted dates (about 5 ounces)*, occasionally scraping down sides of bowl, until coarsely textured paste forms. Cover and refrigerate until ready to use. Makes about 1⅓ cups.

Apricot-Orange Filling In 1-quart saucepan, heat *1½ cups dried apricots (about 10 ounces)* and *1 cup water* to boiling over high heat. Reduce heat to low; cover and simmer about 25 minutes or until apricots are very tender, stirring occasionally. Remove saucepan from heat; mash apricots with potato masher or fork until almost smooth. Stir in *⅓ cup sweet orange marmalade*; cover and refrigerate until ready to use. Makes about 1½ cups.

Coffee Cake Glaze Just before using, in small bowl, mix *1 cup confectioners' sugar* with *2 tablespoons milk* until smooth. With spoon, drizzle over cooled coffee cake. Makes about 1 cup.

Almond & Pear Strudel

PREP: 1½ HOURS PLUS COOLING
BAKE: 35 TO 40 MINUTES

Crisp layers of phyllo are wrapped around simmered pears and a sweet almond filling. Cool strudel slightly and enjoy it warm with our rich pear sauce.

STRUDEL FILLING:
4 tablespoons margarine or butter
5 large firm, ripe pears (about 2½ pounds),
    peeled, cored, and cut into ½-inch pieces
1 teaspoon vanilla extract
½ cup packed dark brown sugar
½ cup whole natural almonds, toasted
4 ounces almond paste (about half 7- to 8-ounce
    can or tube)
1 large egg

PHYLLO LAYERS:
¼ cup whole natural almonds, toasted
2 tablespoons plain dried bread crumbs
½ teaspoon ground cinnamon
1 tablespoon plus 1 teaspoon granulated sugar
16 sheets (17" by 12" each) fresh or frozen
    (thawed) phyllo (8 ounces)
½ cup margarine or butter (1 stick), melted
½ cup heavy or whipping cream

1 Prepare Strudel Filling: In 12-inch skillet, melt margarine or butter over medium-high heat. Add pears, vanilla, and ¼ cup dark brown sugar. Cook, uncovered, 15 to 18 minutes, until pears are tender, stirring occasionally. Drain pear mixture in colander set over large bowl; reserve drained pear liquid. Cool pears completely.

2 In food processor with knife blade attached, blend toasted almonds with remaining ¼ cup dark brown sugar until almonds are finely ground. Add almond paste and egg and process until mixture is smooth. Transfer almond mixture to small bowl; set aside.

3 Prepare Phyllo Layers: Preheat oven to 400°F. In food processor with knife blade attached, blend toasted almonds, dried bread crumbs, cinnamon, and 1 tablespoon granulated sugar until finely ground. Transfer to small bowl; set aside.

4 On waxed paper, arrange 1 phyllo sheet; brush with some melted margarine or butter. Top with second phyllo sheet; brush with some margarine or butter, then sprinkle with 1 tablespoon bread-crumb mixture. Continue layering phyllo, brushing each sheet with melted margarine or butter (reserving about 1 tablespoon melted margarine or butter for brushing completed roll) and sprinkling every other sheet with 1 tablespoon bread-crumb mixture except last layer.

5 Starting along one long side of layered phyllo, with metal spatula, gently spread almond-paste mixture about ¾ inch from edges to cover about one-third of phyllo rectangle. Spoon cooled pears over almond mixture.

6 From side with filling, roll phyllo, jelly-roll fashion, using waxed paper to help lift roll.

7 Place roll diagonally on large cookie sheet, seam side down. Tuck in ends of roll for a finished look. Brush with remaining 1 tablespoon melted margarine or butter and sprinkle with remaining 1 teaspoon sugar.

8 Bake strudel 35 to 40 minutes, until phyllo is golden and filling is hot. Cool on cookie sheet on wire rack about 20 minutes before slicing.

9 While strudel is cooling, in 1-quart saucepan, heat cream and drained pear liquid to boiling over high heat, stirring constantly; boil 1 minute. Serve strudel warm with warm pear sauce. Makes 14 servings.

Each serving with pear sauce: About 330 calories, 5 g protein, 34 g carbohydrate, 20 g total fat (5 g saturated), 27 mg cholesterol, 230 mg sodium.

Overnight Sticky Buns

PREP: 1 HOUR PLUS RISING AND COOLING
BAKE: ABOUT 30 MINUTES

Make these yummy goodies the night before serving. After a slow overnight rise in the refrigerator, simply bake and enjoy for breakfast.

DOUGH:
1 package active dry yeast
1 teaspoon plus ¼ cup granulated sugar
1 cup cake flour (not self-rising)
¾ cup milk
4 tablespoons margarine or butter, softened
1 teaspoon salt
3 large egg yolks
About 3 cups all-purpose flour

FILLING:
½ cup packed dark brown sugar
¼ cup dried currants
1 tablespoon ground cinnamon
4 tablespoons margarine or butter, melted

TOPPING:
⅔ cup packed dark brown sugar
3 tablespoons margarine or butter
2 tablespoons light corn syrup

Overnight Sticky Buns

2 tablespoons honey
1¼ cups pecans, coarsely chopped

1 Prepare Dough: In cup, stir yeast and 1 teaspoon sugar into ¼ *cup warm water* (105° to 115°F.); let stand until yeast foams, about 5 minutes.

2 In large bowl, with mixer at low speed, blend yeast mixture with cake flour, milk, margarine or butter, salt, egg yolks, 2 cups all-purpose flour, and remaining ¼ cup sugar until blended. With wooden spoon, stir in ¾ cup all-purpose flour.

3 Turn dough onto lightly floured surface and knead until smooth and elastic, about 5 minutes, working in more flour if necessary (about ¼ cup) while kneading.

4 Shape dough into a ball; place in greased large bowl, turning dough over to grease top. Cover and let rise in warm place (80° to 85°F.) until doubled, about 1 hour.

5 Meanwhile, prepare Filling: In small bowl, combine brown sugar, currants, and cinnamon. Reserve melted margarine or butter.

6 Prepare Topping: In 1-quart saucepan, heat brown sugar, margarine or butter, corn syrup, and honey over low heat until melted, stirring occasionally. Grease 13" by 9" metal baking pan; pour melted brown-sugar mixture into pan and sprinkle evenly with pecans; set aside.

7 Punch down dough. Turn dough onto lightly floured surface; cover and let rest 15 minutes. Roll dough into an 18" by 12" rectangle. Brush dough with reserved melted margarine or butter and sprinkle with Filling. Starting at one long side, roll dough jelly-roll fashion; place seam side down. Cut dough crosswise into 20 slices.

8 Place slices, cut sides down, in baking pan with Topping in 4 rows of 5 slices each. Cover pan with plastic wrap; refrigerate at least 12 hours or up to 15 hours.

9 Preheat oven to 375°F. Discard plastic wrap. Bake buns 30 minutes or until golden. Remove pan from oven. Immediately place serving tray or jelly-roll pan over top of baking pan and invert; remove pan. Let buns cool slightly to serve warm, or cool completely to serve later. Makes 20 buns.

Each bun: About 280 calories, 4 g protein, 40 g carbohydrate, 12 g total fat (2 g saturated), 33 mg cholesterol, 205 mg sodium.

DESSERTS

Broiled Brown-Sugar Bananas

PREP: 5 MINUTES • BROIL: 5 MINUTES

A sweet, satisfying dessert with just 4 basic ingredients and only 2 grams of fat!

4 ripe medium bananas (about 1½ pounds), unpeeled
2 tablespoons brown sugar
1 tablespoon lower-fat margarine (40% fat)
⅛ teaspoon ground cinnamon

1 Preheat broiler. Make a lengthwise slit in each unpeeled banana, being careful not to cut all the way through and leaving 1 inch uncut at banana ends.

2 In cup, with fork, blend together brown sugar, margarine, and cinnamon. Place bananas, cut side up, on rack in broiling pan. Spoon brown-sugar mixture into split bananas.

3 Place pan in broiler at closest position to source of heat; broil bananas 5 minutes or until browned. Serve bananas in skins, and use spoons to scoop out fruit. Makes 4 servings.

Each serving: About 150 calories, 1 g protein, 34 g carbohydrate, 2 g total fat (1 g saturated), 0 mg cholesterol, 20 mg sodium.

Cantaloupe Boats

PREP: 10 MINUTES

Drizzle honey and toasted almonds over raspberries, frozen yogurt, and sweet melon for a simple summer treat.

¼ cup sliced almonds
¼ cup honey
1 ripe medium cantaloupe, cut into quarters, with seeds removed
1 pint vanilla frozen yogurt
½ pint raspberries

1 In small nonstick skillet, toast almonds over medium heat just until golden, stirring frequently. Remove skillet from heat and stir in honey; set aside.

2 To serve, place cantaloupe quarters on 4 dessert plates. Top with frozen yogurt, raspberries, and warm almond mixture. Makes 4 servings.

Each serving: About 330 calories, 8 g protein, 64 g carbohydrate, 8 g total fat (3 g saturated), 2 mg cholesterol, 125 mg sodium.

Fast Baked Apples with Oatmeal Streusel

PREP: 8 MINUTES • MICROWAVE: 12 TO 14 MINUTES

Cooking apples in the microwave, rather than the regular oven, yields plumper, juicier, less shriveled fruit—and saves a big chunk of time!

4 large Rome or Cortland apples (about 10 ounces each)
¼ cup packed brown sugar
¼ cup quick-cooking oats, uncooked
2 tablespoons chopped dates
½ teaspoon ground cinnamon
2 teaspoons margarine or butter

1 Core apples, cutting out a 1¼-inch-diameter cylinder from center of each, almost but not all the way through to bottom. Remove peel about one-third of the way down from top. Place apples in shallow 1½-quart ceramic casserole or 8" by 8" glass baking dish.

2 In small bowl, combine brown sugar, oats, dates, and cinnamon. Fill each cored apple with equal amounts of oat mixture. (Mixture will spill over top of apples.) Place ½ teaspoon margarine or butter on top of filling in each apple.

3 Microwave apples, covered, on Medium-High (70% power) until tender, 12 to 14 minutes, turning each apple halfway through cooking time. Spoon cooking liquid from baking dish over apples to serve. Makes 4 servings.

Each serving: About 240 calories, 2 g protein, 54 g carbohydrate, 3 g total fat (1 g saturated), 0 mg cholesterol, 30 mg sodium.

Fast Baked Apples with Oatmeal Streusel ➤

Tropical Banana Splits

PREP: 15 MINUTES

The king of soda-shop desserts is even better made with sorbets and coconut.

¼ cup shredded coconut
2 ripe medium bananas, peeled and each cut lengthwise in half, then crosswise into quarters
1 cup fat-free passionfruit sorbet
1 cup fat-free raspberry sorbet
2 medium kiwifruit, peeled and each cut crosswise into 8 slices

1 In small nonstick skillet, toast coconut over medium heat, stirring frequently.

2 To serve, on each of 4 dessert plates (oval if possible), arrange 2 banana quarters, cut sides up, on opposite sides of plate. Place ¼-cup scoop each of passionfruit and raspberry sorbets between banana quarters. Top with 4 slices kiwifruit and sprinkle with 1 tablespoon toasted coconut. Makes 4 servings.

Each serving: About 230 calories, 1 g protein, 45 g carbohydrate, 3 g total fat (2 g saturated), 0 mg cholesterol, 20 mg sodium.

Country Plum Cobbler

PREP: 20 MINUTES PLUS COOLING
BAKE: 50 TO 60 MINUTES

Comfort food at its best: fresh, sugared summer plums baked until bubbly, under a golden biscuit crust.

2½ pounds ripe red or purple plums (about 10 medium), each cut into quarters
½ cup sugar
2 tablespoons all-purpose flour
1¾ cups reduced-fat all-purpose baking mix
¼ cup yellow cornmeal

Country Plum Cobbler

1 Preheat oven to 400°F. In large bowl, toss plums with sugar and flour. Spoon plum mixture into shallow 2-quart ceramic or glass baking dish. Cover loosely with foil. Bake 30 to 35 minutes, until plums are very tender.

2 Remove baking dish from oven. In medium bowl, stir baking mix and cornmeal with ¾ *cup water* just until combined. Drop 10 heaping spoonfuls of batter randomly on top of plum mixture.

3 Bake cobbler, uncovered, 20 to 25 minutes longer, until biscuits are browned and plum mixture is bubbling. Cool slightly to serve warm, or cool completely to serve later. Reheat if desired. Makes 10 servings.

Each serving: About 190 calories, 3 g protein, 41 g carbohydrate, 2 g total fat (0 g saturated), 0 mg cholesterol, 230 mg sodium.

"Log Cabin" Pudding

PREP: 40 MINUTES PLUS CHILLING

This recipe was given to Associate Production Manager Jeff Dibler's grandmother, Peoble Brehm, by her grade school teacher in the 1920's. Before she died, Brehm made sure that each of her grandchildren knew how to make this family favorite.

2 envelopes unflavored gelatin
1 cup maple-flavor syrup
2 cups milk
1 cup heavy or whipping cream
1 cup pecans, toasted and chopped
30 vanilla wafer cookies, crushed

1 In 2-quart saucepan, evenly sprinkle gelatin over ⅓ *cup cold water*; let stand 1 minute to soften gelatin. Heat over low heat, stirring, 2 to 3 minutes, until gelatin completely dissolves (do not boil). Remove from heat; stir in maple syrup.

2 Pour milk into medium bowl; with wire whisk, stir in gelatin mixture until blended.

3 Set bowl with gelatin mixture in large bowl of ice water. With rubber spatula, stir gelatin mixture until it gets very thick, about 15 minutes. Remove gelatin mixture from bowl of water.

4 In large bowl, with mixer at medium speed, beat cream until stiff peaks form. Fold gelatin mixture and pecans into whipped cream until evenly blended.

5 Sprinkle half of cookie crumbs over bottom of shallow 2½-quart glass or ceramic baking dish. Top with pudding mixture and sprinkle with remaining crumbs. Cover and refrigerate at least 6 hours or overnight. Makes 16 servings.

Each serving: About 200 calories, 3 g protein, 21 g carbohydrate, 12 g total fat (5 g saturated), 29 mg cholesterol, 40 mg sodium.

Skillet Blueberry Crisps

PREP: 10 MINUTES • COOK: 5 MINUTES

Homespun and delicious, but easy to stir up in a saucepan!

1 medium lemon
2 tablespoons brown sugar
2 teaspoons cornstarch
2 teaspoons almond-flavor liqueur
1 tablespoon margarine or butter, softened
1 pint (about 2½ cups) blueberries, rinsed
10 amaretti cookies, coarsely crushed
Confectioners' sugar

1 From lemon, grate ¼ teaspoon peel and squeeze 1 teaspoon juice. In 2-quart saucepan, with spoon, stir lemon peel, lemon juice, brown sugar, cornstarch, almond liqueur, and ½ *cup cold water*.

2 Add margarine or butter and half of blueberries to mixture in saucepan; lightly crush blueberries with potato masher or side of spoon. Cook blueberry mixture over medium heat, stirring constantly until mixture boils. Stir in remaining blueberries and boil 2 minutes longer, stirring.

3 Spoon hot blueberry mixture into 4 dessert or custard cups; top with amaretti-cookie crumbs and sprinkle with confectioners' sugar. Serve warm. Makes 4 servings.

Each serving: About 160 calories, 1 g protein, 30 g carbohydrate, 4 g total fat (1 g saturated), 0 mg cholesterol, 50 mg sodium.

Cool Berry Pudding

PREP: 20 MINUTES PLUS COOLING, AND CHILLING OVERNIGHT • COOK: 8 TO 10 MINUTES

This traditional English dessert is the summer version of bread pudding. Instead of being baked, a variety of berries are heated just until they release their juices, then they are layered with bread and weighted down in a "pudding basin"—or, in this case, a bowl.

12 slices firm white bread, crusts removed
2 cups blueberries
⅔ cup sugar
2 cups sliced strawberries
2 cups raspberries
1 cup blackberries
Whipped cream (optional)
Berries for garnish

1 Arrange bread slices on wire rack to dry out while preparing filling.

2 Meanwhile, in 3-quart saucepan, heat blueberries with sugar to boiling over medium heat, stirring often; boil 1 minute. Stir in strawberries, raspberries, and blackberries, and cook 1 minute longer, stirring. Remove saucepan from heat; cool berry filling to room temperature.

3 Line deep 1½-quart bowl with plastic wrap, allowing ends of plastic wrap to hang over side of bowl. Line bowl with some bread slices, trimming to fit and using scraps to fill in spaces. Spoon 2 cups berry filling into bowl. Cover with a layer of bread, trimming

10 QUICK STRAWBERRY DESSERTS

One of the best things about strawberries is that they're delicious au naturel—whole or sliced—or simply prepared with a few other ingredients. Some of our favorite fast ways to serve a pintful:

Balsamic Berries Toss sliced fruit with 1 tablespoon melted margarine or butter until just coated. Stir in a splash of balsamic vinegar and a pinch of coarsely ground black pepper for a sweet and tangy flavor. Enjoy as is, or spoon over ice cream or angel food cake.

Soft Serve Turn frozen berries into instant ice cream by whirling in a food processor with ½ cup heavy cream until velvety smooth; sweeten as desired.

Supershake In blender, combine berries with 2 scoops vanilla ice cream or frozen yogurt and honey to taste; pour into tall glasses, and serve with straws.

Filled Flowers Cut stem ends from jumbo berries. Cut an X in tip of each and gently spread apart to resemble petals. Lightly sweeten mascarpone or whipped cream cheese, and spoon or pipe into openings.

Elegant Finale Slightly sweeten whole, hulled strawberries. At serving time, spoon into goblets and splash with orange-flavor liqueur.

Blender Sauce (pictured above) Puree half a pint of strawberries with sugar to taste and 1 to 2 tablespoons cassis or berry-flavor liqueur. Add remain-

Blender Sauce

ing half-pint and pulse until coarsely chopped. Serve over ice cream, tapioca or vanilla pudding, sliced peaches, or sponge cake.

Sweetshop Stars Dip large berries (long-stem or not) partway into melted semisweet chocolate. Place on foil- or waxed-paper-lined cookie sheet to set coating, then drizzle with melted white chocolate. Refrigerate up to 4 hours.

Pudding Perfect Alternate layers of sliced strawberries with store-bought or homemade rice pudding to make a perfect parfait.

5-Minute Shortcake Toast slices of pound cake in toaster oven or toaster until lightly golden. Top with sliced berries and sweetened whipped cream.

Big Dippers Dunk plump strawberries, with caps still attached, into plain yogurt, then brown sugar.

to fit. Spoon remaining filling into bowl and top with remaining bread.

4 Cover bowl loosely with plastic wrap. Place a saucer, small enough to fit just inside rim of bowl, on top of plastic wrap. Place several heavy cans on top of saucer to weight down pudding. Refrigerate, on plate to catch any drips, 24 hours or until pudding is firm and bread is saturated with berry juices.

5 Remove cans, saucer, and top layer of plastic wrap. Invert pudding onto serving plate; discard plastic wrap. Spoon juices over pudding. Serve with whipped cream if you like. Garnish with berries. Makes 8 servings.

Each serving without whipped cream: About 195 calories, 3 g protein, 44 g carbohydrate, 2 g total fat (0 g saturated), 0 mg cholesterol, 150 mg sodium.

Strawberry Granita

PREP: 20 MINUTES PLUS FREEZING

A cool finish for a spring meal—and it's made with just 3 basic ingredients.

½ cup sugar
2 pints strawberries, hulled
1 tablespoon fresh lemon juice

1 In 1-quart saucepan, heat sugar and *1 cup water* to boiling over high heat, stirring occasionally. Reduce heat to medium; cook mixture 1 minute or until sugar dissolves completely. Remove saucepan from heat to cool sugar syrup slightly.

2 In food processor with knife blade attached, pulse strawberries until almost smooth. Add sugar syrup and lemon juice to strawberries; pulse just until mixed.

3 Pour strawberry mixture into 9" by 9" metal baking pan. Cover with foil or plastic wrap. Freeze until partially frozen, about 2 hours; stir with fork. Freeze until completely frozen, at least 3 hours longer or overnight.

4 To serve, let granita stand at room temperature 10 minutes to soften slightly. Then, with spoon or fork, scrape across surface of granita to create pebbly texture. Makes about 6 cups or 12 servings.

Each serving: About 45 calories, 0 g protein, 12 g carbohydrate, 0 g total fat, 0 mg cholesterol, 1 mg sodium.

Old-Fashioned Strawberry Ice Cream

PREP: 1 HOUR PLUS CHILLING AND FREEZING

This frosty confection is made with a classic custard-style base.

3 tablespoons all-purpose flour
½ teaspoon salt
1½ cups sugar
3 cups milk
3 large eggs
2 pints strawberries, hulled and crushed
1 tablespoon fresh lemon juice
1½ cups heavy or whipping cream
1 tablespoon vanilla extract

1 In heavy 3-quart saucepan, mix flour, salt, and 1 cup sugar; stir in milk. Cook over medium heat until mixture thickens slightly and boils, stirring frequently. Boil 1 minute.

2 In medium bowl, with wire whisk, beat eggs slightly. Gradually beat about 1 cup hot milk mixture into eggs to warm them slightly and keep them from curdling. Pour egg mixture, in steady stream, into hot milk mixture remaining in saucepan, beating rapidly with whisk to prevent lumps.

3 Cook over low heat, stirring constantly, until mixture thickens and coats the back of a spoon well, about 30 seconds. (Mixture should reach 160°F.) Do not boil or mixture will curdle.

4 Strain custard through sieve into large bowl. Refrigerate until cold, about 3 hours, stirring occasionally. (Or, place bowl with custard in larger bowl filled with ice water to come halfway up side of custard bowl. Chill custard completely, about 20 minutes, stirring every 5 minutes.)

5 While custard is chilling, in medium bowl, stir crushed strawberries with lemon juice and remaining ½ cup sugar; refrigerate at least 20 minutes to blend flavors.

6 Pour custard, cream, vanilla, and strawberry mixture into 4- to 6-quart ice-cream can or freezer chamber of ice-cream maker. Freeze as manufacturer directs. Serve immediately or freeze to harden. Makes about 2½ quarts or 20 servings.

Each serving: About 170 calories, 3 g protein, 21 g carbohydrate, 9 g total fat (5 g saturated), 61 mg cholesterol, 90 mg sodium.

Ricotta Pie

PREP: 50 MINUTES PLUS CHILLING
BAKE: 35 TO 40 MINUTES

Food Director Susan Westmoreland's Aunt Alice used to make this family favorite every Thanksgiving. Eventually, she had to make two pies, because Westmoreland, her brother, Michael, and her cousin, Judith, would have a contest to see who could eat the most!

CRUST:
¾ cup margarine or butter (1½ sticks), softened
⅓ cup sugar
1 large egg
2 teaspoons vanilla extract
2 cups all-purpose flour
¼ teaspoon salt

RICOTTA FILLING:
1 package (8 ounces) cream cheese, softened
¾ cup sugar
¼ teaspoon ground cinnamon
1 container (32 ounces) ricotta cheese
5 large egg whites, beaten

1 Prepare Crust: In large bowl, with mixer at low speed, beat margarine or butter with sugar until blended. Increase speed to high; beat until light and creamy, occasionally scraping bowl with rubber spatula. Reduce speed to medium; beat in egg until blended. Beat in vanilla. With wooden spoon, stir in flour and salt until dough begins to form. With hands, press dough together. Shape dough into a disk and wrap in plastic wrap; refrigerate 30 minutes or until dough is firm enough to handle.

2 Meanwhile, prepare Ricotta Filling: In large bowl, with mixer at low speed, beat cream cheese, sugar, and cinnamon until blended. Increase speed to high; beat until light and creamy. Reduce speed to medium; add ricotta cheese and all but 1 tablespoon egg whites and beat just until blended. Set filling aside.

3 Preheat oven to 400°F. Lightly grease 13" by 9" glass baking dish.

4 With floured hands, press dough onto bottom and up sides of baking dish. Brush reserved egg white over dough. Pour in ricotta mixture; spread evenly. With fingers, gently push edge of dough into scalloped design around top of filling.

5 Bake pie 25 minutes; reduce heat to 350°F. and bake 10 to 15 minutes longer, until center barely jiggles. Cool completely in pan on wire rack. Cover and refrigerate 6 hours or overnight, until well chilled. Makes 20 servings.

Each serving: About 275 calories, 8 g protein, 22 g carbohydrate, 17 g total fat (8 g saturated), 46 mg cholesterol, 210 mg sodium.

Chocolate Pudding

PREP: 5 MINUTES • COOK: 6 MINUTES

Retro food at its best—and who doesn't love chocolate pudding? The good news is this treat has only 2 grams of fat per serving and tastes divine warm or chilled!

⅓ cup sugar
¼ cup cornstarch
3 tablespoons unsweetened cocoa
Pinch salt
2 cups fat-free (skim) milk
1 ounce semisweet chocolate, finely chopped
1 teaspoon vanilla extract

1 In 2-quart saucepan, with wire whisk, mix sugar, cornstarch, cocoa, and salt until combined. Whisk in milk until blended.

2 Heat mixture to boiling over medium heat, stirring constantly. Add chocolate and cook 1 minute, stirring, until chocolate melts and pudding thickens slightly. Remove saucepan from heat; stir in vanilla. Spoon pudding into custard cups; serve warm. Or, cover surface of pudding directly with plastic wrap and refrigerate. Makes 4 servings.

Each serving: About 180 calories, 5 g protein, 37 g carbohydrate, 2 g total fat (0 g saturated), 2 mg cholesterol, 105 mg sodium.

◀ *Ricotta Pie*

Sugar & Spice Ice-Cream Sandwiches

PREP: 10 MINUTES PLUS CHILLING AND FREEZING
BAKE: 10 TO 12 MINUTES PER BATCH

The bar cookies are spiced up with cinnamon, ginger, and a hint of pepper—they're the perfect match for our homemade (or store-bought) ice cream.

1½ cups all-purpose flour
½ cup unsweetened cocoa
2 teaspoons ground ginger
1 teaspoon ground cinnamon
1 teaspoon baking powder
½ teaspoon baking soda
½ teaspoon finely ground black pepper
½ teaspoon salt
1 cup packed dark brown sugar
½ cup margarine or butter (1 stick), softened
1 large egg
1 teaspoon vanilla extract
1 pint strawberry ice cream, softened

1 In medium bowl, combine flour, cocoa, ginger, cinnamon, baking powder, baking soda, pepper, and salt.

2 In large bowl, with mixer at medium speed, beat brown sugar with margarine or butter until creamy. Reduce speed to low; beat in egg and vanilla until well blended. Add flour mixture, beating just until blended.

3 Divide dough into 4 equal pieces. Shape each piece of dough into a 3" by 2" rectangular block 1½ inches high. Wrap each block with waxed paper or plastic wrap and freeze until very firm, at least 1 hour or overnight.

4 Preheat oven to 350°F. Slice 1 cookie-dough block lengthwise into 8 equal slices. Place slices, about 1 inch apart, on large ungreased cookie sheet. Repeat with another block of dough. (Work quickly with dough to prevent cookies from becoming misshapen as the dough softens.)

5 Bake cookies 10 to 12 minutes. Cool completely on cookie sheet. Transfer cookies to plate. Repeat with remaining dough.

6 To make sandwiches, place 16 cookies on 15½" by 10½" jelly-roll pan. Place about 1 heaping table-spoon softened ice cream on top of each cookie. With small metal spatula, spread ice cream on each cookie, almost to edges. Top with remaining cookies to make 16 sandwiches in all. Wrap individually in foil and freeze at least 1 hour or up to 1 week. Makes 16 sandwiches.

Each sandwich: About 200 calories, 3 g protein, 30 g carbohydrate, 9 g total fat (3 g saturated), 29 mg cholesterol, 240 mg sodium.

Pumpkin Cheesecake

PREP: 30 MINUTES PLUS CHILLING
BAKE: 1 HOUR 20 MINUTES

Food Associate Lisa Troland has been baking this dessert "on demand" for years. It's light (in texture) and rich at the same time.

CRUMB CRUST:
1 cup graham-cracker crumbs
3 tablespoons margarine or butter, melted
2 tablespoons sugar

PUMPKIN FILLING:
2 packages (8 ounces each) cream cheese, softened
1¼ cups sugar
1 can (16 ounces) solid-pack pumpkin (not pumpkin-pie mix)
¾ cup sour cream
2 tablespoons bourbon or 2 teaspoons vanilla extract
1 teaspoon ground cinnamon
½ teaspoon ground allspice
¼ teaspoon salt
4 large eggs

SOUR-CREAM TOPPING:
1 cup sour cream
3 tablespoons sugar
1 teaspoon vanilla extract
Crystallized ginger strips for garnish

1 Prepare Crumb Crust: Preheat oven to 350°F. In 9" by 3" springform pan, with fork, stir graham-cracker crumbs, melted margarine or butter, and sugar until moistened. With hand, press mixture onto bottom of pan. Tightly wrap outside of pan with heavy-duty foil to prevent leakage when baking in water bath later. Bake crust 10 minutes. Cool completely in pan on wire rack.

2 Prepare Pumpkin Filling: In large bowl, with mixer at medium speed, beat cream cheese until smooth; slowly beat in sugar until blended, about 1 minute, scraping bowl often with rubber spatula. With mixer at low speed, beat in pumpkin, sour cream, bourbon or vanilla, cinnamon, allspice, and salt. Add eggs, 1 at a time, beating just until blended after each addition.

3 Pour pumpkin mixture into crust and place in large roasting pan. Place pan on oven rack. Carefully pour enough boiling water into pan to come 1 inch up side of springform pan. Bake cheesecake 1 hour 10 minutes or until center barely jiggles.

4 Meanwhile, prepare Sour-Cream Topping: In small bowl, with wire whisk, beat sour cream, sugar, and vanilla until blended. Remove cheesecake from water bath, leaving water bath in oven, and spread sour-cream mixture evenly over top. Return cake to water bath and bake 5 minutes longer.

5 Remove cheesecake from water bath and transfer to wire rack; discard foil. With small knife, loosen cheesecake from side of pan to help prevent cracking during cooling. Cool cheesecake completely. Cover and refrigerate cheesecake at least 6 hours or overnight, until well chilled. Remove side of pan to serve. Garnish with crystallized ginger. Makes 16 servings.

Each serving: About 310 calories, 5 g protein, 30 g carbohydrate, 20 g total fat (10 g saturated), 95 mg cholesterol, 225 mg sodium.

Pumpkin Cheesecake

Mocha-Banana Trifle

PREP: 1 HOUR PLUS CHILLING • COOK: 10 MINUTES

CUSTARDS:
1 tablespoon instant espresso-coffee powder
6 large eggs
¾ cup sugar
⅓ cup cornstarch
4 cups milk
4 tablespoons margarine or butter
2 tablespoons vanilla extract

FUDGE SAUCE:
⅔ cup sugar
½ cup heavy or whipping cream
⅓ cup unsweetened cocoa
3 tablespoons margarine or butter

1 package (12 ounces) vanilla-wafer cookies
   (about 90 cookies)
6 small ripe bananas (1¾ pounds), sliced
1 cup heavy or whipping cream

1 Prepare Custards: In cup, dissolve espresso powder in *1 tablespoon hot tap water*. In large bowl, with wire whisk, beat eggs.

2 In 3-quart saucepan, combine sugar and cornstarch. With wire whisk, beat in milk until blended. Heat mixture to simmering over medium-high heat. While constantly beating with whisk, gradually pour about half of simmering milk mixture into eggs. Return egg mixture to saucepan and cook over low heat, whisking constantly, until mixture thickens and begins to bubble around edge of pan (mixture will not appear to boil vigorously); simmer 1 minute. Remove saucepan from heat; stir in margarine or butter and vanilla.

3 Pour half of custard into medium bowl; cover surface directly with plastic wrap to prevent skin from forming. Pour remaining custard into another medium bowl; stir in espresso mixture until blended; cover surface with plastic wrap. Do not refrigerate.

4 Prepare Fudge Sauce: In 1-quart saucepan, cook sugar, cream, cocoa, and margarine or butter over medium heat until mixture is smooth and boils; set aside.

5 To layer trifle: In 4-quart glass trifle or deep serving bowl, place 1 layer of vanilla-wafer cookies (about 30 cookies). Spoon warm espresso custard on top of cookies; top with half of sliced bananas and half of warm fudge. Place another layer of cookies (about 30) on top of fudge; top with warm vanilla custard. Top with remaining bananas, fudge, and cookies.

6 In small bowl, with mixer at medium speed, beat cream until stiff peaks form; spoon over top layer of cookies. Cover trifle loosely with plastic wrap and refrigerate 6 hours or overnight. Makes 24 servings.

Each serving: About 270 calories, 4 g protein, 33 g carbohydrate, 14 g total fat (6 g saturated), 88 mg cholesterol, 125 mg sodium.

Christmas Pudding with Hard Sauce

PREP: 1 HOUR • COOK: ABOUT 2 HOURS

This is the perfect recipe to prepare ahead since the flavor improves as the pudding "ages." If making ahead, cool puddings in bowls completely after cooking, then wrap well and refrigerate up to 1 month (or freeze up to 3 months). To serve, re-steam pudding (thawed, if frozen), covered, as directed in step 5, for 1 hour. If making the hard sauce ahead, cover and refrigerate up to 1 month.

PLUM PUDDING:
2¼ cups all-purpose flour
1 cup fresh bread crumbs
1 teaspoon baking powder
1 teaspoon ground cinnamon
½ teaspoon salt
¼ teaspoon ground nutmeg
¼ teaspoon ground cloves
1 cup pitted prunes, chopped
1 cup pitted dates, chopped
¾ cup dark seedless raisins
½ cup walnuts, toasted and chopped
1 medium Granny Smith apple, peeled, cored,
   and coarsely shredded
1 teaspoon grated fresh lemon peel
1 cup margarine or butter (2 sticks), softened
1 cup packed light brown sugar
2 large eggs
⅔ cup buttermilk
½ cup dark molasses
⅓ cup dark rum or brandy

HARD SAUCE:
1 cup butter (2 sticks), softened (do not use margarine)
2 cups confectioners' sugar
¼ cup dark rum or brandy
1 teaspoon vanilla extract

1 Heavily grease two 1-quart heat-safe bowls. Cut 2 pieces of foil, one to cover top of each bowl, allowing 1-inch overhang. Grease one side of each piece of foil; set aside.

2 Prepare Plum Pudding: In large bowl, combine first 7 ingredients. Add prunes, dates, raisins, walnuts, apple, and lemon peel to flour mixture. With hands, thoroughly toss mixture until fruits are well coated and separate. Set aside.

3 In another large bowl, with mixer at low speed, beat margarine or butter with brown sugar. Increase speed to high; beat until creamy, about 1 minute. At medium speed, add eggs, 1 at a time, beating well after each addition. Beat in buttermilk, molasses, and rum (mixture will look curdled). With spoon, stir margarine mixture into flour mixture until blended.

4 Spoon batter into prepared bowls; cover with foil, greased side down. Tie foil tightly in place with string around outside of bowls so pudding surface does not get wet from steam.

5 Place a metal cookie cutter into each of two 5- or 6-quart saucepots. (The cookie cutters are used as trivets so bowls remain elevated during steaming.) Pour in *water to measure 1½ inches*. Set bowls on top of cookie cutters. Cover saucepots and heat water to boiling over high heat. Reduce heat to low; simmer puddings about 2 hours or until toothpick inserted through foil into center comes out clean.

6 Meanwhile, prepare Hard Sauce: In small bowl, with mixer at medium speed, beat butter until smooth. At low speed, gradually beat in confectioners' sugar until creamy. Beat in rum or brandy and vanilla. Spoon into 1 or 2 decorative crocks or bowls. Cover and chill until serving time. Makes about 2 cups.

7 When puddings are done, cool in bowls on wire racks 5 minutes. Remove foil; loosen puddings with small spatula or knife and invert onto serving dishes. Serve hot with Hard Sauce. Makes 2 puddings, each 8 servings.

Each serving of pudding without hard sauce: About 365 calories, 4 g protein, 56 g carbohydrate, 15 g total fat (3 g saturated), 27 mg cholesterol, 290 mg sodium.

Each tablespoon hard sauce: About 85 calories, 0 g protein, 8 g carbohydrate, 6 g total fat (4 g saturated), 15 mg cholesterol, 60 mg sodium.

PLUM PUDDING'S RICH HISTORY

Homey plum pudding dates back to the 1700's. It quickly became a December tradition, the cap on the family holiday meal—and it remains so today.

Some experts say it was first made with prunes; others note that plum is simply another word for raisin when used in desserts. In any case, the sweet ending is a pudding in the British sense of the word, which encompasses not just the creamy spoonable version, but all kinds of desserts, from cakes to pies.

Originally, plum pudding was a steamed or boiled mixture of fruits, nuts, spices, and suet, often flamed with brandy or rum. Today, the suet—available mainly from the butcher—has been replaced by more convenient margarine or butter (our choices for best flavor), or shortening.

Most lovers of this classic dish wouldn't think of serving it without hard sauce: a blend of butter, sugar, and flavoring—usually brandy, rum, or

Christmas Pudding with Hard Sauce

whiskey—that's beaten, then chilled until hard. (The British call it brandy butter or rum butter.) A scoop of vanilla ice cream or some whipped cream is an Americanized accompaniment—a soft, cool contrast to the hot pudding.

Easy Napoleons

PREP: 45 MINUTES • BAKE: 10 MINUTES

The phyllo triangles can be made 1 day ahead and stored, tightly covered, at room temperature; assemble Napoleons just before serving.

1 large egg white
Pinch salt
4 sheets (about 16" by 12" each) fresh or frozen (thawed) phyllo
2 tablespoons margarine or butter, melted
⅓ cup plus 1 tablespoon sugar
½ cup sliced natural almonds
1 pint strawberries
¾ cup heavy or whipping cream
½ teaspoon vanilla extract

1 Preheat oven to 375°F. In small bowl, lightly beat egg white and salt with *1 teaspoon water*; set aside.

2 Place 1 phyllo sheet on work surface; brush with melted margarine or butter and sprinkle with 1 rounded tablespoon sugar. Top with a second phyllo sheet; brush with melted margarine or butter and sprinkle with 1 rounded tablespoon sugar. Repeat layering with phyllo, melted margarine or butter, and sugar 1 more time. Top with remaining phyllo and brush with egg-white mixture.

3 Cut phyllo stack lengthwise into 3 strips, then cut each strip crosswise into 4 squares. Cut each square diagonally in half to make 24 triangles in all. Place triangles on ungreased large cookie sheet; sprinkle with sliced almonds and 1 rounded tablespoon sugar.

4 Bake phyllo triangles 10 minutes or until golden; transfer to wire racks to cool.

5 Just before serving, hull and thinly slice strawberries. In small bowl, with mixer at medium speed, beat cream with vanilla and remaining 1 tablespoon sugar until stiff peaks form.

6 To assemble, place 1 phyllo triangle in center of each of 8 dessert plates. Top each with about 1 tablespoon whipped cream and about 1 rounded tablespoon sliced strawberries. Place a second phyllo triangle on top of each, rotating it so that points of second triangle are angled slightly away from points of first triangle. Repeat with remaining cream and strawberries; top with a third triangle. Serve immediately. Makes 8 servings.

Each serving: About 220 calories, 4 g protein, 19 g carbohydrate, 15 g total fat (6 g saturated), 31 mg cholesterol, 115 mg sodium.

Easy Napoleon

PIES & CAKES

Double Blueberry Pie

PREP: 30 MINUTES PLUS 5 HOURS CHILLING
BAKE: 8 MINUTES

We've updated an old New England classic with a spiced cookie crust.

30 gingersnaps
2 tablespoons plus ½ cup sugar
5 tablespoons margarine or butter, melted
2 tablespoons cornstarch
3 pints blueberries
Whipped cream (optional)

1 In food processor with knife blade attached or in blender at high speed, blend gingersnaps and 2 tablespoons sugar until fine crumbs form.

2 Preheat oven to 375°F. In 9-inch pie plate, with fork, stir crumbs with melted margarine or butter until moistened. With hand, press mixture onto bottom and up side of pie plate, making a small rim. Bake crust 8 minutes. Cool crust on wire rack.

3 Meanwhile, in 2-quart saucepan, mix cornstarch with *2 tablespoons cold water* until blended. Add half the blueberries and remaining ½ cup sugar to cornstarch mixture; heat to boiling over medium-high heat, pressing blueberries against side of saucepan with back of spoon. Boil 1 minute, stirring constantly. Remove saucepan from heat; stir in remaining blueberries.

4 Pour blueberry mixture into crust. Cover with plastic wrap and refrigerate until well chilled, about 5 hours. Serve with whipped cream if you like. Makes 10 servings.

Each serving without whipped cream: About 240 calories, 2 g protein, 42 g carbohydrate, 8 g total fat (2 g saturated), 0 mg cholesterol, 220 mg sodium.

Peach Tarte Tatin

PREP: 1 HOUR PLUS 1 HOUR COOLING
BAKE: 25 MINUTES

We love this tart with its caramelized-peach filling. Serve warm with a scoop of vanilla ice cream.

1½ cups all-purpose flour
½ teaspoon salt
3 tablespoons plus 1 cup sugar
¼ cup shortening
10 tablespoons margarine or butter (1¼ sticks)
1 tablespoon fresh lemon juice
11 firm, slightly ripe medium peaches (about 3¾ pounds), peeled, pitted, and each cut in half

1 In medium bowl, stir flour, salt, and 3 tablespoons sugar. With pastry blender or two knives used scissor-fashion, cut in shortening and 4 tablespoons margarine or butter until mixture resembles coarse crumbs.

2 Sprinkle 3 *to 4 tablespoons cold water*, 1 tablespoon at a time, into flour mixture, mixing with a fork after each addition until dough is just moist enough to hold together.

3 Shape dough into a disk; wrap with plastic wrap and refrigerate until firm, about 30 minutes.

4 Meanwhile, in heavy 12-inch skillet with oven-safe handle, heat lemon juice, remaining 1 cup sugar, and 6 tablespoons margarine or butter over medium-high heat until mixture boils. Place peaches in skillet, pitted side down. Cook 10 minutes. Carefully turn peaches over; cook 8 to 12 minutes longer, until syrup is caramelized and thickened.

5 Preheat oven to 425°F. Just before peaches are done, on lightly floured surface, with floured rolling pin, roll dough into a 14-inch round. Place dough on top of peaches in skillet; fold edge of dough under to form a rim around edge of peaches. With knife, cut six ¼-inch slits in dough so steam can escape during baking. Bake tart 25 minutes or until crust is golden.

6 When tart is done, place large platter over top of tart. Quickly turn skillet upside down to invert tart. Cool 1 hour to serve warm or cool completely to serve later. Makes 12 servings.

Each serving: About 300 calories, 2 g protein, 44 g carbohydrate, 14 g total fat (3 g saturated), 0 mg cholesterol, 215 mg sodium.

Peach Tarte Tatin ➤

Dutch Apple Pie

PREP: 40 MINUTES PLUS COOLING
BAKE: 1 HOUR 30 MINUTES

Alice Garbarini Hurley, GH's senior copy writer, loves to make this orange-spiced, streusel-topped fruit pie for Thanksgiving. She adapted it from one of her favorite cookbooks, *Sweets for Saints & Sinners* by Janice Feuer and Veronica di Rosa.

PIE CRUST:
1½ cups all-purpose flour
½ teaspoon salt
4 tablespoons margarine or butter
¼ cup shortening

APPLE FILLING:
2 pounds Granny Smith apples (about 4 large)
2 tablespoons fresh lemon juice
1 container (8 ounces) sour cream
¾ cup granulated sugar
2 tablespoons all-purpose flour
1 teaspoon vanilla extract
⅛ teaspoon salt
1 large egg

STREUSEL TOPPING:
¾ cup all-purpose flour
½ cup walnuts, toasted and chopped
¼ cup packed brown sugar
¼ cup granulated sugar
1 teaspoon ground cinnamon
1 teaspoon grated fresh orange peel
4 tablespoons cold margarine or butter

1 Prepare Pie Crust: In medium bowl, mix flour and salt. With pastry blender or two knives used scissor-fashion, cut in margarine or butter with shortening until mixture resembles coarse crumbs. Sprinkle about *4 tablespoons cold water*, 1 tablespoon at a time, into flour mixture, mixing lightly with fork after each addition until dough is just moist enough to hold together. Shape dough into a disk.

2 On lightly floured surface, with floured rolling pin, roll dough into a round 2 inches larger in diameter than inverted 9½-inch deep-dish pie plate. Ease dough into pie plate; trim edge, leaving 1-inch over-hang. Fold overhang under; pinch to form decorative edge. Cover and refrigerate pie shell.

3 Meanwhile, preheat oven to 400°F. Prepare Apple Filling: Peel, core, and cut apples into ¼-inch-thick slices. In large bowl, toss apples with lemon juice. In medium bowl, with wire whisk or fork, beat sour cream, sugar, flour, vanilla, salt, and egg just until blended. Stir sour-cream mixture into apple mixture; spoon into chilled pie shell.

4 Place sheet of foil under pie plate; crimp foil edges to form a rim to catch any drips during baking. Bake pie 1 hour, covering loosely with foil if apples are browning too quickly.

GH INSTITUTE REPORT

KING PINS

Rolling dough for pies and cookies can go smoothly or lead to a sticky mess—but many a seasoned baker will tell you that the secret is in the rolling pin. We asked our Institute bakers to try out 8 different models on classic pie pastry and cookie dough (see Holiday Sugar Cookies, page 234) to see which made the task easy. Unanimously, our testers preferred wooden ones (whether new versions or a slim, decades-old tapered model that belonged to a staffer's grandmother) over marble, plastic filled with ice water, nonstick, and stainless steel. Why? They said wood "held on" better to a dusting of flour, so the dough didn't stick.

The favorites weighed about 1½ pounds—heavy enough to tackle the dough but not so hefty that they were unwieldy to use and store (like the 4½-pound marble one). Still, there was a split decision. Some testers liked the 20-inch French-style boxwood pin without handles, below, saying it was simpler to roll the dough to an even thickness by using their palms to control the pressure. At $40, it's a good investment for serious bakers. Others were more comfortable with the homey 12-inch maple model (also below) with ball bearings in the handles to help turn the pin. One staffer likened its smooth, gliding action to "ice skates on a frozen pond." It's reasonably priced at $16.

5 While pie is baking, prepare Streusel Topping: In medium bowl, stir flour, walnuts, brown sugar, granulated sugar, cinnamon, and orange peel. With fingertips, blend in cold margarine or butter until mixture resembles coarse crumbs.

6 After pie has baked 1 hour, turn oven control to 350°F. Sprinkle Streusel Topping evenly over apples. Bake pie 30 minutes longer or until filling is hot and bubbly and top is golden. Cool pie on wire rack 1 hour to serve warm. Or cool completely to serve at room temperature later. Makes 10 servings.

Each serving: About 470 calories, 5 g protein, 62 g carbohydrate, 24 g total fat (7 g saturated), 31 mg cholesterol, 275 mg sodium.

Lattice-Top Pineapple Tart

PREP: 45 MINUTES PLUS CHILLING AND COOLING
BAKE: 35 TO 40 MINUTES

At Thanksgiving, Debby Goldsmith, associate food director, bakes this delicious pineapple tart especially for her father, Del, whose family lived in the Caribbean for many years. Del's sister, Vera, was the original tart maker, but now Goldsmith does the honors. She and her family love it with sliced sharp Cheddar cheese on top.

COOKIE CRUST:
¾ cup butter (1½ sticks), softened (don't use margarine)
⅓ cup plus 1 teaspoon granulated sugar
1 large egg, beaten
2 teaspoons vanilla extract
2 cups all-purpose flour
¼ teaspoon salt

PINEAPPLE FILLING:
1 can (20 ounces) crushed pineapple in unsweetened pineapple juice
⅓ cup packed light brown sugar
2 tablespoons fresh lemon juice
1 tablespoon butter, softened

1 Prepare Cookie Crust: In large bowl, with mixer at low speed, beat butter and ⅓ cup granulated sugar until blended. Increase speed to high; beat until light and creamy, occasionally scraping bowl with rubber spatula. Reduce speed to medium; beat in all but 1 tablespoon egg (cover and refrigerate remaining egg). Beat in vanilla. With wooden spoon, stir in flour and salt until dough begins to form. With hands, press dough together. Divide dough into 2 pieces, 1 slightly larger than the other. Shape each piece into a disk and wrap each with plastic wrap; refrigerate 30 minutes or until dough is firm enough to roll.

2 While dough is chilling, prepare Pineapple Filling: In 10-inch skillet, heat pineapple with its juice, brown sugar, and lemon juice to boiling over medium-high heat. Cook, stirring often, until liquid evaporates, about 15 minutes. Stir in butter. Spoon pineapple mixture into medium bowl; cover and refrigerate until cooled.

3 Preheat oven to 375°F. Remove both pieces of dough from refrigerator. With floured hands, press larger piece of dough into 9-inch round tart pan with removable bottom. Refrigerate 15 minutes.

4 Meanwhile, on lightly floured waxed paper, roll remaining piece of dough into 10-inch round. With pastry wheel or knife, cut dough into ten ¾-inch-wide strips. Refrigerate strips 15 minutes or until easy to handle.

5 Spread pineapple mixture over dough in tart pan to ½ inch from edge. Place 5 strips, about ¾ inch apart, across tart. Repeat with 5 more strips placed diagonally across first ones, trimming ends, to make a diamond lattice pattern. Press ends to seal. With hands, roll dough trimmings into ¼-inch-thick ropes. Press ropes around edge of tart to create a finished edge. (If ropes break, just press pieces together.)

6 Mix *1 teaspoon water* into reserved egg; use to brush over lattice and edge. Sprinkle lattice and edge with remaining 1 teaspoon granulated sugar. Bake tart 35 to 40 minutes, until crust is golden. Cool tart in pan on wire rack. Makes 10 servings.

Each serving: About 320 calories, 4 g protein, 43 g carbohydrate, 16 g total fat (9 g saturated), 61 mg cholesterol, 215 mg sodium.

Farm-Stand Cherry Pie

PREP: 45 MINUTES PLUS 3 HOURS CHILLING AND
COOLING • BAKE: 45 TO 50 MINUTES

This beautiful pie in a rustic cornmeal crust
delights both the eye and the taste buds.

1½ cups all-purpose flour
⅓ cup plus 1 tablespoon cornmeal
⅔ cup plus 1 teaspoon sugar
½ teaspoon plus ⅛ teaspoon salt
½ cup cold margarine or butter (1 stick)
2 tablespoons plus 1 teaspoon cornstarch
1½ pounds dark sweet cherries, pitted
1 large egg white

1 Preheat oven to 425°F. In medium bowl, mix flour,
⅓ cup cornmeal, ⅓ cup sugar, and ½ teaspoon salt.

With pastry blender or two knives used scissor-fashion, cut in margarine or butter until mixture resembles coarse crumbs. Sprinkle *4 to 5 tablespoons cold water*, 1 tablespoon at a time, into flour mixture, mixing with hands until dough comes together (it will feel dry at first). Shape into a ball.

2 Sprinkle large cookie sheet with remaining 1 tablespoon cornmeal. Place dampened towel under cookie sheet to prevent it from slipping. With floured rolling pin, roll dough, on cookie sheet, into a 13-inch round. With long metal spatula, gently loosen round from cookie sheet.

3 In large bowl, combine ⅓ cup sugar with cornstarch. Sprinkle half of sugar mixture over center of dough round, leaving a 2½-inch border all around. Add cherries and any cherry juice to sugar mixture remaining in bowl; toss well. With slotted spoon, spoon cherry mixture over sugared area on dough round (reserve any cherry-juice mixture in bowl). Fold dough up around cherries, leaving a 4-inch opening in center. Pinch dough to seal any cracks.

Farm-Stand Cherry Pie

4 In cup, beat egg white with remaining ⅛ teaspoon salt. Brush egg-white mixture over dough; sprinkle with remaining 1 teaspoon sugar. Pour cherry-juice mixture through opening in top of pie. Refrigerate until well chilled, about 30 minutes. Bake pie 45 to 50 minutes until crust is golden brown and cherry mixture is gently bubbling, covering pie loosely with foil during last 10 minutes of baking to prevent over-browning.

5 As soon as pie is done, use long metal spatula to loosen it from cookie sheet to prevent sticking. Cool pie 15 minutes on cookie sheet, then slide onto wire rack to cool completely. Makes 6 servings.

Each serving: About 460 calories, 6 g protein, 74 g carbohydrate, 17 g total fat (3 g saturated), 0 mg cholesterol, 435 mg sodium.

Bumbleberry Pie

PREP: 1 HOUR PLUS CHILLING AND COOLING
BAKE: ABOUT 1 HOUR 20 MINUTES

The Inn at Kristofer's, in Wisconsin's scenic Door County, goes through more than 20 of these beauties per week—and serves each slice warm, with a scoop of French vanilla ice cream. The "bumbleberry" name is a spin on the jumble of berries used, according to the inn's co-proprietor Terri Milligan. Her recipe combines Door County's wonderful tart cherries with sweet summer berries. Feel free to substitute whatever you have on hand (frozen cherries from the supermarket work too). When pitting fresh cherries, reserve any juice and add it to the filling.

½ teaspoon salt
2¼ cups plus 2 tablespoons all-purpose flour
½ cup margarine or butter (1 stick)
¼ cup shortening
1½ pounds tart cherries, pitted, or 3 cups frozen pitted tart cherries
3 cups assorted berries, such as blueberries, raspberries, and blackberries
¼ cup cornstarch
1 cup plus 2 teaspoons sugar
3 tablespoons milk or cream
1 large egg

1 In large bowl, mix salt and 2¼ cups flour. With pastry blender or two knives used scissor-fashion, cut in margarine or butter with shortening until mixture resembles coarse crumbs. Sprinkle 4 *to 6 tablespoons cold water*, 1 tablespoon at a time, into flour mixture, mixing lightly with a fork after each addition until dough is just moist enough to hold together. Shape dough into 2 balls, 1 slightly larger than the other. Cover with plastic wrap and refrigerate 30 minutes.

2 Meanwhile, in large bowl, toss cherries and berries with cornstarch, 1 cup sugar, and remaining 2 tablespoons flour.

3 Preheat oven to 425°F. On lightly floured surface, with floured rolling pin, roll larger ball of dough into a round 1½ inches larger in diameter than inverted 9-inch pie plate. Gently ease dough into pie plate; trim edge, leaving 1-inch overhang. Spoon cherry mixture into pie crust.

4 Roll remaining dough for top crust into 10-inch round. Center round over filling in bottom crust. Trim edge, leaving 1-inch overhang. Fold overhang under; bring up over pie-plate rim and pinch to form high fluted edge. Reroll trimmings. With floured cookie cutter or knife, cut out decorations.

5 In small bowl, with wire whisk or fork, mix milk and egg until blended. Lightly brush top of pie with egg mixture. Arrange decorations on top of pie; brush decorations with egg mixture. Cut short slashes in top crust to allow steam to escape during baking. Sprinkle remaining 2 teaspoons sugar over top of pie.

6 Place sheet of foil underneath pie plate; crimp foil edges to form a rim to catch any drips during baking. Bake pie 20 minutes. Turn oven control to 375°F. and bake 55 to 60 minutes longer, until crust is brown and filling is bubbly. Cover pie loosely with foil if crust is browning too quickly. Cool pie on wire rack 1 hour to serve warm. Or, cool completely to serve later. Makes 10 servings.

Each serving: About 385 calories, 5 g protein, 59 g carbohydrate, 16 g total fat (4 g saturated), 22 mg cholesterol, 240 mg sodium.

Plum Frangipane Tart

PREP: 20 MINUTES PLUS 2 HOURS COOLING
BAKE: 1 HOUR 30 MINUTES

Frangipane, a rich almond-flavored filling, is used in many pastries and cakes. For this tart, the filling can be topped with red or black plums—it's equally good with either kind.

1¾ cups all-purpose flour
3 tablespoons plus ½ cup sugar
¾ teaspoon salt
½ cup shortening
1 tube or can (7 to 8 ounces) almond paste,
    broken into 1-inch pieces
4 tablespoons butter, softened
2 large eggs
2 teaspoons vanilla extract
1¼ pounds ripe plums (about 5 medium), each
    cut into 6 wedges

1 Preheat oven to 375°F. In medium bowl, with fork, stir 1½ cups flour, 3 tablespoons sugar, and ½ teaspoon salt. With pastry blender or two knives used scissor-fashion, cut shortening into flour mixture until mixture resembles coarse crumbs. Add 3 *to 4 tablespoons cold water*, 1 tablespoon at a time, mixing lightly with fork after each addition, until dough is just moist enough to hold together.

2 On lightly floured surface, with floured rolling pin, roll dough into a 14-inch round. Ease dough round into 11" by 1" round tart pan with removable bottom. Fold overhang in and press against side of tart pan to form a rim ⅛ inch above edge of pan.

3 Line tart shell with foil and fill with pie weights, dried beans, or uncooked rice. Bake tart shell 20 minutes; remove foil with weights and bake 10 to 15 minutes longer until golden. (If crust puffs up during baking, gently press it down with back of spoon.)

4 Meanwhile, prepare filling: In large bowl, with mixer at low speed, beat almond paste, butter, remaining ½ cup sugar, and ¼ teaspoon salt until crumbly. Increase speed to medium-high and beat until combined, constantly scraping bowl with rubber spatula, about 3 minutes. (It's okay if there are tiny lumps.) Add eggs and vanilla extract; beat until smooth. With spoon, stir in remaining ¼ cup flour.

5 Pour filling into warm tart shell. Arrange plums in concentric circles over filling. Bake tart 50 to 60 minutes, until golden. Cool tart in pan on wire rack. When cool, carefully remove side from pan. Makes 12 servings.

Each serving: About 340 calories, 5 g protein, 38 g carbohydrate, 19 g total fat (4 g saturated), 36 mg cholesterol, 195 mg sodium.

Fig Frangipane Tart

PREP: 30 MINUTES PLUS CHILLING
BAKE: 45 TO 50 MINUTES

Here a layer of frangipane is studded with fresh figs and baked in a sweet pastry crust.

CRUST:
¾ cup butter (1½ sticks), softened
⅓ cup sugar
2 large egg yolks
1 teaspoon vanilla extract
2 cups all-purpose flour

FRANGIPANE FILLING:
1 tube or can (7 to 8 ounces) almond paste,
    broken into 1-inch pieces
4 tablespoons butter, softened
2 large eggs
1 tablespoon all-purpose flour
2 pints small figs (about 1½ pounds), trimmed
    and each cut into quarters
1 tablespoon sugar

1 Prepare Crust: In large bowl, with mixer at low speed, beat butter with sugar until blended. Increase speed to high; beat until creamy, about 2 minutes, constantly scraping bowl with rubber spatula. Beat in egg yolks, vanilla, and *1 tablespoon plus 1 teaspoon cold water*. At low speed, beat in flour until dough is just moist enough to hold together.

2 Shape dough into a disk; wrap with plastic wrap and refrigerate until cold, about 30 minutes.

3 Preheat oven to 375°F. With floured hands, press dough into 11" by 8" by 1" rectangular or 11" by 1" round tart pan with removable bottom. Refrigerate while preparing Frangipane Filling.

Fig Facts

Plump, fresh figs are sweet and fat-free. For a quick summer dessert, try them sliced and drizzled with honey or a little heavy cream. But figs are highly perishable, so to get your money's worth (about $2 to $3 per pint, or up to $1 apiece for large figs), remember to:

• Buy fruit that is heavy, smells fresh (not musty), and is soft to the touch.

• Use figs promptly; they'll keep, refrigerated, for only a day or two.

• Rinse gently. The entire fruit is edible, skin and all—just discard the stem.

When it comes to choosing (unless you live in sunny California), you may have to take what you can get—many supermarkets don't carry several different varieties of fresh figs all at once. Any of these will work fine in our tart:

Adriatic Named for the Adriatic Sea, an arm of the Mediterranean, this fig has pale pink flesh and light green skin. Its high sugar content, retained as the fruit dries to a golden shade, makes this a blue-ribbon choice for fig bars and pastry fillings.

Black Mission (or Mission) Named for the Spanish missionaries who planted fig trees along the fertile California coast. This fruit has deep-purple or black skin and tender, pink flesh. It's popular in recipes calling for dried or fresh figs, such as compotes or chutneys.

Calimyrna The Smyrna fig comes from the ancient Turkish city that once went by that name, but the Calimyrna is its descendant, grown in Cal-

Fig Frangipane Tart

ifornia. This large, greenish-yellow fig is known for its sweet crunch (thanks to many tiny edible seeds) and appealing nutlike flavor; it's the best-selling dried variety.

Kadota A favorite for canning and preserving, this fig is the American version of the Italian Dattato. Its thick skin is a pretty amber when ripe; the flesh is purple and practically seedless.

Per serving (2 medium fresh or dried figs): 75 to 100 calories, 4 g fiber.

---

4 Prepare Frangipane Filling: In medium bowl, with mixer at low speed, beat almond paste and butter until blended. Increase speed to high; beat until light and fluffy, about 2 minutes, constantly scraping bowl with rubber spatula. Reduce speed to medium; add eggs and beat until blended. (It's okay if there are tiny bits of almond paste in mixture.) With spoon, stir in flour.

5 Spread filling over dough in pan. Arrange figs, cut side up, close together on filling; sprinkle with sugar.

Place sheet of foil under tart pan; crimp foil edges to form a rim to catch any drips during baking.

6 Bake tart 45 to 50 minutes, until center is golden. Cool tart in pan on wire rack. When cool, carefully remove side of pan. Makes 12 servings.

Each serving: About 390 calories, 6 g protein, 43 g carbohydrate, 23 g total fat (11 g saturated), 112 mg cholesterol, 170 mg sodium.

Butternut Squash Pie

PREP: 30 MINUTES • BAKE: 40 TO 45 MINUTES

This truly American recipe has been in Photo Editor Maya Kaimal's family since the early part of the century. Her mother's dad, John Vernon Augusta, was one of 8 children, all of whom adored pie, so this version reflects not only the family's Boston heritage, but also a love of great pie! Try it the way Kaimal's family serves it—warm, with whipped cream.

PIE CRUST:
1½ cups all-purpose flour
2 tablespoons sugar
½ teaspoon salt
4 tablespoons cold margarine or butter
¼ cup shortening

SQUASH FILLING:
1½ cups cooked, mashed butternut squash (from about a 1½-pound squash)*
1 cup milk
⅔ cup packed brown sugar
½ cup heavy or whipping cream
2 tablespoons granulated sugar
1 tablespoon margarine or butter, melted
1¼ teaspoons ground cinnamon
½ teaspoon ground ginger
½ teaspoon ground nutmeg
¼ teaspoon ground cloves
⅛ teaspoon salt
2 large eggs

1 Prepare Pie Crust: In medium bowl, mix flour, sugar, and salt. With pastry blender or two knives used scissor-fashion, cut in margarine or butter with shortening until mixture resembles coarse crumbs. Sprinkle about *4 tablespoons cold water*, 1 tablespoon at a time, into flour mixture, mixing lightly with fork after each addition until dough is just moist enough to hold together. Shape dough into a disk.

2 On lightly floured surface, with floured rolling pin, roll dough into a round 2 inches larger in diameter than inverted 9-inch pie plate. Ease dough into pie plate; trim edge, leaving 1-inch overhang. Fold overhang under; pinch to form decorative edge. Cover and refrigerate pie shell.

3 Meanwhile, preheat oven to 425°F. Make a foil shield for edge of crust: Cut 12-inch square piece of foil; fold into quarters. Cut out center and round off edges, leaving a 2½-inch-wide ring. Unfold ring; set aside. Prepare Squash Filling: In large bowl, with wire whisk, beat all filling ingredients until blended. Pour squash mixture into pie shell.

4 Place foil shield over edge of crust to prevent over-browning. Bake pie 40 to 45 minutes, until knife inserted 1 inch from edge comes out clean. Cool pie on wire rack. Makes 10 servings.

*To cook squash in microwave oven: Cut squash lengthwise in half; remove seeds. In shallow microwave-safe baking dish, place squash cut side down in ½ inch water. Cook on High about 6 minutes; turn squash over and cook 6 minutes longer or until fork-tender. Or, to cook in conventional oven, place squash halves in shallow pan and bake at 400°F. 35 to 45 minutes until tender.

Each serving: About 325 calories, 5 g protein, 39 g carbohydrate, 17 g total fat (6 g saturated), 62 mg cholesterol, 245 mg sodium.

Coconut Cream Pie

PREP: 35 MINUTES PLUS CHILLING • BAKE: 20 MINUTES

Mary Jane Ogilvie Silvia, engineering department coordinator, remembers her mother, Scottish-born Margaret Ogilvie, baking this pie every Thanksgiving in Lancaster, Pennsylvania.

PIE CRUST:
1 cup all-purpose flour
½ cup sweetened shredded coconut, toasted
6 tablespoons cold margarine or butter, cut into small pieces
2 tablespoons sugar
Nonstick cooking spray

FOOD EDITOR'S TIP

Q Are cream of coconut and coconut cream the same thing?

A No. Coconut cream, available in Asian and Hispanic specialty stores, is pressed and rehydrated coconut meat. It resembles vegetable shortening, and is used in some Asian and Caribbean cooking for deep-frying. Cream of coconut, a sweeter, thicker version of coconut milk, contains added sugar and stabilizers. It's used in piña coladas (and similar drinks) and in our Coconut Cream Pie (above); you'll find it where cocktail mixers are sold.

FILLING:
2 cups milk
1 can (8½ ounces) cream of coconut (not coconut milk)
⅓ cup cornstarch
¼ teaspoon salt
4 large egg yolks
2 tablespoons margarine or butter
1 teaspoon vanilla extract

TOPPING:
1 cup heavy or whipping cream
2 tablespoons sugar
½ teaspoon vanilla extract
2 tablespoons sweetened shredded coconut, toasted

1 Prepare Pie Crust: Preheat oven to 375°F. Place all crust ingredients and *1 tablespoon cold water* into food processor with knife blade attached. Blend ingredients, pulsing processor on and off, until dough just comes together.

2 Spray 9-inch pie plate with nonstick cooking spray. Press dough evenly onto bottom and up side of pie plate, making a small rim. Bake pie shell 20 minutes or until golden, covering edge with foil if necessary during last 10 minutes to prevent overbrowning. Cool on wire rack.

3 While pie shell is cooling, prepare Filling: In 3-quart saucepan, with wire whisk, mix milk, cream of coconut, cornstarch, and salt until blended. Cook over medium heat until mixture thickens and begins to bubble around side of pan, about 7 minutes, stirring constantly; boil 1 minute.

4 In small bowl, with wire whisk or fork, beat egg yolks slightly. Into yolks, beat small amount of hot milk mixture. Slowly pour yolk mixture back into milk mixture, stirring rapidly to prevent lumping. Over low heat, cook about 2 minutes, stirring constantly, until very thick (mixture should be about 160°F.).

5 Remove saucepan from heat; stir in margarine or butter and vanilla. Spoon hot filling into pie shell. Place plastic wrap directly on surface of filling and refrigerate pie 4 hours or until filling is cold and set.

6 To serve, prepare Topping: In bowl, with mixer at medium speed, beat cream and sugar to stiff peaks. Beat in vanilla. Spread whipped cream over filling. Sprinkle with coconut. Makes 10 servings.

Each serving: About 425 calories, 5 g protein, 40 g carbohydrate, 28 g total fat (14 g saturated), 124 mg cholesterol, 235 mg sodium.

Frozen Strawberry Margarita Pie

PREP: 25 MINUTES PLUS FREEZING • BAKE: 10 MINUTES

If you love margaritas, you'll love this—the delectable filling is made with whipped cream and fresh lime juice.

CRUMB CRUST:
1½ cups vanilla wafer crumbs
5 tablespoons margarine or butter, melted
½ teaspoon grated fresh lime peel

STRAWBERRY FILLING:
1 pint strawberries
2 limes
1 can (14 ounces) sweetened condensed milk
2 tablespoons orange-flavor liqueur
1 cup heavy or whipping cream

1 Prepare Crumb Crust: Preheat oven to 375°F. In 9-inch pie plate, with fork, stir crust ingredients until crumbs are moistened. Press mixture onto bottom and up side of pie plate, making a slight rim. Bake crust 10 minutes. Cool crust in pie plate on wire rack.

2 Prepare Strawberry Filling: Hull 2 cups strawberries; reserve remaining berries for garnish. From limes, grate 1 teaspoon peel and squeeze ¼ cup juice. In food processor with knife blade attached, pulse hulled berries with lime peel and juice, undiluted sweetened condensed milk, and liqueur until almost smooth. Transfer mixture to large bowl.

3 In small bowl, with mixer at medium speed, beat ⅔ cup cream until stiff peaks form; reserve remaining unwhipped cream for garnish. Gently fold whipped cream into strawberry mixture, one-third at a time.

4 Pour filling into cooled crust. Freeze at least 4 hours or until almost firm. (If not serving pie on the same day, wrap frozen pie in foil or plastic wrap and freeze up to 1 week.)

5 If pie freezes completely, let it stand at room temperature 10 minutes before serving for easier slicing. Meanwhile, cut each reserved strawberry in half. In small bowl, with mixer at medium speed, beat remaining ⅓ cup cream just until stiff peaks form. Mound whipped cream in center of pie and top with strawberry halves. Makes 10 servings.

Each serving: About 360 calories, 5 g protein, 39 g carbohydrate, 21 g total fat (9 g saturated), 57 mg cholesterol, 180 mg sodium.

Berry Banana-Cream Tart

PREP: 45 MINUTES PLUS CHILLING • BAKE: 30 MINUTES

The pretty top layer of glazed strawberries is easy to achieve with a quick brush of melted apple jelly.

TART SHELL:
1½ cups all-purpose flour
½ teaspoon salt
½ cup margarine or butter (1 stick)
2 tablespoons shortening

BANANA-CREAM FILLING:
2¼ cups milk
4 large egg yolks
⅔ cup sugar
¼ cup cornstarch
¼ cup all-purpose flour
1 tablespoon vanilla extract
½ cup heavy or whipping cream
2 ripe medium bananas

TOPPING:
About 1 pint strawberries
2 tablespoons apple jelly
Mint leaves for garnish

1 Prepare Tart Shell: In medium bowl, with fork, stir flour and salt. With pastry blender or two knives used scissor-fashion, cut in margarine or butter with shortening until mixture resembles coarse crumbs. Sprinkle about *4 tablespoons cold water*, 1 tablespoon at a time, into flour mixture, mixing lightly with fork after each addition until dough is just moist enough to hold together. Shape dough into a disk; wrap with plastic wrap and refrigerate 30 minutes or until firm enough to roll.

2 Meanwhile, prepare Banana-Cream Filling: In 3-quart saucepan, heat 2 cups milk to simmering over medium-high heat. In large bowl, whisk egg yolks, sugar, and remaining ¼ cup milk until blended; whisk in cornstarch and flour until smooth. While constantly beating with wire whisk, gradually pour about half of simmering milk into bowl with yolk

mixture. Return yolk mixture to saucepan and cook until mixture thickens and boils, stirring constantly. Reduce heat to low and cook, stirring constantly, about 2 minutes longer. Remove saucepan from heat; stir in vanilla.

3 Transfer filling to medium bowl; cover surface directly with plastic wrap to prevent skin from forming and refrigerate at least 1 hour.

4 While filling is chilling, preheat oven to 425°F. On lightly floured surface, with floured rolling pin, roll dough into a 14-inch round. Press dough onto bottom and up side of 11" by 1" round tart pan with removable bottom. Fold overhang in and press against side of tart pan to form a rim ⅛ inch above edge of pan. With fork, prick dough at 1-inch intervals to prevent puffing and shrinking during baking.

5 Line tart shell with foil and fill with pie weights, dried beans, or uncooked rice. Bake tart shell 20 minutes; remove foil with weights and bake 10 minutes longer or until golden. Cool tart shell in pan on wire rack.

6 In small bowl, with mixer at high speed, beat cream until stiff peaks form. Thinly slice bananas. Fold whipped cream and bananas into filling mixture. Spoon filling into cooled tart shell.

7 Prepare Topping: Hull and thinly slice strawberries. Arrange slices in concentric circles on top of filling. Refrigerate up to 4 hours.

8 Just before serving, in small saucepan, melt apple jelly over medium-high heat, stirring constantly. With pastry brush, brush apple jelly over strawberries. Garnish pie with mint leaves. Makes 12 servings.

Each serving: About 325 calories, 5 g protein, 39 g carbohydrate, 17 g total fat (6 g saturated), 91 mg cholesterol, 220 mg sodium.

Strawberry Icebox Cake

PREP: 30 MINUTES PLUS CHILLING

1½ pints strawberries
1½ cups heavy or whipping cream
3 tablespoons confectioners' sugar
1 teaspoon vanilla extract
2 tablespoons strawberry preserves
35 chocolate wafer cookies (about one 9-ounce package)

1 Hull and thinly slice 1 pint strawberries; reserve rest for garnish.

2 In large bowl, with mixer at medium speed, beat cream, sugar, and vanilla until stiff peaks form. Spoon 2 cups whipped cream into another bowl; cover and refrigerate.

3 With rubber spatula, gently fold sliced strawberries and preserves into remaining whipped cream.

4 On 1 side of each of 6 cookies, spread about 1 heaping tablespoon strawberry cream. Stack cookies on top of one another. Top stack with a plain cookie. Repeat stacking cookies with strawberry cream until all cookies and cream are used, making 5 stacks of 7 cookies each.

5 Turn each stack on its side. Place stacks next to one another, with rounded edges touching, to form a rectangle on platter. Frost with reserved whipped cream; cover and refrigerate cake at least 5 hours or overnight to allow cookies to soften.

FOOD EDITOR'S TIP

A I hate to pass strawberries up when they are in season, but I don't always have an immediate need for them. Can they be successfully frozen?

Q Sure, just follow these guidelines: Don't wash or remove caps before freezing; washing removes the natural protective coating, and the caps help lock in flavor, texture, and nutrients. Freeze unwashed berries on a cookie sheet for about 1 hour, until hard; then transfer to a freezer container or a freezer-weight self-sealing bag. After freezing, the berries may not be pristine enough for a tart, but will work well in shortcakes, smoothies, and sauces. To serve, rinse without thawing. (Exception: Commercially frozen whole strawberries are already washed.)

6 To serve, hull reserved strawberries; cut each into quarters. Garnish platter with strawberries. Makes 10 servings.

Each serving: About 270 calories, 3 g protein, 28 g carbohydrate, 17 g total fat (9 g saturated), 49 mg cholesterol, 165 mg sodium.

Cranberry-Raisin Fruitcake

PREP: 20 MINUTES PLUS COOLING
BAKE: ABOUT 1 HOUR 15 MINUTES

This type of fruitcake is known as "white fruitcake" because it's light rather than dark. You can bake it up to 1 month ahead, but don't glaze it until the day it will be served.

2⅔ cups walnuts, toasted
1½ cups golden raisins
1 cup dried cranberries
1 tablespoon plus 2 cups all-purpose flour
1¼ cups sugar
1 cup margarine or butter (2 sticks), softened
5 large eggs
½ cup brandy
1 tablespoon vanilla extract
2 teaspoons baking powder
1 teaspoon salt
⅓ cup apple jelly

1 Preheat oven to 325°F. Grease 9-inch tube pan with removable bottom.

2 Set aside ⅔ cup walnut halves or large pieces to decorate top of cake; coarsely chop remaining walnuts. In medium bowl, toss chopped walnuts with raisins, dried cranberries, and 1 tablespoon flour; set aside.

3 In large bowl, with mixer at low speed, beat sugar with margarine or butter until blended. Increase speed to high; beat until creamy, about 2 minutes, constantly scraping bowl with rubber spatula.

4 With mixer at low speed, add eggs, brandy, vanilla, baking powder, salt, and remaining 2 cups flour; beat until well blended. With spoon, stir in raisin mixture (batter may look curdled).

5 Spoon batter into pan. Scatter reserved walnuts on top of batter. Bake cake about 1 hour and 15 minutes or until wooden skewer or toothpick inserted in center comes out clean.

6 Cool cake in pan on wire rack 10 minutes. With small metal spatula, loosen cake from side of pan. Invert cake onto plate and remove side of pan. Loosen bottom of pan from cake and remove. Immediately invert cake onto wire rack to cool completely.

7 When fruitcake is cold, melt apple jelly in small saucepan over low heat. Brush cake with melted apple jelly. Or, wrap and refrigerate cake up to 1 month, then brush with jelly before serving. Makes 24 servings.

Each serving: About 315 calories, 5 g protein, 37 g carbohydrate, 17 g total fat (3 g saturated), 44 mg cholesterol, 240 mg sodium.

Cannoli Cake Roll

• •

PREP: 1 HOUR 30 MINUTES PLUS COOLING
AND CHILLING • BAKE: 10 MINUTES

This sweet finale has a rich ricotta and cream cheese filling, rolled into an orange-liqueur-spiked sponge cake—with whipped-cream frosting!

CAKE:
5 large eggs, separated
1 teaspoon vanilla extract
½ cup plus 1 tablespoon granulated sugar
¼ teaspoon cream of tartar
¼ teaspoon salt
¾ cup cake flour (not self-rising)
2 tablespoons orange-flavor liqueur
Confectioners' sugar

RICOTTA FILLING:
1¼ cups ricotta cheese
4 ounces reduced-fat cream cheese (Neufchâtel)
½ cup confectioners' sugar
½ teaspoon vanilla extract
¼ teaspoon ground cinnamon
¼ cup semisweet-chocolate mini pieces

FROSTING:
¾ cup heavy or whipping cream
3 tablespoons confectioners' sugar
2 tablespoons orange-flavor liqueur
½ teaspoon vanilla extract
¼ cup pistachio nuts, chopped
1 tablespoon semisweet-chocolate mini pieces

1 Prepare Cake: Preheat oven to 375°F. Grease 15½" by 10½" jelly-roll pan; line with waxed paper; grease paper and dust with flour.

2 In small bowl, with mixer at high speed, beat egg yolks, vanilla, and ¼ cup granulated sugar until very thick and lemon-colored, about 5 minutes. Transfer beaten yolk mixture to a large bowl and set aside.

3 In another large bowl, with clean beaters and with mixer at high speed, beat egg whites, cream of tartar, and salt until soft peaks form. Beating at high speed, gradually sprinkle in ¼ cup granulated sugar until sugar dissolves and whites stand in stiff peaks.

4 With rubber spatula or wire whisk, gently fold beaten egg whites into beaten egg yolks, one-third at a time. Sift and fold flour, one-third at a time, into egg mixture.

5 With metal spatula, spread batter evenly in pan. Bake 10 minutes or until top of cake springs back when lightly touched with finger.

6 Meanwhile, in cup, mix orange liqueur with *1 tablespoon water* and remaining 1 tablespoon granulated sugar until sugar dissolves.

7 Sprinkle clean cloth towel with confectioners' sugar. When cake is done, immediately invert hot cake onto towel. Carefully peel off waxed paper and discard. Brush cake with orange-liqueur mixture. Starting from a long side, roll cake with towel jelly-roll fashion. Cool cake roll, seam side down, on wire rack until completely cool, about 1 hour.

8 Meanwhile, prepare Ricotta Filling: In food processor with knife blade attached, blend all filling ingredients, except chocolate pieces, until smooth. Transfer filling to bowl; stir in chocolate pieces. Cover and refrigerate filling while cake cools.

9 Assemble cake: Gently unroll cooled cake. With metal spatula, spread filling over cake almost to edges. Starting from same long side, roll cake without towel. Place rolled cake, seam side down, on platter.

10 Prepare Frosting: In small bowl, with mixer at medium speed, beat heavy cream and confectioners' sugar until soft peaks form. With rubber spatula, fold in orange liqueur and vanilla. Spread whipped-cream frosting over cake. Refrigerate cake at least 2 hours before serving. Sprinkle top of cake with pistachios and chocolate just before serving. Makes 14 servings.

Each serving: About 255 calories, 7 g protein, 26 g carbohydrate, 13 g total fat (7 g saturated), 111 mg cholesterol, 120 mg sodium.

Chocolate Truffle Cake

PREP: 1 HOUR PLUS OVERNIGHT CHILLING
BAKE: 35 MINUTES

This exceptionally rich dessert must be baked a day ahead for optimum flavor and texture. For easy serving, dip knife in hot water before cutting each slice.

1 cup (2 sticks) butter (do not use margarine)
14 squares (1 ounce each) semisweet chocolate
2 squares (1 ounce each) unsweetened chocolate
9 large eggs, separated
½ cup sugar
¼ teaspoon cream of tartar
Confectioners' sugar for decorating

1 Preheat oven to 300°F. Remove bottom from 9" by 3" springform pan and cover with foil, wrapping foil around to the underside (this will make it easier to remove cake from pan). Replace bottom. Grease and flour foil bottom and side of pan.

2 In large glass bowl, combine butter and both kinds of chocolate. In microwave oven, cook, uncovered, on Medium (50%), 2½ minutes; stir. Return choco-late mixture to microwave oven; cook 2 to 2½ minutes longer until almost melted; stir until smooth. (Or, in heavy 2-quart saucepan, heat butter and both kinds of chocolate over low heat until melted, stirring frequently. Pour chocolate mixture into large bowl.)

3 In small bowl, with mixer at high speed, beat egg yolks and sugar until very thick and lemon-colored, about 5 minutes. Add egg-yolk mixture to chocolate mixture, stirring with rubber spatula until blended.

4 In another large bowl, with clean beaters, and with mixer at high speed, beat egg whites and cream of tar-tar until soft peaks form. With rubber spatula or wire whisk, gently fold beaten egg whites into chocolate mixture, one-third at a time.

5 Pour batter into pan, spreading evenly. Bake 35 minutes. (Do not overbake. The cake will firm upon standing and chilling.) Cool cake completely in pan on wire rack. Then, refrigerate overnight in pan.

6 To remove cake from pan, run a hot knife around edge of cake, then lift off side of pan. Invert cake onto cake plate; unwrap foil from bottom and lift off bottom of pan. Carefully peel foil from cake.

7 Let cake stand 1 hour at room temperature before serving. Just before serving, decorate cake: Sprinkle confectioners' sugar through fine sieve over star sten-cil for a pretty design.* Or, dust top of cake with con-fectioners' sugar. Makes 24 servings.

*A store-bought doily makes an easy stencil, or you can create your own design on lightweight cardboard or a manila file folder. Cut cardboard at least 1 inch larger all around than the cake's surface. Cut out stars of different sizes or your own design using a mat knife. Place stencil over cake and sprinkle with con-fectioners' sugar, as we did, or try cocoa, ground nuts, or grated chocolate.

Each serving without confectioners' sugar: About 200 calories, 4 g protein, 17 g carbohydrate, 14 g total fat (6 g saturated), 100 mg cholesterol, 110 mg sodium.

Chocolate Truffle Cake

COOKIES

Holiday Sugar Cookies

PREP: 1 HOUR PLUS COOLING AND DECORATING
BAKE: 10 TO 12 MINUTES PER BATCH

Use this basic dough to make these pretty iced cutouts or a batch of our Stained-Glass Cookies (at right).

3 cups all-purpose flour
1 teaspoon baking powder
¼ teaspoon salt
1 cup sugar
½ cup margarine or butter (1 stick), softened
½ cup shortening
2 large eggs
2 teaspoons vanilla extract
Ornamental Frosting (page 237)

1 Into large bowl, measure flour, baking powder, and salt. In another large bowl, with mixer at medium speed, beat sugar, margarine or butter, and shortening until creamy. Reduce speed to low; add eggs, 1 at a time, and vanilla; beat until blended.

2 Beat in flour mixture just until blended. Divide dough into 4 equal pieces. Wrap each piece with plastic wrap and refrigerate 30 minutes (dough will be soft).

3 Preheat oven to 350°F. On well-floured surface, with floured rolling pin, roll 1 piece of dough ⅛ inch thick. With floured 3- to 4-inch assorted cookie cutters, cut dough into as many cookies as possible; reserve trimmings. With pancake turner, place cookies, about 1 inch apart, on large ungreased cookie sheet.

4 Bake cookies 10 to 12 minutes, until lightly browned. Transfer cookies to wire rack to cool. Repeat with remaining dough and trimmings.

5 When cookies are cool, prepare Ornamental Frosting; use to decorate cookies as desired. Set cookies aside to allow frosting to dry completely, about 1 hour. Store cookies in tightly covered container. Makes about 5 dozen cookies.

Each cookie without frosting: About 65 calories, 1 g protein, 8 g carbohydrate, 4 g total fat (1 g saturated), 7 mg cholesterol, 40 mg sodium.

Stained-Glass Cookies

PREP: 1 HOUR 20 MINUTES PLUS COOLING
BAKE: 10 TO 12 MINUTES PER BATCH

Use cookie cutters and crushed sour balls to create cookie ornaments that are good enough to eat.

Holiday Sugar Cookie dough (at left)
1 package (10 to 12 ounces) hard candy, such as sour balls in assorted colors*

1 Prepare Holiday Sugar Cookie dough as in steps 1 and 2.

2 While dough is chilling, group candies by color and place in separate heavy-duty self-sealing plastic bags. Place 1 bag on towel-covered work surface. With meat mallet or rolling pin, lightly crush candy into small pieces, being careful not to crush until fine and powdery. Repeat with remaining candy.

3 Preheat oven to 350°F. Roll and cut dough as in step 3 of Holiday Sugar Cookies, but place cutout cookies on large cookie sheet lined with foil.

4 With mini cookie cutters, canapé cutters, or knife, cut 1 or more small shapes from each large cookie; remove small cutout pieces and reserve for rerolling. Place some crushed candy in cutouts of each cookie. With drinking straw, make a hole in top of each cookie for hanging.

5 Bake cookies 10 to 12 minutes, until lightly browned. Cool cookies completely on cookie sheet. Repeat with remaining dough and trimmings.

6 For wreath, tree, or window decorations, tie ribbons or nylon fishing line through hole in each cookie to make loop for hanging. Makes about 5 dozen cookies.

*Do not use red-and-white-swirled peppermint candies—they won't melt in the oven.

Each cookie: About 90 calories, 1 g protein, 14 g carbohydrate, 4 g total fat (1 g saturated), 7 mg cholesterol, 40 mg sodium.

Stained-Glass Cookies ➤

Raspberry Linzer Thumbprint Cookies

PREP: 45 MINUTES PLUS COOLING
BAKE: 20 MINUTES PER BATCH

These cookies have all the delicious flavors of a traditional linzertorte (linzer tart)—a buttery crust with ground nuts and a raspberry jam filling. But, they're much easier to make.

1⅓ cups hazelnuts (filberts)
½ cup sugar
¾ cup margarine or butter (1½ sticks), cut up
1 teaspoon vanilla extract
¼ teaspoon salt
1¾ cups all-purpose flour
¼ cup seedless red raspberry jam

1 Preheat oven to 350°F. Place 1 cup hazelnuts in 9" by 9" metal baking pan. Bake 15 minutes or until toasted, shaking pan occasionally. Wrap hot hazelnuts in clean cloth towel. With hands, roll hazelnuts back and forth to remove most of skins. Cool nuts completely.

2 In food processor with knife blade attached, blend toasted hazelnuts with sugar until finely ground. Add margarine or butter, vanilla, and salt, and process until blended. Add flour and process until evenly mixed. Remove knife blade, and press dough together with hand.

3 Finely chop remaining ⅓ cup hazelnuts; spread on piece of waxed paper. Roll dough into 1-inch balls (dough may be slightly crumbly), using about 2 teaspoons dough for each ball. Roll balls in nuts, gently pressing nuts onto dough.

4 Place balls, about 1½ inches apart, on ungreased large cookie sheet. With thumb, make small indentation in center of each ball. Fill each indentation with ¼ teaspoon jam. Bake cookies 20 minutes or until lightly golden around edges. Transfer cookies to wire rack to cool. Repeat with remaining balls and jam. Store cookies in tightly covered container. Makes about 4 dozen cookies.

Each cookie: About 75 calories, 1 g protein, 7 g carbohydrate, 5 g total fat (1 g saturated), 0 mg cholesterol, 50 mg sodium.

Mostaccioli

PREP: 45 MINUTES PLUS COOLING
BAKE: 8 TO 10 MINUTES PER BATCH

These cakelike chocolate spice cookies are an Italian tradition.

COOKIES:
2 cups all-purpose flour
½ cup unsweetened cocoa
1½ teaspoons baking powder
1 teaspoon ground cinnamon
½ teaspoon ground cloves
¼ teaspoon salt
⅔ cup granulated sugar
½ cup margarine or butter (1 stick), softened
1 large egg
½ cup milk

CHOCOLATE GLAZE:
3 tablespoons unsweetened cocoa
1¼ cups confectioners' sugar

1 Preheat oven to 400°F. Prepare Cookies: In medium bowl, combine flour, cocoa, baking powder, cinnamon, cloves, and salt. In large bowl, with mixer at low speed, beat granulated sugar with margarine or butter until blended. Increase speed to high; beat until light and creamy. At low speed, beat in egg until blended. Alternately beat in flour mixture and milk, beginning and ending with flour mixture.

2 With hands dusted with cocoa, roll about 2 level teaspoons dough into 1-inch balls. Place balls, about 2 inches apart, on ungreased large cookie sheet. Bake cookies 8 to 10 minutes, until puffed (they will look dry and slightly cracked). Transfer cookies to wire rack to cool. Repeat with remaining dough.

3 Prepare Chocolate Glaze: In medium bowl, with wire whisk or fork, mix cocoa with 3 *tablespoons plus 1 teaspoon boiling water* until smooth. Gradually stir in confectioners' sugar and blend well. Dip top of each cooled cookie into glaze. Place cookies on wire rack set over waxed paper to catch any drips. Allow glaze to set, about 10 minutes. Store cookies in tightly covered container with waxed paper between the layers. Makes about 5 dozen cookies.

Each cookie: About 50 calories, 1 g protein, 9 g carbohydrate, 2 g total fat (0 g saturated), 4 mg cholesterol, 40 mg sodium.

GH Gingerbread Cutouts

PREP: 55 MINUTES PLUS COOLING AND DECORATING
BAKE: 12 MINUTES PER BATCH

Our favorite gingerbread cookie! You mix it all up right in a saucepan—no mixer required. And the dough is ready to roll out as soon as it's made.

½ cup sugar
½ cup light molasses
1½ teaspoons ground ginger
1 teaspoon ground allspice
1 teaspoon ground cinnamon
1 teaspoon ground cloves
2 teaspoons baking soda
½ cup margarine or butter (1 stick), cut into chunks
1 large egg, beaten
3½ cups all-purpose flour
Ornamental Frosting (at right)

1 In 3-quart saucepan, heat sugar, molasses, ginger, allspice, cinnamon, and cloves to boiling over medium heat, stirring occasionally. Remove saucepan from heat; stir in baking soda (mixture will foam up in pan). Stir in margarine or butter until melted. With fork, stir in egg, then flour.

2 On lightly floured surface, knead dough until thoroughly mixed. Divide dough in half; wrap half of dough with plastic wrap and set aside.

3 Preheat oven to 325°F. With floured rolling pin, roll half of dough slightly thinner than ¼ inch. With floured 3- to 4-inch assorted cookie cutters, cut dough into as many cookies as possible; reserve trimmings. Place cookies, about ½ inch apart, on ungreased large cookie sheet. Reroll trimmings and cut out more cookies. If you like, with drinking straw, make a hole in top of each cookie for hanging.

4 Bake cookies 12 minutes or until edges begin to brown. Transfer cookies to wire racks to cool. Repeat with remaining dough.

5 When cookies are cool, prepare Ornamental Frosting; use to decorate cookies as desired. Set cookies aside to allow frosting to dry completely, about 1 hour. Store cookies in tightly covered container.

6 For wreath, tree, or window decorations, tie ribbon or clear nylon fishing line through hole in each cookie to make loop for hanging. Makes about 3 dozen cookies.

Each cookie without frosting: About 90 calories, 1 g protein, 15 g carbohydrate, 3 g total fat (1 g saturated), 6 mg cholesterol, 105 mg sodium.

ORNAMENTAL FROSTING

We used this hard-drying frosting—tinted different colors with food coloring—to decorate GH Gingerbread Cutouts (at left) and Holiday Sugar Cookies (page 234).

1 package (16 ounces) confectioners' sugar
3 tablespoons meringue powder*
Assorted food colorings (optional)

1 In bowl, with mixer at medium speed, beat confectioners' sugar, meringue powder, and *⅓ cup warm water* until blended and mixture is so stiff that knife drawn through it leaves a clean-cut path, about 5 minutes.

2 If you like, tint frosting with food colorings as desired; keep covered with plastic wrap to prevent drying out. With small metal spatula, artists' paintbrush, or decorating bag with small writing tips, decorate cookies with frosting. (You may need to thin frosting with a little warm water to obtain the right spreading or piping consistency.) Makes about 3 cups.

*Meringue powder is available in specialty stores wherever cake-decorating equipment is sold.

Each tablespoon: About 40 calories, 0 g protein, 10 g carbohydrate, 0 g total fat, 0 mg cholesterol, 3 mg sodium.

Fruitcake Drops

PREP: 30 MINUTES PLUS COOLING
BAKE: 10 TO 12 MINUTES PER BATCH

Chock-full of fruit, these are a delicious treat for breakfast or snack time!

1¾ cups all-purpose flour
½ teaspoon baking soda
¼ teaspoon salt
1 cup packed light brown sugar
6 tablespoons margarine or butter (¾ stick), softened
2 tablespoons shortening
1 large egg
1 cup pitted prunes, coarsely chopped
1 cup golden raisins
½ cup red candied cherries, coarsely chopped
½ cup sweetened shredded coconut

3 ounces white chocolate, Swiss confectionery bar, or white baking bar

1 Preheat oven to 375°F. Grease large cookie sheet.

2 In large bowl, combine flour, baking soda, and salt; set aside.

3 In another large bowl, with mixer at low speed, beat brown sugar, margarine or butter, and shortening until blended, occasionally scraping bowl with rubber spatula. Increase speed to high; beat until creamy, about 2 minutes. At low speed, beat in egg until blended. Add flour mixture, prunes, raisins, cherries, and coconut, and beat just until blended.

4 Drop dough by rounded tablespoons, about 2 inches apart, onto cookie sheet. Bake 10 to 12 minutes, until golden around edges (cookies will be soft). Transfer cookies to wire rack to cool. Repeat with remaining dough.

5 In heavy small saucepan, melt white chocolate over very low heat, stirring frequently, until smooth.

ROVER'S REWARD

PREP: 1 HOUR PLUS COOLING • BAKE: 30 TO 40 MINUTES PLUS DRYING

Humans aren't the only creatures who appreciate cookies.

1 package active dry yeast
1 teaspoon sugar
2 cups all-purpose flour
2 cups whole-wheat flour
2 cups cornmeal
2 cups old-fashioned oats, uncooked
1 cup loosely packed fresh mint leaves, chopped
1 cup loosely packed fresh parsley leaves, chopped
½ cup toasted wheat germ
1 can (13¾ to 14½ ounces) beef broth
¾ cup milk

1 Preheat oven to 350°F. In small bowl, combine yeast, sugar, and ¼ cup warm water (105° to 115°F.). Let stand until yeast foams, about 5 minutes.

2 In very large bowl, combine all-purpose flour, whole wheat flour, cornmeal, oats, mint, parsley, and wheat germ. With wooden spoon, stir in yeast mixture, broth, and milk until combined. With hands, knead dough in bowl until blended, about 1 minute.

3 Divide dough in half. Cover 1 piece with plastic wrap to prevent drying out. Place remaining piece of dough on lightly floured surface. With floured rolling pin, roll dough to ¼-inch thickness. With large (about 5 inches) or small (about 2 inches) cookie cutter, such as bone or mailman, cut out as many biscuits as possible, reserving trimmings. With spatula, transfer biscuits to large ungreased cookie sheet. Reroll trimmings and cut more biscuits. Repeat with remaining dough.

4 Bake small biscuits 30 minutes, bake large biscuits 40 minutes. Turn oven off; leave biscuits in oven 1 hour to dry out.

5 Transfer biscuits from cookie sheet to wire rack. When cool, store at room temperature in tightly covered container up to 3 months. Makes about 4 dozen large biscuits or 24 dozen small biscuits.

Each large biscuit: About 90 calories, 4 g protein, 17 g carbohydrate, 1 g total fat (0 g saturated), 1 mg cholesterol, 30 mg sodium.

On sheet of waxed paper, arrange cookies in 1 layer. Using spoon, drizzle white chocolate over cookies. Allow white chocolate to set, refrigerating if necessary. Store cookies in tightly covered container with waxed paper between the layers. Makes about 3 dozen cookies.

Each cookie: About 130 calories, 1 g protein, 22 g carbohydrate, 4 g total fat (2 g saturated), 6 mg cholesterol, 70 mg sodium.

Vanilla Spritz Cookies

PREP: 15 MINUTES PLUS COOLING
BAKE: 12 TO 14 MINUTES PER BATCH

Our classic spritz dough is firm enough to be used with a cookie press or a decorating bag fitted with a large star tip. To really do justice to these melt-in-your-mouth cookies, we recommend using butter—they'll not only taste better but hold their shape better too.

1 cup margarine or butter (2 sticks), softened
¾ cup sugar
1 large egg yolk
1 teaspoon vanilla extract
2 cups all-purpose flour
Red candied cherries, each cut in half, for
  garnish

1 Preheat oven to 375°F. In large bowl, with mixer at medium speed, beat margarine or butter with sugar until creamy. Beat in egg yolk and vanilla until blended. At low speed, beat in flour just until blended, occasionally scraping bowl with rubber spatula.

2 Spoon half of dough into large decorating bag with large star tip (¾-inch diameter opening). Pipe dough into rosettes (about 1½ inches in diameter), about 1 inch apart, onto ungreased large cookie sheet. If you like, place a cherry half in center of some or all of the cookies before baking.

3 Bake cookies 12 to 14 minutes, until lightly browned around the edges. Let cookies remain on cookie sheet on wire rack 3 minutes to cool slightly. Then, transfer cookies to wire rack to cool completely. Repeat with remaining dough. Store cookies in tightly covered container. Makes about 4½ dozen cookies.

Each cookie without candied cherry: About 60 calories, 1 g protein, 6 g carbohydrate, 4 g total fat (1 g saturated), 4 mg cholesterol, 45 mg sodium.

Moravian Spice Crisps

PREP: 30 MINUTES PLUS COOLING
BAKE: 8 TO 10 MINUTES PER BATCH

Moravians, members of a Protestant religious group, have been rolling out ultrathin, spice cookies since they settled in Winston-Salem, North Carolina, in the 1700's. Our recipe is a close replica of those delicate cookies—but without the rolling!

¾ cup all-purpose flour
½ teaspoon baking powder
½ teaspoon ground cinnamon
½ teaspoon ground ginger
½ teaspoon ground white pepper
¼ teaspoon ground cloves
¼ teaspoon baking soda
¼ teaspoon salt
⅓ cup packed light brown sugar
3 tablespoons margarine or butter, softened
¼ cup mild molasses

1 Preheat oven to 350°F. Grease large cookie sheet.

2 In large bowl, combine flour, baking powder, cinnamon, ginger, white pepper, cloves, baking soda, and salt; set aside.

3 In another large bowl, with mixer at low speed, beat brown sugar with margarine or butter until blended. Increase speed to high; beat until creamy, about 2 minutes. At medium speed, beat in molasses until blended. With spoon, stir in flour mixture.

4 Drop dough by rounded teaspoons, about 4 inches apart, onto cookie sheet. With finger, press each into a 2-inch round. Bake 8 to 10 minutes, until cookies spread and darken. Let cookies remain on cookie sheet on wire rack 3 minutes to cool slightly. Transfer cookies to wire rack to cool completely. Repeat with remaining dough. Store cookies in tightly covered container. Makes about 3 dozen cookies.

Each cookie: About 30 calories, 0 g protein, 6 g carbohydrate, 1 g total fat (0 g saturated), 0 mg cholesterol, 45 mg sodium.

Almond Crescents

PREP: 45 MINUTES PLUS CHILLING AND COOLING
BAKE: 20 MINUTES PER BATCH

A classic holiday favorite, these cookies also make a welcome gift. Butter is essential to the exquisite texture and flavor; we don't recommend substituting margarine.

1 cup blanched almonds
¼ teaspoon salt
½ cup granulated sugar
1 cup butter (2 sticks), softened
2 cups all-purpose flour
1 teaspoon almond extract
½ teaspoon vanilla extract
¾ cup confectioners' sugar

1 Preheat oven to 350°F. Place almonds in 9" by 9" metal baking pan. Bake almonds 8 to 10 minutes, until lightly toasted. Cool completely. Turn off oven.

2 In food processor with knife blade attached, blend almonds with salt and ¼ cup granulated sugar until almonds are very finely ground.

3 In large bowl, with mixer at low speed, beat butter and remaining ¼ cup granulated sugar until blended, occasionally scraping bowl with rubber spatula. Increase speed to high; beat until light and creamy, about 3 minutes. Reduce speed to low; gradually beat in flour, almond extract, vanilla, and ground-almond mixture until blended. Divide dough in half; wrap each with plastic wrap and refrigerate 1 hour or until dough is firm enough to handle. (Or, place dough in freezer 30 minutes.)

4 Preheat oven to 325°F. Working with half of dough at a time, with lightly floured hands, shape dough by rounded teaspoons into 2" by ½" crescents. Place crescents, about 1 inch apart, on ungreased cookie sheet. Bake cookies 20 minutes or until lightly browned around the edges. Transfer cookies to wire rack. Immediately sprinkle confectioners' sugar through sieve over hot cookies until well coated; cool completely.

5 Repeat with remaining dough. Store cookies in tightly covered container, placing waxed paper between layers if necessary. Makes about 6 dozen cookies.

Each cookie: About 55 calories, 1 g protein, 6 g carbohydrate, 4 g total fat (2 g saturated), 7 mg cholesterol, 35 mg sodium.

Chocolate-Cherry Biscotti

PREP: 30 MINUTES PLUS COOLING • BAKE: 50 MINUTES

Pairing rich cocoa with tart dried cherries makes the beloved crunchy twice-baked Italian cookie even more appealing.

2½ cups all-purpose flour
¾ cup unsweetened cocoa
1 tablespoon baking powder
½ teaspoon salt
1⅓ cups sugar
½ cup margarine or butter (1 stick), softened
3 large eggs
2 squares (1 ounce each) semisweet chocolate, melted
1 teaspoon instant espresso-coffee powder
¾ cup dried tart cherries, coarsely chopped

1 Preheat oven to 350° F. Grease and flour large cookie sheet. In large bowl, mix flour, cocoa, baking powder, and salt.

2 In another large bowl, with mixer at medium speed, beat sugar with margarine or butter until creamy. At low speed, add eggs, 1 at a time, then chocolate, and beat until mixed.

3 Dissolve espresso-coffee powder in *1 teaspoon hot water*; beat into chocolate mixture. Add flour mixture, and beat just until blended. With hands, knead in cherries until combined.

4 On floured surface, with floured hands, divide dough in half. Shape each half into a 12" by 3" log. With pastry brush, brush off excess flour. Place logs, about 3 inches apart, on cookie sheet. Bake logs 30 minutes. Cool logs on cookie sheet on wire rack 10 minutes or until easy to handle.

5 Place 1 log on cutting board. With serrated knife, cut log crosswise into ¾-inch-thick diagonal slices. Repeat with remaining log. Place slices, cut side down, on same cookie sheet. Bake slices 20 to 25 minutes to allow biscotti to dry out. Transfer biscotti to wire racks to cool completely. (Biscotti will harden as they cool.) Store biscotti in tightly covered container. Makes about 3 dozen biscotti.

Each biscotti: About 110 calories, 2 g protein, 18 g carbohydrate, 4 g total fat (1 g saturated), 18 mg cholesterol, 100 mg sodium.

Old-Fashioned Hermits

PREP: 10 MINUTES PLUS COOLING • BAKE: 10 MINUTES

A new guilt-free stash for your cookie jar—soft spice bars to please kids of all ages.

1 cup all-purpose flour
⅓ cup dark seedless raisins
⅓ cup packed dark brown sugar
1¼ teaspoons ground ginger
1 teaspoon ground cinnamon
½ teaspoon baking powder
¼ teaspoon salt
¼ cup mild molasses
3 tablespoons margarine or butter, melted
1 teaspoon vanilla extract
1 large egg white

1 Preheat oven to 375°F. Spray large cookie sheet with nonstick cooking spray.

2 In large bowl, with spoon, stir flour, raisins, brown sugar, ginger, cinnamon, baking powder, and salt until combined.

Old-Fashioned Hermits

3 Stir in molasses, melted margarine or butter, vanilla, and egg white just until blended.

4 With metal spatula, spread batter in two 12" by 2" strips, about 2 inches apart, on cookie sheet. Bake 10 minutes. While hot, with serrated knife, cut strips crosswise into 1½-inch-wide bars. Transfer bars to wire rack to cool. If not serving right away, store bars in tightly covered container. Makes about 16 bars.

Each bar: About 90 calories, 1 g protein, 16 g carbohydrate, 2 g total fat (0 g saturated), 0 mg cholesterol, 80 mg sodium.

White-Chocolate Macadamia Cookies

PREP: 15 MINUTES • BAKE: 8 TO 10 MINUTES PER BATCH

An easy recipe to make for the chocolate-chip-cookie lovers on your gift list.

1¼ cups all-purpose flour
¾ cup sugar
½ cup margarine or butter (1 stick), softened
1 teaspoon vanilla extract
½ teaspoon baking soda
½ teaspoon salt
1 large egg
8 ounces white chocolate, Swiss confectionery bar, or white baking bar, chopped
1 jar (7 ounces) macadamia nuts, chopped

1 Preheat oven to 375°F. In large bowl, combine flour, sugar, margarine or butter, vanilla, baking soda, salt, and egg. With mixer at medium speed, beat ingredients until blended, occasionally scraping bowl with rubber spatula. With spoon, stir in white chocolate and macadamia nuts.

2 Drop mixture by rounded teaspoons, about 2 inches apart, onto ungreased large cookie sheet. Bake cookies 8 to 10 minutes, until lightly browned. Transfer cookies to wire rack to cool. Repeat with remaining dough. Store cookies in tightly covered container. Makes about 6 dozen cookies.

Each cookie: About 65 calories, 1 g protein, 6 g carbohydrate, 5 g total fat (1 g saturated), 4 mg cholesterol, 50 mg sodium.

Shortcut Rugelach

PREP: 35 MINUTES PLUS THAWING AND COOLING
BAKE: 15 TO 17 MINUTES PER BATCH

Rugelach are usually made with a cream-cheese dough that's rolled into a crescent shape around a filling. This simplified version uses prepared puff pastry, and the results are every bit as good, in half the time.

1 package (17¼ ounces) frozen puff-pastry
   sheets
1 cup dark seedless raisins
⅔ cup walnuts
⅔ cup plus 2 teaspoons sugar
1 teaspoon ground cinnamon
1 large egg white

1 Remove 1 puff-pastry sheet from freezer; let stand at room temperature, about 20 minutes, to thaw as label directs.

2 While pastry is thawing, in food processor with knife blade attached, blend raisins, walnuts, ⅔ cup sugar, and ¾ teaspoon cinnamon until raisins and walnuts are finely chopped.

3 In small bowl, lightly beat egg white with *1 teaspoon water*. In another small bowl, mix remaining 2 teaspoons sugar and ¼ teaspoon cinnamon. Set both bowls aside.

4 Preheat oven to 375°F. Grease large cookie sheet. Remove second puff-pastry sheet from freezer; thaw as above.

5 Meanwhile, on lightly floured surface, with floured rolling pin, roll thawed puff-pastry sheet into a 14" by 12" rectangle. Cut pastry crosswise in half to make two 7" by 12" rectangles. Divide raisin mixture into fourths. Sprinkle one-fourth of raisin mixture (rounded ½ cup) on 1 rectangle, leaving ¾-inch border along a 12-inch side. Repeat with another one-fourth of raisin mixture on second rectangle. Lightly brush border on each rectangle with some egg-white mixture. Roll each pastry rectangle, jelly-roll fashion, starting from 12-inch side with filling; pinch seam to seal.

6 Brush rolls with some egg-white mixture, and sprinkle with half of sugar-cinnamon mixture. Cut each roll crosswise into 12 (about 1-inch-thick) pieces. Place pieces, about 1½ inches apart, seam side down on cookie sheet. Bake cookies 15 to 17 minutes, until puffed and golden. Transfer cookies to wire rack to cool. Repeat, using second puff-pastry sheet and remaining ingredients. Store cookies in tightly covered container. Makes 4 dozen cookies.

Each cookie: About 90 calories, 1 g protein, 10 g carbohydrate, 5 g total fat (1 g saturated), 0 mg cholesterol, 25 mg sodium.

COOKIE STRATEGIES

Home-baked cookies make one of the most irresistible of desserts, but the effort involved in mixing up a batch of cookies at the last minute can be a great deterrent. Here are some advance-preparation strategies from our experts:

• Most unbaked cookie doughs—except those for delicate layered sweets like our Fresh Lemon Bars (page 245)—can be frozen, then defrosted for baking later. Divide the dough into several portions, and wrap each in foil, then place in freezer-weight self-sealing plastic bags. Label the bags with contents and date; raw dough will keep for up to 2 months in the freezer. To use it, simply defrost in the refrigerator or on the counter and bake cookies according to recipe.

• To take the process a step further, freeze uncooked drop cookies individually. Spoon dough onto cookie sheets, freeze until firm, then place in labeled freezer-weight self-sealing plastic bags. When ready to bake, arrange dough on cookie sheets, let warm to room temperature, and bake as usual (for a smaller batch, use your toaster oven).

• You can also freeze baked, iced, and decorated cookies for up to 3 months. Cool them completely, then place in sturdy freezer containers with waxed paper between layers. To serve, simply unwrap, place on a plate, and allow to come to room temperature.

• Cut and store bar cookies in the pan they were baked in; cover it with foil or plastic wrap. (Some 13" by 9" pans even come with convenient snap-on plastic lids.)

Pine-Nut Tassies

PREP: 40 MINUTES PLUS CHILLING AND COOLING
BAKE: 30 MINUTES

These miniature tarts have a special cream-cheese crust.

1 cup pine nuts (pignoli)
1 package (3 ounces) cream cheese, softened
½ cup (1 stick) plus 1 tablespoon margarine or butter, softened
1 cup all-purpose flour
2 tablespoons granulated sugar
⅔ cup packed light brown sugar
1 large egg
1 teaspoon vanilla extract

1 Preheat oven to 350°F. Place ¾ cup pine nuts in 9" by 9" metal baking pan. Bake pine nuts 8 to 10 minutes, until lightly toasted. Cool completely.

2 Meanwhile, in large bowl, with mixer at high speed, beat cream cheese with ½ cup margarine or butter (1 stick) until creamy. Reduce speed to low; add flour and granulated sugar, and beat until well mixed. Cover bowl with plastic wrap; refrigerate 30 minutes.

3 In food processor with knife blade attached, blend toasted pine nuts with brown sugar until pine nuts are finely ground.

4 In medium bowl, with spoon, combine pine-nut mixture with egg, vanilla, and remaining 1 tablespoon margarine or butter.

5 With floured hands, divide chilled dough into 24 equal pieces (dough will be very soft). With floured fingertips, gently press each piece of dough evenly onto bottom and up sides of twenty-four 1¾" by 1" ungreased miniature muffin-pan cups. Spoon filling by heaping teaspoons into each pastry cup; sprinkle with remaining ¼ cup pine nuts.

6 Bake 30 minutes or until filling is set and crust is golden. With tip of knife, loosen cookie cups from muffin-pan cups, and place on wire rack to cool completely. Store cookies in tightly covered container. Makes 2 dozen cookies.

Each cookie: About 125 calories, 2 g protein, 12 g carbohydrate, 8 g total fat (2 g saturated), 13 mg cholesterol, 75 mg sodium.

Chocolate & Peanut Butter Brownies

PREP: 20 MINUTES PLUS 2 HOURS COOLING
BAKE: 25 TO 30 MINUTES

Irresistible to anyone—at any age—with a sweet tooth.

2½ cups all-purpose flour
1½ teaspoons baking powder
½ teaspoon salt
1¾ cups packed light brown sugar
1 cup creamy peanut butter
½ cup margarine or butter (1 stick), slightly softened
3 large eggs
2 teaspoons vanilla extract
3 squares (1 ounce each) semisweet chocolate, melted
1 square (1 ounce) unsweetened chocolate, melted
1 package (6 ounces) semisweet-chocolate pieces

1 Preheat oven to 350°F. In medium bowl, mix flour, baking powder, and salt.

2 In large bowl, with mixer at medium speed, beat brown sugar, peanut butter, and margarine or butter until smooth, about 2 minutes. Reduce speed to low. Beat in eggs and vanilla; beat until smooth. Beat in flour mixture just until combined (dough will be stiff).

3 Place one-third of dough (about 1¾ cups) in another large bowl. Stir in melted chocolate until blended; fold in ¾ cup semisweet-chocolate pieces.

4 Pat half of remaining peanut-butter dough into ungreased 13" by 9" metal baking pan. In random pattern, drop chocolate dough and remaining peanut-butter dough on top of peanut-butter layer; pat down with hand. Sprinkle with remaining chocolate pieces.

5 Bake 25 to 30 minutes until toothpick inserted in center comes out clean. Cool in pan on rack. Makes 24 bars.

Each bar: About 270 calories, 5 g protein, 36 g carbohydrate, 13 g total fat (2 g saturated), 27 mg cholesterol, 190 mg sodium.

Browned-Butter Shortbread

PREP: 15 MINUTES PLUS CHILLING AND COOLING
BAKE: 40 TO 45 MINUTES

Browning some of the butter first gives our shortbread a deep, rich flavor. You can bake it in either a standard cake or tart pan or a shortbread mold.

12 tablespoons unsalted butter (1½ sticks),
  slightly softened (no substitutions)
½ cup sugar
1¾ cups all-purpose flour
½ teaspoon salt

1 In heavy 2-quart saucepan, melt 6 tablespoons butter over low heat. Cook butter 8 to 12 minutes, stirring occasionally, until butter solids at bottom of pan are a rich brown color and butter has a nutty aroma. (Be careful not to overbrown butter; it will have a bitter flavor.) Pour browned butter into small bowl; refrigerate until almost firm, about 35 minutes.

2 Preheat oven to 350°F. In large bowl, with mixer at medium speed, beat sugar with cooled browned butter and remaining 6 tablespoons softened butter until creamy.

3 With hand, mix flour and salt into butter mixture just until crumbs form. (Do not overwork dough; shortbread will be tough.) Pat shortbread crumbs into ungreased 9-inch round tart pan with removable bottom or cake pan.

4 Bake shortbread 40 to 45 minutes, until browned around the edge. Let cool in pan on wire rack 10 minutes.

5 Remove shortbread from pan to cutting board. While still warm, cut shortbread into 16 wedges. Cool wedges completely on wire rack. Store cookies in tightly covered container. Makes 16 cookies.

Each cookie: About 150 calories, 2 g protein, 17 g carbohydrate, 9 g total fat (5 g saturated), 23 mg cholesterol, 70 mg sodium.

Fresh Lemon Bars

PREP: 15 MINUTES PLUS COOLING • BAKE: 35 MINUTES

A classic American sweet that has been winning over kids and adults for years. Our recipe is super simple, with a crispy cookie bottom and a tangy lemon custard.

1½ cups plus 3 tablespoons all-purpose flour
½ cup plus 1 tablespoon confectioners' sugar
¾ cup margarine or butter (1½ sticks), cut into
  small pieces
2 large lemons
3 large eggs
1 cup granulated sugar
½ teaspoon baking powder
½ teaspoon salt

1 Preheat oven to 350°F. Line 13" by 9" metal baking pan with foil; lightly grease foil.

2 In medium bowl, combine 1½ cups flour and ½ cup confectioners' sugar. With pastry blender or two knives used scissor-fashion, cut in margarine or butter until mixture resembles coarse crumbs.

3 Sprinkle crumb mixture evenly in pan. With floured hands, firmly pat crumbs onto bottom of pan to form a crust. Bake crust 15 to 17 minutes until lightly browned.

4 Meanwhile, grate peel from lemons to equal 1 teaspoon and squeeze juice to equal ⅓ cup. In large bowl, with mixer at high speed, beat eggs until thick and lemon-colored, about 3 minutes. Reduce speed to low; add lemon juice, lemon peel, granulated sugar, baking powder, salt, and remaining 3 tablespoons flour, and beat until blended, occasionally scraping bowl.

5 Pour lemon filling over warm crust. Bake 15 minutes or until filling is just set and golden around edges. Transfer pan to wire rack. Place remaining 1 tablespoon confectioners' sugar in sieve and sprinkle over warm filling. Cool completely in pan on wire rack.

6 When cool, cut lengthwise into 3 strips, then cut each strip crosswise into 12 bars. To store, cover pan and refrigerate. Makes 36 bars.

Each bar: About 90 calories, 1 g protein, 12 g carbohydrate, 4 g total fat (1 g saturated), 18 mg cholesterol, 90 mg sodium.

◀ *Browned-Butter Shortbread (top)*
and Fresh Lemon Bars

INDEX

CREDITS

Cover: Mark Thomas. Page 7: Steffen Thalemann. Page 8 (left): Michael Grand. Page 8 (middle & right): Steve Wisbauer. Pages 9 & 10: Steve Wisbauer. Page 11 (illustration): Lisa Blackshear. Page 11 (photo): David Hamsley. Pages 12 & 13: Steve Wisbauer. Page 14 (top): David Hamsley. Page 14 (bottom): Michael Grand. Pages 15 & 16: Steve Wisbauer. Page 17 (all): Michael Grand. Page 18: Julia Gran. Pages 23 & 24: Steven Mark Needham. Page 29: Carlos Marrero. Page 30: Steven Mark Needham. Page 35: Mary Ellen Bartley. Page 36: Rita Maas. Page 41: Ann Stratton. Page 42: Brian Hagiwara. Pages 44, 47, 49, 51, & 53: Ann Stratton. Pagea 57 & 59: Mark Thomas. Page 64: Brian Hagiwara. Page 67: Ann Stratton. Pages 68 & 72: Brian Hagiwara. Page 75: Mark Thomas. Page 76: Tom McWilliam. Pages 79 & 82: Mark Thomas. Page 84: Alan Richardson. Page 89: Mark Thomas. Page 90 (all): Brian Hagiwara. Page 92: Alan Richardson. Page 97: Mark Thomas. Page 101: Tom McWilliam. Pages 102 & 104: Brian Hagiwara. Pages 109, 112, 116, 120, 122, & 124: Alan Richardson. Page 126: Steve Wisbauer. Page 128: Alan Richardson. Page 131: Brian Hagiwara. Pages 134 & 136: Alan Richardson. Pages 139 & 145: Brian Hagiwara. Page 146: Mark Thomas. Page 148: Harry Campbell. Page 150: Mark Thomas. Page 152: Brian Hagiwara. Page 155: Alan Richardson. Page 156: Ann Stratton. Pages 161 & 164: Brian Hagiwara. Pages 166 & 171: Mark Thomas. Page 172: Christopher Irion. Page 177: Brian Hagiwara. Pages 178 & 185: Ann Stratton. Page 188: Steven Mark Needham. Pages 191, 193, 197, 198 (all), & 202: Simon Metz. Page 205: Brian Hagiwara. Page 206: Peter Ardito. Page 208: Ann Stratton. Pages 210 & 213: Brian Hagiwara. Page 215: Mary Ellen Bartley. Page 216: Ann Stratton. Page 219: Steven Mark Needham. Page 220: David Hamsley. Page 222: Steven Mark Needham. Page 225: Alan Richardson. Page 229: Ann Stratton. Page 232: Mark Thomas. Page 235: Alan Richardson. Page 238: Mary Ellen Bartley. Page 241: Brian Hagiwara. Page 244: Alan Richardson.

Special thanks to the following gourmet dinner clubs who contributed to this volume: Elliot Feldstein and other dinner-club members in Scarsdale, New York; Chris Howland and other dinner-club members in Seattle, Washington; Donna Bower and other dinner-club members in Parker, Colorado.

METRIC CONVERSIONS

LENGTH

If you know:	Multiply by:	To find:
INCHES	25.0	MILLIMETERS
INCHES	2.5	CENTIMETERS
FEET	30.0	CENTIMETERS
YARDS	0.9	METERS
MILES	1.6	KILOMETERS
MILLIMETERS	0.04	INCHES
CENTIMETERS	0.4	INCHES
METERS	3.3	FEET
METERS	1.1	YARDS
KILOMETERS	0.6	MILES

VOLUME

If you know:	Multiply by:	To find:
TEASPOONS	5.0	MILLILITERS
TABLESPOONS	15.0	MILLILITERS
FLUID OUNCES	30.0	MILLILITERS
CUPS	0.24	LITERS
PINTS	0.47	LITERS
QUARTS	0.95	LITERS
GALLONS	3.8	LITERS
MILLILITERS	0.03	FLUID OUNCES
LITERS	4.2	CUPS
LITERS	2.1	PINTS
LITERS	1.06	QUARTS
LITERS	0.26	GALLONS

WEIGHT

If you know:	Multiply by:	To find:
OUNCES	28.0	GRAMS
POUNDS	0.45	KILOGRAMS
GRAMS	0.035	OUNCES
KILOGRAMS	2.2	POUNDS

TEMPERATURE

If you know:	Multiply by:	To find:
DEGREES FAHRENHEIT	0.56 (AFTER SUBTRACTING 32)	DEGREES CELSIUS
DEGREES CELSIUS	1.8 (THEN ADD 32)	DEGREES FAHRENHEIT